Children

49 MUSICIANS SHAPING

of the

A NEW BLUES TRADITION

Blues

Art Tipaldi

Backbeat
Books
San Francisco

Published by Backbeat Books
600 Harrison Street, San Francisco, CA 94107
www.backbeatbooks.com
E-mail: books@musicplayer.com
An imprint of the Music Player Network
United Entertainment Media, Inc.

Distributed to the book trade in the US and Canada by
Publishers Group West, 1700 Fourth Street, Berkeley, CA 94710

Distributed to the music trade in the US and Canada by
Hal Leonard Publishing, P.O. Box 13819, Milwaukee, WI 53213

Cover Design by Richard Leeds
Text Design by Saroyan Humphrey
Page Composition by Margaret Copeland
Front Cover Photo of Luther and Bernard Allison by Robert Barclay
Back Cover Photos by Art Tipaldi

Library of Congress Cataloging-in-Publication Data

Tipaldi, Art.
    Children of the blues : 49 musicians shaping a new blues tradition / by Art
Tipaldi.
        p. cm.
    Discography: p.
    Includes index.
    ISBN 0-87930-700-5
        1. Blues musicians—United States—Interviews.

ML385 .T57 2001
781.643'092'273—dc21
[B]
                                                                2001043709

Printed in the United States of America

02 03 04 05 06   10 9 8 7 6 5 4 3 2 1

This is dedicated to those who have searched,
those who continue to search, those who are searching,
those who will search out the blues.

CONTENTS

ACKNOWLEDGMENTS

BECAUSE THIS BOOK is essentially about the master-apprentice relationship in the blues, I must acknowledge my mentors, who have shown me how to move with integrity, sincerity, and respect. I am indebted to Bill Ferris, Peter Guralnick, Bruce Iglauer, and Dick Waterman for teaching me firsthand.

I am also grateful to the men and women profiled within this volume, who granted me access to their lives and their art. I am likewise indebted to numerous other musicians who have shared their stories and memories. Hopefully they will become the center of the next effort.

I am greatly indebted to B.B. King, John Lee Hooker, and Bonnie Raitt for offering their endorsement and support of my effort.

I must thank the many editors and publishers who afforded me the chance to discover the writer within, especially my dear friend Bob Vorel, of *Blues Revue*, for sensing my commitment and providing the opportunity to begin the journey. Each editor I have worked with has pushed me to uncover a new facet of style. Thanks to Andy Robble, who told me always to write from the heart, to my many other editors—Angel Rosemond, Harry Sleeper, Kim Ahern, Janet Reynolds, Brian Owens, Lisa Danforth, Craig Gill, Sean Glennon, Alister Highet, and Rich and Maureen Delgrosso—and to Jas Obrecht, whose friendship and guidance as editor and mentor have always been invaluable.

Thanks to Margaret Flowers, who as friend and knowing reader validated the work's direction, read drafts, and kept me focused.

Special thanks to Chris Kreiser, my current editor at *Blues Revue*, who edited the manuscript and offered suggestions and advice crucial to refining its scope.

Thanks to my friends in blues music, who provided many opportunities to grow on the journey: Peter Aschoff, Dave Bartlett, Rick Bates, Cat Bauer,

Mike Beck, Chuck Bloomingburg, John Boncimino, Rick Booth, John Cain, Dave Carpenter, Tommy Couch, Jr., Stew Crossen, Jerry Del Giudice, Don Denley, Doug Engel, Jim English, Bruce Feiner, Marci Ferris, Roger Finck, Josten Forsberg, Michael Franks, Randy Freil, Mindy Giles, Jerry Gordon, John Hahn, Steve Hetch, Bev Howell, Chad Kassem, Lenny Lewis, Teo Leyasmeyer, Marc Lipkin, Andy McKaie, Pat Mitchell, Miki Mulvehill, Roger Nabor, David Nelson, Marc Norberg, Shirley Mae Owens, Bob Porter, Richard Rosenblatt, Thomas Ruf, David Sanjek, Art Simas, Howard Stovall, Bonnie Tallman, Sandra Tooze, Reuben Williams, Cary Wolfson. Special thanks to my friend Steve Walbridge; who booked many of these performers in our local clubs and festivals, thus giving me the chance to write about them; and Michael Cloeren, who has been a close friend throughout this blues journey. I apologize to anyone I've forgotten.

And I must thank my buddies in the photo pits across the world— Robert Barclay, Connor Grimes, Niles Frantz, Tom Hazeltine, David Horwitz, Jef Jaison, Kathy Minke, Nappy Niles, Butch Ruth, Jim Saley, Scott Saltzman, Bob Sekinger, and Chuck Winans—as well as my colleagues in blues education: T.J. Wheeler, Fruteland Jackson, and Hawkeye Herman.

My personal gratitude goes to the folks at Backbeat Books for understanding the reach of this book. Thanks to Matt Kelsey, Dorothy Cox, Richard Johnston, Nancy Tabor, Larissa Berry, Jay Kahn, and Nina Lesowitz.

Thanks go to my friends David Bernstein, Bob Brown, Mark Caron, Scott Leven, and Greg Trimmer, who have shared friendship, sports, and music discussions over the years. Special thanks to all my students during the 29 years I've taught high school English. Each one of you has been an important part of me.

My deepest thanks go to my family: my mother, Rose, and my father, Art, for their foresight in giving birth to a Sagittarius; my sisters, Lorraine and Marilyn, who, like me, carry the musical genes of our ancestors; and my daughters, Allison and Katie, who've listened to more blues than any teenagers probably should.

A most heartfelt acknowledgment goes to my best friend and wife, Bonnie. When I first saw her face in a crowd, nearly 35 years ago, I never imagined the rich future we were to share. I have found no truer friend. Her laughter and encouragement continue to be central to my life. Each day, she too discovers the magic of the blues.

INTRODUCTION

You don't choose the blues—it chooses you. Whether it's in the first wail of a harmonica, the pierce of a guitar note, the sting of glass on metal, the left-handed boogie-woogie bass, or a voice that rips you inside out, the blues plays hide-and-seek until it's ready to be found. Once found, it's hard to resist. In many ways it requires the musician and the listener to sign a pact at the crossroads, a pact dedicated to search and self-discovery. Once under the spell, each musician walks on from the crossroads looking to stir magic from the ordinary. Many musicians will tread the path of blues rock, screaming for Stevie Ray Vaughan or Jimi Hendrix covers. Others will meander to cities like Chicago and Houston and Memphis, listening to Muddy Waters or B.B. King, or John Lee Hooker or Albert Collins, or Freddie King or Howlin' Wolf on their Walkman. Still others will jump and swing their blues with a jazz flavor. And there are many devotees who will travel by foot on the dusty back roads of the South, fueled by a purpose—searching for the blues.

For the listener, it's the same story told a hundred ways in a hundred voices. Elmore James's slide, Little Walter's harp, Koko Taylor's growl, Albert Collins's single note, Son House's intensity, Mississippi John Hurt's smile, Fred McDowell's spirit, Robert Johnson's pain.

Though simple, blues can take a lifetime to absorb. As B.B. King once told me, "If you really want to play, you have to put the time into it. You have to express yourself when you play. Some people will just play the notes. Some will say to you, 'Anybody can play the blues,' but that doesn't mean everybody'll like it. It's a very simple music, but I think that simplicity makes we that play the blues work harder at it."

It cannot be learned from a music book or video; in its purest form, it must be passed knee to knee, mouth to mouth, eye to eye. This music, more than any other, is rooted in the passing of traditions. On long rides to gigs, in predawn hotel rooms, or around bandstands, real education transpires. Every young apprentice is an empty canvas to be saturated with the approaches and techniques that must be absorbed.

This book presents the first-person recollections of 49 children of the blues who have sat with the musical fathers and today carry the real definitions of the blues. Since many of us have never traveled in the front seat of the van with Muddy Waters or Albert Collins and shared their stories and many in future generations will never sit backstage with B.B. King, these snapshots present to every new generation of interested fans the unique opportunity to sit in those smoky rooms and learn intimately what the blues is really about.

At the same time, these profiles chronicle the personal journeys that these "children" have embarked upon in forging musical careers outside the mainstream of American popular culture.

Though blues was created from a variety of musical sources by a rebellious younger generation of newly freed African Americans early in the 20th century, younger African Americans in the 1960s turned their backs on the music of their grandparents. Older African Americans chose the intelligent approach of jazz to assimilate into the dominant culture. As commercial interests discovered the hugely marketable aspects of rock and roll and blues rock, the contemporary world was given a version of blues that fit more into the clothing of rock and roll, and authentic blues forms became endangered species, existing only in tiny holdouts.

In the 1960s, blues was the true underground music, surviving mainly in tiny bars throughout the African American inner cities. The blues revival that began in the 1960s was fueled primarily by a young, white audience. Taj Mahal remembers the paradox of the Newport Folk Festivals in the early 1960s: "The bulk of the talent was all black. And I was one of 100 black people there among 30,000 young, white Americans."

The musicians chosen for this book represent various corners of that blues revival. Early in the 1960s, you could find the music in places like Watts and the Ash Grove in Los Angeles, Greenwich Village, the South and West sides of Chicago, the Club 47 in Cambridge, and the Newport Folk Festivals. People like John Hammond, Rory Block, Taj Mahal, and Paul Rishell searched out the rediscovered elders from the 1930s at Newport and other East Coast venues. At the same time, Rod Piazza, Al Blake, and James Harman traveled to the storied ghetto clubs in Watts to watch a West Coast version of the blues through George "Harmonica" Smith, T-Bone Walker, and Big Joe Turner. Charlie Musselwhite sat knee to knee with the blues in Memphis and Chicago; Delbert McClinton, Sherman Robertson, and

Jimmie Vaughan could not avoid the Texas grit of Albert Collins or Gatemouth Brown. All the while, Chicago's Bobby Rush and Mississippi's Big Jack Johnson worked at keeping the earliest traditions of the blues alive in clubs and jukes far from mainstream America.

By 1967, other teens had become integral parts of the blues revival. Junior Watson was listening to every blues act coming through Berkeley. Fred Kaplan was playing R&B at low-rider parties. Dave Maxwell lived in every blues haunt in Boston. Duke Robillard had formed the initial version of Roomful of Blues. Bob Margolin was preparing to become Muddy Waters's guitarist. Doug MacLeod was working Virginia coffee houses with Ernest Banks. Joe Louis Walker had moved to San Francisco and was living with Michael Bloomfield. Kim Wilson and Robert Cray were beginning real schooling in the blues. Lil' Ed Williams watched his uncle J.B. Hutto at family gatherings. Carl Weathersby was immersed in music at every family gathering. Tommy Shannon played Woodstock behind Johnny Winter. Coco Montoya was spellbound by an Albert King performance. Debbie Davies studied guitar after hearing Eric Clapton solos. Kenny Brown was sitting on a porch in Mississippi learning from rural masters. Because these teenagers had dedicated themselves to learning the blues verbatim, they were poised to breathe new life into the music.

In a genetic sense, some of the musicians profiled in this book actually are children of real blues fathers. That younger generation of Bernard Allison, Ronnie and Wayne Brooks, Kenny Neal, Shemekia Copeland, Lucky Peterson, and Jimmy D. Lane embodies the traditions of the past grafted onto the contemporary seedlings. Coupled with Keb' Mo', they stand at the vanguard of the next blues generation.

And some are actual fathers who function as significant links in the transmission of tradition. They too have learned from an older generation willing to teach and then have instructed not only their own offspring, but others willing to become caretakers of the art form. In this way, Luther Allison, Lonnie Brooks, and Johnny "Clyde" Copeland represent the purest form of parenting blues ethics. There are other parents, like Jimmy Rogers, Raful Neal, and James Peterson, who have also raised legitimate blues children.

Certain younger musicians have chosen to partner with an older, experienced blues master. This type of bond demonstrates the suppressing of individual ego in favor of mutual respect. Texan Anson Funderburgh's long-term partnership with Mississippian Sam Myers, fiery guitarist Smokin' Joe Kubek's association with jazz guitar-influenced Bnois King, and the three-woman, equal partnership of Ann Rabson, Gaye Adegbalola, and Andra McIntosh of Saffire are proof that as each partner thrives, the whole created is greater than the sum of what the individuals bring to the relationship.

To understand how these subjects fit into the genealogy of the blues, we must understand a fundamental definition of the blues. B.B. King simplified the definition when he told me, "The blues is the source. Blues is about life as we lived it in the past, as we live it today, and as we will live it tomorrow. It's life, with all the emotion and passions. As long as we have them, we'll have blues. We blues singers tell stories about basic feelings of human beings: pain, happiness, fear, courage, confusion, and desire told in simple stories. That's the genius of the blues."

Distilled, the blues is "the reals": It tells about life the way it is; it sums up the entire human condition. Like all art, the blues freely allows for personality and life experiences to flow through the music played. Because this music comes from the heart of the player, it always retains a spontaneous, of-the-moment quality. In that way, blues grows from the performer, touches audience members individually, and soothes. As the simple, time-honored blues philosophy expresses it: Everything's gonna be alright because the sun is gonna shine on my back door someday.

If music is to move us, it must provide an opening for us to relate the personal story being told to our own experiences. In that way, we personalize the art. It has always been the culminating effect of daily life that invigorates the art created. Charlie Parker said, "If you don't live it, it won't come out of your horn." By discovering the spiritual in the everyday, each musician searches for the key to articulate those common experiences. Contrary to the way commercial interests sell blues, the meaning is in the way each performer offers healing vibes to troubled souls. The self-absorption and overt dedication to technique puts each musician on the identical lifetime journey that every master embarks upon when searching out art. At the same time, these children have observed diligently how to generate their unique spirit from the ordinary, how to let genuine emotion articulate through fingers and breath. Without that personal brushstroke, the art created is only a black-and-white photocopy of an original.

The greats of the blues—B.B. King, Muddy Waters, Otis Spann, Son House, Howlin' Wolf, John Lee Hooker, Albert Collins, Luther Allison, and Johnny "Clyde" Copeland—were emphatic in their instruction that each musician take the form and add to it. These 49—and countless others— have taken that advice to heart and over years discovered the process that combines the traditional forms with contemporary perspectives. In direct contrast to the popular culture that wants it all today regardless of how flimsy the craftsmanship, they've each painstakingly crafted a substantial and lasting musical art.

These musicians were nurtured differently than the originators of the form, because they have grown up in areas far removed from Mississippi porches and Chicago taverns. Many of these blues children are from outside the culture, but they received the identical instruction as earlier generations from within. Author Alex Haley once stated that being raised right in Mississippi meant children sitting at the feet of the family elders on porches and listening to the family stories. First- and second-generation bluesmen sat on these porches, sat on stages, sat in cars, sat in living rooms, sat on buses, sat on stoops and raised the next generation. Kenny Neal distills the process to its essence: "The way we learn in the South is that you don't go ask for tips. You pay attention."

Though most of these musicians can recall the initial rapture on hearing Muddy, the Wolf, Little Walter, or Otis Spann on record, all agree it was the modest, personal gestures that set their life's course. When white, suburban, high school guitar players caught Muddy, they were never barred from the traditions. When B.B. King passed along a broken string, a discarded guitar pick, or an encouraging word, he continued the thread of knowledge he was a mere part of years earlier. A lucky handful remember the ecstasy of being called from the crowd to jam on stage during a show. When a young musician sat after hours with Howlin' Wolf, he learned the generous nature of Wolf in passing down a lick. When a youthful harp player rode in a car with George "Harmonica" Smith, he soaked up lessons of the road. When Albert Collins cut a youngster's head in an onstage guitar duel, he did it in a way that strengthened the precious master-apprentice relationship inherent in the blues.

"When the older cats knew a young musician was serious about the music, they were unselfish in offering help." This was repeated too often in my interviews to credit any one musician. "They wouldn't sit down and say, 'This is how I did that.' They simply played it once for you and assumed you'd learn it. That's how they were taught." Another often-repeated memory.

These two statements reveal the paramount core of the relationship. Like the very best teachers and coaches, many of these unschooled musicians knew intuitively how to teach about the music and encourage young players to develop musical talent.

These artists have learned that to create worthwhile art, you must learn it right, and if that takes years, so be it. Men like B.B. King preach this ethic every day. When musicians who have been playing the music for over 30 years tell me they are still learning, that supports the maxim that true education never stops. That inspires me. It should be obvious that this highly personal journey to that awareness is not embodied in the overnight business of commercialized music

These profiles do not focus solely on the insights of first- and second-generation musicians. Though these men and women initially received their lessons as musical, time has revealed that more subtle humanities necessary to personal survival were conveyed. There is an overwhelming human joy in the stories that recount struggles with personal demons. When addiction to any substance becomes the master force driving artistic creativity, a dark filter restricts all imagination. Though there are arguments that a person must experience all aspects of life to sing the blues, many of the musicians describe their substance addictions as a time when creating music from the heart was secondary to their physical and emotional cravings.

Though some readers may think these interviews relate simply to music, I can tell you they also offer essentials that every individual requires in searching out a personal direction. There are discoveries about the nature of artistic creativity, about how, in the end, it is the voice and vision of each artist that makes art breathe. There are insights about how, in order to create out of spontaneity and intuition, one must lose self-consciousness, surrender to the moment, and enter the zone of creativity. And there are discussions of the difficulty of remaining in that zone when the culture at large ignores your art. Through these stories, I have learned about the drive to become accepted into any peer group, artistic or otherwise, and the work necessary to remain a part of that group.

Underlying all these stories is the dignity these African American elders demonstrated to the children at their feet, a dignity that arises from a people treated as second-class citizens from the other side of the tracks but who gave first-class gifts to the world. Though they've watched their songs be played and sold by others or have signed away their rights to a fast-talking studio for a pittance, these artists have exhibited superior dignity in the face of tremendous exploitation and adversity and have freely shared their musical gifts. As Albert Collins told Coco Montoya often, "If you throw me a brick, I'll give you bread."

Genetic or otherwise, blues traits have been passed along. These blues children have accepted the responsibility of energizing and strengthening the gift they were handed, working as hard in gaining recognition for their work in the art form as their musical fathers. When musicians like Robert Cray, Joe Louis Walker, Rod Piazza, Kim Wilson, Taj Mahal, Charlie Musselwhite, Sherman Robertson, Duke Robillard, Jimmie Vaughan, and Bob Margolin craft their contemporary blues, they continue to respect to the timeless forms pioneered over 50 years ago by these blues innovators. When Rory Block, John Hammond, Paul Rishell, and Doug MacLeod immerse themselves in the acoustic spirit, they evoke the timeless quality of the blues. When Bernard Allison, Jimmy D. Lane, Shemekia Copeland, Kenny Neal, and Ronnie and Wayne Brooks sing and play, it is difficult not to feel their fathers' presence. When newcomers like Keb' Mo' travel to Mississippi to sit on a porch with genuine blues elders, it suggests to the world that the chain of tradition will always survive.

After reading these profiles, there remain major areas of questions to ponder.

- Has modern commercialism sold the world its own profitable definition of the blues that flies against time-honored assumptions?
- Is it primarily because of determined musicians like these that the blues still exists today as a dynamic art form?
- Is it their adherence to the long-established forms they learned that constitutes the basis for the new order of contemporary blues? Or have these musicians placed too much emphasis on honoring their inheritance, thus stagnating the blues form?
- Without being a member of the culture that owns it, what have these revivalists provided the art form?
- Without growing up in the archetypal blues environments of the South or inner cities, is the oral transmission of culture as valid? Or have these modern players discovered relevant approaches that both honor and advance the traditions?
- Since many of the masters and innovators have died, is it necessary that today's untrained blues musicians learn the conventions from the "libraries" within these modern masters of the blues? Or can that heritage be learned from records and videos? And is that transmission as valid?
- To survive in the next century, will it be necessary for blues to marry itself off to a commercial suitor and disregard its essential folk traditions?

In order to move forward, we must be conscious of where we come from and interpret that within the context of today's culture. With an inherent respect for the inheritance, the traditional forms can move forward. Over years these men and women have remained true to the forms they were given, but they have also expanded those forms to include current attitudes.

That combination of respect and innovative spirit has established many of the men and women profiled within these pages as instrumental in solidifying the musical approaches of the area or genre with which they are associated. Chicago musicians were given the recipe for Muddy Waters' and Howlin' Wolf's electric Delta blues and asked to season it for present-day tastes. Many of the bands in the Northeast begin as clones of the Duke

Robillard's Roomful of Blues big band combination of guitar and massive horns. Every Texas blues band arguably begins with the intention of catching lightning in a bottle like the Fabulous Thunderbirds. On the West Coast, there are never-ending permutations of the Rod Piazza, Hollywood Fats, and James Harman bands for startup bands to experiment with. Even today's acoustic revival can be traced back to the influences of Taj Mahal, Rory Block, and John Hammond. Through it all, these people continue to fly at the vanguard, digging deeply into their craft.

The importance of the oral tradition in the African American culture is underscored by the blues. The interviews and stories presented here follow our conversational thread. We sometimes chose paths not always taken. Within every interview, performers explored inner creative forces and shared the origins of their individual drive. In that way, each musician's perceptions are unique and impart meaning differently. These are the words captured on the day of the interview. Like a blues lyric, they are true in the context of the moment. Though there will always be varying perceptions of events and their significance, what is compiled here represents the knowledge, information, judgment, and insights unique to each individual.

I am personally indebted to these friends and all the others who have freely shared their intimate memories of the men and women who've made a lasting mark on the world of music. For any aspiring or veteran musician, there are substantial lessons about how one creates art. Though I'm not a musician, the stories and shared personal wisdom have taught me invaluable lessons on how to participate as an active listener with all music. These individuals have testified that improvisation is not playing mere notes in a scale. It exists more in the feelings and ideas expressed throughout the structure. They have allowed me to hear how musical conversations breathe. They have demonstrated the blues paradox that less is fundamentally more. They have opened my eyes to understand how the more spaces you leave, the more impact it has when you do play. They have laid bare that musically the blues is focused on tension and release. By sharing that awareness with me, they have each continued the cycle of transmission within the oral culture of the blues. I do likewise in hopes of enriching each individual's experience.

People have always wanted to save some of the best to pass on to their children, the future generations. As we celebrate the best of the 20th century and rectify some of its tragic omissions, we cannot overlook these fathers of American music. Without these blues offspring's commitment to tradition and their courage to create, the wisdom, ritual, and unwritten conventions of authentic blues might have been lost forever, existing only in dusty museums and in archival recordings. Instead, the blues art form has been carefully handed down from the generation of originators to their offspring, who today have become both the caretakers and innovators of the blues.

Real Fathers, Real Children, Chicago, and the South

I N MANY WAYS, Chicago in the 1960s was the family living room of the blues. It not only offered symbolic home-style living room atmospheres like Maxwell Street and the variety of clubs like Peppers, Theresa's, and the Checkerboard, it also contained the real homes where boys learned from the men who brought the blues up from the South. In that way, young, white blues enthusiasts mixed on the streets, in the taverns, and in homes with first-generation music makers of all types.

Within this chapter are the stories of four actual children and their talented birth fathers, two with deep musical roots in family backgrounds and one who gracefully demonstrates how, from years of lessons and living, a child grows into a master.

At some point, the real fathers—Luther Allison, Lonnie Brooks, and Johnny "Clyde" Copeland—were also schooled in the music through an older generation. Each recalls how early study metamorphosed into modern genius. While Allison and Copeland tell of their blues trials, Brooks offers a first-class primer in how to parent, and lets his sons tell of the hard blues life he's lived. Through each offspring we understand clearly the dominant role the father plays in fostering a child's talent to maturity. In addition, each child opens a window to the musical contemporaries of his father and the regal way these bluesmen and -women lived their lives. Jimmy D. Lane (son of the great guitarist Jimmy Rogers), Bernard Allison, Shemekia Copeland, Kenny Neal, and Ronnie and Wayne Brooks, all accept the fact that the door to musical opportunities was opened by their father, but they also know they can only survive in the game through hard work and talent.

Bobby Rush was another schooled in the music of Chicago in the 1950s who has taken his brand of soul blues from the chitlin' circuit to stages around the world. Another who sat and listened to a father was Lucky Peterson, who as a teenager worked as the bandleader for Bobby "Blue" Bland and Little Milton.

Big Jack Johnson grew up playing in the Mississippi jukes and today carries the near-extinct juke experience around the world. Carl Weathersby brought his Mississippi musical genes to East Chicago, Indiana. There he met family friend Albert King and began his true Mississippi music education. Through Lil' Ed Williams, readers are again transported into a blues family's living room. As the nephew to J.B. Hutto, Williams learned early and often the importance of music in the family's genes. He also came to inherit another genetic trait from his uncle: substance abuse. Lil' Ed's downward spiral into dependency and his subsequent rebirth offer reason for optimism to anyone caught in the cycle of addiction.

Growing up in the cotton fields of Mississippi, Kenny Brown took guitar lessons from Joe Callicott on the porch of his sharecropper cabin. When Callicott died, Brown began his tenure playing the jukes of rural Mississippi with R.L. Burnside. Like Johnson, Brown provides a precise look at the rural juke experience.

Whether he sat with the bluesmen of Memphis in the 1950s or of Chicago in the 1960s or traveled the world, Charlie Musselwhite offers readers a perfect example of understanding an art form, working within that form, and eventually, by discovering one's individual voice, producing one's own legitimate music.

Luther
Allison

Leave your ego,
Play the music,
Love the people.
—LUTHER ALLISON

THERE ARE MUSICIANS who merely entertain and those who can allow each member of the audience the privilege to enter into the spontaneous, creative process. Luther Allison discovered the rare ability to empower any spectator willing to join his musical spirit. For over 30 years, his intimately passionate performance was as physically, emotionally, and spiritually draining for audience members as for the sweat-drenched Allison. This was the same intense performance that impressed those who witnessed him in the late 1960s and early 1970s.

"Musically, it is the same Luther Allison, but the show has to be different because the material inside me is different," said Allison in 1995. "People who saw Luther Allison 20 years ago [were] sayin' 'Hey man, you ain't lost nothing and you're better than ever.' That means I haven't let anybody down from the beginning. People saw what I had then. Although, I've moved to France, I've been back to America many, many times, I say to these people, 'Where was my support for those last 11 years?'"

His longtime guitar and writing partner James Solberg agrees: "This isn't anything new; he's always been like that, even back to the 1950s. Luther lives to be on that bandstand. The rest of the time he's just a guy sittin' in the truck going to the next gig. But he comes to life onstage. We all have to keep up with him too! I tell the musicians just when you think you're playing as

From his earliest performances, Luther Allison was known
for his nonstop four-hour shows.

hard as you ever could imagine in your entire life, Luther will manage to get you up to another level of intensity and energy. It's funny to turn and look at the drummer and see it look like his heart's about to pop out of his chest tryin' to keep up."

The ultimate vindication of Luther Allison in America occurred in Memphis at the 1996 Handy Awards, where the humble Allison copped five awards for Entertainer of the Year, Guitar Player of the Year, Contemporary Male Blues Artist of the Year, Album of the Year, *Blue Streak*, and Song of the Year, "Cherry Red Wine." After Luther Allison won his third Handy award, host Ruth Brown warned, "Luther, you better stay off my stage!" After his fourth, Allison ran out of words of gratitude and announced, "I'm gonna let my guitar talk!" After his fifth, the guitar spoke Luther's heartfelt gratitude for over an hour.

This prompted *Blues Revue*, in its cover story on Luther in October/November of 1996, to proclaim him the new King of the Blues. His follow-up? Winning three more Handys in 1997, and another Handy sweep of six in 1998, posthumously.

Whenever you talked to Luther, he peppered his speech with the phrase "coming up the ladder." It is this indomitable spirit to ascend one step at a time that characterizes the mission of his life. From his early days apprenticing on Chicago's West Side to his move to Europe in 1984 to his triumphant return to America, Allison came to represent every man's path to self-discovery.

"The originality is in your heart. That's where you can take it. When you can make it without the drugs, without the bottle, then you've got a chance to call yourself original. You have to find it. I've been searching for Luther Allison for a lot of years and I'm hoping that now people hear Luther Allison and can say that's Luther Allison. I'm gonna come out of it with some kind of experience, some kind of survival, because I got a story to tell if I survive. I believe I'm a survivor.

"The music sounds great now. Because I feel so at rest with myself, I'm not fighting like I was fighting before. In the beginning you had to fight being shy, fight being in place, fight to be part of the competition, fight what you look like, fight being wanted by a girl and being rejected and getting laughed at. You had to fight being black and tryin' to fit in the white world. Man, it was so tough."

He was born in Arkansas in 1939, 14th of 15 children. Like so many children of sharecroppers, his first contact with playing music was plucking a piece of wire nailed to the side of the house. When the family moved to Chicago in 1951, he discovered the instrument that would become his voice in the world. "One day when I got out of school, I came in and my brother was playing the guitar. I said 'When you're finished, would you please show me how to play some boogie-woogie on that guitar.' The only thing I had done with a guitar before that was that I played the old broom wire on the house down on the cotton plantation in Arkansas."

Three years later, Allison joined his brother Ollie's gospel group, The Rolling Stones. Then, in 1957, he quit to learn the blues from the streets of Chicago. "I came up the ladder pretty good. I was about 19 when I started drifting into the nightclubs. We hung outside of the clubs on the sidewalks. There was no air conditioning in these clubs. So the musicians would come outside on their break, sit down, drink, and talk to us. It was great! From there we'd get invited onstage and do some head cutting. When that time come, you'd become the talk of your neighborhood," Luther remembered. One of Luther's first gigs was in Bobby Rush's band.

In the mid-'60s, he stood on the same ladder with the new generation of West Side blues guitarists, like Freddie King, Magic Sam, Jimmy Dawkins, Buddy Guy, and Otis Rush. "We had to get it from each other. We all listened to the same people coming up the ladder. There wasn't a lot of people like there is today. There was Muddy Waters, Howlin' Wolf, Little Walter, Jimmy Reed, and Eddie Taylor. B.B. King was the frontrunner. These are our dreams; these are what made us want to go up that ladder. Then you'd see people like Chuck Berry come along, Little Richard, Bo Diddley, and Fats Domino. These guys really showed us where we were headed. We had everything right there on the West and South sides, creating the blues out of the gospel, creating soul music, creating funk, creating rap. What you hear today, we did all this then.

"When I went on the stage on the South side, I was just sharpening my pencil. By the time I got to the West side, about 21 years old, then we started to move. There was Magic Sam, Freddie King, Buddy Guy, and Otis Rush, who became my idol. The guy just had such a beautiful tone coming from the guitar. I lived only two blocks from where Bob Koester found me. Jack's Lounge, where Otis Rush played, was only a half a block from my house. When I was discovered by Delmark, there was a little club called the Triangle Lounge. That's where I started with my light bulb in the corner. There was no stage. My brother Grant doin' some singing. We just put stuff together for our little neighborhood club."

His first record, *Love Me Mama*, was for Bob Koester's Delmark label in 1969. His three recordings with Motown were to be that label's first entry into the blues field. Solberg recalled that, when he first saw Luther Allison in 1971, "From the first second I saw him, he had this aura about him. He had this brittle tone he played so he sounded like his notes were gonna break. I started jamming with him in 1972." Solberg and Allison began their soul mate partnership on the bandstand in 1973. Like Michael Jordan and Scottie Pippen, Solberg and Allison knew intuitively from the start where the other was headed almost before it happened onstage.

"I think he and I had that singular urgency like we were driven by something. We related to each other immediately on that level. Luther and I got so many blues inside of us that we got to beat it over your head to try to get it out. It's difficult for he and I to sit way back and give just a little." In

1976, Allison and Solberg played the Montreux Jazz Festival in Switzerland. Solberg recalled, "The success in Europe was so overwhelming and the failure in the United States was so overwhelming that Luther made the only choice he could." Permanent residence in St. Cloud, France.

"If Count Basie, Willie Dixon, B.B. King, and Miles Davis can go to Europe and pick up European musicians to help make it over there, what's wrong with Luther Allison doin' it that way too?" said Allison. "I remember when I first went to Europe in 1976 for the Montreux Jazz Festival. We took the band from here. Then we started going over once, then twice, then three times a year."

Through the 1980s it was nonstop success in Europe. In the 1990s, Allison still hadn't conquered America. Solberg talked of the plan to bring Luther home. "From 1976, it's been a snowball of success in Europe for Luther. But all Luther ever wanted in his entire life was to come home and be accepted here. In 1993, the whole scenario of trying to bring Luther back to the United States happened. He'd stopped drinking and there was a sincerity of it. When the opportunity came to bring him home, I jumped right in."

With the Alligator release of *Soul Fixin' Man* in 1993, Allison announced he was ready to come home and show off the touch that marries gospel and blues with rock and soul. In addition to his blazing string attacks, Allison's music is also a call to action. Whether he urges people to "Move From the Hood" or asks inhabitants to take stock of the lack of fulfillment city life offers in "Big City," Allison's social activism is a wakeup call to all. "It's called the truth. Doin' something positive for each other. I'm not talking about just black; I'm talking about helping kids and grown people as well who need some direction. You better believe the music will help. The music absolutely heals people. Let's hope I can touch people with my message. If you listen all the way down from the European recordings to the Motown stuff to my performances today and 20 years ago, musically it's the same Luther Allison.

"A lot of people today would not look to the future of our young people. I believe that if I became a star, I could go into every big ghetto and give young people some direction. That can save a lot. We had Muddy. When Muddy and them played in a nightclub, they let us play. They didn't say, 'You ain't got your instrument, so you can't play.' They brought us. They'd sit us right down and tell us if we were gonna do it, to do it right. Not be on drugs, not be drunk, not be full of cigarettes—you gonna do your job right here. They said, 'When you come back to see me, you better show me how you been studyin' when you're away from me.' That was care, man.

"Years ago, B.B. King said, 'You remind me of me when I was ten years younger. I take my hat off to you. You're something else! I don't know how you do it.' As draining as my shows are, if the audience is doin' their job, appreciating what's going on, I'm not so tired at the end of a night's performance. I'm very spontaneous onstage. Right now if I got the chance to play for four hours, I'll still do it. But I don't want people to program it, I don't like to sound like I'm a rehearsed person. To me, if it happens, it's a bonus, man! I tell the people, you've paid for the first 90 minutes. Anything after that, consider that I'm paying for it." Allison laughed.

Solberg remembered the most amazing thing he ever saw Luther do on the bandstand. "Cutting heads with people like Freddie King and Eric Clapton and leave them walking away with their tails between their legs and the crowd cheering Luther on even though it may have been their crowd. Eric didn't take kindly to that headcuttin'. But that was the way Luther grew up."

"I had to work day jobs. I didn't have any other way besides playing music to make money," said Allison. "Many times I put my hand into my pocket to pay my band out of money I made on the day job. I worked for Keystone Steel and Wire, making clothes hangers and nails, and the Caterpillar Tractor Co., and car washes you wouldn't believe. Try to play music at 2 o'clock in the morning in the winter after working in the pits of those early car washes. I worked construction with my brothers. I moved furniture for people on my back up and down stairs to apartment buildings in Chicago. I sold watermelons behind mules during the summertime. But here I am. And I've brought through a beautiful musician, my son Bernard. I hope it doesn't take the world as long to find him as it took the world to find Luther Allison."

Even offstage, Luther Allison's primary mission was always to individually reach people. After his 1996 Handy victories, the warm, gentle nature of Luther Allison intimately touched me. "I hope that now the people believe in Luther Allison. I'm looking for a welcome home so Luther Allison can go on like he should. I hope that I can go in every year and still be recognized and get something back from these great people who have supported Luther Allison and the blues. I feel like I've brought some new ideas to younger musicians about what they should be thinking about today. I'm bringing the love back that my country so missed in me. They didn't see that love in the early days when I was very visible. They didn't know the meaning of the blues then."

On August 12, 1997, Luther Allison departed the blues stage.

He taught each of us many lessons: perseverance, acceptance, redemption, triumph, friendship, and generous, overwhelming love. His most enduring lesson, however, may be the message to live our lives in the precious present. It was these exquisite moments Luther never ignored. Walking down Beale Street after an enormous night of honor at the Handys, Luther always took time to talk individually with every person who stopped him.

Somewhere there is a picture of Luther and a fan holding hands, smiling and laughing, while the rest of the world passed by. Maybe you were the fan he hugged on the stairs of a club or the fan with whom he talked privately for what seemed like eternity. Maybe you were photographed with him on some blues cruise or you were the friend for whom he signed the last autograph of the night, "With love, your friend, Luther Allison."

Perhaps you were the kid he taught a lick to after a show or the friend to whom he proud pappa'd about Bernard. Or the breathless first-timer gasping, "I've never seen anything like this."

Maybe, 20 years ago, you sat with a handful of people while this unknown fireball blazed on well past last call. Or attended school in Madison and forever link Luther with those days. The precious present.

To hold his precious present, Luther assaulted endings. Every night he battled the performer's enemy: curfews and closing times. He extended encores for hours as one song became five became ten. He fought to keep club lights on until every fan had been personally touched.

And he defied the symptoms of his cancer until the final moment, when that precious present had to yield to a superior force.

Solberg spoke of Luther's last guitar session. After Allison's fourth treatment, Solberg and Allison jammed acoustically at Luther's Wisconsin cottage. "We got about a half hour of taping done. The following Monday, four days later, is when he lost consciousness. The very last thing we did together was 'Closer Walk with Thee.' That's the last note he ever played." Solberg's "L.A. Blues" is the most direct tribute to Luther. Lines like "He brought us together with a gift all his own" and "Stars are shinin', no need for us to cry, for he's still playin' the blues for one friend at a time" memorialize the friendship and message he gave to us all. "I robbed a couple of lines outta Luther's favorite old song, 'Oh Precious Lord, Take My Hand' for the chorus," said Solberg.

Mikki Mulvehill, Luther's manager, told me that in his final days, as he drifted in and out of consciousness, Luther warned, "Better tell Muddy and Wolf to be ready 'cause when I get to heaven, I'm not takin' any breaks." The precious present.

Farewell, dear friend, and hold a seat for us all. We will never behold another like you.

Bernard
Allison

There was never a conversation with Luther Allison that didn't include a smile and a proud-father story about his son Bernard's musical career in Europe. On June 10, 1997, exactly two months before he died, Luther sat on my porch, listened to a 1957 Otis Rush recording, and exclaimed, "I was there when this was happening. Muddy and Wolf were doin' their thing, but we were the young guys who wanted to do something different. We wanted to make our own music. We didn't want to copy them. That's what Bernard is tryin' to do."

It was tragically ironic that Luther should have died at the moment Bernard released his first American album on Cannonball and began his first American tour. In Europe, the young Allison has released five CDs and tours constantly with a band that freely mixes funk, jazz, rock, and blues. "In Europe, I normally play for crowds over 1,000, but I realize that I have to start off playing smaller clubs here."

However, he is nervous that fans always come expecting to see a clone of his father. If that's the case, they will be shocked and pleasantly surprised.

"I'm gonna try my best to pick up where he left off, but I can't be Luther Allison—I can only be myself. In the beginning everyone expects me to be exactly like him, but we are two different musicians. We have a lot of similarities, but we also have differences. We're gonna definitely shock a lot of people. I have a seven-piece group in Europe, and we do blues funk mixed with rock."

How did his direction sit with his Chicago blues father? "He was definitely supportive of the directions I was going. He always told me to be a musician and not get labeled, like he was.

During every show, Bernard Allison plays his father's USA guitar.

"Our relationship was like brothers, not father-son. We shared a lot in the music. I helped write and arrange a lot of the songs on his last three Alligator albums. He recorded one of my songs on *Reckless*, "Low Down and Dirty." Much of *Soul Fixin' Man* was my arrangements. Likewise, he'd come to my rehearsals and give me ideas for my group. Within five minutes, he'd be up singing and playing. Off the stage, we were hangin' out in music stores together."

Bernard's Ruf recording, *Times Are Changin'*, relies heavily on the sound that Allison worked on in Europe for the last eight years. Allison's sound is a system very similar to the one Stevie Ray Vaughan used, only it's pro- grammed in a rack unit that is really compact. "Rather than playing it old school through a reverb, each guitar has a program where I can get clarity of sound for whatever each song calls for. For me, it's not about loudness; it's about fineness and clarity in the sound. It plays a big part in who I am musi- cally to know anywhere I go, I will have my sound."

Bernard was born in 1965 and though he spent much of his youth mov- ing back and forth between Illinois and Florida, he still remained close to his father's music. While Luther was absent, Luther's record collection played a major role in shaping the son's direction. "I listened to a lot of my dad's influences. I went through his record collection: Magic Sam, Otis Rush, T-Bone Walker, Lightnin' Hopkins, and B.B. King. Later I got into the next generation that followed, people like Stevie Ray Vaughan, Johnny Winter, and Jimi Hendrix."

Like Ken Griffey Jr. hanging out in baseball locker rooms as a youth, Bernard was always in his father's circle. Luther's longtime guitar mate, James Solberg, recalls festival appearances in the early 1970s, like Ann Arbor, where Bernard the kid would be running onstage throughout the band's set. Experiences like that profoundly affect one's aspirations. "That's when I decided I wanted to be up there like him. I think I was seven."

"I grew up in Florida when I began to play. There were no venues at all in that area, so dad was never able to come there. That's why he didn't know I could play. He was touring the East, Midwest, and Europe. I didn't get a chance to see him until he found out I could play guitar. When we moved to Peoria, he came home preparing to do his live album in Peoria, I hooked up the amplifier and guitar in the basement and started playing his first record, *Love Me Mama*, note for note. He freaked out and said, 'Tonight you're gonna record with me.' That was my first recording, at 12. I played 'You Don't Love Me No More' and 'Sweet Home Chicago.'

"He brought me my first guitar, a Fender Stratocaster. He told me if I wanted to play guitar I had to first get my education. 'I want you to have that first, then you'll have plenty of time for the guitar.' That's what I did. I graduated from high school, and one week out of school I got a call from Koko Taylor asking me to be her lead guitar player.

At 18, Bernard joined his father onstage at the 1983 Chicago Blues Festival, finished high school, and joined Koko Taylor's Blues Machine for three years. "Koko and Pops Taylor taught me the do's and don'ts of the road. They were like my mom and pop. I was able to tour the world and see different cultures. Koko was the only group I played in besides my father's."

Relationships in the 1980s with Johnny Winter and Stevie Ray Vaughan expanded Bernard's guitar foundation. "Johnny basically taught me how to play slide guitar. I never heard anyone play slide like that. I call it 'speed slide.' I met Johnny when I was very young. My dad left me onstage with him. He was playin' circles around me. I was tryin' to play slide, and I couldn't figure out the open tunings. He explained them to me, and couple of weeks later it clicked. We always try and see each other in Texas or Paris."

"I met Stevie in 1983. When I heard him, I knew that he was learning everything I had learned from my dad. I knew exactly where he got his licks from. What amazed me was his attitude. He would share ideas with me, telling me, 'You're playing it wrong, try this.' Guitar players don't tell secrets, but I respect him for passing down what he'd learned." Bernard's live set occasionally contains a blistering 20-minute tribute to Stevie, complete with an explosive five-minute guitar-and-drum duet.

As much as these players were early influences on Bernard, he was the catalyst for putting his good friend Ronnie Baker Brooks back on the stage with his father, Lonnie Brooks. Ronnie had given up serious playing in favor of basketball until he saw Bernard and Luther playing together at the Chicago Fest in 1983. "That's been a very big memory for me, to play in front of all those people. We were on the bill with Lonnie Brooks and his son Ronnie. Ronnie had stopped playin' then and saw me play. We talked and that brought him back to playing. We're very close and we keep in touch. Every time I see him now he thanks me, sayin', 'If it wasn't for you, I might not have picked up the guitar again.'"

Just as the father influenced the son, so too did the son influence the father. Bernard pushed his father to expand the frantic slide guitar that accompanied Luther's signature club walk in his American assault in the 1990s. Luther tackled the slide when he witnessed Bernard's proficiency. "He had great faith in my playing. In fact, I brought him back to playing slide guitar. He saw me playin' slide, and he asked me how I was doin' that. He was only used to the regular tunings, so I taught him open tunings and he's been rippin' away at it ever since."

After leaving Koko's band, Bernard lived and played in London, Ontario, Canada. Then, in 1989, Bernard flew to Europe to record with his father, was asked to lead the band, and, like his father, adopted permanent residency in Europe. "He was the best at working an audience. He could get onstage and have them in his hand within a matter of minutes. I was his bandleader for three years. Even then, we played those four-hour shows. I knew how to pace myself, but watchin' the drummers slowly sink down in their seats after three hours was funny.

"Things really took off from there. Within three years, I received my first record contract. My first record was *The Next Generation*. I got my own group together, and now we're one of the major touring acts in Europe. When American blues acts come to Europe, they open for us. It happened the same way it happened for my dad. I was getting a little frustrated here, went there, was well received and treated right. It's a shame it happens that way, but this is nothing new. Look at Hendrix or Memphis Slim. The European audiences don't hold back. In Europe, families come to the shows. You don't really see that here except at festivals. In Europe, we're the Bernard Allison Group, not the Bernard Allison Blues Band. That's because my father didn't want me to become labeled, because it cuts the audience down."

As Bernard began filling houses in Europe, Luther cautioned him about returning to America. He never filled Bernard with unrealistic expectations. Rather, he advised his son to establish himself first with the people, saying notoriety will inevitably follow. "He knew my capabilities. He told me that I was going to have to play smaller venues, deal with the bar scene, and travel in a van all over again. From there, I can move to bigger clubs and festival bookings."

Bernard has slowly climbed the ladder of musical acceptance since his first trip to America, in May of 1997. His first tour of the United States was in the fall of 1997, immediately following Luther's death. But he returns to Europe each winter to continue building his European audience and expanding his musical style. According to Bernard, playing only in America might put him in the same club-and-festival circuit, playing the same music, becoming too comfortable in the consistency of that environment.

"So many blues acts do the same show over and over. I think I offer something new to fans. You never know what I'm gonna do because I never know what I'm gonna do. I feel the crowd out and vibe off of the people. If I hit 'em with something funky and they don't respond, I know to try something with more rock in it. I know when I hit the straight blues, they'll definitely respond. In every show, I like to see how wide I can go."

Nothing ignites a blue streak in a crowd quicker than when the performer leaves the stage and takes the music to the people. Though many musicians feel the call to abandon the safety net of the stage, few actually risk crossing the line. "I basically play two shows. After the walk at the end of the first set, people are blown away. They're on telephones calling friends telling them to come down fast. I can't do the walk in the second set, so I normally end with two slide tunes, "Lowdown and Dirty" and my speed slide, which is even higher energy then the walk. Once audiences hear the speed slide, they go over the top. When I come back for an encore, I try and do a song that'll mellow 'em out and bring 'em back down after the speed slide. Those are some of the little things that I learned from my dad.

"Most people consider musicians untouchable stars. That's too high in the sky for me. I try to keep the communication with them person to person," said Allison. "Since not many people do that, it's a very effective way to reach audiences. If you hide on the stage, you only see a few people. By walking the crowd, I can mingle with the people and talk to individuals. Regardless of how big I get, I don't ever think I could stay on the stage. This is all part of the family vibe that I try to create at every show."

Part of a younger generation of players who are now making a mark, Bernard encompasses his father's spirit and vision. "I always make a point to record one of my father's songs. Though my pop's gone, for me he's not gone anywhere. He's looking down at me every minute. He knew where my heart was and what I wanted to do. I'm followin' what he wanted me to do. Somebody needs to carry the music to the youth." Any Bernard show will have stirring covers of Luther's songs, like "Bad Love" or Luther's famous marathon encore song, "I'm Going Down," all played with Bernard's eerie, Luther-like vocal attack. Yet the addition of a blasting horn section with its jazzy excursions into musical landscapes singles out Bernard's musical breadth from today's guitar-laden bands.

Listen close to "Don't Be Confused" on *Times Are Changin'*, Bernard's recorded tribute to his father. "It's the kind of song that reaches anyone who has lost a family member. I also talk about his struggles, saying some things he never really had the chance to say. That was the most difficult song to record. Musically it wasn't a problem, but vocally it was real hard to deliver. It's only been since December of 1998 that I'm able to finish the song live."

Though Bernard has catalogued a lifetime of memories of Luther, one stands out. "My special memory was the first time he saw my last European group. I could see the look in his eyes that said, 'Wow!' He could see how much I had learned from him and that really made him a proud father. He's always wanted to have the big band behind him, and he could see I was doing the sound. He could see his son doing more than one thing."

Bernard is a distinctive "son of the blues," for he possesses the requisite guitar feel and vocal intonations necessary to push his blues into the next century. He knows the energy level necessary to hold audiences and combines enough showmanship and spontaneity to push the performance in fresh, innovative directions each night.

Luther always told me the future of the blues depended on kids like Bernard playing the music their way, like Luther did in the 1960s. Scary, weird, ironic, but like his dad, Bernard is making his first musical waves in America at almost the same age Luther hit the Ann Arbor Blues Festival stage in 1969. Let's hope the country doesn't ignore another Allison, only to discover that burning talent too late.

Lonnie, Ronnie Baker, and Wayne Baker Brooks

We all know Lonnie Brooks is committed to the blues, but not many understand the devotion he brought to parenting his musically talented offspring, Ronnie Baker Brooks and Wayne Baker Brooks. From the beginning, Lonnie instilled a love of the music for the music's sake, the drive for his sons to make it on their own, and the safe family environment where success or failure could be accepted.

Most parents who want great things for their children push aggressively instead of guiding gently. Lonnie's approach was much gentler, with an innate understanding of the psychology of child-rearing.

"I played with my kids. I didn't drive them to anything," said Lonnie. "They wanted to do it. They enjoyed it because I made it look like fun to them. If somebody doesn't want to do something, and you demand, they're not gonna do their best and you can ruin it. Look, I'm proud of my kids. My daddy was good to me, he took care of me, but he wasn't interested in what I did. I know what it means to show you care about your kids. That's what's wrong with a lot of kids today, fathers don't spend time with them, and they grow up on the wrong end."

"He was real cool with that gentle criticism," said Ronnie. "When someone is starting out, you have to be careful about what to say to them. That's what he was like. He didn't want to make it look like I was doing it all wrong. If he had said the wrong thing about my playing, I might give it up."

Though Wayne came into the music much later, he was still given the same encouragement and nurturing. "He never pushed me. I was 21 when I told dad I wanted to play guitar. He showed me a lick and said, 'Do it like this.' I did that, and I knew this was what I wanted to do for the rest of my life."

Ronnie and Wayne both feel that though their father may have opened the door to a music career, without any talent they would have been quickly forgotten.

Ronnie said, "I don't want anyone to think I got my break because of my dad. I might have gotten to the door because of the name, but I got through that door because of myself. Without real talent, you won't last long in the business. I know that as long as I'm on this earth, I'm gonna be Lonnie Brooks' son. I'm able to deal with that—on my own. And that's what I want people to understand. I'm always gonna be his son and I'm willing to accept that. But I don't want my peers to think I only got here because of Dad."

Wayne, who only started playing guitar in 1991, concurs. "I know from growing up in a family where someone is a superstar that you've got to fill big shoes. I knew that if I didn't get it myself, I didn't deserve it. Even though I know I'll ride on my dad's name for the rest of my life, I wanted to prove to myself that I can do it without ridin' on my dad's name."

Today, the bond between father and sons runs deep. Ronnie uses his father as a sounding board for the songs he writes. "I've been fortunate to have songs make his CDs. Selling the song to Dad is hard, because Dad has to feel the song. I used to be terrified when I wanted him to check out songs I was writing. He's given me confidence by putting my songs on albums. Now I'll ask him to critique songs and tell me what I need to do to make songs better. He doesn't get on me negatively, but he says what he thinks about them in a very positive way. In that way, he tells me exactly what I need to do with them."

"I call it Blues University," laughed Wayne. "I want a good reputation, so I watch how my dad takes care of the business. I'm taking the same approaches as my dad did and doing it with professionalism."

"The one thing I always try to tell them is to mean what you play. Play it straight from the heart. If you can do that, people will feel what you feel," said Lonnie.

"I can't play it if I don't feel it," said Ronnie. "My dad always said, 'Be yourself, don't be another me, and play it from the heart. Don't ever be jealous of someone, because you can get it too if you work at it.' He always preached to learn what I could from anybody and make it me.

"I didn't know much about the responsibilities of being a bandleader until I started getting my own band. Once I started doing that, I started appreciating more what my dad was doing. I used the lessons he taught me to keep my own band running," said Ronnie.

Today, both sons front their own bands that play the music they grew up hearing and playing, mixing funk, rock, jazz, and other modern music with Chicago blues. In the fall of 1998, Ronnie released his first solo CD,

Lonnie Brooks (right) taught his sons Ronnie
Baker Brooks (left) and Wayne Baker Brooks the
showmanship necessary to every performance.

Golddigger, while Wayne coauthored the book *Blues for Dummies*. Clearly, Lonnie and Jeannine Brooks have raised men to carry music, values, and traditions into the next century.

Ronnie was born in 1968 and took to the guitar very quickly. By six, he was an integral part of the Brooks family band. "I started teaching him at six years old. I used to have a little rehearsal with the band and have fun with my kids. Wayne was beatin' on a shoebox or pan for the drums, Ronnie was playing the bass line on a guitar, and I'd be playing lead," remembered Lonnie.

Three years later, Ronnie hounded his dad for the chance to get onstage. Before he left for Europe, his father told him to learn two songs all the way through, and when he returned, Ronnie would get his chance.

"He was away for three months. I knew the songs, but this gave me the time to learn them where I could just play them real easy," said Ronnie.

Ronnie remembers well the party that night at Pepper's Hideout. "I played "Messin' With the Kid" and "Reconsider Baby" with my dad. I had a mood ring on and that mood ring was changin' all kinds of colors. I was nervous before I got onstage. Then, once I got on there, it felt like that was what I was born to do. I knew that at a younger age, but not for sure, not until I played onstage. I knew that this was me expressing myself."

Lonnie also recalls the night. "Nine years old, and he played "Messin' With the Kid" perfect. I let him play like I promised. Had a suit made like mine. People thought I just had him up there as a gimmick; they still thought it was me playing. When he got to his solo, I took my hands off the guitar and held them up in the air. Boy, when the people seen that, they started throwin' him money! He made more money in one night than I did!"

"I got a standing ovation, people were throwin' money onstage. My dad still teases me, saying, 'I used to make $30 a night, and then he come around and makes $90 in one night,'" laughed Ronnie.

How exactly did Lonnie know Ronnie was to be the first of Brooks' nine children to follow in his guitar footsteps?

"It's a funny thing. I was playing at a club on 63rd Street in Chicago, and I got home at the time my wife was to go to work. She was mad at me for coming in late. It was early, and the kids get up as soon as she was up, so I made me a pallet on the floor. I took my acoustic guitar and went to sleep.

"Then, I heard these notes being picked; he was playing the strings. I woke up and saw that. Other kids, older than Ronnie, pull on the strings. He didn't do that. He was playing just like I played 'em. He just didn't know how to note it. He had that touch already, and I heard that. After that, I started showing him. I saw that when I started showing him something, he never forgot it. That boy learned everything so fast."

Lonnie's pride and joy balanced with a pain that every parent experiences during the rebellious teenage years. That was when Ronnie begged out of playing the guitar in favor of basketball. "None of my friends were playing music. I felt like I wasn't being a kid. When I went with my friends, they were all into sports and I was sittin' home practicing a guitar. I always wanted to be accepted by my friends. I put the guitar down and started playing basketball. I took basketball real serious.

"I think when I quit totally was something that really hurt my dad. He'd accept me doing both, but I didn't play guitar at all. The thing I love him for is that he stuck it out and supported me even though it hurt him. He said, 'Well, Ronnie, if this is what you want to do.' He'd be up all night playing at clubs and then be at my games the next morning. That made me feel good, but I never realized what I was doing to my dad. He was crushed behind that."

"When he stopped playing music, it broke my heart," said Lonnie. "I didn't let him know how it hurt. I went to all his games. I made it look like I didn't care, that way he'd come back to it. When Ronnie told me he didn't want to play music, he was gonna play basketball, I could have said, 'No! You're gonna play the guitar.' If I'd done that, he wouldn't be where he is today.

"On weekends, I'd go out with him. In 1983, we ran into Bernard and Luther Allison at the Chicago Blues Fest. I was lookin' at Bernard up there with Luther, and it hit me again. Bernard came up to me and said, 'We got enough Michael Jordans, we need some more B.B. Kings.' That got the spark back again. It just took me until after high school for it to really sink in. My father always preached, 'Get your education first. No matter what you do, music or sports, you're going to school.' After I graduated, I took to the music even more because I started traveling with him."

In retrospect, the basketball experience indirectly taught Ronnie about playing on the bandstand. "Playing basketball gave me a sense of the teamwork necessary for a band. My coach used to preach to us that if we learned from basketball, it will help us in life. That helped me with the band. I know that everyone can't shoot the ball at the same time. To make it work, everybody's got to have a role. I accepted that role with my dad's band. I know we've got a team here. Dad is the Michael Jordan or the coach. I know the ball will get passed to me onstage, and I'm learnin' how to deal with that with my own band today."

When 18-year-old Ronnie asked for permission to tour with his father, Jeannine also seemed to direct both Brooks men. "She used us both to watch each other. She told my dad to take me on the road with him to keep an eye on me. Mom wanted me to go on the road to watch over my dad and make sure he was alright. We were both there watching each other," laughed Ronnie.

Going on the road with his father in 1985 was much harder than Ronnie thought. "When he came back and said he wanted to play again, I kinda ripped him a bit," said the elder Brooks. "I told him he might play one tune, but he was gonna have to carry my guitar and set up my amps. I tried to make it real hard for him. He was out there with me a pretty good while before he worked himself into the band."

When the opportunity arose to add Ronnie as the second guitar, Lonnie faced up to the criticism. "It happened that the guitar player left without notice. We were going on the road with George Thorogood and the cat wouldn't go with us. If I'd had a week or so, I could have found another guitar player, but without a notice, I couldn't find anyone who could learn my tunes in a day.

"But here was Ronnie, who already knew the stuff. At the time, he was a little weak, and I heard a lot of people talkin', 'Lonnie Brooks ought to be ashamed of himself, got his son out there playing the guitar knowing he ain't ready.' If they ain't no good, they ain't gonna make it. That boy stayed on that guitar and learned my tunes better than I did. He was 18 when he got with me, but started playing full time in 1988."

Life on the road has put Ronnie in personal contact with the artists willing to share stories and lessons. "I treasure the friendships with Jimmy Rogers, Luther Allison, Buddy Guy, Junior Wells, Albert Collins. Koko Taylor is like my blues mama. I've known her over 20 years. Son Seals and Hubert Sumlin would come by the house and share music too. Some shared lessons by showing, some by talking.

"I learned so much on the tour we did with Junior, B.B. King, Buddy Guy, Koko, and my dad. That was probably the best fun I ever had in my lifetime. Every young guy should experience what I experienced on that tour. It was awesome. We'd be on the bus playing acoustic stuff. There was no inhibitions about the playing because everybody was just being themselves. Everybody was together talking about experiences and telling jokes. It was like being in school. I would sit in the corner and just watch and listen.

"B.B. would tell me, 'Boy, if I had it like you have it, I'd be a monster too!' He was tellin' me about not having this kind of stuff where people get together and play for each other when he was coming up. 'I had to go see one person here, another there. I could never get backstage to 'em.'

"B.B. is the biggest gentleman in the world. He can make everybody feel great. He was telling me, 'Hey man, just go on and do it.' I've been fortunate enough to be around him watchin'. He's the best, definitely the king. And he doesn't let it go to his head.

"Sometimes on the tour, I'd tell him he was sounding great. He'd say, 'Look son, I'm doing what I'm doing, but your dad is just as good. We've just got different styles.' For somebody of his stature to say that about my dad—he didn't have to say that. He made sure I realized that my dad is just as good as B.B. King. That made me feel real proud as the son of Lonnie Brooks.

"I remember sittin' backstage at a show we did one time with Koko, years ago when Pops Taylor was still alive. They sat me down and talked to me about stickin' with my dad. They told me that bein' with my dad was the best thing I could do, that I'd learn a lot but also be helpin' him.

"I remember Junior Wells tellin' me, 'If you don't feel it, you can't make the people feel it.' I always remember that. My dad was getting on me when I first tried singin', and I remember him askin' Willie Dixon to tell me about singin'. Willie said, 'Man, it ain't nothing to it. You just gotta mean what you say. Look at Howlin' Wolf. He wasn't a great singer, but he meant every word he sang.' Those are the kinds of things I learned from Willie, Koko, Junior.

"Albert Collins and Buddy Guy always told me to 'play your ass off because you never know who's watchin'.' I always remember Albert being like a member of the family. We got into music, but he would go beyond that. As a person, Albert was a sweetheart to me. Next to my father, he's probably the only other guy who has really, really touched me in a way others haven't. All the others have touched me, but Albert gave me that spark, man, that lifted the playing.

"My dad gave me all the tools and the want to do it. Albert made me believe I could do it. To see him have the time to talk to me made me feel so good and took me to a whole other level. Albert said, 'Keep your ears open to everybody.' He didn't say go steal, take what they do and find a place for it. I'm never gonna play Albert Collins's licks. But I can try and play a lick with the same spirit. That's what I try and do with all the musicians I listen to.

"He was the same way as B.B. He'd tell me, 'I ain't doing nothing your daddy isn't doin'.' The motivation in his playing just touched me. I felt him. I remember one night when Albert had just started hittin' the next level. He came to where my dad was playin' in Chicago. Man, did they get into it onstage. The back of my hair just stood up. I was froze. I couldn't move, I was so amazed. The vibe, the people there, the musicians, and Albert and Dad was like sparks flyin' on the stage. Right then I was sayin',' 'For sure, that's what I want to do.' And Albert was always tellin' me, 'You can do it'."

Then there is requisite the headcuttin', ass-kicking lesson imperative to the master-apprentice relationship in the blues. Ask anyone who played with Collins and they have their own personal version of Ronnie's experience. "I always wanted to play with him, and I never got the nerve. Once, when we were in Japan, our keyboard player asked Albert to let me sit in with him. Now, before we went on, we were backstage shootin' dice to pass time, havin' fun, you know. We started off shooting for guitar picks. Then it started getting serious. We started playing for some yen. I'd won some money off Albert.

"At the end of the show, Albert was playin' "Frosty," and he called me onstage and he took that out on me. 'Come on out here, Brother Ron.' He was standin' by his amp, lookin' at me, sayin', 'Go ahead, get your solo.' I'm doin' all I can do. Then he hit that one note, and it just cut me down. I looked at him and he had a look on his face that said, 'I gotcha.' From then on I was in la-la land. Afterwards he said, 'I had to get you back. You took all my money.' He told me that nobody'd ever beat him like that, and I'd have to take him out to breakfast the next morning."

Ronnie's lessons from Luther Allison are at the center of his commitment. Ronnie experienced what so many of us around Luther did; once he looked into your eyes, you were somehow changed. "When we started playing, he and I got into this zone where I forgot where I was. I didn't even know what I was playing. It was like that every time he called me up. The first time was at Bruce Iglauer's wedding, in 1996. We just locked in and forgot where we were. It was more than music. There was something spiritual there. From that, every time we'd see each other, he called me out. He said I gave him energy, that's why he called me out. He definitely gave me energy. It was an honor to be onstage with him. Luther gave you every ounce in him and lived more in 15 minutes than most people live in their lives."

Wayne was born in 1970 and, though he also played music in the family living room, it was not until 1991, at the age of 21, that music called. "I was into things like basketball during school. I was thinking about taking up drums, but they didn't come as easy as guitar did. I felt like I finally found something I could do. From that point, I listened to everything. In the beginning, when I was learning, I'd go to the clubs and I wouldn't tell people who I was. I just wanted to get up there in the jams and have people appreciate it, knowing it was that they liked me for me, not as Lonnie Brooks's son.

"When I first began, I used to practice 18 hours a day. I really wanted to get it right before I got onstage. I didn't want people to say, 'Lonnie Brooks' son can't play. Why is he picking up the guitar?' I was thinking that, when I got onstage, I wouldn't be a beginner, I'd be more like an intermediate. It's an everyday learning process of everything for me.

"The first song I ever played was 'Sweet Home Chicago.' Once the people were screamin' and yellin' and I got that rush, I thought, 'I want to do this for the rest of my life.' It was an adrenaline high that went through my entire body like a drug. I felt like I was glowing just from the people's applause."

Ronnie has his own most amazing stories of his dad to contribute. "The most amazing thing was being at home with us kids, playing with us on the floor, wrestling, then going to the show that evening and killing the people. He used to do the Chicago Fest and we'd play with him in the morning, then he'd go out at night and killed them. Everybody's tryin' to get next to him, and I'm smilin', sayin', 'That's my dad. Y'all don't know it but we were just wrestling together.'"

Another time it was a show in Seattle. "We were onstage when the power went off. We had the crowd in the palm of our hands, the crowd was rockin'. Dad was sayin', 'We got 'em, we can't lose 'em." We were up on a high stage, and he climbed a rafter down off the stage and people were wonderin' what he was doin'. He got in the audience and climbed on one of the chairs and started singin' a cappella to 'em. He kept them people goin'. Probably took 'em to a higher level than he would have if the power had stayed on. It was so obvious that he wasn't gonna let nothing stop him from touchin' them people. Finally, the power came back on and we put the music to the song and that took it even higher. We go back there and people are still talkin' about that show.

"I'm still in awe of him. Sometimes, playing behind him, I'm caught in a daze. I'll close my eyes and be listening and I'll say to myself, 'Thank you Lord.' I know this don't happen to everybody, and I want to enjoy it to the fullest."

Perhaps the truest measure of a man's reputation and character is how others see him and his accomplishments. Amid the children of his contemporaries, Lonnie Brooks is constantly lauded by his musical friends for the outstanding men he has raised. "They'd say to me, 'Man, you must be the proudest person in the world. You got some nice boys.' I guess they expected them to be smokin' pot and getting drunk, havin' an attitude. Everybody wants to adopt my kids in a minute. That's what makes me feel good. All the old players look at them and say, 'I wish my boy'd be like that,' and that makes me feel good."

Johnny "Clyde" and Shemekia Copeland

The stirrings of the blues have always been connected to the heart and soul of its performer. When Johnny "Clyde" Copeland learned in 1989 that he had congestive heart failure, his first step was medication. However, on May 6, 1995, when his heart stopped beating, more drastic measures were necessary.

"I started getting shortness of breath. I couldn't walk up a hill without losing my breath. I couldn't even walk up stairs. I knew something was going wrong. When I went to the doctor, he told me I had the heart of an 83-year-old man," said Copeland.

That's when Copeland became a candidate for the state-of-the-art pump, the left ventricular assist device (LVAD), a machine designed to keep a patient's heart pumping. Essentially, the LVAD consists of two wires running out from Copeland's side. Outside the house, one wire is plugged into the LVAD and the other into the batteries. At home, Copeland was plugged directly into the machine. "I had to plug into it wherever I went. I even plugged into the main machine when I was sleeping. It was like having a guitar cord following me all over the place," laughed Copeland.

Copeland continued touring, though he usually limited his gigs to stay close to his New Jersey home. "The batteries on the LVAD lasted about three hours. When I was ready to go on, I would change the batteries and they would last for a pretty normal set. The first one started malfunctioning on me, so I had to get an operation to get a second one put in me."

Miraculously, this electric pump kept him alive for more than 20 months, until his heart transplant on New Year's Day, 1997. Four months later, on April 4, 1997, Copeland staged his dramatic comeback with a sold-

In 1986, Johnny "Clyde" Copeland won
a Grammy for his album Showdown.

out show at Manny's Car Wash in New York City. From there, Copeland
sprinted with a second chance at life, playing at the 1997 Handy Awards
and the Beale Street Music Festival only six months after the transplant.

"I felt real good. It's taking me a while to get back 'cause I gotta come
back slowly. The first night I went out, I was a little nervous. I had been off
so long, and my coordination between the guitar and the singing, keeping

the lyrics in place, was off. The prognosis on my transplant is very good. I just heard from the hospital, and they said there has been totally no rejection. Right now, I'm touring Texas, California, Memphis, and New England. I'll be going back in the studio in September."

Those days never came. Sadly, Copeland passed away on July 3, 1997, at Columbia Presbyterian Hospital in New York City. Johnny underwent heart surgery a week before his death in order to repair a leaky heart valve and died of complications from that surgery. Copeland, the warrior, had undergone eight heart surgeries since March of 1995.

Copeland was known as the "Texas Twister" for the spin he brings to blues from the Lone Star State. "It took us a long time to get recognized coming out of Texas. No major music people came out of there, so we had to leave Texas to get famous. Everybody was leavin' for Memphis and New Orleans. I'm interested in making sure the Texas musicians get the proper respect. The Delta and Chicago blues had the British invasion. We never had a proper uprising. Guys like Albert Collins, the Thunderbirds, Stevie Ray Vaughan, and myself really had to beat it out and let people know that the scene is happening down there.

"The Texas sound is right between Kansas City swinging horn lines and New Orleans funk. It's not as bluesy as blues; there's a funkier beat. It's blues, but it tells all kinds of stories. Take Lightnin' Hopkins' material—it told stories with a great amount of humor in it."

Innovative and intense guitar players have always dominated the music exported from Texas. "I listened to Gatemouth Brown and T-Bone Walker when I was coming up, and a host of local people, like Johnny "Guitar" Watson and Lowell Fulson. That was our whole world. Freddie King and Albert Collins came along in the '60s. That led to Stevie in the late '70s."

Copeland was born in 1937 in Haynesville, Louisiana, and moved to Houston's Third Ward in 1950. There he became part of Houston's vibrant music scene. "I had the guitar from the time I was 12 years old. I just played what I'd hear. I didn't really get into it until I moved to Houston, 'cause all the kids there were playing. We formed a band called the Dukes of Rhythm and that's when I really got interested. I took one lesson. At the time, I didn't want to play like that. I wanted to learn how to play like T-Bone. He was teaching me this progressive stuff. I wasn't gonna waste my money for this. So I went back to woodsheddin' by myself. I was about 15 then. He learned me some stuff I still remember, stuff like how to run my scales and some great chords I still play. He was gonna make a progressive player outta me, and I didn't want that. I wanted to be a blues singer, I didn't want to be no progressive jazz player."

In 1953, he formed his first blues band, The Dukes of Rhythm, with guitarist Joe Hughes. That was also the year Copeland fell under Albert Collins's spell. "I knew Albert all my life. He was one of the first electric players I heard. He'd play during lunches from 12 to 4 P.M. I'd go see him all the time. I left the Dukes then to go play with Albert Collins. You know, he sounded as good the last time I heard him as he did the first time. He had that everlastin' thing. When I started playing, he would always take time to show me things. He was as nice a guy as there is," said Copeland.

Throughout the next 20 years, Copeland suffered through the soul explosion of the '60s and the deteriorating live music scene in Texas in the 1970s, so he packed his guitar and headed East in 1975. "I moved East because my management was from Springfield and Worchester, Massachusetts, and they knew that area pretty well. We rented a place in West Brookfield, Massachusetts, to get a band together for the first album. We started working the small clubs and then moved back to New York." He lived in Harlem until moving to Teaneck, New Jersey, in the early 1990s.

Though Copeland made numerous recordings (notched on his guitar strap), his most noteworthy are 1986's Grammy winner, *Showdown*, with Albert Collins and Robert Cray, and 1984's *Bringing It All Back Home*, inspired by Copeland's 1982 ten-nation, six-week tour of Africa. "I could tell the root of the blues comes from there. They mostly understood the Delta blues. They was expecting it to be all slow blues. But we surprised them and had the kids up dancin' and on the stage. We were more uplifting then the Delta blues they'd heard. The tour and record that came out of it has been very uplifting for my career.

"The trip to Africa was shocking at first; I liked the language and the people so I decided to try and write songs there. Paul Simon went to South Africa to record after me, but we have to remember that he had a great budget to work with. I did it on a very low budget, and I was the first to attempt to do that kind of tour. I found that the African people liked to give, so I picked up a lot of lines and licks from what they'd show me."

Nor does Copeland neglect blues roots in America. "The blues is not dead yet. One of the reasons I fight so hard is that I think our people and parents deserve to be recognized. I know what my daddy went through as a sharecropper, so I always try and do my best for audiences because I know that they understand what they are listening to."

During his medical battles, one element was constant at every Copeland show: the set opener by his teenage daughter Shemekia. Copeland knew intuitively this was the child born to sing. In retrospect, it appears that he fought so hard and hung so strong in the face of personal catastrophe until she was ready to fly on her own. Copeland told me in April of 1997, "It sure

In 2001, 21-year-old Shemekia Copeland's album Wicked *was nominated for a Grammy. She also won a W.C. Handy Award for Contemporary Female Artist and Album of the Year.*

is a thrill watching my daughter perform. She's a real blues person. She's been doin' it all her life, but she only started doing it regularly after I got sick. I'm able to just sit back in the audience and enjoy her singing."

Shemekia Copeland is blessed with the savvy to grip a capacity club in her hands for a full 90-minute show or wrap herself into the fabric of a venue with much smaller attendance. This is one of the greatest lessons her father, the late Johnny "Clyde" Copeland, passed on to his daughter.

"When my dad died, people would tell me about seeing him play a set for 15 people like he was playing at Madison Square Garden. Then, with ten people at the second set, he'd play it even better. My dad always said if it wasn't for the fans, musicians would be nothing. Every place I go is not a packed house and nobody knows who I am yet, so I have to give it my best, no matter how many people are in the audience."

Though she's just a kid who was born in 1979, Shemekia feels ready to carry the torch passed to her by her father. "I never knew I wanted to sing. My dad knew ever since I was a baby that I was gonna be a singer. He'd say, 'This child is gonna be a singer.' People have been tellin' me that I was the only child he'd say that about," said Shemekia.

Unlike the precocious preteen hamming-it-up shows for the family, this

child was embarrassed every time her father made her sing. Instead of bringing down family functions, she would hide behind a curtain or couch and sing
from there. The confidence to sing in front of people came slowly. At eight,
she was called on Harlem's famed Cotton Club stage by her father to sing
"Stingy," a song the elder Copeland had written especially for Shemekia.

"My mother dragged me to the club. When my dad saw me in the audience, he announced that his baby was gonna come up and sing. I was eight
years old and scared to death. I wasn't serious about it. When I was 12, my
dad put together a bigger show at the Cotton Club for me. Another cute
thing, but I still wasn't serious about it. I was just into being a kid."

This blues diva comes into the music world from the most improbable
of blues locales, Harlem. Though the Big Apple has traditionally been a jazz
center, Shemekia's here to champion its big-city blues. Earlier blues voices
may have learned by hangin' out on Delta porches or in South Side Chicago
taverns. Copeland's real music lessons came each day on the streets. City
experiences mature children quickly, and Shemekia admits she has seen
more blues each day than most people see in a lifetime. The Harlem she
walked exposed her to a richly diverse music in the air, from guitar players
on corners, saxophone duos in subway stations, and bands in every neighborhood park. "When I sing 'Ghetto Child,' I can tell you, because of what
I saw in Harlem, I really mean it," said Copeland.

The artistic calling burned hot when her father became sick. "I don't
know what happened to me. It was a weird thing, but at that moment, I just
wanted to sing. My dad always said to me, 'You have to have the need to
sing. People have to hear that need in your voice.' He told me that I'd always
been a singer, but I never needed it. Nobody wants to listen to someone
singing just to earn some extra money. You've gotta sing because you need
it. It's like a drug for me now. When I'm not singing, I'm sick."

Through the years of opening for her father, Shemekia came to gradually understand the virtues of Johnny Copeland. "My dad liked me to think
by opening for him that I was doin' him a favor, but in reality he did it all
for me. I knew he didn't have all the strength he needed to do all those
shows, but he would do them so I would get the exposure. There were
nights I knew he didn't feel like performing, but I know now that he did it
for me because he wanted the people to hear me."

One of the principles Johnny Copeland instilled in all musicians he
tutored was to be original. This lesson was not lost on his daughter. Though
his spirit flows naturally in her vision, Shemekia has set out to avoid the
artistic suicide that comes with photocopying originals. Where Copeland
the elder played a mean Texas guitar, Copeland the younger brings a bold
and sassy vocal interpretation to all she sings. Whether she pays homage to

her father on one of his songs or interprets blues standards, Shemekia bangs them out with an intensely full-throated swaggering. But she also understands the need to write original material to reach people. "I want to be responsible for creating something that will last and touch people. I don't want to just copy other people's stuff. Most of the songs I sing are my own. I am Shemekia, so I have to have my own material. I can't copy my father, he wouldn't have wanted it."

She's more than just a blues shouter. She's a maturing singer who understands with each song she sings exactly what she is capable of. As she passionately belts out words or clings to syllables, Copeland is constantly discovering new ways her voice can express. The material written for her by John Hahn, Jon and Sally Tiven, and Copeland herself allows her to sing songs crafted for her. This ownership allows her to sing what she feels and to touch listeners of every age.

In nearly every live show, Copeland's tour de force performance comes when she walks the club singing the chorus to "Ghetto Child" without amplification. "I really enjoy being able to sing without using the microphone because it makes me feel really close to the audience. It's a much more natural way for me to sing. When the band plays as quietly as possible, and I'm singing without the mic, it's much easier on my voice."

At the Cambridge House of Blues Fifth Anniversary party in November of 1997, Shemekia Copeland was opening the show and royalty was in the house. Koko Taylor sat in the sound room and watched. Teo Leyasmeyer, who books the club and played in Johnny's band, remembered that night. "Koko was cheering her on, and Koko looked at me and said, 'Damn, that song sounds just like Etta James.' This is coming from Koko Taylor. She took Shemekia aside and had a private conversation with her, told her some of the pitfalls to watch out for in the business and as a woman. She told Shemekia, 'Don't start getting into this "I need a drink or two to sing because I'm nervous," because in ten years, you're gonna need a bottle.'

"When Koko did her set, she stopped and she said, 'This whole generation has gotten into rap, and there are very few black kids who are continuing in the blues traditions. I want to congratulate Shemekia for doing what she's doing. I wish her all the luck because she's gonna be the future of this music.' Shemekia had tears in her eyes. It was a perfect moment," said Leyasmeyer.

Shemekia also remembered the night. "She's one of my biggest singer influences. She told me about things to avoid in the business. To leave all the negativity, the drugs and alcohol, alone. She told me that we've lost so many talented artists already from that stupid stuff. I grew up in Harlem until I was 15, and there were a lot of temptations, but I never let myself go to any of them. That's why I think I can handle this music business. She said, 'Baby, you gonna have your good nights and your bad nights. But you gotta keep doin' it.' She always says to me, 'Look to the hills.' I think I take that in so many ways. I think she's talking about God, looking towards him."

There have been other memorable lessons passed along from the friends of her father. Copeland has opened often for B.B. King and Buddy Guy. B.B. especially has given her advice about longevity in the blues. She has sat on his tour bus night after night and listened to his wisdom.

The women vocalists have passed along lessons about voice and diction to Copeland. It is in her vocal interpretation of her originals that Shemekia's soul shines brightly. It's crucial that every singer discovers how to tell a story within a song in a way that enables the audience to believe every word. It is this intangible ability to become the song and compel listeners to trust her assertions that singles out Copeland's mesmerizing vocal magic. "My songs are those types of songs that I do have to sell. I call it flirting with the audience. People have to know what I'm talking about. They have to believe me, or there's no point. When I listen to Ruth Brown or see her live, I like to watch her attitude more than anything. She has more class in her little finger than most of us do in our entire bodies. But Ruth also has sass. I want to be that classy, sassy entertainer.

"I take little things from everybody. I've watched Koko and I love the power of her growl, how she can walk out there and take control of the stage. When I listen to people like Mahalia Jackson, I hear her singing like a bird. When she hums, everybody can hear her. She doesn't even have to sing a note and everybody knows she's up there. I love that sassy attitude that Bessie Smith and Big Mama Thornton have. When I listen to the older singers, like O.V. Wright, Jackie Wilson, and Sam Cooke, I just want to sound as much like them as possible. When the older singers opened their mouth, you knew exactly who it was because nobody sounded like them."

Without any formal vocal training, Shemekia relied on the genetic gifts of her father's musical heritage. Phrasing, inflection, intonation, vibrato, and growl were all intuitively within her soul, waiting to explode. "I think what sets me apart is that I listen to everything and everybody. I'm very versatile because I adopt something from every vocalist I consider an idol. Eventually these small items become part of my voice. When I hear myself, I don't think that I sound like anybody else," said Copeland.

Armed with incredibly high standards, Copeland grades every performance. Rarely does a performance earn three stars. "I'm my worst critic. I'm always saying to myself, 'Mekia, you did all this wrong.' That's just the way I've always been. I'm hard on myself in life too. I know there's so many things I have to learn before it can even start thinking about giving myself a five."

The only recorded duet with her dad is the rockin' "Tumblin' Dice" on the Rolling Stones tribute CD, *Paint It Blue*. When questioned about the experience, Shemekia giggles and laughs throughout the story. "That was so cool! Daddy was sittin' in the kitchen listening to the tapes saying, 'I don't know if I can do this, baby.' I went to the mall that day. Something made me call home that day. My brother was yelling that the producer, John Snyder, wanted me at the studio.

"John had me do the background vocals on that song. It's the first thing I ever did with my dad that was recorded. I'm a pretty strong person; I don't cry a lot. But one day I was coming home from work, listening to my daddy and me singing that song on the CD player. Though I had been listening to it for a long time, it really hit me hard that day. I cried all the way home.

"The most memorable thing I saw my daddy do was his performance at the Handy Awards that May in 1997. My dad was upset because each performer could only play two songs. Everybody else was playing long sets. He said, 'I'm just gonna do what I have to do.' He was in the middle of "Kasavubu" and the curtains came down and he kept right on playing. Those curtains went right back up."

John Hahn, her manager and family friend, and Alligator Records' Bruce Iglauer agree on Copeland's strengths and future. Both admit she has her father's blues voice, yet at the same time she is endowed with a gospel delivery that adds gospel-like embellishments to her phrasings. The other quality is more intangible. "Mekia has that smile and attitude that reaches across the lights," said Hahn. "The people just respond to her. It's the Johnny Copeland smile. She's had this all along, it's not an act she just started."

Iglauer agreed. "I believe she'll be the next great female blues artist. I'd like to not change her music, but reach beyond the hard-core blues audience. Because her voice and personality are so accessible, Shemekia can reach beyond that."

Both look ahead and liken her growth to that of an athlete, but with one huge difference. "There is nothing more exciting than starting new talent," said Iglauer. "I've seen so much growing up in such a short amount of time. She's still finding out what she can do. Watching her grow is a big part of the excitement. The potential to grow, unlike athletes who peak by the time they are 30, Shemekia's growth is a lifetime thing."

Again Hahn concurred. She's the natural. It's a wonderful thing to watch because every six months she changes."

After she exploded on the blues scene with her first CD in 1998, Copeland on her second CD, *Wicked*, is like Tiger Woods three years after his first tournament win. It was so good that it earned a 2001 Grammy nomination as Contemporary Blues Album of the Year.

"I got to walk on the red carpet," said Copeland. "I was excited about being there with the people who I respect. I was sitting next to Koko Taylor, Taj Mahal, and Bobby Rush. My name was the first name they read off in the category. For 30 seconds, everybody from the industry saw my name."

Though she didn't win a Grammy, Taj Mahal did, and Copeland was given a great perspective. "After they announced the winner, Koko said to me, 'Every race horse can't win.' I know that hopefully one day I'll have another chance to go back and win one."

You might think that a Grammy nomination is the pinnacle of success. Not for Copeland. "Being nominated two years in a row as Entertainer of the Year in the Blues Foundation's Handy Awards has meant more to me than the Grammy nomination. I work really hard on my stage performance and for people to recognize that effort means a lot to me. I don't have to win, but to be the only woman nominated with B.B. King, Taj Mahal, and Rod Piazza means that people are recognizing that I'm doing my best."

Today, though life's curtain has descended on Johnny Copeland, the musical soul of this master will always play on through his daughter. "I know how much he looked out for me when he was here. Now he's watchin' me every minute. For as long as I live, he and his music will live through me. I feel his spirit every night onstage. I know that sometimes I get tired because night after night on the road is rough. Sometimes I can't even talk, let alone sing, but I believe that God and my father give me the strength to do this. I know he's up there with me."

Kenny
Brown

Say "blues" and everyone thinks of something different. Some hear Chicago harp, others perceive Texas guitar, while still others dream of acoustic guitars on rural Delta porches. Few remember to include the blues played in Mississippi hill country by men like R.L. Burnside and Junior Kimbrough. Their raw, nerve-jangling, rough-edged, juke-distorted tones will likely turn first-time listeners away. However, this is merely the clear extension of the music played by John Lee Hooker, Son Hibler, Mississippi Fred McDowell, and Joe Callicott.

It's easy to find kids sittin' on South Side street corners or standin' in Austin record shops, but you need only look as far as Kenny Brown to discover one of the hill region's dedicated standard-bearers. Brown has been R.L. Burnside's long-haired slide guitar foil since 1971, when as a timid 18-year-old he approached Burnside for lessons. Burnside readily furnished Brown the same lessons he was offered at that age. "He's been with me before any of my kids were big enough to play. When Joe Callicott passed, he came to my house and asked me to teach him how to play. He was doing some cotton, and I was working days on the plantation, but we'd sit up till two or three in the morning playing. After eight months, I knew he was ready to play with me in the jukes," remembered Burnside.

"I remember the first one R.L. took me to was pretty wild. It seemed like we drove forever down these country roads that looked like tunnels from the overgrown trees. We'd come to this old house in the clearing. At quarter to ten, there was hardly anybody in there; at quarter after ten, the place was damn near packed. After we played a little while, R.L. said, 'Brown, you can keep playing, I'm going to go in back and gamble a little

***Kenny Brown first performed in the juke joints of North
Mississippi when he was a timid 18-year-old.***

while.' I looked around and I'm the only white person in the place. I'm
scared to death. So I did what I knew. I started playing, and the people loved
it. A little while later R.L. came back in and started playing with me. I think
he was just testing me."

Burnside also remembers Brown's juke initiation. "The first time, he was
kinda nervous. At that time, you didn't see black and white people at the
same place. I was busy gambling, so I told him to play one while I gambled.

He said, 'Man, I can't play no guitar in front of all these people.' I said, 'Ain't nobody gonna bother you. If they bother you, they got to bother me.' He played a song. When he started the second one, they all started hollering, 'Play that thing, white boy!' From then on, I knew he had it."

Brown was born in 1953 in Alabama but moved back to Nesbit, Mississippi, when he was six months. Like every kid growing up in Mississippi, Brown found the music hard to ignore. "The first thing I ever remember hearing was Johnny Cash on the radio when I was five. I remember my dad and my cousins taking me to see Elvis once. When I was about six, we had a friend who was about ten years older who lived with us for a little while. He told me he used to sneak me out of the house, and we'd go out to my mom's Chevy, and we'd lay down in the seats and turn on that Nashville station that was playing blues.

"He also showed me some licks on guitar when I was about six. There was this guy that had picnics right across the road from my house, and they would play the fife and drum all night. My mom told me that they would have to whip me to make me come inside when it was dark because I'd be sitting on the bank listening to the music. And then I'd go to bed and have the window open and listen to it, sometimes all night. I probably had a lot driven into my head subconsciously."

Brown received his first guitar at ten, when he and his brother sold seed packages from the back of comic books door to door for the prizes. "My brother got a BB gun and I got a plastic guitar. I started learning some things, and then my mom bought me a Kay arch-top acoustic and I started taking some lessons. But I was getting frustrated."

As Brown was fiddling with the guitar, a black family moved in to the sharecropper cabin next door. Kenny's brother told him, "Go over to that old man, old Joe next door, he plays guitar pretty good too, and get him to show you something."

"I went over there and talked to him, and it was Joe Callicott. He told me to come on over, and I started going over any time I had any free time to hang with Joe. I was 12 at the time. He was like a father to me. He'd teach me things about riding horses, hunting, and what to do if I was ever in a juke joint and a fight broke out—to grab a pool stick and back up in a corner. That way you can keep them off of you.

"I remember, the first song we played, at the end he slapped me on the leg and said, 'That's it, boy.' I'd go over there just about every day. When I was about 15, he was getting ready to teach me how to sing. With Joe, it was all acoustic. Joe didn't even like electric guitars. I got an electric guitar, and I took it over to show Joe how loud it would get. All he said was, 'Turn that down!' Joe was all acoustic." Most of Brown's instruction came in the clipped talk of the region; a mere five words, 'Hit it like this, boy' were the most words offered.

Callicott's death in 1969 hit Brown hard then and continues to affect him today. "He was 72, I think, when he died. I was getting my driver's license, and he used to tell me, 'Drive for yourself and the other fellow too.' His wife said when he died his last words were talking to me. He rolled over in bed and said, 'Kenny, drive for yourself and for the other fellow too. And always be a good boy.' Those were his last words.

"A lot of people probably wouldn't believe this, but since he's been dead, he's come to me a couple of times in the night. I still get chills, especially when I'm doing one of his songs. 'You Don't Know My Mind' (aka "Laughing to Keep From Crying") was his favorite, and it's my favorite too. I've played it just about every show I've ever done. And everybody loves it. After he died, I remember his wife said, 'What are me and Kenny going to do?' She just passed away recently, she was 92."

Here's the weird part. In 1968, George Mitchell recorded Callicott for the Arhoolie record *Mississippi Delta Blues, Vol. 2*. The recording had Callicott on one side and R.L. Burnside on the other. In the liner notes Mitchell wrote, "Last time we were there, in April of 1968, Callicott had a student to brag about, a 10-year-old white boy from down the road who brought his guitar to Joe's almost every day to learn from one of the best of the living masters of a dying musical form." That boy was Kenny Brown.

Callicott died before Brown ever met R.L., and Kenny has been playing with R.L. since 1969. "Years later, I was in Memphis at a friend's house, and he was showing me this Arhoolie album with Joe on one side and R.L. on the other. I'm reading through the liner notes, and I realized that little boy was me! That's weird, how the two men I've played with never met each other, but here they are on the same recording, and I'm mentioned in the liner notes. That was really the first time I knew what I was put here for."

"There were a lot of hippies that used to come down to Joe's house. When I was 14 I met this one guy, Bobbie Ray Watson, and I started hanging with him. He taught me some slide and introduced me to Johnny Woods, a harmonica player who used to play with Fred McDowell. I got to know Johnny, and played with him off and on for about 20 years, until he died in 1990.

"I learned a lot of stuff from him about Mississippi Fred. Someone wrote somewhere that I learned directly from Fred, but that isn't exactly true. It was in a more roundabout way. Playing with Johnny Woods, it feels like I learned from Fred. And I've listened to Fred's records."

The two guitar approaches Brown relies heavily on today are McDowell's droning slide techniques and Callicott's finger-picking style.

These men, together with everything else Brown was exposed to, like picnics with Othar Turner and his proximity to the Hemphill clan, contribute
to the characteristics of North Mississippi blues.

"There's a small area from Oxford to Holly Springs, Senatobia, and
Coldwater where a lot of those people that play that style, like Jessie Mae
Hemphill, Junior, R.L., Fred McDowell, and Johnny Woods, have similar
traits in their music.

"The music here is a lot different from the Delta. It comes from the fife
and drum music which was real popular up in the hills. I heard it when I was
just a kid growing up. It's real droning and repetitive, percussive. The Delta
music is more structured, with the three chord changes. You could almost
say it's a little more sophisticated, but none of the Mississippi stuff is real
sophisticated. This stuff is just real, maybe no chord changes. The rhythms
and feelings are what drive it."

These unorthodox rhythms can play havoc with rhythmic foot-tappers
who continually anticipate changes, sometimes with band members too.
"We'll play a song we've been playing the same way for 20 years and I'll get
comfortable and look off into the crowd, and suddenly R.L.'ll change everything. You definitely gotta follow those guys, especially R.L."

These juke joint ordeals cemented Brown's blues calling as the white kid
destined to carry on black music. Still, Brown met with some suspicion as
the white kid playing black music. "When I was seven, I used to listen to
Othar Turner playing over at the picnics. I didn't know who he was. Years
later, Othar invited me down to his picnic to play. I went down there and I
asked if it was alright if I played something, and he said yeah. I started getting my electric guitar and amplifier out, and I overheard Othar's wife say
to him, 'Now don't you let that white boy run all our peoples off.' I thought,
'I'll show her.' I started playing, and she was the first one who jumped up
and started dancing."

Another time, on Jackson, Mississippi's infamous Farrish Street, Brown
disregarded the popular wisdom and found a club where he could plug in.
"I rode down there, and there were guys getting equipment out of their car.
I pulled up and said, 'Y'all playing here tonight? 'Y'all mind people sitting
in?' They said, 'We let people sit in. I went back that night, and I walked
through the door with my guitar and plugged it in and went to playing. I
played with an all-black band, a guy named King Edward, down there
around Jackson for a while."

The jukes today have changed, and Brown doesn't recommend using this
as a blues player's step to the major leagues. "The jukes today are a lot worse
because of the crack problem. I don't go to as many places as I used to. For
one thing, there aren't as many. They started disappearing when the police

started clamping down on the crack problems. Junior's was always a real cool place. There's not a crack problem there." However, the Kimbrough juke burned down in 2000.

"Junior's was a big part of my education since I returned from Austin, Texas, in 1986. Johnny Woods first took me down to Junior's. Junior used to have these house parties on Sundays. It started out he was just practicing with his band. Then there got to be so many people coming in there, he'd do a little bootleg and stuff. Johnny played with them and took me down there. I hit it off with Junior, so I've been playing with him off and on since."

From his juke joint seat with both Kimbrough and Burnside, Brown can dissect each man's approach to his music. "Junior played more structured, although still with that droning. He has some songs that make a full chord change. R.L.'s got songs that he won't be hitting but two notes with his left hand, back and forth to the two notes with his left finger. The right hand is really keeping the rhythm chugging. Neither of these guys play with a pick; they use their thumb and the fingers on their right hand. With both, it won't ever be on a regular timing. Jim Dickinson told me one time that the best way to keep up with those guys is to count in two's or three's, not four's. He said that came from an African thing they still follow in their timing. But sometimes I don't even count or tap my foot, I just feel it."

Today, Brown straddles the fence of touring the country with R.L. and recording his own music. His CD *Goin' Back to Mississippi* accurately catalogues the various music Mississippi has given the world and touches on the styles and techniques Brown has been exposed to over the years. At times Brown's guitar awakens the music of the Mississippi hills; at other times he is the raucous rock and roll that awakened Memphis. His respect of all that comes in between labels Brown a genuine keeper of the flame.

Big Jack
Johnson

From the earliest days of the 20th century to the present, rural juke joints in Mississippi have been incubators for the blues. In the days of sharecropping, these tin-roofed country digs were the weekend hot spots for releasing pent-up frustrations after the back-breaking sharecropping work from the week. As bootleggers hawked moonshine, musicians cutting their teeth provided all the entertainment African Americans needed. Men like Charley Patton, Son House, Robert Johnson, and, later, Muddy Waters, Johnny Shines, Howlin' Wolf, and Honeyboy Edwards worked each weekend at the art of the blues.

There are still juke joints in Mississippi. They have names like Red's, the Do Drop Inn, Smitty's, and the Playboy Club, and they continue to allow Mississippi musicians the woodshedding necessary to develop style. Younger musicians like David Thompson, Lonnie Pitchford, Lonnie Shields, Kenny Brown, Super Chikan, Kenny Kimbrough, the Burnside offspring, and David Malone, and newcomers like the North Mississippi All Stars learned the subtleties of this rural music from masters like the late Junior Kimbrough, the late Roosevelt "Bubba" Barnes, the late Frank Frost, Sam Carr, R.L. Burnside, Othar Turner, and Big Jack Johnson.

The most famous of these is Junior Kimbrough's Juke Joint. Drive down Route 4 in Holly Springs, Mississippi, on any Sunday night and Junior Kimbrough's Juke Joint glows warmly. Set the length of a car off this rural highway, it is one of precious few hangouts where you can feel the origins of the blues.

By 8:30, 20 cars are already parked helter-skelter on the gravel shoulder. A $2 cover and a "How y'all doin'" will get you in. A pool table sits dead center, furniture pulled from a scrap heap fronts cinderblock walls, Junior

***Raised in Clarkesdale, Mississippi, Big Jack Johnson carries
Mississippi Delta blues throughout the world.***

or a relative pulls lukewarm cans of beer from a refrigerator circa 1960.
There are welcoming handshakes and greetings; Junior Kimbrough's juke
encourages a lively mix of black and white.

Seated on a chair from an ancient kitchenette, R.L. Burnside, a Sunday
regular, begins to play Muddy Waters's "I Can't Be Satisfied" solo. Close
your eyes and it's Muddy in the jukes of Clarkesdale in 1941. R.L.'s percussive playing requires no other support. Younger patrons surround the
pool table, while older regulars gyrate slowly to R.L.'s hypnotic rhythms,
which spread through the air like the viney kudzu that overspreads and
defines much of the landscape.

These rural jukes dotting the Mississippi landscape provided a porch to
shape styles. "As I grew up, I played in mostly black jukes," said Burnside.
"Those were the good days. Back then, there'd be a lot of dancing going on
from 8 P.M. until 3:00 or 4:00 in the morning. Places like Junior's only
opened one night. It wasn't too violent then; you could go out and have
yourself some fun. I played acoustic back then 'cause people really liked the
country blues sound. After rock and roll came out, people wanted electric.
Today, I won't play in a lot of the town bars in Mississippi because the young
people are getting too wild."

Because many of us in today's world will never open the door to a back-woods Mississippi juke joint, Big Jack Johnson hopes his time on the stage will approximate that vanishing world. Just as many of the Mississippi men who cut their teeth in jukes have died, many of the jukes have also faded away. With the last authentic juke, Junior Kimbrough's in Holly Springs, Mississippi, destroyed by an early morning fire in April 2000 (there are currently plans to rebuild), musicians like Johnson who've spent their lives playing every Mississippi juke and roadhouse are the last remnants of that soon-to-be-extinct experience.

As a 22-year-old, Johnson began his playing in the jukes of Mississippi in 1962 as the junior member of the Jelly Roll Kings. "In those days the people were on the plantations. Once the places closed up in the towns like Clarkesdale, the people drove to the jukes out in the country," remembered Johnson. "Most times, we'd play at Smitty's in the town, and the guys who owned the jukes in the country would ask us to play for them after hours. After midnight, we'd go out in the country and, man, you'd see the cars followin' us out to the juke lined up like a funeral.

"Once there, there'd be gambling, dancing, hot dogs, buffalo fish, and white lightning. We called it Joe Louis whiskey because it exploded! We'd be up all weekend drinkin' that whiskey, eyes all red. We played our brains out. We'd start playing on Fridays and end up on Monday morning. In those days we played every juke, bar, and roadhouse in Mississippi and Arkansas. We didn't know how good we was back then. We had such a good time singin' and playin'. Today I look back through the past and see it and I don't believe what went on with us."

As good as those times were, Johnson has also witnessed the jukes beginning to die out in the 1980s. Once the sharecropping on plantations was replaced by a mechanized labor force and chemicals were used in the fields to kill the grass that African American laborers had chopped back, the people moved from the land. When they moved to find new employment in Mississippi, the music also moved, into casinos. Today, Johnson sees the proliferation of casinos up and down Highway 61, the blues highway, as the sad, modern juke joint for Mississippi's people.

"I managed a plantation for 37 years and I ran three jukes. I came back to Mississippi in 1998 and there's nothing out here, no houses or anything, just land. I started crying, it was real sad. Ain't no more juke houses too, because the casinos have come to town. People go there, get their whiskey free, hear the music free, and if they got a dime, they can try their best to hit with it." Johnson was so disgusted by the lure of these modern jukes, he penned the song "Sweet Home Mississippi." Played to the tune of "Sweet

Home Chicago," the song sings of the effect of these 24-7 casinos, like Sam's, the Horseshoe, Lady Luck, and Harrah's, sprouting up everywhere in the state.

Johnson was born in Lambert, Mississippi, in 1940 and grew up helping a hard-working family cultivate the Mississippi land. "When I was growing up in the 1940s, we all had to go to the fields to pick cotton. With a big family of 15, that was 15 cotton sacks in the field. We used a mule. There used to be a thousand mules in the fields. Now they have tractors that can do 12 rows."

And there was always music around the family. As with so many other Mississippi children, Johnson's first instrument was a one-string. "My daddy did snuff and bought his snuff in the glass bottles. We'd use the glass bottles. There was plenty of baling wire because we bailed a lot of hay. We had plenty of staples because we used them on the fences. I stapled the wire against the wall down here and up there, I took that snuff bottle and broke off that thing and went to slidin' up and down the wire like Muddy Waters. Shoot, I could do it right now.

"When I was 17, I went to a guy's house for his daughter's birthday party. There was no music, so I put up a strand of wire on the side of the house. I started playing the wire and I had the whole yard dancin'. And I made the girl too.

"I knew early I wanted to be a musician. My daddy had fiddles and banjos and mandolins all around the place. My daddy played that stuff called the breakdown on the violin. He showed me how to chord, A-B-C-D, and that was good to me. I was listening to music like "Baby, Please Don't Go," "Catfish Blues," and "Good Morning, Little School Girl," and I started playing around the house. Then my daddy'd say, 'Let's go play with this band and that band.'

"I grew up listening to the Grand Ole Opry when I first started. I'd hear Hank Snow, Gene Autry, Hank Williams, and Johnny Cash. There was a lot of country on the radio. It was hard to hear blues guys. The only guy you could really hear on the radio was Eddie "Cleanhead" Vinson and Blind Lemon Jefferson. Then I heard B.B. King and Elmore James on radio and I jumped on them guys' case. Then I heard Albert King and Freddie King and Muddy on the slide and I wanted to do that. And the Wolf? I loved the Wolf's singin' and his guitar players. I can't take just one part—I have to get all these out in my playing.

"I didn't see B.B. until I was 22. Before that I'd seen Albert King. To see Albert King at that time'll make your hair stand up. He was tough. I'll never forget, it was at the Masonic Hall in Clarksdale. I had a chance to play with Sonny Boy Williamson and Robert Nighthawk in the 1960s. The way they played their music is not like they play it today. Nobody plays it like that anymore. They played the music with a feeling."

That was about the same time that Johnson met Sam Carr and Frank Frost, two veterans of the Mississippi jukes. "I met Frank in 1960. I was playing with a band called the Esquires. Frank and Sam came from St. Louis to see their mothers and help 'em get their crops outta the fields. While they were down here, they played at a little place in the woods. There was so much work for them to do, they stayed down here. They were playing at the Savoy Theater in Clarkesdale and looking for another guitar player to hook up with. And they come and got me. I was 19 when I started playing with them. Frank was blowing harmonica through a rack, playing guitar and organ, and Sam was keeping rhythm on the drums. Sam and Frank liked the way I played. And we've been hooked up ever since."

Frost and Carr came with their own impressive musical résumé. Frost learned harmonica from Willie Foster and Sonny Boy Williamson and played guitar in Williamson's band from 1956 to 1959. Carr learned his musicianship from his father, Delta guitarist Robert Nighthawk. They both toured with Williamson and Nighthawk.

"You'd think it was three or four people, and it was just those two. Frank was one of the best. He was singing, had a rack on his neck for harmonica, playing guitar and keyboards at the same time. The people down South had never seen this. Frank was hell with a guitar. I learned a lot about guitar and how to sing from him. I learned how to not be shy. He'd walk the floor and be playing behind his head all the time. I saw him doing it, and I wanted to do it like him.

"There's not a better drummer than Sam. He knows how to fill 'em up. You can sit him outside a building and hear him play a two-piece drum set, and you'll swear he has a full set. He's got this lick he puts down that nobody's got but him. I try my best to instruct my drummers how to put that lick down because if they can learn that lick, they'll have something nobody else got. But it's hard to get over."

The trio recorded *Hey Boss Man* in 1963 as Frank Frost and the Nighthawks for Sam Phillips Sun Records. Their second album, recorded for Jewel Records, used Scotty Moore as its producer. After those recordings, the group worked their jobs by day and played the jukes by night.

Johnson's nickname, the Oil Man, originates from his daytime occupation, delivering Shell oil to over 300 Delta residents. "I was an oil man, I drove a tractor and combine, I was runnin' a farm and a snap bean picker, potato digger, peanut thresher, and I worked in the gin. I did all that in the 1960s and 1970s during the day and played my music at night."

When Chicago blues fan and founder of Earwig Records Michael Frank traveled to Clarkesdale in 1975 and saw the Jelly Roll Kings at Johnson's Black Fox juke, he knew they had to be recorded. In 1978, Frank recorded the first Jelly Roll Kings CD on Earwig. That opened more doors here and abroad for the band to play. But after 25 years together, the Jelly Roll Kings separated in 1987.

"Frank moved away to Greenville and started playing with guys around there. Sam also started playing with different people. Whenever Sam did get us together, we did go out and play. I had a lot of songs written in my mind that I wanted to do but I couldn't do as a sideman behind Frank. With Frank the leader of the band, I couldn't play the way I wanted to. I couldn't go out and shoot my shot because I didn't want him thinking I was trying to overplay him. I didn't want to upset the man. Once I got on my own, I had to come out and do what I had to do, to push myself out there because I had so much to offer.

"Michael Frank asked me if I wanted to do a CD, and that's when I really started concentrating on my own songs. That was the *Oil Man* CD in 1987. Then he asked me about doing another one and I did *Daddy, When Is Mama Coming Home?*". Since that 1987 debut, Johnson has recorded six solo ventures that display the evolution of his singing, playing, and song writing.

Johnson's music reaches back beyond today's electric imitators of the blues, beyond the British invasion, beyond Sam Phillips and the Chess brothers, beyond Robert Johnson, back to the taproot of the blues. When Johnson plays the blues, he does so in the same manner as first-generation Mississippi bluesmen, all feeling and no formula. In fact, Johnson is the primary link in the blues chain that connects directly to Charley Patton, the so-called conscience of the Delta. Johnson, like Patton, plays a highly rhythmic and percussive guitar that puts people on dance floors. If Patton was to pick up an electric guitar today, he'd probably sound very much like Big Jack.

As song writers, Patton and Johnson can both also be called the heart and soul of the region. As chroniclers of their time and place, they have recorded historical snapshots in the oral folk tradition. Patton took a Delta occurrence like the 1927 flood of the Mississippi River and turned it into the song "High Water Everywhere." Johnson turned the Clarkesdale ice storm of 1994 into one of his biggest-selling regional songs, "Ice Storm Blues." Patton sang of the problems of establishing relationships, sheriffs arresting moonshiners, and the evils of abuse; Johnson writes of relationships, AIDS, casinos, crack-headed women, and youth violence.

"The songs ideas just kinda hit me. I see things every day in the world, all the time, that I could sing about. There's so many people out here, and I've got to find something to get to them. I can't be saying the same thing. It won't get me anywhere. Everybody did Muddy's "Hootchie-Cootchie

Man" and "Sweet Home Chicago," but you've got to get out of that line. Like "Crack-Headed Woman." That's right, she's out there and her kids home by themselves, all these other men hangin' out at the house, and I sing that she's got to leave that line alone. I'm a Christian man and I believe in singing about the right things. That's why I sing what I sing. Maybe 50 years from now, people'll realize what I'm tryin' to say and it might turn something around."

Early blues singers like Patton created their music spontaneously in the jukes. Then they took those songs that were 30 minutes long and crafted a concise, three-minute work that fit nicely on 78s. Johnson's songwriting also follows that tradition. "I don't carry a notebook around. All these ideas are in my head. I go in the studio with no book or nothing. I just start to sing all this stuff and put my music to it. I did that on the second CD. I get these things in my head and set 'em aside in my head and go back and sing 'em later. My wife calls it amazing."

Johnson always takes what he's learned from the men he sat behind and the jukes he's played and then delivers real Mississippi blues around the world. "Most guys stand up on the stage and just tap their foot to the same beat. Anybody can keep up that noise. The people are comin' to hear you for something. They can hear music on the radio. They're comin' to see me for something. Too many guys are playing without that sadness, they're playing too happy. There's got to be some meanness to it. Most bands can't give it to them. You gotta come out to hear Jack Johnson. When you leave me, you'll be satisfied.

As so many older musicians pass away, Johnson is one of the last who can keep the music of Mississippi alive. He plays 300 nights a year, keeping the juke experience alive around the world. "Because I came from the jukes, I'm playing the real Mississippi blues. People are always sayin', 'You got to hear this guy play' because I recreate the juke. When I see the people up dancin', I've done my job and turned the place into a juke. If you're playing the real stuff, somebody's gonna turn around. If you start walkin' out that door and I pick up my guitar, I'll bet you'll stop and turn around and come back and want to know who that is. There's something in my playing that'll make you turn around and come back. That's the Mississippi thing."

Jimmy D. Lane

Though normally the ties of tradition connect from father to child, often it takes an outsider to awaken one's genetic heritage. Take the case of Chicago's Jimmy Rogers, aka Jimmy Lane. Rogers was at the forefront of the Chess sound as the guitarist in the Muddy Waters band throughout the 1950s. In the 1960s every blues musician in Chicago and throughout the country had spent time at the Rogers house. And though those times were special in retrospect, to his son, guitarist and songwriter Jimmy D. Lane, this was just Dad and his friends—until the younger Lane heard another Jimi, Hendrix.

"Jimmy Rogers gave me life," said Lane, "but Jimi Hendrix was one of the reasons I felt a calling to the music. My dad taught me the respect for the music and traditions, but Jimi Hendrix showed me where it could go. The first time he laid a real heavy impression on me was in late 1983, when I'd just left the military, and I heard "Hey Joe." When I heard "Hey Joe," that just changed my whole life. Listening to this cat play, I knew immediately what I wanted to do. I've heard that song thousands of times since, but I've never heard it in that powerful a way. I describe that experience in the same way a preacher tells of hearing his calling, an 'I see the light' experience.

"I didn't say I can do that, I said I want to do that. I used all the money I had in my pocket and bought a $59 Harmony guitar from the very pawnshop they used in the *Blues Brothers* movie. I think it was Art's Pawn Shop, right off King Drive. I still have that receipt. I sat down and had to learn that song."

He started listening to Eric Clapton, Cream, Ten Years After, and Hendrix first. "When I read how they were all listening to the music my dad

The son of guitarist Jimmy Rogers, Jimmy D. Lane heard Jimi Hendrix's "Hey Joe" when he was 18, went to Art's Pawn Shop, and bought his first guitar.

played, I started listening to the old man. I knew these cats and took them for granted at the time. These were guys my old man worked with who would come by and talk shop. I started putting it together. This is Mr. Morganfield. This is Mr. Burnett. That's Shakey Horton.

"These men were able to take everyday experiences and put them into their music in a way that touches everyday people. That's the magic of their art. That makes blues what it is, livin' life every day. If you take that away from it, you have music with no substance.

"You'd hear Walter blow something like "Quarter to Twelve" and you can hear the melancholy tone and mood. Thinking about the stories I'd heard about Walter makes that melancholy fit the song. That was Walter coming out of the harp. To hear the runs the old man put behind Muddy and on his own stuff was exactly from his personality. Very subtle, very tasteful. Adding what enhances the music was his personality.

"Wolf made quite an impression. He was very dramatic, with a lot of charisma. I didn't understand those things at the time, but I knew there was something different about him. He was a flamboyant man who put on a show just walking into a room. That was Wolf's character. It was always that way. Those cats were who they were on record in life."

Rogers was born in 1965 and received his first guitar when he was eight, from Shakey Jake. Throughout those years, the Rogers home was one jam session after another. "I would pick up an instrument all the time and try and join in. First, I had a little plastic guitar and they would give me the 'ain't that cute?' routine. After I began to get more serious with it, they got more serious with me. Louis and Dave Myers would say thing like, 'Put that thing down. You ain't gonna do this.' It made me feel real bad when they said stuff like that.

"One of two things can happen. You either drop it and forget about it altogether or take it as a challenge and you get better. I took the lesson as their way of trying to encourage me to go on and do it right. One day, James Cotton took it a step further when he told me, 'You got to get it for yourself. Nobody's gonna give it to you.' I remember that to this day. I recently saw James in Chicago and came onstage doing an acoustic set. I asked him if he remembered telling me that. He said, 'I sure do. You listened didn't you?' I smiled and said, 'It's with me forever like Samsonite luggage.'"

After Lane bought his first Harmony, he would go to the different jams in the city to watch everybody. At the same time, he was trying to get his own band together. "I would lock myself in the room and only come out to eat. When I'd wake up, the guitar was on the bed with me. After work and a shower, it was the guitar again, just in my room, playing. My father heard what he had to hear, some Muddy stuff, some of his stuff. One night in the fall of 1987 at a club called Willy's in Chicago was the first night I played with him. I've played with him ever since. I was very nervous that night, hoping not to make a mistake. I'm worried about, Will this chord work? Or will I throw him off if I put this chord here? He was looking at me, laughing all night, and I figured everything was all right. I knew that he knew I could handle it. He let me know in his own ways that everything was alright."

In all the years on the road together and private in-house moments, what were the most amazing things this son witnessed his father do? "Seeing him take a hand-held propane torch and thawing out the pipes in the house so we could have heat in the winter. Standing right there while he did it, and then knowing he probably went out and played that night. One night at this club, I saw him doing a shuffle in E, and his hand was movin' so fast I couldn't believe it. He was in his 40s at the time and that blew me away. Another time we were doing a European tour in 1991 in Norway. We're onstage and there were about 20,000 people singin' "Walkin' by Myself" in English. I looked at him and he had this smile on his face like he was king of the world. I was thinking how proud I was to be his son."

And his son also witnessed his father's acceptance and honor within the rock world. "I was very happy for him when I watched the way Mick, Eric, and Taj greeted him. These guys always have said that the only reason they were here was because of the blues guys like my father. You hear all the hype about cats like Clapton, but he always made sure my dad was paid. I remember a conversation he and Eric had right after Eric lost his son. I remember Eric getting advice from the old man about how to deal with that loss. The old man had lost two children, and Eric wanted advice about how to deal with that.

"They had very, very high respect for him. They all felt as though they knew him through the music. He didn't mind that because that was the kind of guy he was. He always talked to people as a very genuine man. He never was judgmental, and he accepted those guys and was very grateful that they looked at him and respected him and the music as they did. He loved nothing more than to sit out here on the fish bank. We'd be ridin' on the road and I'd look over at him and ask, 'You OK pop?' and he'd answer, 'Boy, this sure is a nice fishing day, isn't it?' We're on our way through the mountains of Colorado and he's talking about sitting on the fish bank.

Rogers and many other blues artists never got that same respect from their record labels. "When people say I never went to college, I say I went to the college of Chess. The old man would talk about how Chess would do things to them. When Willie Mabon asked for his royalty off "I Don't Know," Chess blackballed him. He couldn't play a cafe in the city. He said to hell with the U.S. and took off to France. He lived there until he died. I learned how they did all those artists. It's very heartbreaking because my dad was a big part of it. These guys were ripped off because so many of them couldn't read or write.

"My old man wrote songs that made Billboard charts. They sold his records all over the world, and he was paid a fee of $42.75 per session. If Chess received a check during a six-month time period for $10,000, Chess would probably send him $700 and he would feed and clothe six kids on that. They put him down as a cowriter on songs he'd written. He should have been receiving much more. To make it right, when MCA purchased the Chess catalogue, they found out about the backlog Chess owed. I guess MCA made a stipulation of the contract that we will not buy the catalogue unless Chess straightened it out. So here come checks every other week that should have been mailed out in the 1960s. I'm satisfied with the fact that before my old man passed, he was able to enjoy a little bit of what he was supposed to enjoy back when I was a child. Those stories have made me very cautious of the recording industry.

"With everything Chess did to my old man, I never saw him bitter about that. He would hunch his shoulders, open both palms of his hands in the air, and say, 'We're out here working.'"

Because of this, Lane had his eyes wide open when looking for his own record deals. "The label I'm with now, Analogue Productions and Blue Heaven Studios with Chad Kassem, gives me complete freedom in the studio. I've also been hired as music director of the company, so we can do blues the way I think it should be done. I think blues is best when it is natural, spontaneous, and untampered, like our conversation. I like blues in its natural form. Two tracks, no overdubbing, letting the people create the music as they feel it. So what the people hear is what you would hear from the stage. When you have to mix and do this or that to it, it takes away from what the artist was trying to achieve."

As is the case with Bernard Allison and Shemekia Copeland, Jimmy D. also now has to temper his career goals with the loss of his father to cancer in 1997. "Certain times I'll hear a song that will bring something back to me either about playing somewhere, or when he'd take us to the park as kids, or putting strings on the guitar after I'd broke them and put it back in the case so he wouldn't find it broken. I'll still see that clear today. It was a Gibson LS 335 and he was putting the stings on it and running the notes he did when he tuned it up, and I'm sitting there with my little plastic guitar watchin' him."

Then there's Rogers' final recording on his son's *Legacy* CD. "That was the last recording we did. "One-Room Shack" was the last song he ever played a guitar on. We did a couple of takes of that song. I remember the look in his eyes and the effort he put forth in getting that song right. What he said at the beginning, in hindsight turned out to be passing the torch on. I'll always cherish the thoughts of that session. I'm so glad we videotaped that session."

Shortly after his father's death, Lane explained the grieving process. "I don't listen to those songs yet. I can't right now, I'm not ready. It's still a day-by-day thing. I'm still dealing with the fact that I can't just call him up and go out on the lake fishing with him. Just yesterday, I was watchin' television and I was thinking about when we'd be loading up to go on the road, hooking up the trailer, waiting for Ted Harvey to drive up. We'd put a movie on and be laughing and joking up and down the highway from gig to gig. I miss all that.

"I'm constantly humbled by the fans who come and not only offer condolences, but also tell stories about what Jimmy Rogers meant. I have a stack of faxes and e-mails where people tell about meeting my father and what he said to them. It blew me away. I knew he reached a lot of people with his music; I never knew the extent. I know he didn't have an idea or clue what his impact on the music world was. One man named his first child Jimmy after the old man.

"You learn every day. You can never learn everything. Every day I pick up an instrument I'm learnin' something new. I saw my dad learning up till the day he died. He would say that, and I've lived to understand what he meant when he said it. They were tellin' the truth. When I see players with attitudes about how good they are, I remember what they were tellin' me and I think this guy's not gonna learn with that mentality. Those players think they have arrived already. It's so simple, but so hard to master. It's the brass ring you're always chasing. It's right here and you think you can sneak up and grab it, but as soon as you get your hands on it, it finds another way out. It's an evolving thing.

"The hardest thing to master is opening up the key to your vulnerability. On my dad's song "Out on the Road," he's playing notes on that song that make you want to cry. You can hear the vulnerability when you hear the tone on the guitar, when you hear his voice. You can hear that they are coming from the same place. You're trying to express as much truth in your music as possible.

"I think I am my own musician. I never introduce myself as Jimmy Rogers's son, because if I make it I want to make as myself. It seems tacky to ride his name. I've never done that. I just want people to give me a listen and see what I sound like. I'm sure people say this is only because I'm Jimmy Rogers's son, and I simply answer them, 'Thank you very much.' He is my pop and I'm very proud of that. But I still did have to do the work once he opened the door."

Charlie
Musselwhite

In a day when so many musicians stay safe, the risky musical outlook of Charlie Musselwhite is very refreshing. Instead of rehashing from a narrow perspective, Musselwhite's music always looks to broaden the scope of the blues. In that way, he plays hard-edged blues, up-tempo swingin' shuffles, dark jazz, a little rockabilly, some New Orleans swamp, and even Latin-flavored blues from Rio or Cuba.

"My advice to any harp new player is: Don't imitate anybody. Be yourself. Playing what you feel inside is really the key. I call it following the will of the music. When you're playing that way, you're having fun with it. When you're having fun, you're learning. If you set it up like work, you're not gonna get the feeling in the music part," said Musselwhite.

"There's nothing wrong with memorizing tunes like 'Juke' if that's what you choose to do. I remember Paul Butterfield and I walkin' down the street doing 'Juke' just vocally. If you want to learn harmonica, you can learn the classic tunes, but you should go on from there.

"I'm always thinkin' about the different places I try to get at musically. It's like reachin' into this unknown, strange room to try and find the spark. There's a level where you play the stuff you just know by rote from years of playin' the traditional, but I'm always waiting for that door to open to the next level.

"When I can slide through, things become more spontaneous. When I get really lucky, I go over the top into where it really takes off. I feel like I'm standin' next to the tracks and there's a train highballin' right by the end of my nose. I can't even grab a hold of it. I can only just try to keep up with it. It's so fleeting, it's like trying to capture a moonbeam. You can't think at all

Charlie Musselwhite has always said, "Even though you may like other types of music, you'll always have a place in your heart for the blues."

or you lose it, you're just a witness to it. The more I play, it's easier to find that magical door."

The Musselwhite piece "Blues Overtook Me" aptly describes his early blues conversion. Born in Kosciusko, Mississippi, in 1944, he soon relocated with the family to Memphis. Living there from 1947 to 1962, he couldn't avoid the music of the city. "Some of my earliest memories are of the voices of the people who sang in the fields that I heard growing up in Memphis. When I was a little kid I liked to go to Cypress Creek in the summertime because it was cool. I'd lay up on the shady side of the creek and hear people singin' in the fields. Man, it just wrapped itself around me. The feeling in that music—it described just how I felt. It came inside me and said, 'It's O.K.' It affected me so strongly I just wanted to be able to make that sound for myself.

"There was a street called Scott Street that ran under a bridge off of Summer Avenue. I think I was about eight or nine when I was able to take the bus home from downtown alone. I would get off the bus early so I could walk under the bridge and go down Scott Street by the sawmill. There was a guy who was only known as the Scott Street blues singer who would stand out there with the guitar. He was one of my biggest influences. He played just down the street from where I grew up. He was real accessible to me. He'd be playin' for people who were getting off from workin' at the sawmill. I would watch his hands, go home and figure out how to make the chords, tryin' to figure out those little runs."

From there, he became friends with Memphis music legends Furry Lewis, Gus Cannon, and Will Shade. He would go to Lewis' or Shade's house all the time, playing, talking, listening to the ball game, and drinking. "In some ways, they passed on lessons of life and your place in the world. There was always a steady stream of people coming by, and many of them were musicians. That's where I met guys like Earl Bell, Abe McNeil, Son Smith, and Johnny Moment. It was just hangin' out in a living room playing and swappin' stories. Often there wouldn't be any music played at all. But often there would be a jam session happening. Red Robey would come around with his fiddle. Memphis Willie B would also come around. He played guitar and harp on a rack. He was a big influence on me too.

"All of these guys were very willing to show me things on the guitar. They were real flattered because black kids my age weren't interested in their music. It was unusual for a white kid to be interested in their music. I sure felt pride when I learned something from them and then showed it off the next time. I remember the last time I went back to Memphis to visit from Chicago, I went to Will Shade's house. He was really sick, and he asked me to play some harmonica. I played some harmonica, and he just smiled and said, 'Go on, boy. I can tell you been up in Chicago now.' He asked me not to forget about him. It was real sad, and I hated to say goodbye that day. I didn't know that would be the last time I would see him.

"The majority of Beale Street was all black. Even though the businesses on the street catered to the black people, they were owned by whites. In those days, Beale Street all depended on your attitude. If you walked down the streets swaggering or putting out a superior attitude or you weren't respectful, then you weren't welcome. As long as you were respectful to the people on Beale, you probably were OK. Playing the music helped with acceptance in that part of town. As soon as they heard me play, everything was OK.

"Playing in Memphis was strictly for my own gratification. There was something in me that needed to be satisfied. I just wanted to play for myself and learn from these guys. The Buddhists talk about getting something through transmission. Looking back on those days, I was soaking it up it through transmission.

"When I lived in Memphis, it was popular to go over to West Memphis, Arkansas. The law was very loose over there, so the nightclubs were very easy to get into. If you were underage and could hold your liquor, you were OK. One place was called The Plantation Inn and they always had a blues band playing there. This band could play whatever was popular for the dancers, but they knew every blues I ever asked them to play.

"Another club was Danny's. Charlie Rich had been a bouncer there and played piano when the band took a break. This was strictly a hillbilly-type place, and guys like Eddie Bond or Charlie Feathers would play there. Besides Arkansas, there were clubs on the outskirts of Memphis. All these places were very rough. There's a couple still going after all these years, The Hi-Hat and Hernando's Hideaway."

For radio, Charlie had his choice of Rufus Thomas's show or listening to the incomparable Dewey Phillips. "I remember every night when Rufus Thomas came on the radio on WDIA, 'Your all-colored station.' His theme song was "Hootin' Blues" by Sonny Terry. I thought that was just great. As I'd be driving around in my car, I'd roll down the windows and turn it all the way up! It sounded so cool. Also, in Memphis you could pick up WLAC from Nashville.

"Man! I was crazy about Dewey Phillips. I think his show was called *Red, Hot, and Blue*, and that's exactly what it was. He was way wilder than Rufus or anybody else. Rufus was very colorful, but he was smart and played it safe. Dewey did not cater to anybody. That's probably why he didn't last as long as he was alive. He made the establishment nervous and shook people up because they thought of him as being out of control, a loose cannon."

Musselwhite grew up on those streets with another Mississippi transplant, Elvis. Charlie remembers seeing him on Beale Street in those days. He also notes that when Elvis' songs took that area by storm, it validated the music Musselwhite and others wanted to play.

"He gave us faith. Things got easier for musicians after Elvis because he was one of us, not Pat Boone or a Top 40 kind of guy singing the music you heard on the radio. When Elvis became popular, that confirmed our belief in ourselves, that we did have something that was valid in the world. That encouraged other people to be more active in the music they knew."

In 1962, Musselwhite moved to Chicago looking for work, but he was still shy about playing music in public. "My immediate concern was finding a job 'cause I was broke and hungry. I was walkin' down Wells Street in Old Town looking for a job. I heard some piano coming out of this basement bar with windows on the sidewalk. I looked in and there was Little Brother Montgomery. He was the very first live blues I heard in Chicago."

Every day, Musselwhite drove his exterminator truck through the city and beheld blues poster after poster advertising the likes of Muddy Waters and Howlin' Wolf shows. "There were all these people who I listened to on records for years right there every night. Every night of the week, you could go out and hear great blues. For me this was just the greatest experience. I was like a sponge in the ocean, absorbing feeling and technique.

"John Lee Granderson was one of the first musicians I hooked up with in Chicago. I loved his guitar playing. I always thought he was overlooked, that he had more talent than anybody ever seemed to give him credit for. His singing and guitar playing were very subtle and tasty. He played on the street with Robert Nighthawk and Johnny Young. Sometimes me and John Lee would play in these little coffee houses for a few bucks.

"I spent the most time in Chicago playing with Big Joe Williams. He was livin' in the basement of the Jazz Record Mart, and I got a job at the Jazz Record Mart. I needed a place to stay, so we both ended up living there. There were bars, Maxwell Street, and coffee houses, anybody that had any money, you'd play for them. We would walk around streets in Chicago like Clark Street, which was one of the roughest streets in the city. In fact, it was one of the rougher streets I've ever seen. Joe and I just loved to go down to King's Tavern and the Queen's Paradise on Clark Street and sit back and watch the show. It always happened that the roughest ones were our favorite ones. There'd be fights all the time. I never walked on Clark Street in those days that I didn't see some blood on the sidewalks.

"Playing harp with his guitar was a great experience and made sense to me immediately. Joe was one of those guys, like Lightnin' Hopkins and John Lee Hooker, who made these changes whenever he felt like it. I really had to be on my toes when I played with him and learn to anticipate when he was going to make those changes. From that I developed the ear to be able to do that. That skill has helped me out endlessly. It helped me feel where the music was going to go without having to think about it.

"Big Joe and I would laugh together sometime until we would be in tears, laughing and tellin' stories. We also talked a lot about the meaning of life and what life was all about. As hard a life as he had and all the hard experiences he'd had, his spirit never gave in. He could get bitter, but I never saw that in him way often. Big Joe couldn't write his own name. One time he wanted to learn to write his name and we went through making the letters, and he would take a pencil, paper, and eraser and he would try over and over again. He never did get it. Yet he knew every highway."

Gradually, Charlie found the places where he could begin to sit in with the blues legends he had been hearing on radio or records. "I played with Muddy many times in those days. Muddy and Wolf were the two stars of Chicago blues then. I had been going to Pepper's Lounge to listen to Muddy. Pepper's Lounge was Muddy's home club. After he knew I could play, he would always call me up to sit in. It got to the point where I didn't know if I wanted to go there. I'd hide so he wouldn't see me and call me up. Although it was very exciting and a thrill to be up there with those guys, I wasn't comfortable onstage. It was still scary. It wasn't my dream.

"The thing about Muddy and Wolf was that they had a whole lot going for them that was distinctive from the others. They had a voice, they had a look, they had a personality and charisma that made them stand out from everybody else. Anybody might have been able to play what they played, but nobody else could be a Howlin' Wolf. You could mimic him, but he did it like nobody else did it. Muddy, the same way. The other guys in Chicago had their own strengths, but they just didn't have as much of it as Wolf or Muddy. When those guys walked into a place, even if you didn't see 'em, you felt the room change."

Chicago was home to the reinvention of the harmonica from tiny dime store toy to amplified and distorted Mississippi sax. At the center of the harmonica innovations was Little Walter. It didn't take Musselwhite and Walter long to find each other. "I knew Little Walter real well. He was a nice guy, but he was a scrapper. He wouldn't take any bullshit from anybody. It didn't matter how big you were—pound for pound, he was the toughest guy I ever knew.

"As a harp player, he was really innovative. He played a real modern style. That's interesting, because today, if the harp purist hears somebody playing something that goes beyond Little Walter, they will say it's not right. If they had lived when Little Walter lived, they probably would have said that what he was playing wasn't right because he wasn't playing the style that came before him. Little Walter always insisted that I sit in and would buy me drinks and act like he was loanin' me money when he was actually giving me money.

"I'm sure Little Walter was influenced by the jazz saxophone, because the popular groups at the time were people like Louis Jordan or the riffing

horn sections like T-Bone Walker. It would be a natural thing for a harp player to play those riffs. You couldn't help it. When I lived at those record
stores in Chicago, I'd play harp along with the jazz records that we played.

"The word all around Chicago was that Big Walter Horton taught Little
Walter and Sonny Boy Williamson. I've heard that from so many people for
so long, that I've come to believe that he was a big influence on both of
those guys. What I learned from those guys were techniques that they never
recorded, like the different positions I play in. I learned that stuff from
them. But I get criticism because purists feel that since they didn't record
that, they probably didn't play that technique. So I get accused of not being
in the tradition, when, in fact, I sat with tradition and that's where I learned
those techniques from.

"There was a place called Rose and Kelly's Blue Lounge where I used
to play. There was a lot of harp players in that place every night. Walter
Horton lived down the street, so he would always be in there. Carey Bell
and Charles Edwards would be in there too. We would sit in a line of five
or six onstage and take turns playing out runs. When we were finished,
we'd pass the harmonica to the next guy until it got to Big Walter. It always
ended with him. He would always have some new trick to blow everybody
away. I could see how guys like Little Walter or Sonny Boy would hear this
guy and be impressed. Horton's strength was his precise and big tone. I
don't think I ever heard him play a wrong note. I tell all young harp players to listen to the feeling, the feeling's the thing. Tone is just the expression of the feeling. If it don't have any tone or feeling, it doesn't matter
how much you play or how much technique you have, it doesn't amount
to anything.

"For me, feeling was what it was all about. If a guy played only one note
but had a lot of feeling in it, that was enough. It doesn't take a lot of notes.
I always thought that everyone had their own blues inside. That's what you
were trying to reach."

Is it the harp player's phrasing and dynamics that tell the story? "That's
interesting, I never thought about that. I just play what I think sounds right.
I guess you could say that I'm trying to tell a story, but I've always really
liked the way notes go together to make a statement. I'm always just tryin'
to play what I feel in my heart and make it count. Each note should mean
something.

"There's guys out there who just play and play and play. It's like some
kind of technique exercise. I'm thinkin', 'Where's the music at?' There's no
feeling. The bombardment of sound doesn't give the audience any space to
feel the story. I can't follow the story if it's told at 100 mph because the
sound overrides everything.

"It's like in conversation. If somebody comes up to you and starts jabberin' at 100 mph, you'll never understand what he's tryin' to say. Some people speak poetically; they speak a few words that can paint a complete picture. That's where the art is. Like a Japanese brush painting, just a few strokes say the whole thing. And it makes you feel good when you see it."

In 1967, after Musselwhite released his first album on Vanguard, which included the short version of his signature song, "Cristo Redentor," he was offered a month's work in San Francisco. "When I went to California, I saw people in big clubs paying good money to blues musicians. I saw that I could actually make a living playing music. I guess you could say I was one of the first to bring the blues to Haight-Ashbury. It was really far out. There were all these people with tie-dyed shirts and real long hair, and I've got my shades on and a black suit and my hair slicked back, and they say to me, 'Man, you're really weird!' They were real open to everything and they liked the music. Those hippie disc jockeys on the underground radio who played whatever they wanted to play really turned people on to other kinds of music, like blues. I've lived in the Napa area ever since."

From the earliest days in Memphis and Chicago, to be on a stage anywhere and to play for an audience scared the young Musselwhite, so he reached for quick hits of Southern courage in a bottle. That led to his whole drinking problem. "That was the only way I could get onstage. Drinking is an old tradition in the South. At the most, I was drinking at least two quarts of hard liquor every day. All the musicians I knew were heavy drinkers. I was one of those people who could consume vast amounts and still keep walkin' and not falling down sick. Me and Otis Spann would be at Pepper's Lounge drinking whiskey at 6 A.M. when they opened."

It was in the late 1980s that Musselwhite found the courage to take control and step onstage sober. "I had gotten sick of it, and I was trying to quit. I felt like I was trapped in this nightmare. I had been cutting down, but I couldn't make that last hurdle of getting on the stage sober.

"Then on my way to work, I heard about Jennifer McClure stuck in that well in Texas. I was really hit with this picture of how small my little situation was compared to hers. How brave she was being down there in a real life-and-death situation singing nursery rhymes to herself, and me just whining about this thing in my control. That got my attention, and I kinda made a silent prayer to her that I would not drink until she got out."

That night Musselwhite performed clean for the first time. "I was scared to death, my knees felt like jelly. I thought I was just gonna fall over because my legs felt like they were gonna just crumble under me. I was extremely self-conscious, but I felt so great after that night. I still had to keep my promise to her," he declared.

"By the time she got out, I was out too. I just needed that time. When I finally saw that I could get on the stage and play sober, I wondered why I waited so long. The alcohol had me hypnotized: 'Oh no, you can't get up there and play sober. Get that outta your mind. You drink me first, don't forget that.'" The irony is that today Musselwhite lives in the Napa Valley, surrounded by vineyards, with no interest in it or fear of it. "Taking control of my life was like taking control of my music," said Musselwhite.

Today there is a resurgence of blues clubs, blues in advertising, blues societies, and blues festivals. Musselwhite believes this music is the cure for what ails modern society. "In today's world, the blues is the antidote to all the things that lack a human quality. I think it's especially true the way our politics is so blatantly uncaring. Sometimes I feel I'm on a ship of fools in a sea of chaos. I think we're heading in the right direction. The blues thrives not through any advertising campaign mounted by some big company. It's grown from the grassroots efforts of small blues societies that start newsletters and put on small festivals. It's really from the people; they've just demanded it. Even though you may like other types of music, you'll always have a place in your heart for blues."

Musselwhite has taken the people's instrument and found blues expression in all mediums. "Melody was a statement I was always looking for. I would find it in all kinds of music, too: folk music from around the world, classical, and jazz. To me blues is more than just music—it has a spiritual, healing nature. Although from time to time I have strayed away from the 1-4-5 chord change, that don't mean I've strayed away from blues and my perception of it. I like to think I've always followed the music of the heart."

Kenny Neal

When talking about parents and children, we may think of the phrase the apple doesn't fall far from the tree. Anyone who's watched Raful Neal work a crowd or a harmonica can see where son Kenny Neal inherits his genius.

Kenny has always been one of the brightest, most multitalented musicians on the blues scene. He'll walk outside any bar playin' Tampa Red's "It Hurts Me Too." Mid-song, he'll reach in his pocket, pull out a battered Marine Band harmonica, and wail harmonica techniques he learned from his father. When the mood strikes, he'll pick up a lap steel in favor of his time-worn Telecaster and slide swamp-toned magic. He'll take the bass off the shoulder of his brother Darnell and funkify the blues. When he hands it back to Darnell, Kenny will go behind and finger the notes while Darnell slaps the strings. Then they'll blow minds by reversing the fingering, never losing the groove. And he'll never stop smiling. These are all elements of any Kenny Neal performance.

"Kenny Ray loves his music," said his father, Raful. "When he comes home from the road, I'll be telling him to get some rest and he'll come to the club and play all night. He never gets tired. He knows how to get across to the people. He got that from me. Back in the day when we'd go to a club and it was down and everybody was lookin' like they were sad, I'd start playing good, fast, dancin' music to get 'em up. He learned to do that from me."

As a teenager, Raful played harmonica in a band that included a young guitar player named Buddy Guy. When Guy left for Chicago in 1957, Neal decided to stay put in Louisiana and raise his family. He never realized that from his Baton Rouge home he would produce offspring to carry the music into the next century. He and Shirley Neal, both products of broken homes,

***Whether playing the harmonica, guitar, or lap steel guitar,
Kenny Neal is one of the brightest talents in blues today.***

made a marriage pact to build their own family tree. It is their unselfish commitment that holds this musical clan together.

Though his oldest son, Kenny, is the most well-known child of this Baton Rouge blues legend, eight of Raful's ten children are world-class musicians. Meet the Neal household: Frederick, Graylon, and Darnell have been with Kenny's band since they were teenagers. Noel Neal is one of the most sought-after bassists in the blues, playing with Lucky Peterson, Buddy Guy, James Cotton, Koko Taylor, Lonnie Brooks, Sherman Robertson, and Larry McCray. "Lil' Ray" Neal is a well-respected jazz guitarist who splits his gig time between Bobby "Blue" Bland, Little Milton, and his own group. Larry and Ronnie Neal are percussionists and always ready to hit the pavement with the family.

"We grew up with the music. We saw our brothers playin' when we were young. The house was always all the kids playing. It comes from our dad. He spreads it all around," said Frederick. "You just pick up whatever instrument is around and fumble with it. It just comes natural to catch something in your head and learn it on the guitar or keyboards."

The daughters of Raful and his wife, Shirley, are also accustomed to the music spotlight. At the 1997 King Biscuit Festival in Helena, Arkansas, Jackie Neal, with her flamboyant stage presence, played tag with brother

Kenny in a crowd-pleasing sibling rivalry. There are identical twins Charlene and Darlene, who also occasionally sing with the clan.

At that 1997 King Biscuit Festival, the Neal family was booked as the headline act in place of the late Johnny "Clyde" Copeland. Before patriarch Raful took the stage, he told me, "There is no prouder moment for me than performing onstage with my children."

The blues Raful has taught his children grows in the swampy backwater of Louisiana. It was first stirred and later served to the world by great bluesmen of Louisiana like Guitar Kelly, Lazy Lester, Lonesome Sundown, Tabby Thomas, Silas Hogan, and Guitar Slim. Primarily it's a loose and uncertain beat cooked in a pot of guitar and harmonica gumbo that emanates from the Bayou state. Simmered for years, this blues differs from the blues of the Delta, Chicago, and Texas.

Kenny hears in swamp blues the varied cultural influences that came together in the swamps and bayous of Louisiana. "I think it's different here mainly because of the Cajun influences. You had guitar-pickers who began by singing in the fields. When they got a hold of a guitar, they were jammin' with people with accordions. That mixture of French music with gospel, field hollers, call-and-response songs, and the African music from the Caribbean makes us in Louisiana so different."

The loyalty to music and family was instilled early in each child. Raful began taking four-year-old Kenny, dressed in cowboy boots, along to his own local gigs and remembers watching him dancing on tabletops in time with the music. "Me and Slim Harpo used to be at the house getting new licks on the harmonica all the time Kenny was growin' up," said Raful. "Slim'd give Kenny Ray the harmonica all the time. He wasn't playing the harmonica then, but he'd be listening to what Slim played."

Kenny tells it slightly differently. His first harmonica did come from Slim Harpo, but more as a pacifier to a crying three-year-old. "He was playing with us kids and closed us in a trailer that they hauled equipment in," said Kenny. "I got scared in the dark and started to freak out. He was trying to soothe me with the harmonica. It wasn't something like 'take this harmonica and learn how to play.' It was like you'd give a kid a piece of candy. That was his way of soothing me when I got to crying."

By ten, with the guidance of his father, Kenny began making sense first of the piano, then of the bass. "I had a nephew playin' in my band who had a bass rig always set up at the house because he lived with me. Kenny Ray started messin' with the bass. Rudy Richard and I taught him a lot about playin' the bass. He was the first, and the other kids followed him," said Raful.

"I felt great havin' my son up there. You take a bricklayer and he'll take his son out and teach him how to lay bricks, or a carpenter'll show his son how to build houses. I was showin' him what I know. I had gone through a lot of hard times with the blues, and I didn't really want him to play blues. I wanted him to play some kind of rock or Top Ten, like Rick James. There was more profitability in that." But it was the blues that held Kenny's interest.

"I took a liking to the blues because it was my first love in music," said Kenny. "Everything else was secondary. I was hearing music in the house all the time. That's what my father did for a living, so I was always around it. It's like a kid wanting to do what his dad did."

To ensure that Kenny learned good habits, Raful knew he had to be the enforcer of a strict practice regiment. "I was a drill sergeant with him and practice. If he was gonna play, I wanted him to be good. I would roll my eyes and raise a little hell until he got it right. He caught more hell than all the other kids because he was the oldest. I didn't want no lazy guitar player," laughed Raful.

Though Raful may think of his methods as harsh, his son remembers that there was no need to be strict when it came to music. "He might have thought he was drilling me, but it was something I was enjoying," said Kenny. "It was like throwing the rabbit in the briar patch. I was right at home with it. We did more playing then we did practicing. Making the jobs was more important to me and my dad."

Kenny's first job in the blues came as the bass player in his dad's band. When the regular bassist canceled, 13-year-old Kenny volunteered to sit in. "I had been practicing around the house, and I told him that I could make the job. That's how I started playing bass. After that, the other bass player was history. I was so excited on days with a job that I would be ready mid-day to do a gig that night. Because I admired my dad, it was always nice to be able to share the stage and play with him."

By the time Kenny was 19, family friend Buddy Guy hired him to handle the bass chores in the Buddy Guy-Junior Wells band from 1975 to 1979. After playing with his father's band, Kenny found traveling with Buddy and Junior almost relaxing. "I'll bet they were pretty surprised at the way I carried myself and approached the job. I think when I left to go on the road, my dad had it much more together than they did. I was overprepared when he turned me loose with them. I knew about dealing with band members, gigs, life on the road.

"But I'd only seen the little juke joints in the South. I never saw the part where we were getting our hotels paid for and where we were getting paid to fly over to Europe. I hadn't seen that part of the music business. When I saw what Buddy and Junior were doing, playing the same type of music as my dad was, I thought, 'My dad would have been real big if he'd had this opportunity.' That's what motivated me to go on my own."

To go it on his own, Kenny understood he needed to be in front, not hidden in the rhythm section. Imagine his father and mother's disappointment when their world traveling son came home, locked the bass away, and began making noise on the guitar. "After he left Buddy, he didn't want to be a back man no more," remembered Raful. "He wanted to come out front. He told me he wanted to play guitar. I told him there were already too many good guitar players in the world—you better stick with your bass. But he was determined to learn."

"My mom thought I'd lost my mind," laughed Kenny. "She was so proud of me traveling all over Europe with Buddy, and I come back home not wanting to see the bass again. They would get together and laugh at me, saying, 'We need to admit: this kid, he's losing it.'

"I couldn't express myself like I wanted to on the bass. I knew that I would have to move to a lead instrument. It was hours of practice every day. I would crank up my stereo system during the day and put on live albums of people like Albert Collins and Albert King. I put my amp through the system and I would blend my guitar to theirs. I did that every day just trying to figure out the licks.

"I had the opportunity of traveling with Buddy, so I knew that in order to learn it, I had to woodshed. Not just learning the licks, but finding yourself and finding the coordination of being able to strum rhythm and sing is not that easy. You say one thing and your hand does another one. It was hard to get the coordination at first."

But Kenny also relied on the time-honored master-apprentice method of learning. "The way we learn in the South is that you don't go ask for tips. You pay attention. I had hot guitar players from here like James Johnson and Rudy Richard, who is my idol. I looked at it as an opportunity to jump on it."

The first-born's drive to take charge encouraged Neal to forge his own blues identity, first with the Neal Brothers Blues Band in Toronto in the mid-1980s and then with his highly successful recordings since his 1987 solo debut. "Even though I play a lot, I take a lot of pride in each project and each song I record. I work on each song until I like it, because it says something about me. I don't know where that comes from. I just like to create. Even when I'm doing other projects, like building cars or working with wood, I'm the same way. I like to sit back and look at the outcome and say, 'That's pretty neat!' When a project's finished, I like to look back at the little things that took work and time to get it right. That's the approach I take with my music.

"Each day when I play, I'm always curious about whether I'm sounding good. It's never perfect to me. Something can always be better. The audience and my brothers might think it's great, but I'm always picking out certain things and telling my brothers what to try in places. That's just me and the music. I'm always finding something, so I'm always growing and getting better. I would never want to stop that, because it makes the music better all the time. I feel good because I'm watching it grow every year."

The portfolio produced by his frantic pace includes five albums on Alligator Records, a role in 1991 on Broadway, three exceptional releases on Telarc, a joint Telarc effort with Tab Benoit and Debbie Davies, guest appearances on Telarc's *Tribute to Howlin' Wolf* and *Tribute to Willie Dixon*, and nonstop touring as the leader of the Kenny Neal band and a member of the Neal Family band. With constant demands on his talent, something had to give.

Kenny took a well-deserved vacation from his intensive touring for most of March and April of 1999 and worked every day, from early morning until late in the evening, restoring his pride and joy, a 1947 Buick Special, to be road-ready on April 24, 1999. "Working on cars was always something I did back in the day. Welding, sanding, painting—I restored the car and my soul.

"Before this time off, I looked at pictures of the people who I've played with and saw how many had died. I realized I owed it to them to keep myself and the music alive. This is something I can contribute to the blues by being there and keeping it going. When I started playing again, the music felt so clean and fresh. I found that an hour and a half isn't enough time because I've got so much music in me."

Rebirth and renewal are necessary for an artist to search out fresh visions. Often, the daily rigors of touring can cloud the purity of vision, the time to get it right, both inside and outside. So, just as Kenny brings cars back to life, he also has brought his music back to life, spot-welding his seasoned blues onto a foundation of varied musical approaches.

Today, the younger Neal looks back at a photo album that documents time spent with nearly every major blues musician. Offer a name, Kenny will start an "I remember" story. "Many of the guys out here on my circuit don't have a clue. It's not their fault. I was just lucky enough to come in on the later part of their lives and got a chance to share the music with them. I'm one of the few out there today who can dig up tapes of me and Sonny Terry and Brownie McGhee or me and Lightnin' Hopkins or Big Mama Thornton and all the musicians from Louisiana. I've got a tape with me on bass with Professor Longhair and Memphis Slim on keyboards.

"As a teenager, I did a trio with Lightnin' year after year between touring with Buddy. Lightnin' was the type that would feed off the audience. Once the audience showed they loved him, you had to pry him off the stage. When I first played with him, he didn't know what was going on, because I was so young. I learned his style, so I could play under him and with him. I came up and started playing all these old songs. When he found that out, every time he'd come up, he would be asking, 'Where's my boy from Louisiana at? He around here?'

"When I look through my scrapbook I can see that a lot of my goals have been reached. I've shared the stage with all of them, so it's not anything in this business I can have that's better than those experiences. When people ask me what my goals are, I say that I've already done that."

The greatest lesson they all taught Kenny was a simple one. "They made me aware that you don't get rich playing the type of music I'm in. But I think I'm gonna prove 'em wrong on that one day." In that way, Neal wants to be the son who will carry the blues of his musical fathers further than they did.

"It's a lifetime thing for me. It's not something I jumped on because of a trend. All the guys who get the big record deals and use blues to do that doesn't really bother me, because I think as long as I'm alive, I'm carrying a tradition that I'll carry forever. One day I'll fit in my spot. I don't think I can grow and be successful by just having a hit record. I have to earn it. That's the way I want it to be, to earn my place in the music."

But Kenny also understands the mentoring inherent and does the same for today's generation of blues kid as Raful, Buddy, and others did for him. "I encourage them. If I see room for them to do something that will better their playing or presence, I'm straight up when I tell 'em. I always compliment them when they're doing well, because that keeps it going. I deal with them on their level. I don't act like I'm Kenny Neal, a big star. When we're playing, we're all playing together. They don't feel intimidated. I think that helps them in moving further with their thing by being down to earth."

Like many other first-born children, Kenny Neal possess a tremendous drive to please, on one hand, yet also to exceed or transcend his parents. "I always wanted to show him that I was really dedicated to it. I still do that today. I've also ended up outgrowing my dad musically. It's strange. He gave it to me and I kept runnin' with it. I've grown much bigger than my dad in popularity. The audiences don't know how much respect and credit I want to give him.

"I like to let him know that I really appreciate what he gave me. Now I'm starting to take him on tour with me to introduce him to my audience. The main reason I bought my bus is because I'm touring a lot with Pops. Instead of him sitting in a hot trailer or tight dressing room, I want him to have a comfortable place to rest when we get to a show.

"A lot of people would get frustrated. But for me, I'm so happy to be able to make a living doing what I'm doing. Even though we've never won a Grammy or a million-seller, it's still all good to me. It's really just rewarding to know I can be able to make a living off something we took from home."

But the offspring of Raful and Shirley took away more than just music. "We come from a large family and we weren't very wealthy, but we were rich in love and music. That's what counts," said Kenny. "Every night I play, I feel my dad in me because that's where I came from," Kenny told me in Helena in October of 1997. "I don't care if I'm 5,000 miles away, Pops is always in my heart when I'm playing."

Lucky
Peterson

Most five-year-olds dabble with finger paints and recite the alphabet to proud grandparents. Lucky Peterson was not like most toddlers. At three, he began pounding on the family drum set; at four he started playing the Hammond B-3 organ; by five he was guesting on Johnny Carson's *Tonight Show*.

At five, Peterson recorded a single, "1-2-3-4," with Willie Dixon, which became a national R&B hit. That lead to an album called *Our Future* and the appearance on *The Tonight Show*. "I guess it tripped people out seeing a five-year-old kid playing organ on the Johnny Carson show," said Peterson." By eight, I had already cut a couple of records, been on *What's My Line?*, the Johnny Carson show, *To Tell the Truth*, all those national shows."

At seven, he recorded his second album, *The Father, Son, and the Blues*, with his guitar-playing father, James Peterson. At an age when most children were signing up for summer camp or joining scouts, young Lucky began touring the country as the child prodigy of the blues.

"I fronted my own groups and played local bars and clubs after those appearances. But my father and mother were real concerned about my education. When I went on the road, I had a tutor. The laws were so bad, I wasn't able to be in the clubs at that age, so they'd sneak me in, put a lookout at the door so I could finish a set, then they'd rush me out."

Unlike today, there was no national media frenzy for musically gifted children. During the mid-'70s, this ten-year-old phenom was known only within the blues world. When the family returned to Buffalo, New York, Peterson started hanging out at his dad's famous blues night spot, the Governor's Inn. It was here he began taking advanced placement courses in the blues. Regulars at the Inn, like Buddy Guy, Junior Wells, Muddy Waters,

***When he was only five, Lucky Peterson appeared on the
Tonight Show. Today he electrifies crowds on the B-3 or guitar.***

James Cotton, Freddie King, and John Lee Hooker, taught young Lucky the
fundamentals of the blues, while his father provided the day-to-day instruction to learn the music right. "If it wasn't for my father, I wouldn't be where
I am today. He's the one put it there. He took the time to teach me. He
made sure that I had everything to work with. He made sure that I knew
the first notes. He introduced me to the music business. And by owning a
club, he put me right in the middle of the music.

"He wasn't able to teach me the roots of the blues; I got that from watching him. He taught me what I need to do and how you do it. But he kept me around people who could teach me, like Buddy Guy, Junior Wells, Howlin' Wolf, Koko Taylor, Freddie King, Jimmy Reed, John Lee Hooker. Those are the people who stayed at our house when they came to Buffalo. My mother would cook for them, and they would take me to the store and play with me. They'd joke, 'When you get big enough, we're gonna have you on the road.'

"But my best teacher was my father. I got my butt whooped when I didn't do it right, so I had to do it right," laughed Peterson. "My dad was a strict teacher. Looking back, I'm glad he did it that way. He was the type of father who made sure, after my schoolwork was done, that I practiced in the garage. If I got on the stage and sounded like crap, he'd tell me to never pick up a guitar again.

"One night I was playing in the club with him and I was learning the guitar. I know I sounded bad on it. He snatched the guitar out of my hand and said to go sit down and never pick up a guitar again. That hurt my feelings, but it made me go home and get the B.B. King and Little Milton albums. I took my turntable down from 33 ⅓ to 16 so I could learn it lick for lick. I wanted to learn it so well that it would impress him. That's exactly what he was tryin' to do with me. That's the discipline foundation I work from today.

"I learned how to work a crowd from him. He'd play standing on his head, you never knew what my old man would do," said Peterson. Things haven't changed for Lucky's father. It was the elder Peterson who entered the Pocono Fest in 1996 playing guitar while riding the chair lift down the mountain.

By 17, Peterson had shed his "Future of the Blues" tag. In fact, most knowledgeable blues fans began wondering what ever happened to the child star. Upon finishing high school, Peterson was ready to begin his doctoral work in the blues, four years as bandleader for one of the blues' biggest stars, Little Milton.

"Little Milton came to Florida, and his band was caught in a snowstorm in Memphis. He and my father are real good friends, so he called my dad and told him he needed a band for the show. My father told him about me and my band. I rehearsed the band before we went to the show, and we played it all right that Friday night. The next night, Saturday, he played Tampa. We didn't know whether we were playing again, so the whole band went to the job. We saw the bus and knew his band made it. When I walked in, he said he needed a keyboard player. I played and got two standing ovations. After that, he called me back to the dressing room and offered me a job with him. I said, 'Yeah.' He said before I give you this job, I have to talk to your mother and father.

"My mother told him to take me, because I was getting into trouble. She said, 'I'd rather he be with you.' She figured I wouldn't get into trouble with Little Milton. My father didn't want me to go at first, but he knew he was only a phone call away. I was there for four years.

"That was the first time I played with a big name. Getting onstage the first night was fun, but the first night when I knew I was away from home and on my own was real fun. It was in Ft. Lauderdale. I was on my own and I was playing music and I was getting paid playing music. That was real exciting. Eventually it got to where I felt like I had to start creating something. After the fun died down, it was time to start rehearsing the band, learning different things, and creating different things."

Peterson took over bandleader responsibilities at the age 17. "Milton knew, at 17, I had the ability to play and to be his bandleader, and he could see I knew what I was doing. It was also a chance for him to take me up under his wing and show me stuff about the music I didn't know. I really didn't start paying attention to those lessons until I got with Milton."

What sage advice did the master pass on to his willing student? "Number one, Milton told me to be a perfectionist in your music and in whatever you do. He also said to make sure you love what you do," recalled Peterson. "I also learned that soul guitar and stage presence from Milton. I didn't really start to play the guitar until I played with Milton. About the second year with Milton, I decided to pick up the guitar. I used to take care of his guitar and I'd always mess around with it and say I can do this. I played at a jam session in Japan, and he looked at me like 'I can see you ain't gonna be around here long.'"

After graduating from the College of Little Milton, Peterson enrolled for another three years as the bandleader with vocalist Bobby "Blue" Bland. "I was his bandleader at 23 years old. When the other bandleader left, I was the only one left who knew Bobby's music. As the bandleader, there was a lot of responsibility on me. But it was also nice to have that responsibility. He expects his music to be right every night. For everybody to be on time and perform at 200 percent. He expects that the show's running the same, if not better, every night. He never wants to have the show worse than the night before. He wants every night to be good. Those experiences let me know how things need to run and how the music needs to be—what the job consists of.

"He showed me how to make the blues swing. The jazz swing part of my music is part of what I learned from him. I left after four years because it was time to see if I was able to do my own thing."

Playing with Bland put Peterson on many shows with B.B. King. This put Peterson in front of concert audiences and B.B. King. "Bobby was doing more of a concert thing than Milton. So that exposed me to a different audience. I was 23 or 24, and this was the first time I ran into B.B. King. Playing with Bobby, I started running into B.B. a lot. B.B. was very encouraging to me. He is the king of the blues, and every time I turned on something, it was B.B. King. I did a couple of things with him, and he was always telling me to make sure to keep on playing and get some of the weight off me, because when you get my age, it's gonna be hard to lose it," laughed Peterson. " He was always very encouraging and telling me to make sure to keep on playing."

But there were also survival lessons King passed down to Peterson. "God bless the child that has his own. They all told me to be sure and put a nest egg aside, to make sure you save something for when you get older."

Solo since 1989, Lucky is music's foremost triple threat. First and foremost, Peterson is a monster on the B-3. His mastery of the B-3 has made him a sought-after session player who can be found on the recordings of Etta James, James Cotton, Wynton Marsalis, and Junior Wells. On guitar, he can play searing guitar licks à la Luther Allison or swing like Little Milton. As a voice, Peterson reach a gospel-like testifyin' or soulful excitement. Peterson continues to be able to interchange B-3 and guitar onstage at will.

The roles Peterson plays, from producer to bandleader, have taught him invaluable lessons about the music. He's matured and learned there are times to suppress one's ego for the good of the music, to play a submissive role in the background instead of putting his music out front. "There's a balance; you have to be a follower to be a leader. It's like playing on a basketball team, passin' the ball around so everybody has the chance to hold the ball and showcase his talent."

In talking about his 1998 CD *Move*, Peterson explained, "This is the album that has been in me for 32 years." Why has it taken so long to get out? "Experience, age, the time to be able to record this on my own without anybody telling me how to do it. Finally, with a major label, Verve, I'm able to start calling the shots. When I started this CD, I wanted to go deep. I'm doing the same music, I'm just putting power and youth behind it." said Peterson.

Peterson revives old classics like "Let's Go Get Stoned," "It's Your Thing," and Prince's "Purple Rain" with mixtures of funk and jazz, but with a blues approach, while originals like "Move," "I'm Back Again," and "Move On You" combine mature songwriting with Peterson's instrumental expertise on everything with keys or strings.

This CD and his self-titled 2000 CD *Lucky Peterson* are redefining the sound of modern soul blues. Like every original who has come before,

Peterson sprinkles in some of this and some of that and designs a music that defies categorization. Part soul blues, part blues rock, part gospel, part sexy R&B, part genuine blues, Peterson's music is always redefining the industry's arbitrary boundaries.

"Energy and youth. I'm doing the same music I grew up hearing, just with more energy. I'm really not doing anything the older generation hasn't done. I'm just putting power and youth behind it. The sounds of the younger generation—funk, rap, and hip-hop rhythms—all fit in with the blues I play because the blues is about everyday life. I've always put more time into the playing of the music than I put time into the writing of lyrics. For me, the music always comes first. I hear the groove first, then I look for the hook and take it from there."

With all the experiences and lessons under his belt, Peterson is exploring and accomplishing what newcomers to the blues are only trying to play. "It's just been a matter of being there and having done it. I've sat with blues players younger players will never have the chance to learn from."

Bobby Rush

Since the 1950s, Bobby Rush has performed almost exclusively on the chitlin' circuit, the route of black clubs and theaters throughout the nation. In the mid-1990s he expanded his touring to include as many mainstream blues festivals and clubs as possible. The result has been multiple W.C. Handy nominations, including Entertainer of the Year.

"God give me the gift of the entertainer," said Rush. "Life is like a wheel. You put a mark on it and then you roll it. Sometime it come right back around to your mark and sometime it don't. I'm so thankful and blessed to see the wheel turn for me again. I'm lucky. The wheel's been marked for me and come back around two or three times.

"I think people want to be entertained, and within a few minutes people are gonna say that Bobby Rush is about entertainment. You can be taught to play a guitar, you can be taught to blow a harp, but you can't be taught to be an entertainer. You've got to be born to do what I do. People like Elvis Presley, Ray Charles, B.B. King were all born entertainers. There's a whole lot of musicians, there's only a few entertainers."

Growing up in rural Arkansas, Rush began his musical education at an early age. The radio played country and western music and the Grand Ole Opry out of Nashville, Tennessee. Rush first mastered the ham bone and blew some harp. At six, Rush was given his first guitar by a first cousin, John Scott. When he began playing the Arkansas jukes, Rush played guitar and harmonica. When he formed his first bands, he played the drums.

"Harp was my first instrument at home. But I think the first time I was in a gig, I bought me a set a drums, because I didn't have a drummer. And I had a harp rack around my neck, playing drums, blowing a little harp, playing a whole lot of drums. But I wasn't really a drummer—I just didn't have a drummer."

In 1998, Bobby Rush became the first to be honored with
the Blues Foundation's B.B. King Humanitarian Award.

That, coupled with Rush's early lessons from his father about contracting land and workers, has paid off in building a solid musical career. "My father was an independent person who told me to never work for anyone. That's where I got my independence from. He would contract to pick this whole field. Then he would hire a few people to pick it, but most of it was family. We would pick like a bail and a half or two bails a day. But then he would hire his neighbors to pick the rest and pay them some of what he was getting from the owner of the land."

Rush took that lesson and carried it into his career as a musician. He learned early on that the bandleader was like the land contractor and that the man who owned the equipment wielded a certain amount of power and could never be fired. "I probably was the worst player, but I owned all the instruments, and I owned a station wagon. I could get people to play for me because I had good instruments, the amplifier was the best at the time. I had the good credit. I could go to Sears and Roebuck and buy an amplifier that cost $50. I owned everything but the guitars. And I was in a position that I could hire and fire. They couldn't afford to tell me I couldn't play, because they didn't have a job after that," laughed Rush.

As a teenager, Rush left Arkansas in 1946 for Chicago, returned to

Arkansas, and formed his first band in late 1951 to play at an Arkansas juke called Jitter Bugs, in Pine Bluff. "Maybe 30 people, fried fish, and moonshine. When I first played, I didn't have a drum. I had a guy with a snare just playing behind me; it was just myself and my guitar and my harp around my neck. We knew a couple tunes and we would play a couple songs a night. People would go wild.

"I think I was making $3.50 a night with all the chitlin's and fish I could eat, but it was a good time. It was my way of learning. At the time, I knew I couldn't play as well as I would like to play, but it was my way of learning. I look back on it now, and the owner knew I couldn't play as well, but he was giving me a chance to learn, giving me $3 a night. Eventually, I got to where I was getting $12 a night. I would give my guy $5 a night and I would keep the rest of the money."

In 1954, before returning to Chicago, Rush employed Elmore James for nearly a month in a Pine Bluff band. "Elmore was playing good, but he was a woman hound, a real lady hound dog. I think he knew how to play, but he didn't play the slide as well as his cousin, Boyd Gimball, who was also in the band. He was the man. Boyd just didn't have the vocal thing like Elmore. He was a much better player. But at the time people didn't know him. He was probably a little bit older than Elmore, maybe a year or two, and like a daddy image to all of us."

When Rush arrived in the Windy City in 1956, he immediately formed bands that attracted many of the city's younger musicians, like Luther Allison, Freddie King, Eddie Boyd, Tyronne Davis, and Willie Mabon, into his band. Many of these talented players learned from Rush before moving on. But it was Rush's close association with the enigmatic Little Walter that taught him the most, witnessing, first hand, Walter's abilities on harmonica that solidified Rush's commitment to the instrument.

"Little Walter was really causing me to lay with the harp as long as I did, because at one time I didn't want to stick with the harp anymore. One time, Walter went to Illinois and had all this money in his car. He went in two hours before the gig and set the whole bar up. Now the bar didn't hold about ten or 15 people, and with 50 cents for a bottle of beer that wasn't that much money, but to me as a broke kid it seemed like a whole lot of money.

"After a couple of hours, he said, 'Blood' (he called me Blood), 'I done run out of money. Let's go get some more money.' My thought was he was going home to get the money. Now, he's got the bar set up, we got four or five ladies at the bar, he's calling me brother, and all these women are hanging around me. 'This is it!' I'm thinking. 'I don't want to go nowhere.'

"So he goes to his car half drunk, and I said, 'You need me to drive?' And he says, 'No, I'm going to get some money.' So he opened his trunk, and it was full of money. There were one dollar bills, five dollar bills, maybe a few tens, but it was packed. Looking back, it was probably $500, but to me, with no money in my pockets, it looked like a million dollars. He got him a handful and then said, 'Get you some.' So I also got a handful. I probably had around $20 and stuffed them in my pocket. When he closed his trunk, there were dollar bills sticking out of the trunk, and he was trying to tuck them back in and pull them out.

"I said to myself, 'Whatever I'm gonna do in life is gonna be by the harp.' I never saw this kind of money in my life. I was enthused. I've been with $2 to my name, and this harp player's got a trunk full of money. I put the guitar down and decided, 'I'm not playing no more guitar. It's the harp, harp, harp.' To me, the only way to make it rich was from the harp."

But their friendship also became one of student and teacher for Rush. "He was the kind of guy who would tell you to listen to this rhythm, and if you caught the rhythm, he would move to another rhythm. He wouldn't go back to show you that rhythm anymore. He would say, 'Hey, play that like you play it. Don't play it like I play it—play it like you play it.' I would take his riff and put my own thing in it. You could blow one note with Walter, and if he wanted it, he got it. He would hang out around guys who he was supposed to be teaching, and if you blew something different, he'd take what you had and be gone with it. He was just that fast. He was a smart learner, a smart stealer, a good thief.

"At that time, if you picked up a harp, anything you played was so much like Little Walter. I wouldn't come up and jam with Little Walter because he would just cut your neck, because everyone was so into Walter there was nothing you could do. Sometimes, I would go by Walter's place, and I wouldn't sit in with Walter, but I would sit in with his band with Luther Tucker.

"I didn't know at the time that he was learning from me. Apparently he liked what I was doing. And he was probably learning from what I was doing, and I did not know he was. Walter would teach you, but if you blew something different, he would pick it up."

Rush also witnessed Little Walter's dark side. "Walter was so fond of what he was doing that nobody could really tell Walter what to do onstage. Because he was the harp man, who around could tell him how to play? In the 1960s, he stopped doing what he was doing when he first met me. He'd listen to young guys play and just steal what they was doing. I know that we used to listen to some Sonny Boy, but after a while he stopped listening to the Sonny Boy. I don't know if he thought he had it all or he just didn't care.

"For the last years of his life he got deeper and deeper into his drinking. He would just not play unless he was pretty loaded. His last years before he passed, he just didn't get up to do what he used to do. I was around him all that time. Either he thought he was up above it or he just wasn't enthused anymore about what he was doing."

In those days in Chicago, a young Rush also met and befriended Muddy Waters and Howlin' Wolf. As friendly and supportive as they were, Rush regrets that he avoided their musical advice and support. "I would see them at least two to three times a week, and was even invited out more than that. But I would just pull away. Sometime Muddy and Wolf would invite me by and I would not go. I'd say, 'I'm not going to where these old guys are. I'm going to hang around with the young cats, more in my age bracket.' These guys were 40 years old, and at 21, I didn't want to be hanging around the old guys. God forgive me for that, but I just didn't know it.

"I would come up onstage with Muddy and Wolf. I would come in, and they would ask me to sit in, and they would introduce me to the house. I had my band and we used to have a jam session, and try to cut a little head, hoping that the band would hire you one day.

"Muddy Waters would call me 'Blood,' and he literally begged me to do the American Folk Blues Festival overseas with him and Jimmy Reed. Willie Dixon literally begged me. He was a friend of me and my family, and my wife knew him and his wife, and he just literally begged me to do some of his songs and do the overseas bit. At the time, I wasn't interested in his song or the overseas. I was doing alright with where I was, and some of the things I just didn't have knowledge of. I regret not doing some of those things. But I was carving my way in that chitlin' circuit, and I just didn't have the knowledge of where it would lead me. I don't regret it, but if I could do it over again, I think I would be more kind to the men who were trying to get me to do it, because they looked up to me as a son."

It was Rush's commitment to beginning a career as an entertainer on the black chitlin' circuit that became the road he followed. "I remember in the early 1950s I was probably one of the first black men to be hired on Rush Street in Chicago. I was hired after I auditioned with four white guys. When I went to do the job, I returned with four black guys. It was ten minutes before the show and he needed a band, so I integrated. They let me play the first set like that, but told me to get the other guys for later in the night because they couldn't stand for that integration in there.

"After the set, the boss wanted to see me. I know I'm fired. He cursed me down: 'What are you trying to do, integrate my place?' I said, 'No sir.' He's got this guy standing at the door with the machine gun on his back, I mean real Al Capone. He said, 'You got a nerve to come in and integrate my place.' Then he says, 'But you're good' and laughs. I stayed there for about a year and a half.

"Then I had a job at Walton's Corner for about 15 years, as a bandleader in Chicago. For a long time, I was playing four or five days a week, and I was making as much if not more than Muddy Waters and Wolf. The club I was working was a bow tie club. The guys I knew couldn't associate with where I worked at. That made it rough for me and separated me from those guys. Where Junior Wells and them was playin' out making $15 a night, I was comfortable at the time makin' $40 to $50 a night. That was unbelievable in them days. But I think, really, that's my downfall, because I did so well as a young man in Chicago, at this earlier stage in my life, and it took me away from my recording ability. I thought, why should I record when I was making $50 or $60 in those times.

"I'm so creative because I came up in a creative area. I learned so much and I took bits and pieces from everyone. Muddy didn't need a microphone. He was so powerful, he could do it naturally. He would just say something and then laugh, 'Ha, ha, ha.' I mean, no put on. But he was a very good dresser. I learned the dress styles from Muddy Waters. And I learned being self-contained and self-stylish from Howlin' Wolf, because he was so different. He didn't care what you did or what anyone was doing. I learned my swiftness from Little Walter, because he was so swift with the things he did. I learned my songwriting ability from Louis Jordan. There was so many things I learned about each one, and I took a bit of this and a bit of that and put them into Bobby Rush."

Though Rush worked the harmonica and guitar on the bandstand, he's made his name on the chitlin' circuit as an entertainer. Those lessons came from men like Bobby "Blue" Bland and B.B. King's showmanship and professionalism. "The deepest friendship in the music is probably with Bobby Bland. We don't talk to each other on a everyday basis, but that's a deep, embedded friendship with Bobby Bland and I. Bobby Bland has taught me about style and staying power. You may hear Muddy Waters's name mentioned more on the blues circuit, but Bobby Bland is the biggest artist by far. He probably sold as many records as B.B. King.

"I think the advice he gave me was the way he carried himself in the music business. And I listened and watched how he got over with nothing to go on. Because the time he was coming on was earlier than me, and he had nothing to go on. Bobby "Blue" Bland didn't tell me anything, but I could see what he was about, and that's very neat.

"One thing about B.B. is that B.B. made it popular for a lot of us, black and white, because he stand as a bluesman. He definitely had opened the doors that we would not have been able to get through. He made it possible for a lot of us because when you relate to the blues, you relate B.B. King."

Rush learned early about the Jim Crow problems that faced a black man playing clubs in the South. "I didn't have any problems in the South because we knew how to get by. I'd go to a hotel and get their phone number, go across the street to a pay phone, and call the hotel manager. I would change my voice and tell him I was Emit Ellis, manager of a band looking for rooms for this bunch of black guys. He'd say, "I'll get a couple of rooms for the boys." Meantime I'd just went there and was told they had no rooms, you understand? I'd just changed my voice and asked if they could help me out. Most of the time it worked. I'd go by there and say, 'Listen, Mr. Ellis called about some rooms for us?' He'd say, 'Yeah, man, he just called us. C'mon.' There were still a couple that put me on the spot asking to come by and pay in advance 'cause the hotel wasn't gonna accept money from them black guys. You gotta do that to get a room to sleep."

Today Rush continues to be a major force on the chitlin' circuit, but he has also brought his show into primarily-white clubs and festivals with great success. Making the music color-blind is the message behind the man. "People wanted me to change what I do to fit in with the white club. I said, 'No way. This ain't about no white and black issue, this is about good music.' The other blues guy is doin' the blues, but he's sellin' out because he's doin' music he thinks white people like, singin' 'Sweet Home Chicago.'

"I want to cross over into the white market, but I don't want to cross over and cross out. I mean I don't want to cross out the ghetto, the chitlin' circuit, the black people, because those are the roots and foundation. That's where I come from. Why should I record something for white people and then record something different for black people? I just want people to throw this black and white issue away. Let's make good music that's for everybody, because the music don't have no color."

His current shows typically mix African Americans who remember his riotous shows with audiences just discovering this 40-year veteran. By mid-show, Rush has all colors, all sexes, and all ages winking along with him. "I'm the shoeshine boy from the early part of the century. People lined up for the shoeshine boy to shine their shoes, but it was the entertainment he was doin' while he was shinin'. I'm the Cab Calloway that people come to see, the real guy, the average guy who speaks the truth," said Rush.

Rush uses his warning sticker well. He prowls the stage and taunts audiences like a terrorist holding a hand grenade with the pin removed. At any moment, some provocative dance or suggestive line could explode the show's R rating. Whether his gyrating dancers' nonstop hips and tight clothes punctuate every sexual reference he utters to the "fellas" or he utilizes his own good looks and boasts his omnipotent sexual prowess to the ladies, Rush always adds his sly wink to put the show into the realm it really belongs, to ridicule outdated Puritan sexual mores we hold in high regard.

"It's been stated a few times that my show is too risqué for audiences. This is ridiculous, because if I was Tom Jones, they would say nothing. If you look on TV and you see a man sellin' a car on TV, there's always a lady with a short dress helpin'. Within the first three minutes, I know what to do and when to do it," said Rush.

The flip side of this erotic and ribald Rush is Rush the reborn human and devoted husband. In 1992, his spiritual rebirth helped him to realize that the music he played was to be his religious vocation. Through that music, Rush could begin to bring black and white together. "I don't want people to think I'm a religious nut, but I do want people to know where I'm coming from. I live the kind of life now that'll set examples. I still got things that I'm working on. I guess the blues is one of the weaknesses that I have. I'm hopin' to get stronger about all the weaknesses I have. My promise is to do the blues and be the one to start this ball rolling. If I can touch one person, I'm effective. That's a start. That's what it's about."

Thus, the man who holds up gigantic panties and coyly asks, "Has anybody seen my woman?" also attends a bible study class every Wednesday night. The man who crows, "I ain't hen-pecked, just pecked by the right hen," runs a prison ministry with his wife of over 40 years and uses his tour bus to transport rural African American voters in Jackson, Mississippi, to the polls every November. "I'm pretty tied in with groups helpin' out black kids who have never been voting. I don't let people talk about black and white issues to me. We're not about that in the South. We're about problem solving in the community." His efforts have not gone unnoticed. In addition to his numerous civic awards, Rush was awarded the Blues Foundation's first ever B.B. King Humanitarian Award in 1998 for his unselfish community service.

"When Muddy Waters was recording 40 years ago, he didn't have black and white issues in mind. He was just recording a good song. If it wasn't for the white blues lovers and the blues society people, I don't know what the blues would be today. Blacks seem to say, 'I don't want to be reminded of the slavery when I hear the blues. In my biblical readings, I've learned that you have to remember history in order to know where you're going."

Carl
Weathersby

When the older cats come through, all they heard was the blues. When I come through I could hear anything, so my sound has soul, blues, and R&B in it. It would be different if all I heard was Muddy Waters. That would have all I'd be tryin' to do. Everybody's playing the heck out of the guitar nowadays; I wanted to do a different variation with the music," said Carl Weathersby. "It's hard to label what's coming out of me. The biggest thing I give is real, honest expressions. Most of the guys I see playing blues are playing it artificial. They have tube screamers and wah-wahs and it comes off synthetic. Whatever I do is from the heart. When it comes from there, it'll reach there."

Weathersby is another in the cache of young African American blues guitarists who hail from Chicago and is trying to expand the blues to fit into the modern urban realities. Windy City players like Lurrie Bell, Ronnie Baker Brooks, Melvin Taylor, Lil' Ed Williams, Johnny B. Moore, Vaan Shaw, Chico Banks, and Rico MacFarland are pushing the blues envelope by fusing all the music they've heard into their aggressive string attack.

Born into a musical Mississippi family, Carl Weathersby has been playing the guitar for over 30 years. After touring with Albert King and Little Milton, Weathersby in 1982 became an essential part of Billy Branch's Sons of Blues. In January 1996, Weathersby announced it was his time to step out. It has been the release of his Evidence CDs that has jump-started his solo career.

"I left the SOBs because I needed a different direction. Most harp players, with the exception of Sugar Blue, are stuck in the 1950s. As a guitar player, that accompaniment is the first stuff you learned how to play on the guitar. There's no growth that way whatsoever. I needed to be doin' my own

Carl Weathersby's blues is a funky mix of
soul, R&B, gospel, and deep blues.

stuff. I've been with Billy Branch a long time, and doing what he thought we should be doin'. I needed to do what I thought needed to be done."

The primary obstacle Weathersby and these other capable African American guitar players face is the lack of notoriety. "Getting gigs isn't hard; getting gigs that are worth doing is the tough part." Though he has released critically acclaimed CDs, Weathersby admits it hasn't gotten any easier getting bookings. "There's a festival where I live, almost walking distance from me, and they're offering me $200. Yet they want to bring in acts from the West Coast and pay them ten times that and give them the keys to the city. That's good for those guys, but it should be good for me too.

"Nobody's getting any press or credit because they're busy promoting Kenny Wayne Shepherd, Jonny Lang, and all those cats. More power to 'em, but I would like to open up for one of them and get some of that recognition."

Through it all, Weathersby has discovered an inner strength necessary to survive while trying to build a career. At an age when most musicians opt for a stylistic security blanket, Weathersby has chosen to reinvent himself and follow his vision. "When I left Billy Branch and the SOBs, I couldn't just go out and play. People were expecting a continuation from me. When I started over, I had to work to develop a following. In the beginning, every place I went, they were trying to make a rock player out of me. I don't use fuzz pedals or wah-wahs. If that was what I gotta have to do to sell records, I'd rather go to Mississippi and get a truck. Finally it hit everybody to just let me do what I wanted to do."

This has been instrumental in moving Weathersby to the next level. Fans across the country, touched by Carl's gentle offstage demeanor and blistering onstage performance always told Carl he had the stuff. Now the larger blues world is also applauding the Carl Weathersby experience. Starting over can be a humbling, sometimes lonely, experience. In 1996, when he began touring on his own, the bookings were scarce. Promoters asked, "Who is he?" After the gig, the promoters' universally enthusiastic response was, "When can you come back?"

If the blues is about personal connections between performer and individual, then few connect as intimately as Weathersby. His love of playing for the people is obvious. That live experience is one of genuine affection. Before he takes the stage, Carl can be found standing within a circle of fans sharing stories while he fingers the fretboard with his left hand. When he crowd walks, he'll shake hands, talk, sit on blankets, and let children strum the solo. In clubs, he'll share his wireless with those seated and turn table chatter into a song. Then Weathersby will rip off the most intense solo of the day.

"The live show is really what I'm about. I do whatever I can to draw them into the show. It's not a scripted show. I'll borrow lines from different R&B or classic soul songs that the people may know until I get a read on the audience.

"For me, it's just like a linebacker making reads. I watch the eyes and the body language, and that determines what I do. At a classical concert, you play the music exactly as the masters said. But the music I play—blues, gospel, R&B—is not very good unless the people you perform for can feel it. There's always another option people could be doing instead of sitting there listening to me, so I gotta appreciate that and entertain 'em. I know that whoever shows up to one of my shows will not get cheated."

His funky, bluesy R&B blazes with full arrangements, and Weathersby's lyrics tackle real issues, like the violence and lack of opportunity that confront his listeners today. "When I'm writing, I gotta look at today. Ain't too many people pickin' cotton by hand. There's a lot of people in this country without any hope. Kids are born with all kinds of opportunities, and when they turn 16 those opportunities dry up. That's going on in every major city," said Weathersby.

"I talked with Willie Dixon before he died. Once Willie made the connection between 'Baby Doo' Caston and me, it was like I was family. He told me, 'Your blues ain't gonna be the same as mine. You got things buggin' you that didn't even exist when I was coming up.' Remember he said, 'The blues ain't nothing but the facts of life.' That helps me a lot when I'm writing."

Weathersby didn't take a crash course in the blues; he was born into it in Jackson, Mississippi, in 1953. He was related to Willie Dixon's Big Three pianist, Leonard "Baby Doo" Caston. "It's a blood thing to me. It's been in my family forever. Everybody in my family played something. I tell people my family's been messin' around with this blues since it became popular in the 1920s, even before. My father's brothers were drummers, so drums were always around the house. I was playing the drums since I was a little kid. My grandfather played guitar, but every time I tried to mess with it, he'd yell, 'Boy, you'll break that guitar.'

"I was playin' drums in bands in the '60s that had a lot of members—singers and horns—that wasn't getting a lot of money. I thought I might as well let the girls see me. That's when I switched to guitar. Twelve guys in the band getting paid $80. I was about 13 at the time.

"The first time I tried to play guitar, I could. As far as music is concerned, there's some real strong heritage and genes in me. It came a lot easier to me than it came to other people. I've never taken lessons for the guitar. I've had lessons to learn readin' music when I was in school. But I can safely say I didn't learn what I'm doing from the schools in the cities I lived.

"Nobody in the Natchez, Mississippi, area used picks when I was growing up. When you begin playing and you see 100 people playing and nobody's using picks, you think that's how it's done. It's a regional thing. Where I come from in Mississippi, you don't see guys walking around with this big lump of steel on their little finger talkin' 'bout playin' slide. Those cats were usin' forks, spoon, knives, pieces of bottles, polished stones, whatever was handy. I never saw people walkin' around with chunks of steel hangin' off their fingers like I do up here."

Moving from Meadville, Mississippi, to East Chicago, Indiana, in the early 1960s exposed Weathersby to a world beyond traditional rural blues. From late-night Memphis radio, he grooved to Stax and Little Johnny Taylor and the music Isaac Hayes arranged and produced. On Chicago radio, he could hear the Dells, the Radiants, and Motown from Detroit. The different R&B styles from Philadelphia, like the Delphonics, the O'Jays, Bobby Womack, and Harold Melvin and the Blue Notes, also kicked into Weathersby's soul. It was in this environment he would meet and learn from an old friend of his father's, Albert King.

The first time he met King, young Carl tried to impress this mysterious family friend by playing a song he'd just learned, King's own "Crosscut Saw." "I didn't know who he was at first, I just wanted to show off I could play the guitar. They didn't put pictures on 45 records in those days. You could be sittin' next to the man and not even know it. I was sittin' wearin' out the record 'Crosscut Saw,' and I yelled to my daddy, 'I think I got it, Dad.'"

Upon hearing Weathersby's version, the stranger in the living room admonished him, "That ain't the way I played it." "I said, 'What do you mean the way I played it'? He said, 'Boy, that's me on the record. I'm Albert King.' Then he took my guitar and played it. I almost quit playin' there, but he told me to keep playin' it and I'd get it right," said Weathersby.

"He was a very encouraging teacher to me. I played with him on three times from 1979 to 1981. That was like bein' a sponge in the ocean. After I quit playin' for him, I'd still see him. He called me 'Guitar Man' and told me, 'Don't let nobody stop you from playin','" said Weathersby.

"Everybody focuses on the negative, but Albert was a normal person. Onstage, he was just taught to lead in a different manner. Nobody's a born leader. Quite possible the only leaders that Albert was ever around were white straw bosses in Mississippi. Generally, they were ornery people who treated you like you were nothing. That was the way Albert learned how to be a boss.

"He was goal- and achievement-oriented. He didn't compromise. He wanted to get the job done. That was the only thing that mattered. He was a little harsh, but I saw him see himself as a guitar player people went out and paid money to see. His attitude to the band was 'I'm payin' you to do this and that's the way it is.' There was no other way about it. When band members didn't do it the way Albert wanted it done, you'd have trouble. Albert never backed down from anybody. I can't think of anything he was afraid of, including dying. He learned to be like this to survive.

"Yet offstage, Albert was a nice guy who would help you if there was anyway possible. Many times Albert gave money to guys who used to play for him."

Weathersby said King also felt his share of bitterness as others passed him by. "I think he figured people who passed him by might have sold out. That's natural. Look around at today's music. How many people do you hear imitating B.B. King? How many more do you hear playin' Albert's licks? Albert influenced four times the guitar players that B.B. has because Albert was a unique player. Tonally and the way he played made him unique. There's a lot of things I know how he did, but I can't explain them. He did some things that are hard to imitate because of the left-handed way he played the guitar, upside down, and the way he stretched the strings. You can do it, but you have to think about it. He didn't think about what he was gonna play, he'd just play it. When you start thinkin' about it, it takes away something. You become mechanical and unnatural. He never showed me how to play it. In those days they wouldn't show another guitar player exactly how they did something. You had to learn on your own. The most convenient they would make it for you would be that they would play it so you could see 'em doin' it. Then you had to figure it out."

At the same time, Weathersby was part of Little Milton's touring band. "My aunt used to live across the street from Milton. I knew him because my brother played with him. Even today when I see him, he'll ask, 'You still squeezing on that guitar piece? That's the only way you gonna get the blues outta it.' Milton was another one of those guys who can teach you more by doin' what they do than actually sitting down and showing you how to do it. Listening to Milton's records, you can kinda overlook his guitar playing, but see him live and he's a great player."

Weathersby's genuine commitment to the blues has led legendary players to offer invaluable lessons. "Once the older guys knew I was serious, they encouraged me. The guys who actually offered to bring me into their houses and sit down with them and teach me how to play like they did were Eddie Taylor, Johnny Littlejohn, and Robert Lockwood, Jr. Once they saw I really meant what I was doin', they wanted to help too.

"A couple of days after Thanksgiving in 1985, Eddie Taylor and I had set it up for me to spend time with him right after Christmas. He was gonna teach me to play how he played. Those were his exact words. He died on Christmas Day. Johnny Littlejohn was a hell of a player who sat with me in 1993, about a year before he died. What really warmed Eddie and Johnny into my favor was that I was always respectful to these guys. I wasn't tryin' to show them how much faster I could play then them. I just wanted to show that I wanted to play along with you. They all appreciated that.

"Robert Lockwood liked the feistiness in me. At a festival, our rooms were right next to each other. He went and got his guitar and came back, and we set there till the mosquitoes started bitin'. He invited me to come to Cleveland for a month so he could teach me how to play like him. I said, 'Get the hell outta here. I'd have to be in Cleveland two or three years to learn all that stuff you know.' He said he could show me in two or three months.

"Because I'm young enough to not be a dinosaur and old enough to remember how the true guys did it, I feel like I have something that may get lost. I can pass that advice along to people who are just getting started. First thing I tell 'em is that if you're gonna write, write about what you know. You can't write about picking cotton if you live on 110th and Halstead in Chicago, because there's no cotton there. You've got to listen to who else is out there. If 40 guys are all playing with an Ibanez Tube Screamer, why would you get one? You gotta look for and fight for your individuality."

Lil' Ed
Williams

One play of any Lil' Ed record and you will hear generous amounts of the music he inherited. As a child growing up in Chicago, Ed was weaned on the raw boogie recordings of John Lee Hooker and the slippery slide of Elmore James. But it was the family get-togethers in which his uncle, the legendary J.B. Hutto, would lead the family in song that made the greatest impression on Ed and his half-brother, Pookie.

"I was 11 or 12 years old at the time. That would be 1967. He would always come over to the house when he was off the road and stay with us for three or four days at a time. He'd tell us fantastic stories about guys playin' and flippin' onstage. My brother Pookie and I were very excited because we weren't experiencing any of this stuff. He'd always bring his guitar and amps too. Me and Pookie would grab his amp and lug it into the house for our music lessons. First, he'd come in and sit down and start talking with my other uncles. They always sang gospel together, so then they'd start singing old-time gospel songs.

"It was wild and fantastic at the same time. They'd sing gospel first. We'd get all revved up in this gospel thing, with my aunts and mother singin' their gospel too. It'd sound so good. We'd quiet down for a second, Uncle J.B. would pick up his guitar, and then we knew it was party time. He fascinated me because I'd see him with that slide, working the strings like he was still workin' a show. He would pick up the guitar and walk through the house."

Ed's first instrument was a drum his mother bought him when he was 14. She bought his brother a three pickup Tasco guitar the boys restrung for Pookie to play bass. They played on the street every day. Ed remembers the police stopping by this street band and telling them the neighbors were

**With his trademark fez and heavy-duty slide, Lil' Ed took
his blues from the car washes of Chicago to the world.**

complaining about the noise. Times have certainly changed. Ed and Pookie
were getting so good, the police began sittin' to listen. "They were fascinated by how young we were and how good we could play. They knew Uncle
J.B. real good, so they knew about us."

"He had already started teachin' me to play the Elmore James rhythm
patterns on the guitar—all open tuned with a slide. I watched J.B. so close-
ly that I picked up playin' just like that. Once he showed me what I needed

to do, he said, 'Don't let one hand know what the other one is doing.' I had
to keep that in my mind because I was lookin' at my pickin' hand, instead
of lookin' at my chording hand. He told me to look at the chording hand and
pick with the other one. 'Tap your feet and remember how the music flows.
If you lettin' this hand know what the other is doin', you'll get all confused.'"

"When my mom heard me start rhythmin', she bought me a guitar too.
Here I am, playin' the foot drum and rhythm, and Pookie playin' the bass
lines Uncle J.B. taught him on his Tasco guitar," laughed Ed.

When Hutto left for a European tour of three weeks, he told Ed and
Pookie to be ready when he got back. "We both plugged into his amp when
he left. One of my other uncles used to sing for Uncle J.B. when he first
started. He'd sing and me and Pookie would play to his singin'. He really
taught me how to play the slow tunes and how to go with the changes on
fast riffs. He'd be so excited when we found a real good groove, he and my
mother would hug and squeeze us. That made us really want to play."

Then Uncle J.B. came home. "He came home, grabbed his guitar, and
told us to play while he sang. He'd left me a slide, and me and Pookie kicked
off playin'. It amazed him. He yelled, 'Wow! You guys have really been
learnin'.' We worked with him so good that he surprised us and offered to
take us out on a gig the next weekend."

At 17, Lil' Ed played his first show as rhythm guitarist in J.B. Hutto's
band. The boys were packed in the back of a rented panel van and sat on
instruments and drum kits. With Hutto's regular drummer, Ed and Pookie
were playing rhythm guitar and bass, respectively. "I thought it would be a
small club, like the little West Side clubs Pookie and I had been going to in
Chicago. When we got there, it was a big hall with a huge stage. At first I
was real scared. We got on the stage and just ripped the place up. We knew
Uncle J.B.'s music like the back of our hand, because he played so much
around us. We knew exactly what to do the minute he hit a note. He
jumped up and kicked off, and we kicked off right behind him. The people
went wild. That was one of the most wonderful days of my life."

Shortly thereafter, Ed and Pookie began playing out on weekends at local
Chicago clubs as Lil' Ed and the Blues Imperials. The band was originally
going to be called Little J.B. and the Little Hawks, in honor of Hutto. Uncle
J.B. was present at the boys' first gig. "Me and Pookie was out playin' in a
three-piece band at a little bar near our home. Uncle J.B. always wore these
funny old-time gangster hats. We saw that hat sittin' way in the back, lookin'
like Uncle J.B. When we were through playin' the first set, the people weren't
clappin'. Uncle J.B. came up to the stage and said, 'These boys are workin'
hard for you people. Why don't you clap for the boys?' The place went crazy.
He got his guitar out and he started playin' with us. We tore the place up."

For the next 12 years, Ed and his Blues Imperials played every weekend in and around the city. Ed, however, remembered the old blues adage, "Don't quit your day job." He was a player by night, and for ten years worked at a city car wash as a buffer by day. His blues break came in 1984 when Alligator's Bruce Iglauer asked the band to record a track or two for an anthology of young Chicago blues musicians. That recording session ranks as one of Alligator's most historic sessions.

"I didn't know anything about Bruce or Alligator records at the time. We had a lot of material all ready to record. We went into the studio wearin' our work clothes because Pookie and I had to go to the car wash after the session. We started to play and the crew started clappin'. We started thinkin' how cool this was, so we really were gettin' down. I started duck-walkin' and doin' other things I normally do for crowds. This really impressed Bruce. When we were done, he came out and said, 'There's something really special happening here. Let's do an album.' We had already recorded 15 songs. We went on to record 30 songs in two hours."

Mindy Giles remembered the session in the liner notes to *Roughhousin'*: "We'd heard about their raw style and crazy antics, but only Bruce had seen them. They turned the studio into a Saturday night on the West Side. After the second song, Ed yelled, 'Do you want to hear more?' We yelled back, 'Yeah!' Five songs were recorded with no second takes. What we had on tape was the rawest, happiest, gutbucket house-rockin' music we'd heard since Hound Dog Taylor. It took us a minute to decide he should take the next step. Bruce said, 'Ed, let's keep the tape rollin' and make an album!'"

Roughhousin' enabled Ed to tour more extensively and to eventually quit the car wash. Armed with the lessons from Uncle J.B., Lil' Ed was ready to take the blues world by storm.

"Early on, I had to grow outta his shadow. But I wanted to keep in mind the band lessons he taught. I learned how to be a leader watchin' Uncle J.B.'s leadership. He always taught me to stand my ground with my band members, that no matter what happens, even if I mess up, that I am still the leader. He also taught me the way to be a leader. It's not about hollerin' and screamin'. It's about bein' gentle. That's how he treated me, Pookie and his band members. Years ago, when I first started getting my band together, he said, 'This is your first band. By the time you get older, you'll have worked with 200 members.' I didn't pay much attention to it then, but now I know what he meant. He said, 'You're gonna hire 'em and fire 'em. Some'll stick with you, and some'll stab you.'

"I learned a whole lot from bein' able to look at him and watch him play. When I saw him jumpin' off stages or fallin' on his knees, I saw stuff I wanted to do. He'd jump off these stages, fall on his knees. There were a couple of times he slipped and would just lay there in the middle of the floor playin'. It was so amazing to see that. You don't see stuff like that anymore. J.B. learned me that. He said, 'If you fall, as long as you don't hurt yourself, keep going.'

"They called Uncle J.B. a slide slinger, because he played with a heavy slide and could sling it. If you get a heavy slide, you can really get slingin'. A heavy slide'll carry you beyond the last fret without a lot of pressure. Because a glass slide is so much lighter, you have to use more pressure and vibrate the slide more. There's a lot more wrist movement instead of slingin'.

"People either make slides too heavy or too light. I got all kinds of slides—metal, glass, heavy, light. Whatever sounds good to me at that time is what I need. Another thing my Uncle J.B. taught me, never go unprepared. I just reach in the bag, grab one, play with it a minute and if that don't sound good, then I get me another one. I've got a 5/8 socket I'm crazy about. I've tried 'em all. I've got a city water pipe that really cuts. It grips the string and it gives me that gritty sound when I really want to get down with some slow blues. People ask me, 'What kind of metal is it?' I don't know. All I know is it's a water pipe like you have in your basement. It takes a slide player to know what works."

Heavy slide slingin' and open D tuning equips Ed with the necessary tools to forge the sound he craves to reproduce. "Open D is real free. I got a chance to use more fingers and wiggle more. In natural you got to use all your fingers to make one chord. You can use two fingers and make the same chord in open D."

There was another lesson Ed learned from Uncle J.B.'s generation of bluesmen: how to drink and drug. Those Sunday family get-togethers featured music and whiskey. When he began accompanying Uncle J.B. to South Side clubs, alcohol and music were inseparable and very attractive to the youth. "I grew up seeing some of my uncle's flaws. He was a heavy drinker, drinkin' fifths whenever. You had to down a fifth. It was part of playin' the music back then. I've seen him drunk, falling down, and fainting. I didn't like that, but I didn't know that was the alcohol. Then I saw how much better he was after he stopped drinking. That was a good thing for me to see because it gave me strength in my time."

Ed's time came in 1995 when he realized the only way to break the hold alcohol and drugs had on his life was to sacrifice his music. "The more I got on the road, the more I drank or got high. It was getting rough on me. So I decided to take some time off from touring and playing. You have to drop everything. I stopped working with the Blues Imperials for about two years."

Oddly, Lil' Ed works in a profession that encourages its creative minds to use and often abuse these substances. "All I was thinking about was drinking, getting high, and playing for the money to get high some more. It's a cycle. While I'm onstage, I'm thinking about getting a shot of booze or a bag of weed. One day I looked in the mirror and said I gotta change, this is not me, not who I want to be. That's when common sense told me it was time to take control, because I had lost control."

Taking control meant making some hard decisions. It meant no more touring, no more gigs at comfortable old watering holes, no more old friendships. After temporarily disbanding the Blues Imperials, Ed moved in with his original rhythm guitar player, Dave Weld, a sober influence. His then girlfriend, now wife, suggested moving out of the city to her suburban Chicago home. At first, he found the tranquillity too much, but after a few days he knew he could achieve sobriety better in that environment.

Gradually, he began playing again with Weld as a guest headliner in 1996 on Weld's *Keep on Walkin'* CD on Earwig. A few small gigs with Weld and Ed was ready to revive the Blues Imperials. "The very first time I played sober with the Blues Imperials, I was scared to death. We played a festival in Louisville, Kentucky, in the fall of 1997. It was me and thousands of people. Heads as far as I could see.

"It scared me at first. But when I looked out and saw all these people jumpin' for joy, I thought, 'This is what I'm supposed to be doin'.' After the show, people were tellin' me that I sounded better then ever. I got nothing but positive reactions when I told people I'm not drinkin' anymore. Even my band members are tellin' me that I've really got it together. When my band members tell me I'm really kickin' some ass, then I'm working. When I see them jumpin' for joy and havin' a great time with me, I feel like I've found this whole new music that I can explore.

"The music was always there, but it was coming through a fog. Now there ain't no fog. The music is even more intense. I missed a lot of new music techniques I now have discovered. When you're into drinking, smoking pot, and all that stuff, you don't have time to think or to rehearse. I was playin' the same old stuff. Now my mind's open and I'm seein' new doors I want to investigate.

"I moved out of Chicago and into the suburbs. I can come out on my porch at midnight with the moon shining down on my porch and I can sit with my guitar and play. That's when the doors start to open. Now that I'm better, I'm writing better songs, because I feel so good. Here's all this music that I never would have experienced if I'd still been in my alcohol-and-drug thing.

"I'm not the same Lil' Ed that used to drink and get stoned and act the fool. This is the comeback Lil' Ed with a sober mind."

Performances of high flyin' showmanship—Ed on his knees, Ed on the shoulders of a band member, Ed duck-walkin' the club, and his over-the-top

slide guitar playing—pegs Lil' Ed as one of electric slide's most savvy players. The raw, '50s feel to Ed's music continues to keep Uncle J.B.'s approach
vibrant against today's technologically perfect recordings.

"It's gutbucket blues because it's gritty, wild, and crazy. I always listen to
the old-time music of Muddy Waters, Jimmy Reed, John Lee Hooker, and
Howlin' Wolf from the '50s. That really kicks me off. That's what I'm looking for. That's the riffs I try to put into my music. People don't play those
anymore. Everybody's too technical today, looking to get it just right. These
new musicians are good, but they don't have that old-time feel. I'm looking
for that old-time feel. For me, it's if you feel it, play it.

"In the old days, people played music and the audience could feel it.
That's what I want with my music, for people to feel it. A lot of people run
when you say the blues—they think you'll be cryin' all day. That ain't my
kind of blues. My blues is where you can't help tappin' your feet and movin'
your body."

Texas

The blues didn't develop only in Mississippi, Memphis, and Chicago. Texas blues traditions run just as deep. Texas blues has always incorporated a predominant guitar sound. Throughout the 1940s and 1950s, T-Bone Walker, Lightnin' Hopkins, and Gatemouth Brown gave the musical world major innovations in style. In the 1960s and 1970s, Freddie King, Johnny "Clyde" Copeland, Albert Collins, and Johnny Winter carried the guitar torch.

Whether children grew up near Houston's Third Ward, the Gulf Coast, the border towns, the thriving Austin club scene, or the Dallas city sounds, they were hearing the diverse musical sounds from each region.

If the child is father to the man, then early tastes and experiences usually dictate adult musical styles. Growing up in Fort Worth during the 1940s and 1950s, Delbert McClinton heard every type of music from Hank Williams and Bob Wills to Big Joe Turner and Jimmy Reed.

In Houston, the Duke/Peacock label in the 1950s aimed to export the Lone Star guitar tradition. Slingers like Brown, Collins, and Copeland, who all grew up listening to T-Bone Walker bands, began to bulldoze a sound combining elements of swinging Kansas City horn lines with the funky rhythms of New Orleans. A young Sherman Robertson grew up on those Third Ward streets. Now, at the beginning of the 21st century, as modern

Lone Star guitarists are again putting their white-hot brand on the blues, Houston's Sherman Robertson is the explosive chairman of the fretboard. "Twelve o'clock, gunfighter-in-the-street Texas style is what I'm talking about, earthy tones that keep the audience interested, music that won't let you get a beer between songs!"

As a child, Jimmie Vaughan was enamored of the Texas organ trios of the 1950s and the sparse guitar style of Brown, Collins, Johnny "Guitar" Watson, Freddie King, and Guitar Slim. Though Kim Wilson grew to maturity in California, his musical maturity came in Austin. His partnership of West Coast harmonica with Vaughan's Texas guitar ignited the Fabulous Thunderbirds and the 1980s blues revival. That partnership, like any musical partnership, allowed the ideas to flow freely between the members and spark growth to fresh musical vistas. At the same time, Marcia Ball took her New Orleans roots to Austin and began her study of Gulf Coast piano traditions.

The experiences of Tommy Shannon are the perfect bridge between old and new, downfall and redemption. Best known as bass player with Stevie Ray Vaughan, Shannon offers a look into the talents Vaughan possessed, with a detailed description of the addictions he and Vaughan were slave to. Their nosedive and eventual rebirth offers support to any human locked in the dark room of addictions. And like Wilson and Jimmie Vaughan, Shannon also speaks about the vibrant music scene in Austin, its role in the 1980s blues revival, and the effect first-generation musicians had on the young musicians in the city.

The achievements and rewards of partnership are no clearer than in the work of Anson Funderburgh and Sam Myers and Smokin' Joe Kubek and Bnois King. Each relationship demonstrates how, when one suppresses individual ego in favor of mutual respect, the creative output of the whole is greater than any individual contributions.

Marcia Ball

When Marcia Ball crosses her legs and pounds New Orleans R&B on her piano keys, she does so with a lifetime of reverence and devotion to the traditions of that city. Though she's lived in Austin, Texas, since 1970, it is her love of the Crescent City music that continually flows through her fingers.

"I lived on the Texas-Louisiana line, but I was born in Orange, Texas, because that's where the hospital was. Because my home town is on the Louisiana side of the river, I always claim dual citizenship," laughed Ball.

But there is a singular focus to her music. "I call my music R&B in the old-fashioned sense. New Orleans is a piano-and-horn town. Austin's a guitar town. When I started exploring styles of music, there was no place to go as a piano player except Louisiana. When I discovered Professor Longhair in the late 1970s, I knew I had met my maker. Piece by piece I followed the legacy up and down the line. Toots Washington before him. Alan Toussaint, James Booker, and Dr. John were directly in that line.

"Dr. John is a hero of mine because of his entire body of work. He has taken all the influences in me and synthesized them into one beautiful piece of music, "The Litany of the Saints" that he does on the *Going Back to New Orleans* album. He combines a classical composer from New Orleans, the Catholic liturgy and chants with almost a Gregorian sound, the Mardi Gras Indian sounds and rhythms with some Professor Longhair, and he makes this incredible composition that is New Orleans piano. I can only say that's how it should be done. When I hear that, I realize that I am an acolyte at the hands of people like Dr. John.

"Watching Dr. John is horribly frustrating, because those little fingers don't look like they are moving at all. These wonderful dance voicings are coming outta those hands. But as you grow and learn and play, your ears grow. He was talking about the solo recordings he did, *Dr. John Plays Mac Rebennack*, and he said he was scared to make a solo recording. I thought nothing would scare him. That was an interesting comment. When I first heard that record, it was just so over my head. Ten years later, I put it on and I could hear what he meant. A gradual increase in powers and enough listening and playing and I could hear the vulnerability. I've sat in with him, and because we're both piano players, he'll get up and play guitar. I'm terribly nervous at these times."

Nervousness seems odd in someone as veteran as Ball. As a child, the piano and country music engulfed her. "My grandmother played piano and her daughter also played. I was next in line. I started lessons when I was five. By the time I was old enough to know whether I wanted to do it, I was already doing it. People around the house played music for fun and pleasure, just for entertaining each other. One of the reasons why everybody picks up an instrument is to get the attention, and that was definitely a part of it.

"I had music to listen to that was not just kiddie classicals. I was playing "Tin Pan Alley" and "There's a Little Bit of Boogie Goin' On," and I was playing beautiful cocktail music from the 1940s and 1950s." On the radio, the 13-year-old Ball was listening to a combination of country music and the piano-based rock and roll of Fats Domino, Little Richard, and Jerry Lee Lewis.

"At that point, I was just a kid growing up in a small town and playing a piano for fun. I picked up a guitar in high school and played a little folk music. Then in college, I met somebody who I would sing harmony with, and that kind of got me started singing. That led me into being in a rock and roll band in college. Eventually, in 1970, I moved from Baton Rouge to Austin, Texas.

"At that time, Austin wasn't a music scene. A lot of people had just started moving here. Derek O'Brien, Angela Strehli, Lou Ann Barton, Denny Freeman, Doyle Bramhall, Joe Ely, and the Vaughan Brothers all moved down here between 1968 and 1972. Then Willie Nelson moved back to Austin in 1972. That solidified that progressive country scene that I got started in, and culminated in the outlaw country movement and also the urban cowboy phenomenon.

"At that point, I was listening to Tracy Nelson, who already had a couple of records out with Mother Earth. I got in a country band, Freda and the Firedogs, that played real country music and was a success. When that band broke up in 1974, I had to decide what to do, either start a band or join a band. I decided to start a band. It was up to me to decide what we were gonna play, and I went right back to my roots. I had already gone back to

***Marcia Ball, a regular at Jazzfest in New Orleans,
combines the funky rhythms of the Crescent City
with the rocking blues of her home, Austin, Texas.***

Louisiana with some friends and had dug up some of Irma Thomas' records
and tapes to get started with."

Ball's fascination with Thomas traces back to sitting in her audience as
an impressionable 13-year-old. "I've always given a lot of credit to Irma
Thomas. Her influence on me started early and has been consistent. She's
my biggest influence as a singer. When I was growing up, I heard her on the

radio. I had relatives in New Orleans and we spent time in New Orleans when I was growing up, and when I was 13 I saw her on a show in New Orleans, and I never forgot it. That was maybe one of the first and definitely one of the most important live music episodes in my life. Even today, Irma's showmanship, singing, and selection of songs is still real important to me.

"After playing all the kinds of music I've played over the years, I decided to do R&B. I immediately went to Louisiana and found a copy of *New Orleans, Home of the Blues* to learn the songs I wanted to play."

The 1970s was a time of musical experimentation for everyone in Austin. Within the alternatives that were explored in those Austin clubs, bonds of friendship were cemented by kindred spirits. "I played only country music in the mid-1970s. In the late 1970s, I started gradually going over. I had interesting bands and good musicians playing good music. We would do anything we felt like doing. One band, Marcia Ball and the Misery Brothers, was a fabulous band. We would start with "Snapple from the Apple" by Joey Parker and then we'd play "Big River" by Johnny Cash, and then we'd play "I'll Be Dog Gone" by Smokey Robinson. That was a typical set. We did a crazy medley, which was "Crazy Arms" by Billy Price, "Crazy Because I Love You," "Crazy" by Willie Nelson, and "I Go Crazy" by James Brown."

During those years, Ball was meeting the musicians who were to lead Austin's music revolution. Specifically, two Austin women—Angela Strehli and Lou Ann Barton—became soul sisters in a music scene dominated by men.

"Doug Sahm introduced me to Angela in 1972. Angela was playing music at Alexander's, the Armadillo, and Silk Creek at the same time I was playing at those places. We never crossed paths until Doug took me to her house. Lou Ann was already coming to town and hangin' around with people livin' on the notorious 33rd Street near the university in Austin. She said she saw me there hangin' out and jammin' with people at about the same time.

"We were all singers, and for many years we played side-by-side gigs together at Antone's and all these other places. Finally, Angela and I thought we should do something together. We learned 'Little by Little,' and that may have been the first song we did together. Then we did 'It Hurts to Be in Love,' which we later recorded on our Antone's album, *Dreams Come True*, in 1990.

"We have as many differences as we have similarities. The main similarity is that, at some point, we all got turned on to the blues. Even though we have a lot in common, we didn't run together. Our personalities are way different. But it has always been a good support group in a music world of men. A sisterhood seems to form when we all get together and sing. It's a feeling that transcends everything else. The same holds true with Irma Thomas, Tracy Nelson, and me."

It was in the 1990s when Ball solidified her position as one of music's most accomplished piano players, whose varied influences mix together to become unique stylistic statements. "Each piano player does it differently. I play with a heavy bass hand and heavy bass line that I'm sure I'm the bane of the rhythm section. That's quite a bit of the New Orleans influence. The piano can't be a dainty instrument if you are going to try and lead the band. You have to dig in. People didn't see right off that it can be a lead instrument. I learned this from Katie Webster and Carol Fran.

"One of my frustrations is that I wish I had met Katie long before I did. I could have learned so much from her. She's from Lake Charles, which is so close to my home town that I should have known her growing up. When I did finally meet her, I really felt I had met my godmother. She was a powerhouse player and performer, very much in the same style as me. Carol Fran is that way too. Carol is a strong singer with a lot of jazz in her playing, so I'm always learning a lot musically from her."

There were also the Chicago blues influences gleaned from the days of Antone's club. "We played shows with Muddy, but I didn't know him well. At Antone's anniversaries with Hubert Sumlin, Buddy Guy, Junior Wells, Mel Brown, Jimmy Rogers, Pinetop Perkins, Memphis Slim, Willie Smith, Otis Rush, and Albert Collins, I got to pass alongside these great players. I bumped against them and got a little bit from each to put into me. Since I came up in various other fields of music, I don't have as intense a background in the blues as some do. I'm not as versed in the blues. I might actually know more old country and tin pan alley than old blues, so for me there's always something to learn."

The piano traditions of Professor Longhair are within every piano player from New Orleans. Though Ball never played with Professor Longhair, she did see him play a few times. "I never really got to know him. But I've absorbed so much of what he did that so much of my playing is informed by that."

Anyone who grew up with the gumbo in the blood cannot avoid the influence of zydeco master Clifton Chenier. "I mostly learned from his synthesis of styles. He took blues and R&B and put it on the accordion. I hear Otis Spann's attack coming through Clifton's accordion. He taught us all to not be lazy, to get out there and play a real gig. He'd say, 'If all you can do is 45 minutes, why did you even bother to set up? If it's just rock and roll, just go out there and have fun.'

"Chicago piano has strongly influenced me too. The power of Otis Spann and Sunnyland and Pinetop has always been important to me.

Pinetop has licks and sass and is still teaching me. I mix both styles up, and I think what I end up with is Memphis."

As Ball was discovering her own piano approach, she also uncovered the songwriting skills central to her artistic progress. "It's real important for me to be a songwriter. I'm influenced by the songwriting in Austin. I draw a lot of inspiration from the energy of the city, but I tell my own stories. I don't write about someone else's life. I like the creative storytelling aspect of writing. If you open yourself to writing, it is right there, all it's own. The secret is just to be open to it and then to write it down. If you think for a minute you're gonna remember it, write it all down. I have a big stack of notebooks—everything from things to do, to shopping lists, to who called today, to how much we made at the club, to the songs I've been working on.

"I've discovered that you have to sit down with a piece of paper and work at it. You can't wait for inspirations if you really want to create. Sometimes a song is verbally ready before it's musically ready. I write things down often, but I don't sit down at the piano often enough to make songs out of ideas. Recently, I had a song I was working on for a long time, a good idea that I couldn't put together. So I kept it around in the notebook. And finally—it must be five years at least—all the lyrics and the construction of it came together in terms of what it said, the message, the twist that it needed."

Many of her songs chronicle the world she has seen. "Facts of Life" was born when she heard Willie Dixon say, "The blues is the facts of life." "St. Gabriel" is one of the most poignant songs written by Ball. It narrates the true story of a woman imprisoned in this stark and barren Southern Louisiana women's prison for killing her abusive husband. "The Power of Love" fell on me like a gift, as some songs do. And "Daddy Said" is a light, funny song with a cute little twist to it, and yet it's really a touching story. It's a lot of things that I like a song to be.

"I'm just starting to realize the influence of Allen Toussaint in my songwriting. He wrote so much of the music Irma sang. I'm realizing that the body of songs I'm writing, the styles and rhythms and progressions, has him flowing through."

As always, Ball's rich musical gumbo of Cajun, boogie, blues, and soul mixed with the R&B traditions of New Orleans has a swing as natural as her own swinging, crossed legs. "I've learned to play piano just well enough to accompany my singing, and I sing well enough to accompany the piano. Then I'll shake my legs just to distract everybody."

Anson
Funderburgh
and Sam Myers

I t may be that the musical partnership of Anson Funderburgh and Sam Myers represents the perfect pairing of youthful electric guitar and veteran harmonica, of vibrant Texas and seasoned Mississippi. But it was initially their friendship that brought them together to record.

"One of the big secrets to us being together as long as we have is that we were really good friends first," said Anson. "There was never any great master plan of Sam and I ever working together full time. I had a band called Anson Funderburgh and the Rockets since 1978, with Darrell Nulisch as the singer and harmonica player for the first seven-and-a-half years.

"In 1982, we played a little place in Jackson, Mississippi, called George Street Grocery. One of the first times through, Sam's guitar player brought Sam out, and we instantly became good friends. We'd play there for three days at a time. In that time we all got to hang out and become good friends. When he wasn't working, he'd sit in and play with us. There was an after-hours place called the Subway, and we'd go over and see him after we played. During the days, we'd go out to eat, to the movies, and bowl."

Sam also recalled their meeting. "I was still playing out on my own on the chitlin' circuit, and I was working at an Industry for the Blind factory in 1982 when we met. In 1984 was when I started recording with Anson, and I joined his group in 1986. People say we combine Texas and Mississippi styles. For years I've tried to understand the differences in both. I know that there's a Mississippi Delta-style blues. But I never could define what made Texas and Chicago blues different."

"I knew of Sammy from his work with Elmore James in the 1950s, and I

Anson Funderburgh, his wife, Renee, and Sam Myers wrote
"Change in My Pocket," the 2000 W.C. Handy Song of the Year.

had a copy of his 1950s single 'My Love Is Here to Stay.' After that meeting, I thought a recording session with him with a standup bass and swing-style drummer would be really great. We'd already done two records for Black Top and I wanted to do something different, so I got into Hammond Scott's ear about doing a new record." Thus, *My Love Is Here to Stay* was conceived in 1984, as an Anson side project. Nulisch still worked with the band two years after that, with Myers occasionally joining the band onstage. "That was fun because sometimes Sam would get up and play drums behind Darrell, or he'd stand and sing and Darrell would play harmonica."

When Nulisch left in 1986, Anson's choice of replacement was easy: Sam Myers. Sam moved to Dallas in April of 1986, and by May a new partnership was born. "Only real die-hard blues fans knew Sam outside of Mississippi or Alabama. He'd also toured in Europe. That, plus the growing recognition of the Rockets, convinced me he was the right man."

Sam Myers was born in 1936 in Laurel, Mississippi. Between school at Piney Woods, Mississippi, and summers in Chicago, Myers has been playing music since he was seven. "I'd go to Chicago as just a little fella to visit relatives. That's where I had the chance to meet many of the musicians living there. I wasn't able to get into the clubs, but I saw a lot of the musicians who played on Maxwell street. During that time, if you walked the streets of Chicago any day, you could see guys like Muddy Waters or Little Walter on the streets."

It was playing drums with Elmore James that brought Myers into the musical major leagues. "I played with Elmore about 15 years. I started in 1949, when I was 14 or 15." And though Myers remembers much of the music they created, it was their Mississippi moonshine business Sam loves to retell.

"When we were traveling in Mississippi, we had a sideline business going, making moonshine whiskey. It was a very lucrative and popular still, right on the banks of the Pearl River in Jackson, Mississippi. We started in 1955 to about 1959. We never did get caught. We finally gave it up ourselves. We could pump from 250 to 500 gallons of liquor a day. That was a big still. It was hid way back in the woods. When we had some time off from traveling, we'd come to Mississippi and do the still. The people were glad to know we were home. They'd ask, 'How long you guys gonna be around?' They just wanted the juice. We were making a lot more money than playing music, from that still," laughed Myers.

"When I was in Chicago in the 1950s, I'd go to the Palmer House and check out Billie Holiday or Earl Grant. Or I'd see James Moody or some other big jazz cat at Mr. Kelly's. Those were the people I really went out to see. I'd go out to see them because I grew up with horns and the big band sound. A lot of times when I'd walk into those clubs, I'd see Little Walter sittin' in there. Walter listened to horns in the same way other harmonica players listened to him. That's how he'd get that little horn riff sound on the harmonica. He'd hear a riff that a saxophone player would play, and he'd remember it and then transport it to his harmonica.

"I started out as a drummer and trumpet player, and that's why my style is different than a lot of the harmonica players. I picked up the harmonica

Whenever you talk to Sam Myers, be sure to ask him about
when he and Elmore James ran a still in Mississippi.

and transformed what I knew from the trumpet to the harmonica. I still
played the drums in the 1950s with Elmore. During that time's when I
picked up the harmonica. I used to pick up the harmonica off and on. I really decided I'd blow the harmonica because I decided to try something different. I got up from behind the drum set, and I haven't played since then."

At the same time, Plano, Texas, third-grader Anson Funderburgh
received his first guitar. "The lady my mother bought the guitar from gave
me a box of singles. In that box were Freddie King's 'Hideaway,' Bill

Doggett's 'Honky Tonk,' Albert Collins' 'Sno Cone, Parts 1 & 2,' and some old Jimmy Reed stuff. When I heard 'Hideaway,' I thought this was the stuff." From there, Anson listened and learned, and at 15 he was ready for the Dallas stage.

"There was a dance that originated around North Texas called the North Texas Push. It was a really cool dance, like the Shag: you hold hands and dance to beach music, R&B, and blues. When I started playing in nightclubs, you had to know things like 'Running and Hiding' or 'Linda Lou' and 'Honky-Tonk.' That was right up my alley, because I loved that stuff.

"Then I saw B.B. King when I was 16. I got to meet him, set down and talk with him. He'd never remember it, but he gave me a pick and made me feel like I was the only guy in the room. At 16 it made an unbelievable impression on me." Funderburgh's band opened for Albert Collins in 1979 and 1980, and as a green 20-year-old he played twice as the backup guitar player for Lightnin' Hopkins. "That was an amazing experience. I have a tape of it. I did two shows at the Granada Theater, and Doyle Bramhall was the drummer. We did that twice. With Lightnin', it was keep your eyes peeled for the changes."

When he started the Rockets in 1978, it was about the same time as the Fabulous Thunderbirds. Coming from Dallas, they always faced comparisons as just another T-Bird clone. Yet the Vaughan brothers and Anson have always been close friends. "Jimmie's two years older than I am, and I played with Stevie several times. He was a great guy, not a real close friend, but a good friend. He and Jimmie both did so much to help me. I played on that *Butt Rockin'* record with the T-Birds; Jimmie didn't have to do that. They both liked me a lot. And when he lived in Dallas, Stevie would come to see the band.

"He and I had lunch and hung out together right before he died. We were comparing our summer schedules to see if we were gonna be in the vicinity of each other at all. What can I say about somebody like him? He and I shared a lot of things, Jimmie too, because we all have the same love for this kind of music and the same heroes. To both of their success, they not only helped me, but they helped all the world of other musicians by introducing the world to this style of music. Stevie would do 'The Things That I Used to Do' or 'Let The Good Times Roll.' Nobody knew those were Guitar Slim or Earl King songs. So people would go back and listen. When Stevie would do interviews, he'd say something about me or Jimmie, his big brother. Robert Cray was another that helped young players like me by drawing attention to the blues. Those people helped people like me reach larger audiences."

While Anson was copping licks off records, driving Dallas teens to dance, and hanging out with these young Texan guitarists, Myers was traveling

Europe. His first tour, in 1964, just after Elmore died, lasted 18 months. "Even back then blues, jazz, and gospel were big in Europe. It was such a shock to land in Europe and have them sing our songs. I found that people who couldn't even speak English could sing the music. My first performance had the crowd singing our songs without being asked. They weren't able to speak English, but they were able to sing the song, word for word.

"I found out that people in Europe were very wise to the American way of music, that it's highly appreciated. The thing that really startled me was that they craved our music and supported it so much, when in the States, people took it for granted. It's really a sad thing. This is where the music was born. People in the States just take you for granted. You'll get some recognition, but not like you get in Europe," Myers pointed out.

Throughout the 1960s and 1970s, Myers recorded for Bobby Robertson's New Orleans labels. But it's been his union with Funderburgh that has granted Myers a musical rebirth, though now Sam's not behind a drum kit, he's the frontman of this guitar-harmonica ensemble.

"I think Sam has always brought that authenticity to the band. He's also the youngest guy I know. That helps us bring a fresh outlook to the music we play. That's what we have always hoped to do. Whether or not it comes through in the music depends on the listener. Hopefully what we've done is to create something that's our very own. You have your favorite people and you learn from all of those people, and hopefully, over the years, it develops into something that is yours. I think Sam and I have done that over the years. So when people hear that sound, they will immediately say that sounds like Anson and the Rockets with Sam Myers."

The blues-buying public has taken notice. *Sins*, the first record put out by the new band, in 1987, garnered four W.C. Handy awards: Album of the Year, Band of the Year, Song of the Year ("Changing Neighborhoods"), and Blues Instrumentalist, for Myers's harmonica work. Since then, they have won two more Band of the Year Handys. Their albums of the '90s continue to push the casual atmosphere, easy swing, razor-sharp guitar, richly layered keyboards, and Sam's plugged-in jive. Funderburgh lays respectful fills behind Myers' conversational voice, and then his guitar explodes into bursts of Lone Star lightning.

Anson continued, "I really like playing short bursts around Sam's vocals." To listen to the Rockets is to hear Myers' burly voice and Funderburgh's richly textured guitar working to be one. At times these two are so completely in synch, Funderburgh's Strat nearly becomes Myers' voice. That comes from Anson's studied approach onstage. "I study where it comes from and lay back. You have to lay back and give him the freedom so it works. If you play too much, it ruins his freedom. I grew up listening to

Jimmy Reed and Sonny Boy. I have the utmost respect for Louis and David Myers, Robert Lockwood, Jr., and Luther Tucker. This was the music I loved. The songs and the figuring out of the parts that work in the music—it really is so much more intricate than people realize." As always, Funderburgh's fluid guitar work sounds too easy. His Texas shuffles, extended introductions, and efficient solos reflect the polished work of experience.

"Sam's a great showman too. I'm very happy to let Sam be the showman. He doesn't miss a whole lot. He told me a long time ago, 'Anson, I might be blind, but I don't have a blind mind.'"

Myers has been legally blind since he was eight. Operations at eight and again at 14 did little good. Today, Myers walks to and from the stage unaided, shakes hands with friends, and always picks the prettiest girl to dance with. "I never looked at my lack of eyesight as a disadvantage. I just looked at it as, hey, there's nothing that could be done about it. It's just something I have to live with. In some ways it probably helps me as a singer and musician. When people see that you are trying to help yourself instead of looking for charity, they will help you. I can see some, it's not like I'm totally blind. I can see when a crowd stands and cheers."

These live shows are the essence of Funderburgh and Myers. "For Sam and I it's a very personal type of music. No barriers. We try to connect no matter what. That's what we hope people feel like. I think we've always connected well with people. There are some nights where we are in a different zone. We've played enough nights where we can really slip into that groove pretty easily."

Yet Anson admits there are some nights when he's "wearin' the gloves." "It's like putting on a pair of those big old work gloves we used to buy. If you tried to play with those gloves on, it wouldn't sound so good," he laughed. "Whenever I've had a bad night, it feels like I'm playing with a pair of those big old gloves on. Sometimes I still have nights like that, but I still try to get something out. We always try to give 100 percent to our audiences. With a five-man ensemble group, we have to know when one of the players is hitting the groove. If I've got the gloves on one night, maybe the piano player doesn't. Maybe one night Sam is really hot or I'm really hot. Some nights no one is wearing gloves and everyone is in the groove. I have to lay back enough to let the other players follow their inspiration onstage.

"Much of my inspiration comes from watching Sam jump in and out of the truck like a teenager. The biggest lesson he has passed on to me is when I see him give 100 percent whether he plays for 15,000 people or five. That's pretty damn inspiring."

Each offers advice on why this association survives. "You need to put your heads together professionally, see what needs to be put on, toss it up, and see what you can do," said Myers. "It's very important to be friends off-stage. At times I will mention certain things Elmore did or the way his execution was, and Anson seems to nail it down pretty good."

Funderburgh concurred. "One of the big secrets to us being together as long as we have is because we were really good friends first. I feel like Sam's my best friend. I love what I do and I love working with Sam. It brings us to a new level maybe not reachable alone. I think you're right. It works both ways. We've both slung ourselves around to where we really complement one another without whittling away who we both are. It must be a really good combination or it wouldn't have lasted this long."

Smokin' Joe
Kubek
and Bnois King

Smokin' Joe Kubek likens his musical partnership with Bnois King to foods that don't taste quite right unless they are eaten together. "When you're eatin' breakfast and having some toast, you gotta have jam with it. Bnois and I go together like toast and jam. I'm kinda like the toast and he's the jam."

Bnois King honors Kubek with a corresponding, reverent nod. "Joe is one of most gifted guitar players I've ever met. I often told him that if he had chosen to play jazz, if it was in his heart, he could play jazz like I always wanted to play. I know the jazz idiom inside out, but I can't do everything I know. Joe's got the hands and technique to do what I always wanted to do. All the stuff I hear other players doing, he could do because he's that gifted. Joe's one of those people that was born to play the guitar."

Smokin' Joe Kubek and Bnois King are a study in opposites. Kubek slashes away at a powder blue Strat or Flying V with a cigarette in the headstock. He explodes onstage with a rock and blues background born from the guitar traditions of Texas. With over seven guitars onstage and nearly as many foot peddles on the floor, Kubek attacks with a sound all his own. King finesses fat chords from a hollow-body Gibson and belts out blues with his whisper-to-growl voice. There are no peddles at King's feet, and no pick between himself and the warm chordal support he delivers. His background is rooted in the jazz styles of Tal Farlow and Wes Montgomery he heard growing up in Monroe, Louisiana.

Kubek began as a 14-year-old guitar phenom in the Dallas, Texas, area. "I listened to everything from Eddie Taylor to Jimmy Reed to all the Kings

Whenever Smokin' Joe Kubek straps on the guitar,
you know the sparks will fly.

to Muddy. I was more closed minded as a young player. As a kid, it's really hard to sit down and tackle Robert Johnson and Lightnin' Hopkins. I wanted to listen to it, but then I'd always end up putting on the stuff like Albert King's *Years Gone By*. Now I can't get enough of it all."

In the mid-1970s, he was the young blood hanging around stages waiting to be called up. "Yeah, I was one of those 14-year-old phenoms! I used to hang around the big boys and I'd hound 'em to death to call me up for a song. I wouldn't take no for an answer. I was real good at manipulating them into letting me play one more song. I guess they could see the enthusiasm, because I had this look like 'please, please.' They probably felt like they were passing traditions to me."

Kubek remembers one very special night. "I did this B.B. King show in 1976. After the show, I sat with him for a couple of hours passing Lucille back and forth. It made my life! I kept hitting all these licks and showin' him I could do this lick of his and that lick of his. He kept looking at me funny, saying, 'Why don't you do some of your own?' I couldn't think of anything. I accidentally hit this weird, diminished-type lick and he yelled, 'Yeah, that's what I'm talkin' about.' Here I am a young guy about 19 and B.B. King says, 'You remind me of George Benson.' When I heard that at 19, it made my life. He validated what I was doing and gave me the will to survive through all the hard times."

Bnois King's first job in music also came at 15, but it was far different from Kubek's. "My first gig was with a jazz band. It was during the period when the guitar was just becoming a popular instrument in big jazz bands. If people didn't see a guitar, they freaked out. I really couldn't play that well. I was hired as a showpiece. I could play one or two songs. My heroes are Tal Farlow, Kenny Burrell, and Wes Montgomery. I probably heard a lot of T-Bone Walker on the radio, 'cause he was real popular then."

Each guitarist followed a winding and arduous road until meeting the other. Joe survived the musician's life of bar gigs twice a week, jammed around Dallas with Stevie Ray Vaughan, and was to be in Freddie King's band before King died. "It was really hard to play the blues in the mid-1970s. But I wasn't thinking about that back then. All that mattered was that I was playing. One night I was playing and Albert King came up and sat in with us. I was so excited that I went home and I couldn't sleep. I sat there all night and played my guitar. I carry a lot of that tradition to audiences today by letting us know about these greats."

Bnois made his living playing the jazzy background music bar patrons never hear. "Most of the time I played for people who didn't really care that you were there, weren't really into it, and wanted you to turn it down. I would never try to make a living at it again. You talk about tough! Nobody ever really appreciated you."

In 1988, Kubek's three-man group invited King up to play. When they each realized the dynamic directions this unique pairing offered, they aggressively pursued the partnership. King says, "When I started playing with him on Monday night jams, the two guitars first came into play. We just clicked right from the start. Joe had invited guys up, and they sounded decent for a song, but then they'd clash. You've got to be sensitive to the way he plays. You can't just get up there and be waitin' on your turn. Our styles are so different, but somehow we've meshed, and they blend because there never was any competition between us. I've played with other guitar players, but it never worked like this."

Smokin' Joe concurs: "Our gigs together felt real good onstage because we complement each other, and we have a lot of respect for each other. We don't try to run over each other; that's what it's been like since the beginning. The meshing between our styles is effortless. We're tryin' to make it sound as good as it can. Bnois is a monster behind me."

King's chordal studies in jazz accompaniment and his understanding of his role in the band is a major part of their sound. "I'm strictly a support player. His playing makes me want to do more to enhance him. There aren't too many players who can play with Joe. I think our sound is so different because of the mixture. You can get two guitar players that play like Joe, and it wouldn't sound right. But when you stick someone like me with that, it comes out differently. I pay close attention to what Joe does. I'm conscientiously trying to find a spot to play a chord or move a chord to complement what Joe is doing. That's how I was trained as a jazz player. My ears are trained to listen to what somebody is doing and try to lay a bed that enhances what the other player is doing. Other guitar players are only thinking about the right chords to play, waiting on their time to solo. I don't care about soloing! My whole thing is about making Joe sound better. If I play chords that fight with what he's playing, I change it immediately. Because I've played rhythm all my life, I know so many different ways to play it. I always try to find a way to play so you can hear what he's doing and what I'm playing."

In addition to the seamless mesh of styles, their care for and dedication to songwriting also separates this band from the glut of Texas bar bands. Kubek feels their growth: "The partnership has grown in that we're now getting more into being a songwriting team. The songwriting with Bnois is easy."

King recalled that he never envisioned himself as a vocalist or a songwriter. "I never sang before I met Joe, so singing was completely out of my thought process. When I got into this band there wasn't nobody to sing. When I realized that's what I'd be doing, I went out and bought some blues records and learned a bunch of songs real quick. Though I'd always heard it on the radio when I was growing up, I didn't even start really listening to the blues until 1988. I've had a record collection all my life, but it was all jazz.

"Songwriting is something I'm learning how to do," continued King. "The music is basically 12 bars, but the words are harder. I try to write about experiences I know about. The hard part is drawing the picture of the

*Now he plays the blues, but Bnois King began by studying
jazz guitarists such as Kenny Burrell and Tal Farlow.*

experience I'm writing about. You got to whittle words down, and they got
to make sense too. The form is so simple you can't get to wordy. It's got to
be enough words to paint a picture. But we also try to put a little twist into
the songs we write. Maybe a chord you normally wouldn't find in a 12-bar
blues song."

"The band is at its best when we shuffle. We can play a shuffle all night,
man!" laughed Kubek. "It's just the button it pushes, you know, the magic

button. I guess the shuffle we play is that earthy, Texas thing. That's the specialty right there. We got to try different ideas and be more ourselves.

"We're trying to make each album a little different. We got to try different ideas and be more ourselves. There are always extremes, from distortions and pedal effects to jazz. We even try to bring a new sound to the covers we do. A lot of the songs we cover are the songs we've been listenin' to drivin' up and down the highway for years. We fell in love with them and then started doing them in our shows. But we did them our own way."

Each CD and live performance moves the band closer to a recognizable sound of the Smokin' Joe Kubek Band. They delve into guitar extremes, from distortions and pedal effects to the elegant jazz styles King epitomizes. Their partnership on drivin' Texas blues-rock offers stellar examples of how Kubek's explosive guitar and King's soothing voice have united to forge an unparalleled sound. Kubek's wah-wah and reverb on the Hendrix-style instrumentals is proof that where there is Smokin' Joe, there's fire.

At their live shows, the band has carefully ripened into a powerful mixture of self-assured guitar-only muscle and smilin' showmanship. They have ascended each level a step at a time. So as they have become comfortable with the musicianship required, the stage presence also develops. From King's easy banter between songs to Kubek's guitar juggle during bass solos, there are vast amounts of Texas self-confidence.

Does the nickname "Smokin'" come from the flame-throwing guitar Joe brandishes onstage? "That happened when I was 17. We were at a little club in Irving, Texas. They needed a band, and they asked me to put something together quickly. When I got back to the club, they'd put Smokin' Joe Kubek and the Electric Tennis Shoes on the marquee. The club owner just threw that up there, and I've been stuck with it ever since. Can't lay down onstage with that tag."

Together since 1988, Kubek and King realize the blues is a branch of the arts tree where performers must wait in turn to advance each step up the ladder. Through touring, both have glimpsed where they would like to be, but each understands the sustained journey necessary. "You got to be out here a while and wait your turn. Then maybe you'll get to the Charlie Musselwhite level. That would be our next step," revealed King. "I'm starting to feel that to get to that level, we need to continue to play our sound. That's what turns the fans on. Wherever we play, once Joe starts hitting our sound, people start dancing. We used to play a jazz tune or two each night, but I started seeing that altered the mood of the show. People started sitting back like they would at a jazz club. Then we had to win them back again. I'll read the house, and if I see a more sit-down audience, then we'll play one of those.

"I'm starting to feel that we have the modern sound that reaches the next generation of listener. We just need to find ways to reach larger numbers," said King.

Kubek agrees. "There's no way you can just throw together one album and expect to clean up. MTV would be nice. But these days and times, I don't see how it would fit. No offense to music television, but it seems like years ago, music television was a lot hipper and avant-garde than it is now. They're not letting a whole lot of people in on that. We have to tour a lot to get the people to know us. I plan on playing for the rest of my life and putting out a record each year. That's something about the blues—it's really a matter of staying out here, doing it, and waiting your turn."

Until then, these Lone Star guitar slingers endure the 270 nights a year spent roadhousin' and boast the fiery one-two punch few other bands can put match to.

Delbert
McClinton

As his 1998 release is titled, Delbert McClinton is truly one of the "Fortunate Few." Life has surely tried to divert him through these 40 years and there have been bumps on the road McClinton has traveled, but his perseverance is testament that if you sing it with honesty, notoriety will happen.

"I do think that title pretty much says it all. For me, it's been up and it's been down, but it's always been good. There have been some confusing times, but it would be impossible to divert me from this," said McClinton.

The music McClinton delivers is pure American music. It's a mixture of the Texas sounds he heard growing up in the Lone Star State in the 1940s and early 1950s. "You couldn't grow up in Texas in the 1940s and not hear a lot of Bob Wills or Hank Williams, Nat King Cole, and the Ink Spots. That's stuff I still listen to today. In the 1950s, it was the Lamplighters, the Midnighters, the Coasters, Ruth Brown, and Big Mama Thornton—all these raw shouters. That style really got me," continued McClinton. "Deep blues to R&B to a smattering of country to rootsy rock and roll. I grew up with all of that, and I never saw any reason to pick one and shut the others out."

But it was coming home from a hunting adventure when McClinton's ears bagged the biggest trophy. "I was 12 or 13 years old, and I'd been squirrel huntin' with some friends. We were coming back out of the woods and walking across this field in Fort Worth. There was this little black barbecue joint way out in the country. We were coming across that field and I heard 'Honey Hush.' It set me free. I'll never forget that. It was the first time I ever heard that music. That was one of the things I know changed my life."

*Delbert McClinton is known as the young harmonica player
who taught a young John Lennon blues harmonica riffs.*

Though he always sang in the family, it wasn't until then that McClinton picked up a guitar. The harmonica followed as soon as he heard the harp wails of Jimmy Reed. "When I was living in Fort Worth, Jimmy Reed was about as big there as anybody ever was. I remember sitting at a stoplight in Fort Worth first time I ever heard 'Honest I Do' on the radio. Back then, we used to play a gig called Blue Monday at a place called the Skyline Ballroom

Dance Hall on Jacksboro Highway. The place had a convertible top that you could roll back so people would dance under the stars.

"Back then, during segregation, Blue Monday belong to the black musicians and crowd. We were the only white band that I know of to play Blue Monday. At that time, the band was named the Strait Jackets. I was playing some guitar, until we played Blue Monday and saw Jimmy Reed. The stage was built for an orchestra, so they hung sheets across the back half of the stage. Jimmy Reed comes walking out playing the harmonica. That was 1955-56. I'd been playing stuff like 'Dixie' on my harmonica, but the next day I was at T.H. Cohn's buying harmonicas. From 19 to 24, I played on stages in the Fort Worth area with Jimmy Reed, Sonny Boy #2, Howlin' Wolf, Lightnin' Slim, Joe Tex, and Big Joe Turner.

"Jimmy Reed worked in Fort Worth an awful lot. They were great to us. We were backing them up and they couldn't afford not to like what we were doin'. After we backed them up Friday and Saturday nights in Fort Worth, they'd hire us to go to Oklahoma for their Sunday gigs at black clubs. The first place I ever smoked was in the bathroom of Mother's Place in Lawton, Oklahoma, with Sonny Boy. We never had any problems at all at those clubs. One night Buster Brown and Jimmy Reed were playing together. We were gonna back 'em both up. I was so excited. I was sittin' in the dressing room between 'em. I didn't drink at the time. They were passin' a fifth of Old Grand-Dad. I was sittin' between 'em, double-hittin' the bottle with what I thought were small sips. It was a good thing they were there, because they did most of the night with the band. I sure as hell learned that night not to drink with the big boys," laughed McClinton.

"I learned how to play harmonica between Jimmy and Sonny Boy. I'd say, 'How'd you do that?' because I couldn't see anything they were doing. I had lots of time to sit knee to knee with Jimmy and listen to him play. He was always gracious.

"I think Jimmy Reed and both Sonny Boys had that unique harp style. I don't know anybody else who played that way. Nobody played like Jimmy Reed. He played straight into a mic, he didn't hold his hands over it. His was a completely different blues-style harp. Remember, he wore that rig around his neck so he played harp and guitar at the same time. Plus he was playing the high end of the harp much more than other players were. I learned a great deal from both of those guys, but I've never been able to play or ever tried to play like anyone else. Sure, there's some of them within my style at certain points. You learn to choke it down just by listening to them do it, then asking the question of how you do that. It's hard to see what a person's doing with a harmonica, you only get ten holes to do it with. From playing, you learn how to arrange your tongue and how to adjust the air to where you can bend the note. It's just like anything new, you've gotta just keep trying to learn it. It's hard to pass that on to anybody else."

The hard-to-survive music world of Texas then unfolded for Delbert. "I was absolutely possessed by the music. That realization came when I was 17 and did the first recording I ever did. I know from that point I was lost to everything else. It was tough surviving at the music then, but I didn't look at it like that then. Back in the mid-1950s through the '60s, making music was not an honorable thing to do. You had to pay bills like gas and electricity up front. I used to work with guys who only cared how much beer we could buy with the money we were making. You weren't tryin' to make a living. We all slept on somebody's floor. Beer and gas was all that mattered at the time.

"I'll never forget this. When I was 24 years old, a friend's sister approached me at a barbecue one afternoon and asked, 'You still gonna be doin' that when you're 30 years old?' Like why don't you get a real job and work in the paint and body shop like my husband. I smiled and said, 'Well, if I'm lucky.' It was tough. In the first place, you only played these beer joints. It was always, 'Why don't y'all come out this weekend and play for free? If the people like you, we'll have you back next week and I'll still only pay ya $25 for the five of you.'"

But in 1962, the doors opened and the world changed for this 22-year-old. McClinton had recorded a string of 45s when he was asked to add his raw harp to Bruce Channel's hit, "Hey Baby." "I got together with Bruce in early 1962. I met him on the session for 'Hey Baby.' The guy from Fort Worth who was payin' for the session called me regularly to get a band together for the people he was recording. We did four songs and 'Hey Baby' was one of them. I made $25 for 'Hey Baby'."

More importantly, "Hey Baby" led to a trip oversees and gigs throughout England, where McClinton met a group of struggling British musicians, the Beatles. "I was in England a year before the Beatles hit it big and changed the world. You got to put that experience in perspective. They were a great band. How did we know they were fixin' to change the world? At that time in England, there were an awful lot of really good Elvis Presley-type bands. I was around those guys for about four days. They were opening for Bruce's show. I never saw them again."

And the story of McClinton teaching a young John Lennon harmonica riffs? "I did, but when you say that to somebody, they get this mental picture of me sitting with John Lennon. We were just two different bands travelin' on the road. He wanted to play harmonica, so we spent some time together. I can't say how long, maybe a few days. He'd ask, 'How do you do this?' and I'd say, 'Try this or that.' It doesn't matter today, because the story's chiseled in stone that I taught him to play."

American blues and R&B players left their imprint on McClinton throughout the 1960s. "I've played off and on with B.B. King since the '60s. He made a great impression on me, not only with his guitar style, but also with his vocals. I think there's an awful lot of him in my voice. I also think that the Big Joe Turner jump blues sound is great. You just don't hear it anymore like that. Little Richard also made a big impression on me then. I kinda have to shout like him when I sing, that's the way it works. He was and still is a genius to me. And Ray Charles. When I'm on, I'm my favorite singer, me and Ray Charles. No need to say anymore."

What kept McClinton going during the 1960s was the Southern frat house circuit. Here blues, soul, R&B, and any other nonmainstream music was sustained every Friday and Saturday night, *Animal House*-style. "The Southern frat house experience was a wonderful time. I think those places kept the blues alive in the South. These white Southerners brought in black music and gave them a place to play. If we played a frat house joint and it was full, we were doin' great. In Texas, they had a midnight-closing law. We'd play 'til midnight, pack up our stuff, and then play from 1 to 5 A.M. in the morning at after-hours joints."

In the 1970s, the music was constantly changing for McClinton. The road house, honky-tonk, and beer joint became the auditorium in 1977. "By 1977, there were a lot more bigger venues to play. I'm not a household name, I can't fill up a 2,500-seat auditorium in every city on the map. But there's always been enough of the other ones for me. It means I had to work a little more. The thing that's most important about how things have gotten better is that I wouldn't quit, I wouldn't stay out of the way of it. Every time you turned around, there I was, pushin'."

Recently, McClinton has focused on songwriting as much as playing and singing. "There were times when songwriting didn't happen. But I've written more since 1992 than I have in the rest of my life. I think I've finally grown into where I enjoy the writing. Personally, I can get a whole lot said in a very few words; lines to deliver images to smack the listener in the face, that's what I hope to do.

"I have to be inspired by something to write a song. That inspiration can come from anywhere. I don't ever think about life as ideas for songs. The best things I write happen when I hear some groove and that dictates how the words fit. I get inspirations from either words or groove. Either way, if I'm just writing it, I'm also singing how it will go. I can also sit at the piano or guitar and start fooling around, and that will also stimulate my writing.

"I don't write every day. Instead, I expose myself to the environment as much as possible. By that I mean I have pianos and guitars two seconds from me at all times. I usually sit at the piano every day. If I'm not writing something, I'm polishing something that I'm working on. I know people who write every day, and that just doesn't work for me. I've written very good things going into a writing session when I had no ideas. I've also had the opposite happen: I've gone in thinking we were gonna get something and didn't get anything. You never know. It's one of those wonderful things where you get to reach out into infinity, and then have something start to take shape. That's the thing about it, in order for anything to happen, you've got to expose yourself to it. So I expose myself to it a lot, and I'm writing a lot more than I ever did."

Once McClinton pens lyrics, his next step is selling the song to the audience. Without a guitar to strap on, McClinton's only tool is his vocal interpretation. "The only thing that goes through my mind when I sing a song to an audience is to sing it the way I feel it. It's not anything I have to think about. It just happens. It's kind of a testimony. You have to make each song fresh and new every night. What completes the circle after giving it to the audience is when they give it back to the stage. When you're up there really trying to make it count and it gets recognized, people shoot it right back at you. Man, it don't get no better than that. That's as close to magic as there is. I know when everything lines up right and everybody is feeling the same current. That's what I want every night."

Sherman
Robertson

Whether you speak to Sherman Robertson or participate in his show, one feature is obvious: hunger. Within this guitar-slingin' Texan burns an intense fire born nearly 40 years ago that still cuts from the core of his soul. That gnawing hunger manifests itself in the aggressive, guitar-dominated approach Robertson brings to the blues stage and is only momentarily satisfied after his draining performances.

"I figure if the blues is gonna survive, it's gotta have some high energy, like rock. It's gotta have some fire and flash, some in-your-face sound," enthused Robertson. "The sound I'm trying to use is a little more rock, not over the top, but just enough. Twelve o'clock, gunfighter-in-the-street Texas style is what I'm talking about, earthy tones that keep the audience interested, music that won't let you get a beer between songs. When the band's burning behind me, it just kicks my butt and makes me get on. I know some guys like that slow blues riff, but I'm on another page," Robertson said.

Wherever Robertson plays, he talks the talk and then walks the walk by launching into three-hour tracer missile barrages through the hearts of sellout crowds. Robertson hits stages with two speeds, amazing and extra amazing. His jet-propelled workout, accompanied by smiles, grimaces, or looks of wonder or surprise, is solid proof Robertson possesses a healthy dose of superstar showmanship. Whether he stands on tabletops, walks outside to stop midnight traffic on some street, or travels blanket to blanket at festivals, his guitaring never sputters—all proof that Robertson is a charter member of today's contemporary Texas guitar fraternity.

This hunger traces back to growing up in Houston's street-tough Fifth Ward in the 1950s. Though he was born in 1948 in Breaux Bridge, Louisiana, the family moved to Houston's Fifth Ward when Robertson was

*Following in the footsteps of Albert Collins and Johnny
"Clyde" Copeland, Sherman Robertson possesses a healthy
dose of superstar showmanship.*

two. Robertson's time with a guitar began at 13 when he heard Hank
Williams on a TV variety show. "It was country, but he wailed like the
blues." His father bought him a $12 Stella with Black Diamond strings, and
he started banging away until his fingers bled.

Early on, he'd heard a local musician from East Texas, Floyd London,
playing blues. "I learned the blues from listening to him. Then I took lessons

from Clarence Green. It was great because you had the old Duke and Peacock recording studio right down the street. We had these clubs where I caught guys like Junior Parker, Buddy Aces, Piano Slim, Joe Hinton, Gatemouth Brown, Johnny Copeland, and Albert Collins. When I was 12 years old, Albert played two blocks from the house at a place called Walter's Lounge. I used to ride my bike on Sunday evening and lay my ear to the wall. Albert had that old Telecaster ringing just like it always rang. Albert let me sit in one Sunday evening when I was 13 years old.

"The whole two blocks was nothing but music. I was 16 or 17, and my daddy used to take me around to see these guys when they'd come to town. We'd be right up in front and he'd say, 'Could you let my boy get up there and play something?' I didn't have the chops, but I was never shy, so I'd get up there. I ate it, I slept it, I wanted it, I was hungry for it. It's never left, it's always been there." At 17, Robertson was playing enough guitar in a local group, Connie's Combo, to be ready for a six-week stint substituting for Wayne Bennett with Bobby "Blue" Bland. Then, in 1977, he put together his own band, the Crosstown Blues Band. "It was a seven-piece horn band that played seven nights and two matinees locally. I started working everywhere."

"As a kid, Johnny Copeland was one of the guys that I looked up to. Years later, I worked with Johnny for a couple of years. The thing that I learned from Johnny Copeland was, even though it looks good, smells good, and tastes good, you gotta keep pushing. No matter what he was going through, he never lost sight of the music. He said to me once, 'Sherman, all this business stuff ain't worth nothing. Let's just get out there and play the blues.' Johnny told me the real truth. Just play the blues. That's what you started with, that's what you're gonna end up with.

"I got to play with Albert Collins again in St. Louis when I was 32. He called me up and we battled. One thing he told me, he said, 'Hey boy, that shaking that little E you got there. If you keep on shaking it, take it from Albert, your gonna make it all the way.' I have a vibrato where I shake that E note. And it's because I heard him shake it, and it appealed to me.

"Battling Albert onstage was real tricky. He would bite at you and lay back and let you play everything you could play, and then he'd come back and kill ya. But in St. Louis he bit at me, and I took off and then I stopped. And I turned to him and said, 'C'mon Albert, you got it.' And then he had to give everything he had, and then I came around and I ate him up. And he said, 'You're tricky, like me.' We have to carry on that sound."

Albert Collins is famous for saying to young players like Robertson, "Take your time." "That's a real serious quote. And until I learned that, my playing didn't get as good as it could. When I first started playing, speed was the thing, that everybody wants to play so fast. And I heard 'Take your time son' from all the old cats that I learned from. What they was trying to tell you was to take your time because you're gonna burn out quick. It takes years to find out the right notes. I found out after 15 years that I didn't need but three of them in the right places."

It was zydeco master Clifton Chenier who opened doors and etched a lasting imprint on the young guitarist. In 1982, Chenier heard Robertson's band open for him at a Houston festival and quickly asked Robertson to join up. "I played at a festival with Clifton Chenier, and I left with him that same summer. We played on the same show in June, and I left with him in July. When he heard the band, they were playing without me. I was standing next to him backstage. I heard him say, 'Good band, but kinda boring.' Then they called me onstage. When I came off Clifton was saying, 'I gotta meet that guitar guy.' He and my daddy had been raised together in Louisiana. When I called my dad, he said, 'Son, go with him. He's a good man and I trust him.' He was all that too.

"I learned a great deal from him. He's the one who taught me how to do a crowd, how to get it happening every night, no matter where you are. He told me one of the first times when he let me open up for him, 'You doin' everything wrong. It's not about you, it's about the people.' That hurt my feelings, but I paid attention to what he did onstage, and after a while I saw what he was talking about. It's not about the artist, it's about the people. As soon as you give it to them, they give it back to you. That's what he was tryin' to tell me. I think it's my performance separates me from all the new guitar players. Not being egotistical, but so many are still dwelling on 'It's about me and my guitar.' They haven't learned to turn the show over and still be in control."

When Robertson was with Chenier, he began to realize he had something. "I met Les Paul himself. We were playin' at Tramps in New York and *the* Les Paul said to me, 'You're one of the greatest blues players I've ever heard.' Then, years later, when I played with Terrance Simien, Les was giving a class on his guitars. I walked into the room, and he pointed me out, sayin', 'That's the blues-playin' guy.' He remembered me seven years later."

When Chenier began slowing down in 1986, Robertson hooked up with Rockin' Dopsie. "Dopsie was a different kind of guy, more of a businessman, so I learned the business side of the music in the two years with him." It was through Dopsie that Sherman met Paul Simon and played on *Graceland.* "Pencils, tape recorders, and faxes couldn't tell you what it was like to work with Paul. This was a guy that I loved for years, and I never thought I would ever be in the same studio. What I remember most about the Paul Simon session was that when I got through playing, he came to me and said, 'Great rhythms man! Great fuckin' rhythms!' For Paul Simon to tell me that . . . what a rush, you know! As a sideman, those comments made me think, 'What about me? When is my time?' That's what happened in 1990. I knew it was my time."

After seven years of leading his own band and ten years playing as a sideman with Clifton Chenier, Rockin' Dopsie, Terrance Simien, and Johnny "Clyde" Copeland, Robertson was signed by legendary blues producer Mike Vernon after Vernon caught Robertson's incendiary stage show at the Belgium Blues Fest. "When I met Mike, he said, 'You're Freddie King all over again!'"

Robertson's two critically acclaimed Code Blue releases had trouble capturing the clear-cut essence obvious in his live settings. Those brilliant, breaking-free moments were subdued. "When I met Mike and recorded the first CDs, I was a little naive. He was heading someplace and thought I was the guy that could take him there. With my first two CDs, I went in submissive, trying to be what he wanted. It frustrates me. If I get a second chance and open some doors, I'll be the guy that's gonna send my own self through the doors."

That's led fans to see two different Robertsons—the subdued one on his Code Blue recordings and the energetic, in-your-face guitar slinger you saw live. His 1998 disc on Audioquest finally allowed Sherman to be Sherman.

"The way it was done with Audioquest was different from last time. Joe Harley turned the tape on and let me play whatever I wanted. He said, 'I don't wanna disturb you and I don't wanna destroy you.' He left me in control of my own destiny. He didn't dissect me and strip me down. He wanted the sound that he heard in that club to be on this CD. I found out when I record now, I have to go in with Sherman and hope for the best."

This self-confidence is now becoming noticeable in the studio as Robertson is assuming more hands-on control of his destiny. By enlisting his close friends from Little Feat, drummer Richie Hayward and keyboard player Bill Payne, Robertson knew the resulting recordings would exceed his previous studio work. "We finally got a chance to hear the real Sherman Robertson. I needed the security within myself that I could be on that same level and play with Little Feat. It showed me that Sherman Robertson was able to go and work with these kind of guys. They asked, 'Man, where have you been?' I feel something new's going to come out of this. I know that sometimes it doesn't come as fast as we'd like, but it's coming, I can feel it. It's like I'm moving into a new dimension."

The distilled essence of each mentor is evident in every note Robertson plays. Outwardly, the music, man, and audience become one, but inside Robertson lives in lyrics and licks. "Sherman's living every song. When I'm singing a song, I live it. I'm feeling the same thing you feel because I'm no different than you. I don't place myself above the common man. The guitar is singing the words. It's singing the passion. If I'm doing a song that hurts, the guitar is hurting as well."

There are performers who do the show every night with little variation. Robertson's display changes every night. That puts him in the same intense arena as the Luther Allisons. "I've been criticized for doing a different show every night. We don't eat the same food every night. I live every day in my blues, so the show should be spontaneous."

In a club, the show usually starts with Robertson walking to the stage from the rear. This walk energizes an audience but reveals where his string torrent will go. "My audience walk-in tells me right away what they want. When I walk out into that room, I feel whether the crowd wants a high-energy thing or they want a slow-blues night. I let my heart, my mind, and my soul be open. By the second or third number, I've got them.

"I try to prepare in my heart, mind, and soul, a festive delicacy that the people really want. When they walk outta that joint, I want to see everybody smiling. I want to see everybody's soul fed. It took me quite a few years to trust in myself looking for that magic. If I can get that magic, it translates to the audience, and they leave feeling like, 'What the hell just happened?'"

Though the artistic rewards are immense, this nightly vision quest can exact a heavy toll on the performer who attempts to fire blues from the hip. "To be honest with you, I can burn myself out, because I put so much in my show. I'm just like a battery—I wear down too. I need to get away for a while and recharge."

Robertson's primary mission is still performing onstage with his guitar. "I'm still a live performer. My real love is still the guitar. There's no substitute to the rush that kicks in when I strap on my Fender and play for 10,000 people. But to me, it doesn't matter if it's 20 people as long as I have somebody that appreciates the music. I'll always go straight to the heart of the music so it becomes a private, intimate thing between the crowd and myself. After people hear me, I want them saying as they leave, 'When is he coming back?' I want to come out and rip it out of the ballpark like a wild bull. I'm not concerned with whether I get stardom. If it happens, fine. I just want to be a major player in this ball game."

Today, Robertson's hunger is consumed with taking his music to larger audiences. As a veteran of life, he can author volumes about the relationship between the spontaneous inner spirit and excursions on the blues guitar. Unfortunately, the culture dotes on the youth of the genre, avoiding the veterans who have walked the road of life and emerged with a personal voice. Robertson falls in that gap.

"You always have to keep learning. I'm learning how to put the triad together. I'm trying to work on improving my act, the vocals and guitar. I'm still learning more about me and the guitar, opposed to just the guitar and songs. It's a steady learning process of what I need to do.

"The whole thing I see with the music of the young blues players is that they get so much away from the root of the music that they lose the influence. We're using too many words to say, 'I'm hurt, I'm hungry, I'm thirsty.' We're attempt to rewrite the blues, but there is no way. America has thrown away enough. You've always got to come back to the basics. Let's take what was good 40 years ago, and rather than changing it, let's use today's world to make it better. I'm the new guy from the old school."

Tommy
Shannon

It's a testament to one's inner strength to be able to bounce back from life's uncertainties. That resilience of soul and purpose may be one of the most important qualities any person can aspire to. It is only in hindsight, however, that this admirable quality shines through.

In this respect, Tommy Shannon is one of the chosen few. Known mainly for his ten years as the strapping bass behind Stevie Ray Vaughan in Double Trouble, Shannon today touches people in many other intimate and personal ways. From his days as a teenage bass player behind Johnny Winter, to his struggles with substances, to his musical ascendancy with Vaughan, to his descent into addiction, to his recovery and spirituality today, Shannon can offer anyone willing to listen a template for surviving life's trials.

Most everyone crowds Shannon to hear the Vaughan stories. Though he'll readily share those, there's a more crucial Vaughan story Shannon is compelled to tell, about the dark days of their drug and alcohol addictions that hindered every step the duo took.

Blues legend whispers of men like Robert Johnson selling their souls to Legba, the African trickster god who meets blues men at dark, rural crossroads. There, he exchanges or "sells" an earthly musical talent for their souls. Today's musician sells to a different devil. "You don't consciously think, 'I'm selling my soul to the devil.' But as time goes on, you start realizing this behavior [alcohol and drug abuse] is not right. It violates all the values of human decency," said Shannon. "It's not like selling your soul to the devil as much as it is a very sneaky way of trading tomorrow for today.

"That is one of the biggest errors of judgment in life, not only for people who use drugs, but for everyone, because today is really the only thing we have. It's how we handle that and how we choose to look at life. I think

***Tommy Shannon on his work with Stevie Ray Vaughan: "Chris
Layton and I had one goal—to play the best we could for Stevie."***

the beautiful part is when you really make touch with the present, the now,
and you realize that tomorrow is going to take care of itself. There will be
pain and there will be joy, and there will all kinds of changes and experiences. As it unfolds, just participate and don't push your will on it and try
and control everything. Instead, use everything to learn."

In the "anything goes" 1980s, Shannon and Vaughan found that also
included any substance. As the band got more popular, people who had
cocaine or drugs were easily granted backstage access. Those without were
brushed aside. "When we were really still abusing all this stuff, the people
that could really help us couldn't get near us. Only people who had dope
could come on backstage. That's a manic high that forces you into thinking,
'I am so great right now.' I remember I was at this party one night, and I was
kind of struck by this guy because he seemed real calm and clear minded.
He didn't stay very long. I started talking to him and I said, 'Man, here, you
want some cocaine?' He said, 'No thank you, I can't do that stuff anymore.'
I remember I just shriveled inside. And I thought, 'Oh my God, what I'd
give to have that kind of courage.'"

Shannon vividly describes the dark journey before getting to that new
life as a living death with no control anymore. "When you're throwing up
blood and hung over, the easy way to eliminate that pain is turn back to the

alcohol or drugs. That endless cycle of self-destruction sneaks up on you. We used to get high and party all the time, but even back then you could tell no one was very happy. It doesn't matter if you're a musician or what you are, we are all human and we do have something in common. When we start violating our own spirit, it lets us know. It starts nagging at us constantly—either die or start living a life based on spiritual principals. There is no in between, no other way.

"Deep down inside, I knew that someday I was going to hit that brick wall. Stevie and I hit it right about the same time. Chris and Reese were not as addictive in nature. They would drink with us, but they would wake up the next day and not do it. Take some aspirin and go on with their lives. We never stopped. We never had a hangover because we never stopped. There was no human power that could help us.

"I remember about six months before Stevie and I got clean and sober, we knew we were in trouble. It was about four o'clock in the morning and we were sitting in a hotel room in Dallas. We had this big pile of cocaine, probably two ounces, and liquor in the room. And we were sitting there trying to stop, trying to stop, and we were scared, you know? We actually got down on our knees together and prayed. And it was a very sincere, deep prayer. It wasn't a drug-high prayer; it was a pure, desperate cry for help. Now, the thing is, we got up and went back and did some more cocaine and drinking, but the prayer was answered. It's a wonderful thing to discover, after you hit that bottom, that there's a way out."

Shannon calls that prayer the turning point for both. Broken inside, they reached rock bottom. On October 13, 1986, they checked themselves into treatment, Vaughan in Atlanta and Shannon in Austin, and began the 12-step program to recovery. But the question that nags every musician who is also a recovering addict was still to be answered: Will I still be able to play my music?

"Stevie and I were scared to death to go in and do that first record, *In Step*, when we were clean and sober. We were terrified because we had never done anything like that in our lives. We were thinking, 'What if we just don't have it anymore?' Then as we started making the record, we started relaxing a little more and had more and more fun, and we realized we could do this. We discovered a more disciplined and realistic approach instead of the manic approach that drugs gave. You can tell on *In Step* our playing is better than any of our other records. It's like dealing with all the stuff for the first time with your eyes wide open.

"I was so nervous on our first live show that I almost threw up. I kept looking out through these curtains at this outdoor venue. There were about 10,000 people there, and I kept looking out there going, 'Oh, my God!'"

From that day in 1986, Vaughan and Double Trouble set the music scene ablaze like a comet streaking through the night sky. In retrospect, Stevie became that comet, brilliantly lighting the night sky, then disappearing all too quickly. Shannon's greatest test of faith was to come in August of 1990, the day after Vaughan's untimely death. "I was so devastated that I can't even put into words how dark my life was. If I heard the music on the radio, it made about as much sense to me as the sound of a chainsaw. I'd look outside and it'd seem like the trees and the birds were mourning the fact that Stevie died. It was so dark, just like life was gone, a dark path. And the faith that I built in my program recovery started to get very shaky.

"What's so strange is it never once crossed my mind to go drink. All I can say is a power greater than myself was taking care of me because that would have been a perfect opportunity to do that. My faith was crumbled. I couldn't hardly leave my house and go to the store. I was afraid to go outside or go get something to eat. It was like 'Nobody talk to me, don't say nothing to me, please. Just leave me alone.'

"I learned a deep lesson there. The faith that I had up until that time was very shaky. I had to develop a deeper faith and develop the complete reality of death and its permanence and suffering in life. It's a fact. Whether we like it or not, it's the truth. So the faith that I have been building is based upon that reality. It's not based upon getting everything I want. That's not what it's about. For the first four years, that's the kind of faith I had. It's hard to see at first when you actually live through it and you start working and keep working your program and start developing that deeper kind of faith.

"It's not a pessimistic outlook, it's very liberating. Sometimes I get caught up in the games. And when I do, I get miserable. And then I'll work my way out of it, back where I feel that I'm standing on the right ground again and I see the beauty of it. Everything changes. It's like there is constant rebirth too. But if you attach yourself to things, it makes you miserable, because inevitably you're gonna lose them.

"But there's a certain beauty in seeing things as they are and letting them go, enjoying them in the moment, and then, when they pass, seeing the next moment as something brand new, a newness to life. That's where true freedom is. That's where the freedom and the faith really deepen. It's like this old saying: If you can find faith in the middle of hell, then it's pretty real.

"Maybe six weeks later I got to where I'd go out and listen to a band a little bit, and they'd ask me to sit in. I found out it made me feel better to just get up there and play. It wasn't Stevie, which was a letdown, because nobody can do what Stevie did. But it's like I was saying, you need to find enjoyment with what's there. I started enjoying it. And I noticed that it makes me feel better to play, so I started playing more and that started helping me more.

Shannon and Vaughan's experiences date back to the 1970s on the Texas blues scene. The decades distill to single moments that epitomize Stevie Ray Vaughan. "I saw the talent in him when I first met him. It was 1969, and I left Johnny Winter, flew back to Dallas, and I went to a club called the Fog, where all my friends hung out. I was walking in and I heard this guitar player, and it just struck me.

"There was this real awkward-looking, scrawny, 14-year-old kid up there. I knew then that he had something special. Back then he was like all kids. He was copying Eric Clapton and Jimi Hendrix and blues guys. He hadn't developed his own thing yet, but Stevie was so passionate. He loved it so deeply. He put on a guitar and something happened. It's like he went to a different state of consciousness. And you could see it and feel this pure source of energy go right through him.

"In 1978, I hadn't seen him in several years because I had gone through my own troubles with jail. I went to the Rome Inn in Austin, where he was playing, and I could see he was already developing his own style. It just blew me away. I couldn't believe how good he was."

It was almost a spiritual calling that forced Shannon into the band in 1981. "When I joined the band, it was Chris and Stevie, and Jackie Newhouse was playing bass. They were playing in a club in Houston, and I was living in Houston at the time. I looked in the paper and saw that Stevie was playing. I hadn't seen him in a while, so I went down there.

"I walked in and it was like a revelation. Something just hit me right between the eyes, and I knew that's where I belonged. I said, 'Stevie, I belong in this band with you.' And I didn't care who was listening. I had to say it. He asked me to sit in, and we had a great time."

Two weeks later, Newhouse was fired and Vaughan had his longtime musical friend in the band. "We were touring around the country in this milk truck we called the African Queen. We had a couch behind the front seats, and all our equipment behind that. And we had rigged up this bed where you crawled up there and every time you hit the breaks, the bed would slide forward. We were touring around the country in that thing, making $200 each a week. But we loved what we were doing.

"We were like a family. Stevie was not the kind of person who liked to be on his own. We'd do anything for each other. Most important, we all had a common goal and drive. Chris and my role was to play the best we could for Stevie. Stevie never played anything the same way twice, unless it was the main riff of the song or something. But he would just all of a sudden go to a change, knowing we'd be right there. He wouldn't turn around and tell anybody. Sometimes I'd do a bass line running down, walk down and get it to go right down with him. So it was like this intuitive thing we were doing.

"I feel like ultimately that's what a bass player's role is, to be the bridge between drum and Stevie. I don't play all these real fast licks because there is nothing that feels as good as to just find that pulse. When you find that, you follow on to it, and the whole band is doin' it. It feels wonderful, like a sweet spot in time. And it doesn't matter if you're playing one note or a thousand, as long as you're there."

After their 1986 rebirth and their spiritual 20/20 vision, Vaughan and Double Trouble embarked on a road schedule that introduced millions to his music and the music Vaughan honored since childhood. Austin had been the epicenter of Texas blues in the 1970s and 1980s. When Clifford Antone opened Antone's and booked legends like Memphis Slim, Muddy Waters, Buddy Guy, Albert King, Albert Collins, and every other Chicago legend, Jimmie and Stevie Ray Vaughan were always in attendance. "Clifford has had a profound impact on this town and the whole blues scene here. If it wasn't for him, I don't think Jimmie or Stevie would have done as good as they did, because when they were real young, he had this club and he brought in bluesmen like Muddy Waters and Jimmy Reed. Stevie and Jimmie'd be there. Sometimes they'd get to sit in and play with these guys. So Clifford put them through his school of blues."

According to Shannon, when the masters heard the young Vaughan, they knew he had the true inner calling to play. "They could see it. When they'd come to our shows or we played shows with them, they'd be on the side of the stages, smiling and kind of dancing along. You'd see them nudge each other, smile, and point at Stevie like, yeah, that guy is good. And he was so respectful of those guys too. Success never changed him. Those people were his heroes. He knew where that music came from and what his role in it all was. That's one of the beautiful things about Stevie."

In an odd twist, it is Shannon who has been handed the opportunity to channel the music of both Vaughan and the bluesmen he has shared the stage with. "I got to play with Muddy Waters when I was a kid playing with Johnny Winter. That was before we had ever put out a record or anything. We were right here in Austin at the Vulcan Gas Company and Muddy Waters played there with his band. At the end, we had this big jam session. I got up there with Muddy Waters, and I couldn't believe it. It's like, I'm up here with Muddy Waters and he didn't kick me off the stage. I was just a young kid, thinking, 'This is unbelievable—Muddy Waters! It can't possibly get any better than Muddy Waters. That is the purest.' It's the same with people like B.B. King and Albert Collins, those people were all truth. There are no added fringes on the outside. Pure current. And when it gets that pure, what are you going to do to improve it?"

Shannon grew up in Dumas, Texas, and moved to Dallas after he graduated from high school. At that point, his blues education was simple, a
Jimmy Reed song on the radio or Sam Cooke's soulful singing. "Before I
ever heard the term *soul music* it dawned on me that stuff was so different—it touches your soul. But I had no idea until I got out of high school
and moved to Dallas just how deep it was. Working with Johnny Winter
taught me the depth."

At 19, Shannon was blown away by Winter's appearance and talent. "I
met Johnny at the same place I met Stevie in Dallas, this club called The
Fog, down on Lemon Avenue. I was playing in this soul band and Johnny
didn't have a bass player. Johnny blew me away. He was playing and singing
his ass off. I thought, 'God, this guy is beautiful! And he is talented.' He
asked me if I wanted to join the band. So I quit my gig—and I had a good-
paying gig—and moved to Houston.

"When I got with Johnny, I was so ignorant about the blues. I'd listen to
all these new blues bands, and I'd see the writers of the song were names
like Robert Johnson and I'd think, 'He must be a friend of theirs.' Johnny
sat me down one night. He had a whole wall of records, from current all the
way back to field hollers. He took me through the whole collection, playing
and explaining everything about it. He's an encyclopedia of the blues.

"After I went through that process and I listened to all the stuff, all the
way back to the beginning, when I picked up my bass and started playing
the blues, it was just the most natural thing I had ever done. It just seemed
to be there. I owe Johnny that debt of gratitude. Because I had no idea until
I got with Johnny just how and where things really came from.

"We starved our ass off for a while. We couldn't get hired anywhere.
Then we started getting jobs in the Fillmore in New York, the Boston Tea
Party, and, I think, the Back Bay Theater in Boston." Eventually that led
Shannon to play behind Winter at Woodstock in 1969.

Today, the Double Trouble rhythm section is as well known and respected a duo-for-hire as the Memphis Horns. Put Shannon and Layton on a
record and you have something special. "Chris and I are doing our own
record now. We're not trying to recreate what we had with Stevie. There is
one Stevie, and trying to capture that would be a big letdown for everyone
and us. But what we're trying to do is just make a good record. It's gonna
have some good blues on it. It's gonna have some other kind of rock stuff
that's a little different, but it's not a pop album by any means."

Happily, there is an optimistic ending to the years of personal suffering.
Since he plucked his first bass note with Johnny Winter, Shannon, clean and
sober since 1986, has been blessed with the task of interpreting the music

of the legends he has hooked vibes with for three decades. New fans who'll never witness the pure power surge of Vaughan can still behold that magic through Shannon's spirit.

"People have asked me what was the best gig you could ever remember with Stevie, and the only honest answer I could give them was the whole ten years I played for him. Every night he did something amazing. Nothing has been as rewarding as playing with Stevie. That was a once-in-a-lifetime blessing, a perfect situation."

Jimmie Vaughan

Since he began playing the guitar in 1963, Jimmie Vaughan has remained true to music within his soul. Throughout his teenage years in Austin, fronting his first band, Stomp, his 15-year association as founding member of the house-rockin' Fabulous Thunderbird, and his sky-rocketing solo career, Vaughan has continually rediscovered his own personal style of guitar playing, which cuts right to the core of emotion.

"I play exactly what I hear. It's been a lifelong process to get here. It's about feeling, what musicians call 'hearing it.' When you first start playing, you don't hear anything. It's like your intuition. You know just in time before you do it what it's gonna be. It intuitively jumps into your head. All musicians who play for a while build a trust that you learn to try and go with the feeling. A lot of times, even the mistakes are really great, and that fires you up so you just keep chargin' through, not knowing exactly what's gonna happen," said Vaughan.

The road to discovery for Vaughan began in Dallas, Texas, in 1951. The music he heard on the radio filled his head with massive horn charts and the overpowering Hammond B-3's. "As a teenager, I was listening to organ trios along with Slim Harpo, Bo Diddley, and B.B. King. When I first started tryin' to play, the organ trios were real popular."

When he brought his first guitar home, Vaughan did what most kids his age did: put on a record and try and pick along as his little brother watched. "I brought a guitar and records home and got into the blues and started playing. You know, in any family it's normal for little brothers to do what big brothers do. When Stevie started playing, I started showing him tricks I had discovered. About the time I was 15, I ran off from home and left him a guitar. When I saw him a couple of years later, he was a monster," remembered

**"I learned everything I could from the older generation,"
says Jimmie Vaughan. "They were pioneers."**

Vaughan. "I was in awe of his playing. Honest expression just flowed outta him. He was amazing technically, but it was his heart that I thought was the best part of his playing."

Vaughan left Dallas at 19, moved to Austin, and played in a variety of blues bar bands. "Before the T-Birds, there were only a few clubs in town that would play blues. I played with several guys, Louis Cowdrey and Angela Strehli, and we would back up the occasional Bo Diddley show that would come to town in the early '70s. That's when I had quit any hope of working a normal job; I knew it was only music." In 1972 he formed his own group, the Storm.

Jimmie met Kim Wilson in 1974. One year later they formed the Fabulous Thunderbirds with Keith Ferguson and Mike Buck and became the house band at Antone's in Austin. "We couldn't hardly get arrested when we started out," remembered Vaughan. "We were havin' too much fun going out to clubs every night, playing the music that we loved, and earning the money to pay our tab. We didn't care."

They rocked for five years before they were offered a record deal on Chrysalis. But before the T-Bird butt-rockin' style of music hit the airwaves, Vaughan and Wilson had played behind and with every major blues act.

"They all encouraged and pushed us. To be accepted by them, the guys who were and are my heroes, that acceptance and tip of the hat really pushed us to continue doing the things they would continually approve of.

"Early days with the T-Birds was a blast. We had a great time going all over the world. We did everything I'd always dreamed about and more, and yet I never really expected that we'd do any of it. Even though somewhere in the back of your mind, you hoped for that and thought you could, we really weren't thinking about it, because we kept going. We started the same time as Antone's opened. That was perfect because it gave us a place to play. All of a sudden we were the house band, and we had to learn everybody's stuff to back the people from Chicago, California, and Louisiana. It was a great education to play with all the people coming through.

"Bluesmen like Muddy Waters, Buddy Guy, Eddie Taylor, Walter Horton, James Cotton, Lazy Lester, and Albert Collins made strong impressions. Plus we got to see the people who came through with their own bands. We saw the great Little Milton and B.B. King all the time. They all encouraged us and were happily surprised at how we played. They pushed us on and that helped us."

Vaughan tried to continually earn the approval of the Muddy Waters generation by being true to their music. "I learned everything from the older generation, like Muddy Waters. They were pioneers, they were spacemen, but they were very much down to earth," said Vaughan, one of the many guitarists who shared the stage with Waters. "Muddy Waters was the coolest guy you ever met. He was such a power and presence onstage. That's the only way to describe it. Playing with Muddy, it was total chill bumps, because he was one of my greatest heroes. I was scared to death, terrified. Even though I knew the people I was onstage with, after I got home and realized what I had done, then it hit me. It was one of those times stage adrenaline sort of takes care of you and lets you do your thing. Somehow I got through it, and later on I realized what happened."

But Vaughan also remembers stage experiences with Albert Collins and Freddie King. "I especially remember their honesty in playing. I saw Albert a lot because he was from Houston, so he was coming through a lot. He was a wonderful guy offstage. But when he would get onstage, he would kill you and there was nothing you could do about it. Albert was teaching you by example. He would let you go, but once Albert Collins took off on a solo, it was over. There wasn't anything you could do except smile," laughed Vaughan. "Same thing with Freddie King. I played a little with him and saw him play a lot. His power and command of the stage and audience was amazing."

These were the experiences that helped shape Vaughan's uniquely emotional guitar tone. His capo and open E tunings were the sounds he witnessed in the players he saw as he was growing up. Men like Gatemouth Brown, Albert Collins, Johnny "Guitar" Watson, Guitar Slim, and Pee Wee Crayton all come together in Vaughan's direct string attack, where the thumb picks the open E string and another finger simultaneously plucks the corresponding note on a higher string. Vaughan stated, "I started doin' that on the third Thunderbirds album. I'm in E and I've got all those open strings. It just makes me different. My style is sort of that Houston, Gulf Coast style of Guitar Slim, Gatemouth Brown, and Johnny "Guitar" Watson."

In many ways, the T-Bird sound is the blues sound most associated with the 1980s. But in 1989, Vaughan left the Thunderbirds for a variety of reasons. "I wouldn't be the same person without those days. Kim and I had so many memorable nights just playin' Antone's. We went all over the world together and went through a lot of stuff together. I left the band for a lot of reasons. I was tired, drinkin' too much and everything that goes with it. I just wanted to get off the bus and go home. I didn't feel like we were going anywhere."

In 1990, Jimmie and Stevie hooked up and recorded *Family Style* together. Though the tragedy of Stevie's death in 1990 temporarily silenced Jimmie's public guitar playing, the music always was a safe haven of remembrance for Jimmie. "I was really close to Stevie when he died. To be truthful, that year is all sort of blurred. I just didn't want to go out in public and do the interview deal. What do you say? Everybody wanted to tell me how sorry they were, and I just didn't want to talk to anybody. That was real nice of 'em, but I just got tired. I didn't know what to do about it.

"I never stopped playing then. Back then I played every day. I had these archtop acoustic guitars that I played at home constantly. The music was a good place to get lost in. That's what music is for. That's what it's always been for—it's a healer. That's what it does, it makes you feel better. That's why I played my archtop everyday. It's not words—it was something else, a feeling.

"I don't know if you ever get over it, but it does get easier with time. I realized that people are just sharing their loss with me, their feelings. And who better to share them with than me? I understand that. It doesn't bother me now. The tribute we recorded in 1996 helped me a lot. It was like I finally went through a door. Bringing all those people together and doing the tribute was really a big healer for me." Vaughan also won a Grammy for the instrumental "SRV Shuffle" from the tribute. "To have Stevie remembered through the song was very special for me and my mom.

"I think he's in me in every song, like I was in him during songs. We're brothers. There's always something that you share with a brother or sister that you don't share with anybody else, something you both know intuitively without talking. He was as much a teacher to me as I was to him. I was always in awe of his playing. He just had a special way of getting hooked up with whatever it was that leads you down that path of expressing yourself. That thing we keep talking about, honest expression. He was really good at that. It just flowed outta him. I've seen him play some amazing stuff technically, but it was his heart that I thought was the best part of his playing. People saw him, and they knew, 'Something's going on here.'"

Since then, Vaughan released three solo CDs, *Strange Pleasure* in 1994, *Out There* in 1998, and *Do You Get the Blues* in 2001. All contain a mixture of Vaughan originals as they attempt to translate Vaughan's uniquely personal stage show to disc. Though many performers fear the studio experience, considering it sterile and restricting, Vaughan finds the experience quite the opposite. "I actually enjoy going into the studio. After I learned how to get the right sounds and how to work all the stuff, and after I got my head screwed on straight about what I wanted to do and do what I thought was right, it's a real pleasure working in the studio.

"It's like you got this big blank canvas and you got all this paint. When you get in the studio, you've got to be creative. It can be a wonderful place. I always have had a lot to do with the production of my music. Usually I bring the song and try to get a certain thing going and I'm tryin' to get the band to help me bring it out. As long as I know the melody and what the song is about, it works. Because I have to stand up there and sing it, I have to sing something I believe in. That's why I can't sing other people's stuff, because I could never say that in a million years," laughed Vaughan. "It's real expressive to write the song, pick your band, write the arrangement, sing it, play the solo, and end it when you're damn good and ready."

Amid Vaughan's no-frills, aching vocal style, one thing remains constant: the classic Jimmie Vaughan guitar, where less is always more within his heavy, pickless string darts and an emotional tone that can shoot arrows through the hearts of listeners.

In this way Vaughan continually channels decades of genuine Texas music through a modern filter to give listeners his fresh and modernistic brand of Southern musical traditions. "I'm always tryin' to be more honest and relaxed. If you can figure out how to express your real self and if it's honest, then nobody can really say anything about it. That's the goal I'm constantly working on. I feel this stuff, and it somehow fits into the style I've been hearin'. It's my version of the music that I love."

Kim
Wilson

Kim Wilson's story is every person's journey. Whether he talks about the work towards acceptance in a peer group and diligence in continually showing that you belong or he talks about legitimacy within a world that prizes money over honest substance, Wilson talks about human issues we ponder daily.

"American society is about instant gratification," said Wilson, "and forgets the long road that takes you to where you are today. These young kids playing the blues today are very respectful. But I really would like to see young people learning the satisfaction you can get out of being a journeyman player and developing a style through your life that you can take to your old age, one that you can get better and better at, one that changes and evolves as you change and mature. It's all about leaving something legitimate.

"Then you get to the point where you can say 'I finally did something that stands up to everything else I've ever heard.' Then you continue making your way up the ladder of this peer group."

In the house band at Antone's, the legendary Austin music club, Wilson had the opportunity to back nearly every blues legend who came through the club. For Wilson, the experiences with Muddy Waters are etched in his soul. "Muddy said the ultimate stuff about me as a harmonica player and vocalist. He said I was the best guy since Walter. My direction and goal has always been to be in that peer group. Of course my head was full of it, and I talked a lot of trash back then—I was a kid in my 20s. But Muddy was also the first one to humble you too if you got carried away around him. He wasn't gonna take any shit.

"My thing onstage was to blow the old man's mind, to get those good looks out of him. He used to wig out on me. I'd play these things and he'd

*Kim Wilson says the Fabulous Thunderbirds kept the blues
sound alive in the world of rock and roll and disco.*

turn with this scowl on his face and then just start shakin' and shiverin' and
playin' them bottom notes on the guitar behind me. There were times when
it was difficult to play because my mind was blown so bad from being
onstage with Muddy and seeing his reaction to my playing. The adrenaline
was flowin' through that it's hard to even say what I was doin' at that time.

"I knew that if I was to be in that peer group, I had a long way to go, no
matter what Muddy Waters was sayin' about me, even though it was the

greatest thing that ever happened to me in my whole life. I knew that I had to concentrate on holdin' the position he just gave me. All I cared about was that those guys dug me, and the rest of the world could just drop off.

"That was the best thing that ever happened. No money or adulation in the fly-by-night pop world could ever minutely compare to what those days have brought me. I make money and I've had hit records, but that doesn't even compare," said Wilson.

Though they all passed along musical traditions, the most enduring lesson Kim Wilson learned from playing with masters like Muddy Waters and George "Harmonica" Smith was the honest, legitimate expression of the music. "I was raised on legitimacy. Legitimacy has always been 'stickin' to my guns.' There wasn't any other way until I got into the commercial music business, and then legitimacy was pushed aside. In 1998, I met Francis Clay, Muddy's former drummer, for the first time, and he said to me, 'You are so refreshing. Most of these guys out here ain't saying nothing. It's nice to hear somebody with something to say.' You can't put a price on that."

Wilson has strong feelings on the state of legitimacy in today's music. "The further away you get from their original stuff, the more diluted the music gets. It's a really boring, fourth-generation copy diluting a dilution. It's really, really hard to blame the audience when they don't have anything to gauge a musical opinion on. Even though all this legitimate music is right at their fingertips, they don't know where it is because it's not advertised to them. Record companies label rock 'blues' because there is some kind of romantic wave to be ridden. All the stuff they call 'blues' that sells a million records is simply bullshit. I don't think blues even comes into play with these artists.

"Real music is very relaxed anarchy. The relaxation has to be there, or you won't get into the same peer group of the guys you love. You'll always be outside lookin' in."

Know up front that Wilson straddles an artistic fence. He continues to front the commercially successful Fabulous Thunderbirds, and he holds the harmonica chair in the Kim Wilson Blues Revue. Whatever the group backing Wilson, listeners will always hear the honest, legitimate blues Wilson has been part of as a performer since the late 1960s.

According to Wilson, the T-Birds were always playing the blues role in a rock and roll world. "There'll always be people out there who want to hear the rock-and-roll, hit-record side of the band. Lately, we're introducing more of the blues side. In the old days, it was balls to the walls all the time. The T-Birds are getting deeper into the blues. We're getting more into the dynamics of it and the interplay between the band members," said Kim.

"It's a natural thing that too many people are getting away from real blues because they haven't been exposed to it." Laughed Wilson, "Modern-day blues, which is one guy playing a 20-minute solo, usually on a guitar—this is ludicrous to me. But that's the way it is these days."

The days Wilson remembers back to are his early days in Austin, Texas, in 1974, when he, Jimmie Vaughan, Keith Ferguson, and Mike Buck formed the Fabulous Thunderbirds and became the house band at Antone's. "Part of the mission was to create a grittier, more original sound. We tried to bring it to where we felt the music should be. We had a uniqueness to what we did then, because playing those small clubs was conducive to smaller amps and better dynamics. Originally, they labeled us blues-rock. We were always rocky, but we had a legitimacy, because we played good music and used the right standards."

The standards that set the T-Birds apart from other "blues-rock" bands were the places Vaughan and Wilson came from. The road to discovery for Vaughan began in Dallas, Texas, in 1951. Wilson's road also began in 1951, in Detroit. But he grew up in Goleta, California. He began listening to the Motown and Stax music his friends listened to and seeing James Brown and Muddy Waters. Then, at 17, he picked up the harmonica and within three months had put together his first band. He devoured the harp recordings of Junior Well and James Cotton and the live shows of George "Harmonica" Smith.

Rod Piazza remembers one show from those days: "When me and George Smith used to play with the Bacon Fat band in 1969 at the Santa Monica College campus, Kim Wilson was a college student up there. He used to call himself 'Goleta Slim,' and he'd come around and sit in with whatever group was playing when he didn't have a band. He told me years later at Antone's that it was watching me and George Smith playing that 'made me decide to strap on my guns and I wanted to play harmonica.'"

Wilson also remembers his first time playing with Smith: "George Smith really gave me an early break. I was in my late teens, just startin' out. He taught me about showmanship. He was a big hero of mine already, but the first time I met George, I'd been playing for a couple of years. There was this place called the Head Band in the late 1960s in Goleta. I got in there with a fake ID.

"My friend John Phillips would do two or three numbers and then turn the show over to George. At the break, he told me he wanted me to play instead of him. I freaked out. He talked me into it. I got on the bandstand, started playin'. The crowd was going crazy. I got halfway into my third number and here comes my hero, George, jumpin' on the stage with me. I go to leave the stage, and he wouldn't let me. He said, 'You're stayin' up here.' He proceeded to take me along by having me do mirror images of what he was doing. At the end of the night, the club owner handed me a C-note. George Smith asked me to finish out the week with him. For me, that was an early validation."

When Wilson arrived in Austin to stay, before he'd met Jimmie Vaughan, he was hangin' out with Doyle Bramhall and a young kid named Stevie Ray Vaughan. "First time I was in Austin was for about five days. We went to all the clubs and sat in on all the breaks. Stevie was just a kid, but I could tell there was the spark there from the very beginning. 'Course, he'd learned a lot from his brother. He saw his brother playing, and I'm sure that encouraged him to keep going.

"In my mind, Jimmie Vaughan was very influential and was much more responsible for the resurgence of the blues. He was a big influence, along with Hollywood Fats, Junior Watson, and Duke Robillard. You gotta give the resurgence of the true blues to those guys. I think his sound is his main thing. He's one of the few guys who can get a decent sound out of a Strat."

Though they combined a Chicago-style harmonica with high-octane Texas guitar, from the earliest days the T-Birds have carried the blues-rock burden. "In the early days, 1974, we were just kids cuttin' up, with no responsibility. We all came from different musical backgrounds. No one thought much about the future. We were just carryin' on, but we got good in the process. Early on we knew we had something different. It had a lot of attitude that people really went for. We did some things that still stand up."

"We weren't two peas in a pod. There was a lot of things I dug about that style and a lot of things I didn't, especially as an accompaniment to the harp. If you look at guys like Junior Watson and Rusty Zinn, you're really looking at the ultimate accompanists, people who really studied and listened and who are really into setting up a vocalist or solo. In the Thunderbird school, that was never really a strength. The T-Bird style of guitarist has never been conducive to accompanying. It's always been more up front. That has always been frustrating for me as a vocalist and a harp player.

"I felt I hugely compromised many times in the early days, but so did Jimmie. We realized that between the two of us, we had a broad cross-section of styles. We had so many differences that we knew where the crossover was. We knew what would work, so we stuck with what worked. I felt that, at the very beginning, we had a good start but that we had a long way to go."

Five years with Chrysalis produced four albums. But with no major success, Chrysalis dropped them. In 1985, the band was signed by Epic and recorded their mainstream success *Tuff Enuff*. Numbers like the title track and "Wrap It Up" turned the album platinum. This led to another crossover hit, *Powerful Stuff*, in 1987. "With *Tuff Enuff*, we had a very good beginning on what we could do commercially. But I don't think either situation lived up to its potential. The band had a taste of stardom and wanted more. As far as T-Bird stardom goes, it was very, very premature. I don't believe that any of us were stars at that time. At the time I felt the band was stagnating and playing music for basically monetary reasons," said Wilson.

Wilson believed this was draining the artistic creativity from him. "I certainly had a good time while I was doing it, but it really changed for me as the music get much louder and more 'every man for himself' as opposed to a unit or ensemble sound. When it became that way, we parted company. That was very freeing for me."

After a hiatus during which he recorded blues from his soul on the Antone's label, Wilson reformed the T-Birds, with Duke Robillard and Kid Bangham on guitars. In 1995, Wilson again reassembled the band, featuring Kid Ramos, Willie J. Campbell, Gene Taylor, and Fran Christina.

Through the years, Wilson has watched and learned. Tired of listening to suits who never played, he went against the book and formed his own label, Blue Collar, putting his trust in the world of blues fans who thrive on the same legitimate music as Wilson. His *My Blues* attests to the real music continually driving Wilson. "My job is showing people who don't know anything about the blues that it has substance to it. Right now, I really want to cater to the hard-core people, because I think there are a lot of people out there who didn't believe that real blues records could be made anymore. That's old school, but it's the right school.

"I've been wanting to go to the traditional side of recording for a long time, to have my hands on the whole thing. I wanted to know where it was going after I recorded it. This way there were no pressures on me to deliver a more commercial product than I wanted to do. I had total artistic freedom," said Wilson.

Wilson hopes he can raise the standard in today's blues recordings to where it once was and appeal to the fans who are weary of allowing the technological tail to wag the dog and are starved for meaning in the music they buy.

"In any recording, the juice is the room. You gotta have that. On this project, I've gone all the way live to mono. We did mono to recreate the sound everybody wants to hear. No overdubs, very minimal tracking, a few mikes here and there to get that ambient, live-room sound. Different kinds of microphones, mostly old ribbon mikes from the '30s and '40s. We used three or four different rooms on the project, different configurations as far as where you set the musicians. Other than enhancements for tone, you are buying exactly what we sound like.

"I'm not a believer in limitations, but I think that you tailor your voice to the confidence mode. Always trying to extend it, but not an outrageous extension. It's a gradual thing I've done over the last few years. Junior Wells was very much a mentor to me, especially with his vocals. I thought he was one of the best blues singers I ever heard. Later, I really learned and appreciated his harmonica playing more and more. I thought there were a lot of subtleties and refinements in what he did, when he really got serious about it, that were the culmination of many many years of refining a style. Same with my harp playing: I just play all the time—at the house, drivin' the car. I got lost the other night doing that. I was deep in L.A., completely lost on a highway detour because I was bendin' a note."

One thing is always clear, Wilson's honest dedication to both preserve and expand real music. Like the men who passed wisdom along to him 25-30 years ago, Wilson acknowledges the same obligation to spread the authentic traditions of the blues. "What incentive does a kid have today to play blues on a guitar in this modern world?" asked Wilson. "None. They're doing it because they love it, so they need to know what they're doing is right. There isn't much financial or critical reward for doing your homework and learning the music like it's supposed to be learned.

"Kids like Kirk Fletcher and Rusty Zinn are really very diligent about covering all the bases and being proficient on their instrument. They have taken the time to learn the language first. I like that they approach anything contemporary in a very solid traditionally minded approach."

Wilson still yearns for the opportunity to play traditional music in intimate clubs. "Real music happens in the joint, not in a huge hall or giant arena, and there's very few joints left to play," said Wilson. "It's a great musical atmosphere you can't get anywhere else. When you can see the sweat and you can hear directly out of the amplifier, it's like the old days. It's where the real music happens. If I could make a living doing it, I'd be playing small clubs like these all the time."

This commitment is deeply rooted in Wilson's soul. "I want to be the guy who stuck to his guns and was his own man. It's a very difficult world to live in when people like Jimmy Rogers and Junior Wells and Luther Allison are leavin' and it's being taken over by preteen guys who weren't even around and didn't even play with these guys. I'm the last generation of guys that was actually hands-on taught by the creators of the music. They took me under their wing and gave me opportunities. In the end they treated me as an equal. That makes the music I play more personal and more valuable. But I learned much of that from these old guys more than any music. I learned how to be a person. They educated me in humanity."

East Coast

The East Coast has never been looked upon as a thriving blues center. When aspiring blues musicians looked to the big-city sound of New York City, they were faced with big-city jazz traditions grafted onto the blues carried by migrating Southerners. However, through the Newport Folk and Jazz festivals and the growing club scene's promoting of the folk blues revival, the 1960s in Boston and New York played a significant part in keeping the blues alive in the East. Fueled by that folk blues revival and the rediscovery of country blues giants previously thought dead, the Northeast offered a hotbed of clubs and venues for these musicians to resurrect their careers in front of enthusiastic white audiences. Their essential lessons of music and life were not lost on the young, appreciative audiences they played for.

If you couldn't travel to Mississippi porches in the 1960s, Mississippi Delta porches traveled to you. Three East Coast venues—Greenwich Village, the Newport Folk Festival, and Boston coffeehouses—provided aspiring acoustic musicians with in-the-flesh first-generation models. One of the first from the 1960s revival not only to sit with masters of the genre but also to become one himself was John Hammond. Son to the legendary record producer John Hammond, Sr., Hammond was perhaps one of the earliest musicians to revive the blues in the 1960s. Today, he continues to offer fans the most vivid interpretations of Charley Patton, Robert Johnson, and Son House.

Taj Mahal was the oddity in the 1960s, an African American interested in African forms in American music. No white revivalist can offer the accurate insights into the African musical diaspora more clearly than Mahal.

In 1964 in New York's Greenwich Village, a 14-year-old girl, Rory Block, was studying blues off records and participating in jam sessions at Washington Square Park. At the same time, Paul Rishell was making trips to the Village record stores from his Connecticut home and learning the blues from records. The personal epiphany that illuminated the soul of acoustic, country blues in both was meeting Son House.

The Greenwich Village folk scene wasn't the only classroom in the blues university; Boston's "night school" in the 1960s boasted its own classrooms at the Club 47 in Cambridge, the Unicorn Coffee House, Paul's Mall, the Jazz Workshop, and, later in the decade, the Boston Tea Party. In addition, the extensive college scene offered coffeehouse opportunities to many of these first-generation bluesmen, from Mississippi John Hurt to Son House to Muddy Waters to Howlin' Wolf to Rev. Gary Davis to Skip James. Even though the small audiences were very appreciative of these men, a few enthusiastic devotees sat in those audiences.

As high school students in the mid-1960s, Bob Margolin, Duke Robillard, and David Maxwell found their musical path in those places. While Margolin and Maxwell had access to the vibrant Boston club scene, Robillard first pursued solitary study off records and was then able to catch the master players at the Newport Festivals.

Just like their West Coast counterparts, these musicians made their musical marks early. Margolin was Muddy's guitarist when he was 24, Maxwell was friend to Otis Spann in the late '60s and 22-year-old keyboardist with Freddie King, and Robillard was the founder of the jump and swing institution Roomful of Blues in 1967 as a 19-year-old.

Most recently, the three women of Saffire—The Uppity Blues Women, have breathed fresh life into the blues of the classic women singers of the 1920s and 1930s, revived the acoustic music of masters from those days, and yet made their own songwriting statement from their women's perspective.

Rory Block

ory Block has always powered the artistic carousel with a different agenda. Though most everyone visualizes grasping the gold ring of commercialism, her road is a path backward to acoustic landscapes that have not been affected by any commercial interests. In 1964, she heard *Really the Country Blues* and from that moment dedicated her life to learning how to play blues.

"I spent two years of my life with my ear glued to a speaker," said Block. "Out of a deep reverence for the music, I was determined to figure out each and every note and play the great songs with as much accuracy as I could muster."

Few performers can replicate the true mood of country blues like Block does. With her eyes closed, head weaving, fingers flying, strings pulled at (not plucked), and feet stomping, Block turns any performance into a backcountry jukin' reincarnation of the music of Robert Johnson or Son House. This honest commitment to the integrity of the music comes through on every song Block plays. As she travels to the deepest part within her, she also transports the audience.

"I do feel like something takes over when I go into the deepest part of myself, night after night after night. When I get onstage, it's as if the music, which I've been performing and loving for so long, has a life of it's own. Couple that with the audience's energy, and I feel like it carries itself."

As Block penetrates the spirit of each song of her country mentors, like Son House, Charley Patton, Tommy and Robert Johnson, she breathes new life into the music she plays. "You have to tap into the original feeling of a song. There are lot of people who play country blues songs today. But it's few and far between to find someone who actually touches that genuine

*In 1964, Rory Block was a 14-year-old taking part in the
Sunday jam sessions in Washington Square Park with
Maria Muldaur, John Sebastian, and Stefan Grossman.*

spirit and isn't just doing it as an exercise in imitation. When someone actually hits that spirit, it should make your hair stand on end.

"I just play music, and when I hit onto that feeling and get my boat out
onto that the river of spirit, it happens by itself. If I get there, I feel like I'm
back with the original players. It's just an overall sensation."

In attacking her country blues, Block relies more on her ear than any technical deconstruction of the music. "I don't take a song apart technical-ly. It's more intuitive listening and understanding of where the music is going. The difficulty in taking the old music apart in segments is the awk-wardness when you lose the flow of the original."

Within those parameters, Block tackles the music of Robert Johnson dif-ferently than that of Patton or House. "I think Robert was just a genius. With Charley Patton, Son House, and Tommy Johnson, there's this great vibe, and I feel like as long as I'm in the vibe where I feel great, then I'm where I want to be. I can approximate things with other artists because their playing is not as technical as Robert Johnson. He's so technically intensive that I don't want to dishonor it by cutting corners or skipping things. I feel like that's really an art form, so I stay close to the original.

"When you are a genius like Robert, you do things your own way and you obsess with practice until you develop something so intensive. That's obvi-ous in the music he played. Maybe Tommy Johnson and Charley Patton were more a total blend of the atmosphere and mood of the region. Robert was clearly obsessed with being a great guitar player, and that obsession comes through. That's why I get obsessed when I do a Robert Johnson song. I enjoy hearing people play his songs as much like the original as possible. They lose the original beauty when you make one of his songs sound like a standard folk song."

As a child, Block grew up at the center of the Greenwich Village folk explosion of the early 1960s. Her father, Alan Block, supported the music and musicians at his hip Greenwich Village sandal shop. "I spent all my time walking from place to place and thinking or endlessly strumming my Galiano guitar that my mother had acquired at a garage sale for $4. Music had become the absolute center of my being, and nothing mattered more. At the age of ten I figured out "Froggy Went a-Courtin'" by slamming down on the E and then the A strings and plucking out a melody. The guitar was an instrument of wonder and joy, a best friend."

The beauty of the music was tempered by the emotionally dry, exhausting family life of this 14-year-old. More and more, Block gravitat-ed to her musical family. "At 14, with the freedom of adolescence, I was totally lost. I was in so much pain and emptiness from lack of connected-ness. I'm finding that many adolescents quickly identify with those feel-ings of alienation.

"I became part of the Sunday jam sessions in Washington Square Park. People stood around in clusters, pressing together to watch incredible musi-cians playing styles largely unheard of up North. David Grisman, Frank Wakefield, Jodie Stecker, John Herald, Roger Sprung, and Eric Weissberg were some of the bluegrass/country players, and John Sebastian, Maria

Muldaur, Stefan Grossman, Marc Silber, Jack Baker, and others were play-ing ragtime, blues, swing, and early barrelhouse jazz.

"When I first heard the blues, there was no other choice. It's some of the deepest stuff and it takes you to another dimension. The music res-onated inside me, felt real, beautiful, spoke to what was in my heart, moved my soul. It cried out as I cried out, it wept when I wept, it haunted and rolled and wandered as I did. Inspiration is born in the deepest part of the soul, where boundaries don't exist. If you live with your soul extending beyond the borders of your body, you never see boundaries."

If the child is truly mother to the woman, then it was her early vulner-ability and deep human sensibilities coupled with her first-person observa-tions of country blues masters that set Block's artistic journey. Growing up in Greenwich Village during the folk craze of the early 1960s, Block also sat in the presence of country blues rediscoveries.

"For me personally, sitting with many of the older country blues players made a major difference in how I play the music. I did already have this intense, superpowerful connection to the music before I met any of them. But meeting Rev. Gary Davis, Skip James, Mississippi John Hurt, and Son House was such a deeply inspiring experience. Watching Son House play, I felt this aura around him. Talking with him and looking at him showed me his beauty. The power of the music, the story, the passion, and the essence of the music were all in that aura around Son House.

"More than music, the deepest thing I was learning was the spiritual aspects of the music. That the music was about who the person was and the person's life. That, to me, was really the essence of the music. I saw that the notes came out of that feeling. In some way, Son House's presence, a pres-ence that I understood throughout his music, was really more than what the notes within the music was about.

"I met him backstage at the Village Gate in 1965. He virtually radiated a golden light. As I watched him perform, rolling his head back, slamming the strings, and almost choking on the intensity, I learned a deep lesson about the power of the music which became an inseparable part of me. Later, sitting with him at Stefan Grossman's parents' house, I had a chance to play for him. I will never forget his amazement as I played Willie Brown's 'Future Blues.' He kept looking over to Stefan and Dick Waterman and ask-ing, 'Where did she learn to play like this?'

"That was the thing about the older recordings I was listening to. I was getting the notes and feeling from the records. There was this kind of feel-ing on there, almost as if you were sitting with the person. I have no idea how that was accomplished. It's the same thing that happens when you see an old picture from the 1930s. You can look at it and there's a spiritual energy within that picture of what happened then and who the person was that comes through very powerfully. That's the same thing that comes through with some older recordings of this music. Too many people merely get the notes off the record and miss out on the feeling.

"The other thing they gave me was the sense that it didn't matter that I was a 14-year-old white girl living in New York City. All they cared about was that I loved their music, and I loved being in their presence. That was enough for them, to give me an unlimited gift from their wisdom. That's why I think it's so unreal to divide people by any categories at all."

It was categorization that Block fought then and continues to fight now. The industry's first impression watching Rory Block aggressively flail at her guitar strings was, "She plays with the power of a man." Why not, for it was from the rediscovered first-generation bluesmen that Block learned how to play the blues. But early comments like that pigeonhole artists into stifling compartments.

"When I first heard someone say, 'She plays like a man,' I thought if you think that's so surprising, you ain't seen nothing yet! I felt a little empowered by it, but also a little alienated. What are they expecting, and why should a woman not play all out with feeling?"

After years of trying to be another industry round peg, Block returned home to listen to her own spirit. While only a teen mother raising a family, the call back to music came in the form of a dream. "I'd go to sleep every night with the radio on. There was something about Carole King's "You've Got a Friend." It was part dream and part reality. I woke up and I had incorporated it into a dream where I was singing in my voice. When I woke up she was singing, so it went from dream to reality. I said I've got to start doing this again. I knew that if she could do it, I also could do it. Her song somehow made me sure of that.

"I knew early to sing it from the heart, not worry about how everybody categorizes you, about competition or how many records you sell. Just do it for the love of doing it. I was clear about my direction. But it turns out my direction was not commercially acceptable. The music business basically told me they were not interested in country blues. I was told I had to start writing songs using a commercial formula.

"It was when I signed with Rounder in 1981 and wrote 'Lovin' Whiskey' that I became comfortable with my voice as a songwriter." Like most discoveries, finding her unique voice happened quite by accident. Block had written the song, but criticism over her lyrics compelled her to use a personal letter she'd written and drop all songwriting formulas.

"I decided to tell stories with a different type of looking inward, one that looks inward and outward at the same time. It was overly personal, but in a different way. I recorded it, and that's the song that became a gold record in Europe.

"I learned to simply tell the story the way you want to. It appears to be my mission to write songs that are really personal and about really awkward subjects. I feel that if you write it from that place that says, 'We're all in this together and there is really nothing to be ashamed of,' the chances are very great that a lot of people will understand. At first I thought the songs I was writing were too personal. I realized I had nothing to be embarrassed about and that everybody is going through very similar and related experiences. I saw people begin relating right away, and I began realizing that to write these kinds of songs must be my songwriting mission.

"You always hope to continue writing songs of merit. The hardest part is thinking that you've dried up and can't write any more. I still have those feelings, that I can't do it again. I think that's an essential ingredient for me to push forward. I thought that when I wrote 'Mama's Blues,' I thought that when I wrote 'Lovin' Whiskey,' and I thought it when I wrote 'Life Song.'

At was the same time, she discovered her true singing voice. "I have a harder-driving blues voice and a deeper voice that's more relaxed and has a lot of resonance in it and from deep inside the center of my being, the soul or heart. I had the blues voice when I started singing. Years later I was singing soul music. That was the voice I was doing when I was signed to major labels early in my career. They didn't want me to do a soul thing. After writing 'Lovin' Whiskey,' I started feeling I should sound like whatever I wanted to and not worry about fitting into a style. That was very freeing. It's totally removing the outside pressures from yourself. What's left after you free yourself is probably closest to your true self."

In the beginning, Block played the venues that are the bane of every solo act: loud bars with second-rate sound systems. It was then she realized her need for consistency in an inconsistent music world. "Playing bars in the early stages in my career, I felt like I was wearing the wrong clothes. That's the nightmare of being an acoustic artist in an electric world. Once some drunk fell across the stage, saying, 'Play "You're the Reason God Made Oklahoma,"' threw a $100 bill at me, and passed out on the stage. I had to deal with so much insanity like that in the beginning. I needed to start establishing a pattern that made me feel secure." For Block that meant taking her own sound system and road manager on the road.

And it established goals to strive for. "I set my goals early on that I was gonna get out of those places and perform in listening rooms. However, through those days, I learned how be a really good performer and be able to relax and talk to the audience and to keep things going under the most bizarre circumstances."

It was in the 1990s that Block found the balance between these seem-
ingly opposite perspectives of honest writing and faithful adherence to the
country blues idiom. A critically acclaimed string of stirring Rounder recordings alternated between blues and emotionally intense originals. The culmination is 1998's *Confessions*, which achieves near perfection, balancing her
passionate love of country acoustic blues and honest songwriting delivered
with her folk singer's vocal intonations.

When a songwriter like Block puts her memoirs to music, she authors
"Life Song." From tragic events like leaving home at 15, the death of her
son, Thiele, and the tyranny of music business directives to the successes
she has experienced by standing her musical ground and "singin' it from the
heart," Block leaves no stones in her way unturned.

"I always felt these memories were very personal and precious for me,
and I didn't ever want to cheapen them. I always wanted to hold those
experiences close to my heart. In recent years, I began realizing it was something I wanted to talk about, that I didn't cheapen it by talking about it, and
I wanted to explain my sources and inspirations and experiences and frustrations. After keeping it private for a long time, I no longer felt like I could-
n't say the things I wanted to say. I wanted to talk about them." This type
of naked exposure in her lyrics marks Block as a unique and gifted lyricist.

Often when people attend a show of acoustic, country blues, they feel
they are at a museum and need to show reverence—ironic when you realize that this music was created at rural jukes as party music. "I like audience
enthusiasm. Clapping during a great solo is a great way for the audience to
show me they appreciate what I'm playing. As long as the people aren't
drunk out of their minds or disconnected with what I'm playing, they can
holler or cheer or call out song names. Even an occasional smart-aleck
remark is fun. Long ago I learned to enjoy stuff like that.

"Today, I don't really mind it, being lumped together as women in the
blues. We are women in the blues, and we've tried to rise from the underground women of the 1930s who paved the way. The women of today who
do the blues really had to come from nothing. When I first started playing
blues, there were no CD compilations of women blues singers. We had to
reinvent women in blues, clutching our Bessie Smith, Billie Holiday,
Memphis Minnie, Lottie Kimbrough records. Maybe we'll get to the point
up the road where it's just blues."

In a fast world where reverence for the past is easily forgotten, Block
keeps to a high moral road. She is one of the few performers who introduce
each song by identifying the author and some history to the audience. "From
day one, at 14, whenever I've performed blues, without fail I tell you the
original writer. There are many who've not done that, but that's been one

of my obsessions. To keep saying the names of the old performers validates the sense of reverence I feel towards the originators."

From replicating original Delta blues not often reworked by today's country blues players, to writing compelling original vignettes that deal with our world, Block continually navigates a penetrating musical course.

"I have always searched for the deeper side of the music. I've gone to another level, a level where the subjects are very personal, probing songs. After 'Mama's Blues,' people always tell me how much it means to them. Women coming up crying, telling me that the song is all about how they feel all the time. And men tell me they understand their women better after they hear that song.

"I have people coming up to me telling me, 'Somebody's Baby' happened to them. They tell me about giving up their own babies for adoption. I've gone past the thoughts that anything I'm gonna say will make somebody mad. I've accepted the songwriter's vulnerability. When people come to me after a show about how songs like 'Lovin' Whiskey' have changed lives, that's the ultimate reward for me."

John
Hammond

No one has done more to safeguard the country blues traditions than John Hammond. From his career beginnings in 1962, Hammond has been instrumental in replicating authenticity and breathing contemporary life into the genre.

"The blues won't go away. It's a continuum, a historical thing that makes you feel part of history. The blues isn't a passing fad, it isn't rock and roll," said Hammond. "Blues in general is timeless. A good blues song today is just as appropriate as it was 50 years ago because it captures the human condition, which hasn't changed. We're still making the same mistakes. That infinite wisdom of basic life is always there. Almost right away, I realized this was my calling. I loved the music and I felt that I could do this."

Hammond came to the blues through the rock and roll players of the 1950s, like Chuck Berry and Bo Diddley. Since both recorded on Chess, Hammond began to investigate the other artists listed on the albums he owned. He began buying the music of Howlin' Wolf and Muddy Waters. "The stores that would have this kind of music would also sell other blues artists. I saw an album called *The Country Blues*, released in 1957 on Folkways. Names like Blind Boy Fuller intrigued me enough to buy the record. Instantly, I heard where it all came from.

"This was a major discovery for me. I was 16 and just a fan. I hadn't picked up a guitar yet. When I listened to other country artists, like Robert Johnson, it all just crystallized in my head that this was where it all began. This was also the folk boom era in 1959-60, and it seemed that everyone had a guitar. I watched these guys at college playing and thought, 'I can play that.' I got a guitar when I was 18, started playing professionally when I was 19, and, a year after playing professionally, got to record my first album on Vanguard."

John Hammond has played with blues musicians
from Son House and Mississippi John Hurt
to Eric Clapton and Michael Bloomfield.

Though Hammond is the son of John Hammond, the legendary record producer and talent scout who signed Billie Holiday, Bob Dylan, Bruce Springsteen, and Stevie Ray Vaughan to Columbia Records, he relied on his own inner character to govern his career. "I didn't grow up with my dad per se. My parents divorced when I was five. I was one of those teenagers who felt he had been in school much too long. I didn't have a lot of friends in school, and I wasn't a school-oriented person. Subconsciously, I was looking for a way to spring free and make my own way in this world. I was in a position personally at that time where I wanted to be by myself and have my own space and make my own life. I felt very lucky that I had latched onto something that I felt part of in a historical sense."

"I was on shows early on in my career with John Hurt, Mance Lipscomb, Son House, and Bukka White on college gigs. In nightclubs, I worked with Howlin' Wolf and Muddy a bunch of times. I opened shows, hung out, and got to know them all.

"Muddy was the most generous man and one of the greats. I knew Muddy from 1961, when I first met him. I was on gigs with him from 1963 on. He encouraged me incredibly. Muddy was a real country guy. He would sit me down and make me play for him. He'd say, 'I used to play like that.' He told me he only learned to play guitar in open tuning, and it was Jimmy Rogers who showed him how to play in a regular tuning. Onstage he took complete command. As soon as he walked on the bandstand, school was out. He had such presence—completely friendly and open, gracious and unafraid of anything.

"Wolf was different. If you got to know him, he was very open. But if you just saw his stage show, he could scare you. My first gig with Wolf I was probably 20 or 21, at the Ash Grove in Los Angeles. It was terrifying. I opened the show, and I came off the stage and the first person I see is Howlin' Wolf towering over me. He said, 'How in the world did you ever learn to play like that?' I said, 'From records.' He looked at me and said, 'So did I!' Then he said, 'Whatever you do, don't ever stop playing that.' He opened up and told me stuff that to this day I still pinch myself.

"Then he picked up my guitar and played 'Pony Blues.' He told me he learned to play it from Charley Patton and 'Charley would whap me upside the head if I got it wrong.' Imagine that! He also told me his idol as a kid was the yodeling great, Jimmie Rodgers. He said Rodgers inspired him to sing and play. I'm sittin' there with my mouth open ready to drop. Here's Howlin' Wolf, not only talking to me, but opening up."

In many ways, that directly ties Hammond to Patton.

In 1963, Hammond was booked on the stage of the Newport Folk Festival at a point when he was still groping for a voice and point of view on the country blues. "I was on the Newport Festival in 1963, and John Lee Hooker, who was solo acoustic. Rev. Gary Davis too. Brownie and Sonny and Dave Van Ronk. That was my first big show. It totally scared the hell out of me."

Was Hammond nervous playing the music in front of the musicians he'd learned from? "I never thought of the music being owned by anybody. I always thought of it as music I liked. So I never felt like I was usurping any-thing from anybody. I felt like, if you loved the music and you played it, it's yours. I felt like I was at the place I'm supposed to be.

"I was very enthusiastic but without a lot of knowledge about the busi-ness. The Newport Folk Festival in 1963 was one of those turning points, where I not only played well and the audience flipped out, but I also got a manager and agent at the same time, Manny Greenhill of Folklore Productions. He also booked Joan Baez, Doc Watson, Jack Elliott, all the folk-rock, blues guys. All of a sudden, I was being booked professionally all over the country. Within a few years, I was on major tours. I played England in 1965 and hung out and played with Eric Clapton, Brian Jones, John Mayall, Dylan, and Donovan. These people were then in my reality because of where I was.

"I've had so many big moments, but my show at the 1963 Newport Folk Festival stands out as one of the most overwhelming, exciting things I've ever done. To be on the stage with all those great players and feel the over-whelming acceptance by the audience crystallized every feeling I had for the music."

These names carry a star quality today, but the rediscovered country blues artists Hammond learned from in the early 1960s are most dear to his spirit. Hammond played on shows with newly unearthed country bluesmen like Son House, Bukka White, and Lightnin' Hopkins. "I was engaged with a who's who in the country blues. I got to see history right there. The first guy that I actually came into contact with was Big Joe Williams. I met him in Chicago the same year I began playing, through my friend Michael Bloomfield. Big Joe was the real thing. From playing with Big Joe that first time I knew what it was all about. I saw him captivate audiences and blow people's minds. He played gigs with Robert Johnson in the '30s. You name it, he was there. Big Joe saw I had a car, and he conned me into driving him to these gigs outside Chicago and he'd let me play harmonica with him. I was on gigs with John Lee Hooker when he was an acoustic solo player who took the bus to the places he was playing. Then I played with Mississippi John Hurt.

"I worked with John Hurt at the Newport festivals and at the Gaslight in New York. He was one of the sweetest guys in the world. He was such a personable and charming guy that the audiences lapped him up. He enjoyed traveling and meeting people. The more adulation he received, the more he responded.

"The music that he played in the 1960s was exactly the same as what he played on his 1920s recordings. His style is a finger-picking technique very much in the folk style, but it's, for sure, blues. It would sound more

Piedmont than Delta. The effect on a young player like me was that I was seeing it done the way it was done originally. It gives reality to what you hear on records. You see that it's possible."

In many ways, Hammond has experienced the same adversities as these Southern country blues artists of the 1930s. "I got put down for being white and for playing country acoustic blues. As great as I felt about doing what I was doing, there was always some angle that was being taken by the media that this was in some way bizarre. My most severe critics were white writers who gave me racist stuff. I never looked at what I played in a negative way. It always felt like the most natural thing for me."

In a strange, ironic twist, the players who knew the music patted Hammond on the back, while the writers who knew nothing of the music were critical. "I always felt more at ease with the players who were into the music I was into. I couldn't wait to get up on the stage and play. That was what I loved to do. I felt very lucky that I had latched onto something that I felt part of in a historical sense. I was part of a continuum. I felt it really was a calling."

A consummate live performer, Hammond has always unleashed the same fury and abandon in the music as the masters he studies. In any live show, Hammond closes his eyes, throws his head side to side, and attacks the guitar strings, with all ten fingers flailing independently. When he adds the harmonica rack and his free-spirited reed bending, willing showgoers are transported into the timelessness of the blues. "I didn't learn that from the country players I was playing with; I think that came from within. I heard a lot of very good players who were playing it safe. It takes more than just having the ability to play. You have to love it to the point of taking the risk, that is, to follow wherever it takes you. Since I wasn't afraid to create myself, it has taken me a long way."

Anyone who has witnessed Hammond's total immersion in the music wonders where and when Hammond discovered that performance zone. "I didn't know about that zone until I got a guitar. Then I was in the zone. That zone's exactly the same today as when I began. There are 37 years of experiences, but it's still the same feeling that I had when I began.

"I didn't learn that from the players I was playing with. I think that came from within. I know guys who can play, but it's only on the surface. It's not really their major focus. I've heard a lot of very good players who were playing it safe and not able to actually be it. It takes more than just having the ability to play. You have to love it to the point of going with it wherever it takes you. I had that right on. I wasn't afraid to create myself.

"It just happens that I become as one with the music and song. That's what I do. *Confidence* is the word. That's what it's all about. You can pick up on that right away from anyone on the stage. I had that confidence to cross that line right away. Hopefully, I've gotten better, but it's that same feeling."

The John Hammond discography includes over 30 recordings, from his early work on Vanguard in the 1960s to his current critically acclaimed recordings on Point Blank. Through them all, one fact stands out: There are no original songs. "I'm not a writer of songs. When I first hit the scene, everybody was saying you have to write songs or you're never gonna go anywhere or amount to anything. It became a stumbling block for me early on. Though I knew 300 songs, everyone kept saying, 'They're not yours.' I'd write a song and think, 'It's not as good as one I already knew.' I didn't feel that was my focus. I never felt that was the most important thing. The most important thing to me is to put a song across. I felt best at taking a song that had already inspired me and channeling it through so I was making it my own. I feel like I'm part of the tradition, without being one of the innovators.

"I've always felt my strongest ability was to play solo, but I've also over the years worked with a lot of really great players. I'm an acoustic player who can play some electric guitar, so I tend to go with what seems to be hot in the studio," said Hammond.

Today, Hammond is witnessing another blues revival. A major difference, however, is that John Hammond is now the master who young acoustic players must study. "I felt that here was a career that as you got older you earned more respect. I hope too that I've learned things about myself in this journey. This is my life. I've found out about all the downsides, that it can at times be a lot of work. I think that's inspiring that there are these young guys out there playing country blues again. It doesn't matter where your inspiration comes from as long as you're turned on to it. The fact that the body of this music exists in recorded form going back 60 years makes it something that anybody can latch right into."

It is Hammond's choice of slide that best explains his master's outlook. "I still use a Sears 11/16 socket for a slide. Sometimes the simplest things are the best."

Taj
Mahal

The music maxim is simple: Find a successful formula and stick with it. Any change in direction or deviation from that blueprint can spell the death of a recording career. So how does Taj Mahal, with his schizophrenic recording identity, pull it off?

With more on-record personalities than Sybil, Taj can sit on the couch and talk New Orleans R&B to the tune of a Grammy, then come to the next couch session and whisper stories that mix mainland and Hawaiian music—all the while selling his music to a public having a voracious appetite to devour whatever he records. Currently, Taj's involvement with African musical masters from Mali's kora tradition on the critically acclaimed *Kulanjan*, and his endorsement of Tim Duffy's Music Maker Relief Foundation as both creative director in the studio and touring musician on the road have Taj testifying to audiences about the respect demanded by the expansive roots of American blues music.

For Taj, the 1999 *Kulanjan* project embodies his musical and cultural spirit arriving full circle. He'd known about kora players as early as 35 years ago and started thinking about this project seriously ten years ago, when he met African Bassekou Kouyate. "This was beyond any feeling of coming home. This is full circle," said Taj.

"The microphones are listening in on a conversation between a 350-year-old orphan and its long-lost birth parents. I've got so much other music to play. But the point is that after recording with these Africans, basically if I don't play guitar for the rest of my life, that's fine with me."

Any talk with Taj about musical projects becomes a flowing river of African American history and black music. "You're talking about Africans who had flourishing societies. Most people still think only of Africa and

Taj Mahal has won two Grammy Awards, with his second in 2001 for Shoutin' in the Key. *He was also named Blues Band of 2000 by the Blues Foundation's W.C. Handy Awards.*

drums; they have no concept of the great Malian empires where all this music came out of. They were a lettered, written, learned people who had everything destroyed. But before it was destroyed, they designated the clans that would commit physical writing to memory and take the information away and become the oral libraries.

"That's exactly where the Griot tradition comes from. Tumani Diabate, who I'm playing with on *Kulanjan,* is a 71st-generation Griot. His ancestors back were among the first families assigned to be the librarians of the music.

"What we did in the United States was take illusions of the painting, little pieces that were left over from memory, and then stretch that out onto the system that we had to create the songs. Those melodies of blues from the Delta were carried because people weren't allowed to play instruments. This music is a part of what we're composed of; this is in the DNA. It's part of our cultural consciousness, even part of the cosmic consciousness.

"The large majority of Afro-Americans have a hard time dealing with blues, because it comes from such a painful past. The problem is that most people have never been able to get beyond that painful past to find out what the music sounds like on the other side. If you can get around the other side of it—which means that you have to go back and listen to some music that's older than 350 years—you can start to see how it has functioned, in terms of festivities, of burying people, of children coming in the world, of people getting married, it's totally functional music."

To bring an African American audience to an understanding of the blues, Taj feels they need to appreciate the music beyond any color. "With *Kulanjan,* I think that Afro-Americans have the opportunity to not only see the instruments and the musicians, but they also see more about their culture and recognize the faces, the walks, the hands, the voices, and the sounds that are not blues. Afro-American audiences had their eyes really opened up for the first time. This was exciting for them to make this connection and pay a little more attention to this music than before."

Growing up in Springfield, Massachusetts, Taj was the rarity, a young African American who immersed himself in the study of his culture's heritage. Increasingly he began searching out the older forms of African American music that were omitted by white music industry execs who were intent on creating a more digestible mainstream American music. Stung by his discoveries, Taj's self-education took him through Caribbean and Latin music, early jazz and swing, and the blues.

Early on, Taj heard the distinct contrast between the music on popular radio and the music he was hearing in his home. Black expression was omitted to give the music wider appeal. "I started seeing that there was so much of this music and it was so varied compared to what I could actually hear on the radio. I heard my own music from so many different sources. There was a whole bunch of us listening to this music, and we were considered the different guys. The contemporary music didn't scare me off, but I was also listening to Monk, Charles Mingus, and Milt Jackson and hearing the jazz overtones from the music my parents were playing."

Taj describes Springfield in the 1950s as a melting pot of various African

American cultures. "Music was an incredible expression for every part of my life growing up. We were always being introduced to someone from the Caribbean or some African country or a Spanish-speaking country or African Americans from all over the United States." His guitar teacher, Lynnwood Perry, relocated from Durham, North Carolina. "He was deeper than just Piedmont playing. He knew how to play Muddy Waters and John Lee Hooker. The Nichols family that lived around the corner from me were from Stovall, Mississippi, right there in the Delta. I recognized that more people from the North were hip to jazz and R&B, but people from the South were hip to blues and gospel.

"The church was a part of my mother's lifestyle. She came from the South, with a Baptist background. She was a singer within that gospel tradition. My father came through the Caribbean, so I got Caribbean, jazz, swing, bebop, and classical music from my dad.

"I grew up with really a positive attitude toward Africa; not only was it positive, it was also quite unique at the time. I started out knowing about the great traditions of the music and connecting back to the basic cultures in Africa. For me, it's always been an open connection that music was a great part of our ancient civilization and how it shows up in our present civilization. It didn't seem like it was something real different, it was normal.

"I was getting my blues through a combination of records and live experiences of people around playing the music. My friends' parents came to my house and always brought their records. You'd go by somebody's barbecue, and that's what they would be playing. I remember hearing Howlin' Wolf and Muddy Waters on the radio. I heard more of the Louis Jordan, Wyonnie Harris jump and swing at home. The deeper stuff came from going over to friends' houses. I had a friend whose mom was deep into Bobby "Blue" Bland and Elmore James. I didn't hear Robert Johnson until I was 19 or 20."

While studying Agriculture at UMASS Amherst in the early 1960s, Taj planted the musical seeds that have bloomed perennially since. At the time Taj surfaced on the scene, there was a folk blues revival that had young guitar players emulating older Delta and Piedmont African American singers.

"I started out acoustic because it seemed imminent that at some point the powers were gonna pull the plug on the electricity. As an acoustic player, I didn't depend on those powers. I didn't work off the populist theory, which is why it took such a long time for people to figure out what I was doing. I wasn't really worried about it being popular. As long as I really liked and felt deeply enough about it, then I really didn't care.

"I was interested in the music because I felt that something was lost in that transition of blacks trying to assimilate into this society. United States intellectualization has spent 50 years trying to prevent these people from being who they were. Now, anybody could come up and sing whatever they wanted to sing. My point was to be a more well-rounded person. Intelligence meant talking with everybody, not just those in my demographic or genre. That was one of my life's philosophies."

Another is to be the connection between the ancestral qualities of the music and the real ancestors of the music. "I always wanted my ancestors to hear my music and like it. Success is having Lightnin' Hopkins, Joseph Spence, or Mance Lipscomb stay at my house and be happy about the music I was playing. I did not want to be the disconnected African American version of the blues. I wanted to be the connection."

Records may have fueled Taj's fire, but witnessing first-generation country blues masters and discovering their power and gifts at places like the Newport Folk Festival put the match to his calling. "That was one of those powerful events. Here I am, one of 100 black people there among 30,000 young, white Americans. The bulk of the talent was all black. That was confusing to me. Even my brothers and sisters didn't understand what I was up to. It was only later they realized they should have gone and seen these people, because that was the last time some of them ever came around.

"I went to Newport in 1961, '62, '63, so I caught the real stuff. When you've got Mississippi John Hurt, Gus Cannon, Memphis Willie B., Fred McDowell, Furry Lewis, Robert Pete Williams, Lightnin' Hopkins, Bessie Jones, and the Georgia Sea Island Singers, you know where I'm at. I recognized that these were the people I had to see. I realized that, like with the African musicians, I was right on target. That was what I was supposed to be doing. I knew I had to put my energy into acknowledging and giving audience to the masters and the elders of the music.

"I talked to lots of them. They didn't give direction in the sense of saying, 'Now son, I'm passing this on to you.' If there was any insight they gave me, I'm sure it was how to communicate with these older men—and how to listen. That alone gave me hours of being able to listen to senior citizens who had stories to talk about. A kid today trying to find out that stuff basically has the records, but we were lucky to be able to see it."

Still, there were some memorable knee-to-knee lessons passed along from the older generation of musicians. "Back in the '60s, Louis Myers actually said that when I was playing harmonica, I wasn't putting the pieces together. I'm a type of guy, given five pieces of the music, I learn to play each part right and then link it together with the next part. Get to what you can get to first, and then start playing the harder stuff and keep playing the harder stuff until pretty soon you are through it.

"Louis Myers was playing this club with Junior Wells, Fred Below, and his brother, David. He heard me playing some harmonica and walked up to me and said, 'I'm going to show you this one time.' He showed me what it was, and that's been my signature lick in harmonica, the octave sound that you hear when I open up playing 'Leaving Trunk.' Paul Butterfield used to wear me out asking me to play that thing over, and he still couldn't figure it out."

Taj sees the search to discover his unique voice as a development over time, not a never-ending search. "It's like education. I don't think that you can be educated, as much as you are in a process of constantly educating yourself all throughout your life. I was really aware that a lot of the songs that I was singing were songs that were done by other people, and I wondered when was I gonna be able to talk about what was happening in my life.

"It began in the beginning of the '60s and then finally started developing over the years of listening and respecting the different types of dialects that this music came out of. There are a lot of people that don't recognize that. It's like going to any country where there are different kinds of dialects. You have to learn how to speak it, you and people, to really get the best out of it."

In this way, Taj is today's modern link between the traditions of the past and the ear of today. Many who followed these men merely summarized what had already been played. Taj intertwined varied and diverse musical spices into an original musical gumbo. He began pioneering arrangements where popular folk instruments from yesterday, like the banjo, dulcimer, flutes, and tubas, could be added to traditional musical forms.

That set the stage for the eclectic nature of his first three albums on Columbia. Taj threw out the industry rulebook and combined African American musical forms, like spirituals, work songs, blues, R&B, soul, and rock and roll, with calypso, reggae, Cajun, and funk, in bold recordings that defied industry labels and revived forms overlooked by myopic studios. His musical output from those days has held up as the most seminal recordings of the 1960s blues revival. There is a timeless quality to the music and words of real blues, as if its universal message is channeled from voices in the past through voices in the present. The proof of Mahal's vision is in the fact that his groundbreaking debut albums, *Taj Mahal* and *The Natch'l Blues*, released at a time when psychedelic ruled, have indeed stood the test of time. These early albums recorded by Taj reside in that timeless realm.

"Once I discovered what the game was, by the end of the '60s I had put out three major albums. The third one, *Giant Step/De Old Folks at Home*, was the roadmap which everybody for the next 25 years is going to use to really see how to take an old song and hear it in its raw entirety and to develop it either as inspiration for or the actual vehicle to this highly powered and charged music. Once the industry saw that, they basically just left me in the dust. Everybody's all surprised when these young guys today, like Ben Harper, Alvin Youngblood Hart, Corey Harris, Keb' Mo', and Fruteland

Jackson, started popping out and my name came up everywhere as the inspiration." In fact, many of these younger African American musicians pay tribute to Taj, whether in song, like Keb' Mo's "Henry" (Taj was born Henry St. Clair Fredericks in 1942), or in the eclectic approach of recordings like Hart's *Territory* or Harris' *Greens from the Garden.*

In addition to offering traditions to the aforementioned energetic nucleus of African American blues kids, it's also fairly common today to see Taj paired with his musical forebears. He'll sit graciously and speak musical dialects with men like Honeyboy Edwards and Pinetop Perkins, or man an unobtrusive standup bass behind the senior artists of the Music Maker Relief Foundation. Whatever the setting, Taj pulls no punches in lecturing audiences on the importance of this precious music. At one noisy Music Maker show, he chided, "This is traditional American music that the music industry has avoided all these years. Place yourself in the absolute level of respect of what's going on. I don't know how you were raised in your house, but in my house, when you see gray on the face of a person, you give them respect."

Offstage, he sees and explains the importance of this effort in the line. "These are my elders, and I've been given an opportunity to work with these musicians. I'm indebted to these people for staying the course so that I had something to hear. Etta Baker's 87 today and someone I listened to in the 1960s. One of the signature chords in my guitar vocabulary comes from her version of 'Railroad Bill.' I'm playing with Cootie Stark, and because I understand the style we can play right off the top—it goes like this and we're down the road. Cootie has got songs that I have never heard. I'm listening to the lyrics because they are really great and knocking me out. He's 74 and still writing songs.

"As creative consultant, my job is really to stay out of the way of the music. We want the music to feel natural and not feel handled. I'm also a consultant with Tim Duffy when we're doing the business side of things, like making connections with the type of sponsorships which will bring this foundation up even higher."

When he rechristened himself Taj Mahal in 1965, he metamorphosed into the *griot*, the caretaker and preserver of the music, the modern link in the chain of African American oral traditions, the true connection between the many diverse forms of African American music and any student willing to listen. It has been this study of all African American music forms that consumes the life, soul, and being of Taj.

Bob
Margolin

Steady Rollin' Bob Margolin boasts a musical experience few others can claim. From 1973 to 1980, Margolin, who was in his 20s, was the guitarist behind the legendary Muddy Waters. From that seat onstage, Margolin offers the clearest inside view of Muddy and the blues.

Though there are many lessons Muddy taught Margolin, two stand out. "He taught me the language of his style of Chicago blues. The ensemble sound Muddy's famous for was still very much happening when I was part of the group. Rather than lead and rhythm, I learned how each part—guitar, harmonica, and piano—blended with the others. He also taught me his sense of timing. He had a very highly developed sense of rhythm. Trying to get used to it and make it my own way has been very important to me. A lot of today's players don't play with that swinging, behind-the-beat style of playing that he had. It wasn't natural to the way I was playing, so it took me awhile to feel comfortable with that. That's part of what makes the blues not just sound good, but feel good."

The call to be a musician was deeply rooted in Margolin as a youth. A youth from suburban Brookline, Massachusetts, Margolin and his band were playing at all the Boston blues clubs. "I started playing when I was in high school. But when I was in college, I was playing and going to school at the same time and they were working against each other. One of the guys in my band told me to figure which one I was going to concentrate on, that I couldn't do both. Everything was very easy after that. When I heard Muddy Waters, that really slammed me into music pretty heavy. Just hearing his records. The first time I saw him was at the Jazz Workshop in Boston. It was the most powerful music I ever heard in my life."

In 1973, when he was only 21, Steady Rollin' Bob Margolin
joined Muddy Waters's band on guitar.

From there, Margolin began opening for bands like Muddy or just hanging out in places like the Unicorn, the Psychedelic Supermarket, and the Boston Tea Party, watching the shows. The call to the majors was equal parts being in the right place at the right time and being very ready.

"I met him when I opened shows for his gig, and he had been very encouraging to me because I was trying to play his style of Chicago blues. It worked out that he'd just fired Sam Lawhorn on a Sunday night. When he came to town the next day to play Paul's Mall, I was the next guitar player he saw, and Mojo Buford suggested to him that we try it. I didn't sit in, but Muddy asked me to bring a guitar to his hotel room the next day and I impressed him by playing old Chicago blues. The opportunity was there. And because I was very dedicated to his music, I was very aware what it would mean. I knew this would be a great opportunity to learn and take a step into the blues world.

"The first night I played with him, I was just tryin' to get in there and play with what everybody else was doin'. In the beginning, there were a few weeks of honeymoon period. I was trying as hard as I could to play the music the way I thought he wanted me to. For a year or so, I probably wasn't hitting it the way he wanted me to. It really took a few years before I began to feel a strong position in the band. But he was very patient.

"Early on, I would invite myself back to his hotel room after a gig, trying to get him to explain what I could do to avoid the dirty looks. With his help and by positioning myself where I could watch Muddy play, I began to learn how to give him what he wanted to hear. Muddy used to tell me, 'My music is so simple, but so few people can play it right.' He told me that trying to play his music right would hurt, like being in love."

Years and incidents distill to sentences and paragraphs that illuminate the special character of Muddy Waters and others. "The hardest thing to learn from Muddy or the band was a really basic thing that happened right at the beginning of my playing with them. Muddy had a very behind-the-beat feel to his music. You'll tend to want to hit a note before he does. Unless you're up there on the bandstand with him, you don't realize how far behind it is.

"Trying to get that behind-the-beat feel right at the beginning was definitely something that I had to work on before it felt natural. However, once I got used to it, I can't hear music any other way. That's part of what makes Muddy's sound so distinctive. People like Muddy play for tone. Whatever key you're in has a very strong harmonic center that you keep coming back to. That's the best way to describe it musically, but they're also putting a lot of feeling into everything they did to make their stuff sound that way."

To further immerse himself in Muddy's music, Margolin stayed with Muddy whenever the band was playing in and around Chicago. There he'd play Muddy's old songs, tryin' to get it right. Once while Waters relaxed in the kitchen, Margolin sat in the living room and played "I Can't Be Satisfied." "That had been my favorite song long before I'd met Muddy. Each time I tried it, I heard 'Wrong!' from the living room. As well as I thought I knew the song, there were subtle nuances I was missing that were crucial to Muddy, and only by having him sing it for me live was I finally able to play it without him saying anything."

And there were not-so-gentle reprimands from Muddy too. "They were not nurturing, New Age people. When he didn't like what I was playin', Muddy wouldn't tell me the right thing to play. He'd say something like, 'Don't play that again, it makes my dick hurt.'"

In addition to the guitar, Margolin also heard Muddy's commanding voice every night. "You don't get much more powerful than Muddy Waters voice onstage. It's pretty fair to say he really didn't have one little trick. He could sing soft and vulnerable and could also probably throw more testosterone around than anybody.

"Muddy was pretty special, in that he could affect people with his music both in a spiritual way and the personal way too. You can certainly hear the spiritual power he had in the way he plays. The charisma and charm Muddy Waters had was wrapped up in the fact that he was able to affect people spiritually and excite them by what he played."

Standing so close to the core of Chicago blues, Margolin was exposed to rare facets of early Chicago blues. It's one thing to listen from the outside through recordings—it's another matter to be inside the music every night. "Jimmy Rogers told me about the early days in Muddy's band. They didn't just walk on the bandstand and do it; they actually put a lot of stuff together. After the shows, Muddy, Little Walter, and Jimmy Rogers would ride around and really analyze the music, take it apart, and plan and arrange things to go together. Within that band, Walter and Jimmy were considerably younger than Muddy. They were interested in more modern developments that were going on. Jimmy told me that they pulled him towards expanding the musical level, and Muddy kind of kept them grounded in the old stuff. That made their combination pretty exciting.

"Jimmy told me that when Walter tried chromatic on 'I Just Want to Make Love to You,' Muddy told him, 'Don't rehearse on my session!' but that Muddy really liked Walter's innovations when he heard it played back.

"The ensemble sound Muddy's famous for was still very much happening when I was part of the group. It wasn't a question of somebody playing lead guitar and somebody else playing rhythm guitar behind. It was more like a first and second guitar, so that each part blended with each other. I really wanted to get deep into the old style. The type of music that really speaks to me the most of any style is the early Chicago blues.

"There wasn't a whole lot of practice going on when I was in Muddy's band. That ensemble feel is something you just get used to onstage after a while. You find your part, kind of know what you're going to play. I still work with the Tribute Band every now and then, and it's the same groove and the same type of things are taking place from that period. That's what's exciting about a small band—there's a lot of ESP happening, without a lot of things in the way to dilute the power of it.

"For the most part, we stopped playing that style. There were just too many people in the band at that time to play the tight, three- or four-piece ensemble music of those early Chess days. We had a large band, and sometimes the hippest thing to do was to find a part that no one else was doing and stay out of the way."

Through his six-year stint, Margolin was present at Waters' lowest point, in the early 1970s, and also his subsequent rebirth on Blue Sky in the latter part of the decade. "I'd say Muddy's low points at Chess were the *After the Rain* and *Electric Mud* albums. Those came in the late '60s for him. The *Hunk 'n Funk* album was a piece of shit. The producer of that, Ralph Bass, actually did a "We'll fix it when we mix it" to the band. He had the genius idea of recording another version of 'Rollin' and Tumblin'.' That's just what the world needed. In the middle, he came running out of the booth yelling and screaming like there's a fire. The song completely falls apart and starts up again, and he said, 'We'll fix it when we mix it.' It's all right on the album. There's no way that you can interpret it as anything other than a big mess."

Under Johnny Winter's guidance in the late 1970s, Waters scored with three Grammy-winning albums. "It was certainly an honor being on those records, period; however, on most of them, it seemed like there were too many people playing on them. I thought it might have been more effective to have done some of those songs with smaller groups of musicians in the older style of the early ensembles of Muddy. With the larger group, it's hard to isolate on a single musician and listen to the part he plays. On Muddy's recordings, it felt like sometimes there was an extra person or two," recalled Margolin.

"I really learned about running a band from Muddy's good example. He was a very special bandleader on the bandstand. So many good people came out of his band because he would give everybody a chance to play. He used to say, 'If you got a star on the bandstand, you gotta let him shine.' Before he'd come up at every show, he gave the band a chance to play a few instrumentals, even sing if you wanted to. Onstage he would always give out solos and introduce the people in the band."

Ironically, it was business problems with the band in 1980 that caused a split between Muddy and the band. "Towards the end of the time with the band, there were some business problems. Rather than sitting down with the band and talking about them like a family, Muddy let things happen with management, and that turned out to be a situation where everybody, especially Muddy, lost out. That taught me if there's something to straighten out, the band needs to sit down and straighten it out."

Margolin is of the generation of players who put forth an honor-the-father approach to these elders of the blues they played with. For him and others it was more important to be validated by playing the music right. Just as he looked to be validated, he saw Muddy seeking the identical nod from his elders. "There's an album called *Blues with a Feeling*, which are recordings from Newport in the 1960s. Son House was supposed to play and didn't make it, so Muddy went up solo. At one point he did something that sounded and felt like Son, and he said, 'Got the old man pretty good right there.' That's how I felt playing with Muddy. Listening to him say that about someone he idolized was the way I felt about him.

"I see how the stuff is passed on. There does seem to be an informal thing that when older guys see a younger player going for it, they are very encouraging and will take him under their wings, tryin' to teach or show stuff. I remember that a lot of the legendary musicians were that way with me. That was an incredible thrill, and I try to do that with younger ones too over the years.

"For me, that translates to a daily thing that, when I play, I feel that they are watching me, and I know whether they would approve or not. The strange thing is that I have actually had the experience of standing next to Muddy or Jimmy Rogers and had them actually approving or disapproving. In 1990, I did some gigs overseas with Jimmy Rogers. One night while I was playing, he was sitting behind me all night long. I know he was hearing everything I did and judging it. I feel like that is happening all the time, whether they are there physically or not. I still feel Muddy onstage nightly. Even today, I get a spiritual disapproval from Muddy. Those are the kinds of things that happen all the time."

As vital as the music lessons were, Margolin saw more crucial life lessons through the eyes of these men. "They really knew how to forgive and forget. Somebody might get angry with another one day and get over it the next day. I saw how they dealt with the white world. As a suburbanite from Brookline, Massachusetts, I never had to face the same black/white issues they dealt with. Muddy had a very realistic sense of where he was. He was proud of his accomplishment, but he also knew that some band who started last week with a hit on the radio would make a lot more money than he would. Most of the time he just understood it and he'd go out there and play his set.

"One time he got really pissed off. We were playing on the North Shore of Massachusetts in 1977 or 1978. There was a band out called Ace with a song called 'How Long.' Somebody put Muddy on a show with them and put Muddy on first. In the dressing room, I do remember him saying, 'These guys started last month and I've been out here all these years—shit!' That time it bothered him, and that was by far the exception. Most of the time he knew how the world worked and didn't bitch about it. This time he went out there and didn't leave anything for those poor guys. He certainly had the power to do that. He didn't leave anything. He had an awful lot of musical strength, and anytime he wanted to he could rip a place up."

Those life lessons are relevant in regard to Margolin's place in the blues. As the third white member of Muddy's band, Margolin faced the inevitable comments by some that Muddy should only hire black band members. Margolin dismisses any racial boundaries put on the blues. "In the seven years I played with Muddy, none of the band members ever brought up the subject of race. They simply felt if you could play, you could play. Muddy Waters trusted me with his music. That's my validation. Nobody could take that away from me.

"I would be a much different person without these men. They gave me a real perspective and depth and set an example. They set a musical bench-mark that you'll never get to. There's a lot of inspiration there. Today's younger players miss something by not having these men to learn from."

After the breakup of Muddy's band in 1980, Margolin did not sign on with the Legendary Blues Band. Instead he lived in Virginia and played the small blues-bar circuit throughout the mid-Atlantic states with local musi-cians. "I could see that towards the end of the '80s that scene was drying up. If I wanted to continue making a living doing this, I had to start getting out on the national level. The earlier I could have started, the easier it would have been. But I sure did have a less stressful time in the '80s, and I was still making the best music I could make. It was pretty hard to do by the time I had decided to get out on my own."

Today, Margolin's band plays from Muddy's "less is more" blueprint. "That gets the most outta my own guitar playing. The band is starting to understand call and response and how to fill in the cracks. That's what's exciting about a small band—there's a lot of ESP happening, without a lot of things in the way to dilute the power of it.

"There are just three of us. Sometimes we work with guitar-harp-drums and sometimes two guitars and drums. When we don't use bass, I'm play-ing guitar in an early Chicago blues style that thumps bass notes and picks lead lines at the same time. It's more primitive and down-home. Whatever style of music we play, we listen to each other and respond to each other and frame each other. We don't just stand there and play our instruments' standard parts, and we don't sound like bands who do. This is a combina-tion of Muddy Waters's influence, more what he used to do with Little

Walter and Jimmy Rogers than when I was in the band, and what I've learned and developed over thousands of gigs."

The 1990s were especially busy for Margolin. From 1997, he's toured with piano legend, Pinetop Perkins. "When we played in Muddy's band together, I stood onstage between Pine and Mud, and those times were the deepest blues music I will ever experience. Though most of my shows are still done with just me and my band, the many times in the last few years that Pine has been our featured guest are a pure pleasure for me. We try to back him up gracefully and to inspire him to play his best. I enjoy that there is a range of age on our bandstand that spans 62 years between Pine and my bassist/harp/guitar player Tad Walters, with all of us playing the same blues. Pinetop is getting the recognition he deserves now; when I introduce him, fans rush the stage like he was Elvis."

There is also time spent in the Muddy Waters Tribute Band and backing many other Chicago legends. He is a senior writer for *Blues Revue*, with a monthly column. And he is on the Blues Foundation's Board of Directors. Each affords a unique chance to pass on his opinions and lessons.

"Blues is at the crossroads today. It certainly is hard to make a living with the style of music. There's a lot more people trying to play blues today. And though the audience is growing, I doubt it's growing fast enough to support everybody. The entertainment dollar is just getting stretched too thin. It's hard for this music to compete with other forms of entertainment that spend billions to promote themselves. The blues jam that was an incubator and was very vibrant in clubs in the '70s is not happening today as clubs are turning towards other forms of music to happen on their off nights.

"It's very exciting for me as a player to keep Chicago blues alive and growing. But I think the fans themselves are really going to save the music. What separates blues from other forms of music is it's real soulful music and down-to-earth music. So in that way it's attractive to soulful people. If you go out to a blues festival or a blues bar, people in the audience are, generally speaking, not going to be your mainstream Americans who eat whatever they're being served in the media. That's one of the nice things about this music, it brings those kinds of people together."

As everything eventually comes full circle, Margolin today completes the direct line running from Muddy. Margolin's other willing student today is Big Bill Morganfield, son of Muddy Waters. Margolin was instrumental in selling Morganfield to Blind Pig and backing him with former Muddy sidemen to reproduce pure Muddy. Whenever Big Bill duets with Margolin, there is an eerie feeling in the room that Muddy's looking down, smiling at the musical sons his music fathered.

Dave
Maxwell

O nce a fundamental element in the sound of the blues, the piano has been relegated to second-class status by today's guitar-driven blues band. Though its nuances and subtleties have been lost for the larger audience, a dedicated few players still honor the traditions of geniuses as far back as Pine Top Smith and the boogie-woogie pros of the 1930s and synthesize Chicago techniques into the sound they produce today.

Boston's David Maxwell is such a keyboard player. Born in 1950 in Lexington, Massachusetts, a suburb of Boston, Maxwell studied classical piano as a child before moving to jazz and pop as a teenager. But it was hearing the sound of Otis Spann in the old Muddy Waters band that struck a chord. "It was a real eye opener when I first heard him, because it was so different from the commercial sounds around. Boston had the Club 47, the Jazz Workshop, the Unicorn, and Paul's Mall, so as a teenager I could see people I was hearing. I was tryin' to go and sit and play as much as possible. Once that seizes you, you can get really passionately involved," remembered David.

Maxwell recalled those early days in Boston, in the late 1960s. "There were a bunch of kids tryin' to soak up the blues at that point. Bob Margolin and I used to hang out together back then. It was real loose and informal playing then. I got a lot of encouragement from Muddy and the band. I had been sitting in with Muddy, and I did play a gig or two with him at the Jazz Workshop when Spann was sick. That was a real thrill. That's where I first met Paul Oscher, Luther "Snake" Johnson, and S.P. Leary. I wish I had been a regular member of the Muddy Waters band. But with Spann and Pinetop Perkins, it was a tough lineup to crack."

Maxwell had lessons in classical music, and Spann was a self-taught pianist, yet the love and dedication to the music brought them together.

***Pianist David Maxwell toured with Freddie King and Bonnie
Raitt in the early 1970s. Even today, he still sits and learns
from 88-year-old Pinetop Perkins.***

"Otis was very encouraging towards me. It wasn't as though he would teach
me anything. He would sort of let me peer over his shoulder. I'd say, 'Is this
how you played that? Is this it?' He would say, 'This is the way I do it.' He
never said what I was doin' was wrong. I made sure I was here when he was
around, to absorb some of that stuff. I was really infatuated and involved
with the music, so any time with him was very concentrated learning.

"The greats like Spann are hard to copy, because the stuff is so tricky. It
sounds so simple because it just rolled off of him. It was so much an intrin-
sic part of his nature. It wasn't like he was tryin' to play like Otis Spann—
he was Otis Spann."

Spann led Maxwell to those from whom Spann assimilated his style.
This led Maxwell back to Big Maceo, Sunnyland Slim, Johnny Jones, and
Memphis Slim.

"Piano blues was developed from various traditions, starting from the
earliest regional players with very rudimentary or primitive styles. Then the
early boogie-woogie styles developed in the late 1920s. Meade Lux Lewis
and Albert Ammons and Pete Johnson. That's stuff I play a lot and really
enjoy. It's a definite challenge and a nice vehicle to achieve a certain freedom to separate your mind and hands. I think by the '30s a lot of those

styles were set. You can trace the history of these pieces through the record-ings. Then there was the revival in the late 1930s of the boogie style. That was one approach.

"Antecedents of the blues piano in the style of Otis Spann were in play-ers like Sunnyland Slim, Memphis Slim, Leroy Carr, Little Brother Montgomery, Roosevelt Sykes. They had a more melodic, linear sense in their playing and not so much insistence on keeping the driving rhythm in the left hand. There's more of a contemporary ensemble feel, where the phrasing and spaces were very essential."

Like many others, Maxwell was fortunate to have been around soaking up the music at the tail end of the Delta blues revival in the 1960s. As a teenager, he heard Son House, Skip James, and Bukka White, and jammed onstage with John Lee Hooker and Big Mama Thornton in 1969 and 1970, when they came through Boston. Pretty impressive stuff for a 20-year-old.

Equally impressive was the early lesson Skip James offered Maxwell at a Philadelphia gig. "A few friends rounded up an upright piano for Skip James before he died. I was there and I wanted to impress Skip with my playing. I was doin' my best to pound out an Otis Spann impression. He heard me and he stopped me and said with that gentle voice, 'You're alright. But you know, you hit the keys too hard. Why you hittin' the keys so hard?' Essentially, he wasn't a piano player, but he had an approach and style that very gently caressed the keys and allowed for plenty of space in the phrasing.

"My style was too wild, because I was all over the place. That was my thinking back then. As a person, I'm pretty imaginative. There's a certain style associated with blues piano players coming from the Delta to Chicago. It doesn't mean you're all over the keyboards. It means you have to provide certain support and certain phrases and certain key chords at certain times and it's all part of this intricate framework. I understand a lot more about that now than I did then. It took me a long time to develop a sense of phras-ing and stroking the keys to where it became more playing with the music instead of playing at it."

Maxwell describes his techniques as trying to stick to the basics of blues piano traditions and extending it by playing in a way that also emphasizes chordal phrases. "What I'm doing is taking the blues form and materials and vocabulary and trying to work them in my own way. Blues is primarily a vocal art, and the music comes right out of that. I'm at a disadvantage because I can't bend the notes the way a guitar or harp can. But I try to make up for that in the way I touch the keys, in the way I use inflections to approximate vocal techniques."

Though theoretically complicated, the music that is produced sounds so simple. "Kim Wilson's right when he said, 'If it's so simple, how come so few people can play it right?' There are all these important lessons to learn before you can play this simple music correctly. That's what takes a musician a long time to learn."

The mid-1970s gave Maxwell the green light to show off onstage the styles and techniques he'd already accumulated in his style bag: first, Freddie King, the middle of 1972, for a year and a half; then Bonnie Raitt for about a year. There were bands in Boston like John Nicholas's Rhythm Rockers when Ronnie Earl was coming up that offered work until Maxwell finally joined James Cotton and Matt "Guitar" Murphy at the end of the decade. Each experience fit another piece into the musical jigsaw puzzle.

"Freddie King was an extraordinary guitar player and a huge man in his musical passions and human appetites. I was the first white guy who ever played in the band. For me, it was a bit unusual coming out of the suburbs of New England and plungin' right into that atmosphere. We played a fair amount in the South, and we did tours opening for Grand Funk Railroad and Creedence Clearwater Revival."

At that age and in that arena, a kid like Maxwell had to be brash to survive. "I was a little full of myself, and Freddie and I would spar a bit onstage. That was a time when all the piano players around Boston, like Ron Levy, Al Copely, and I, would bump shoulders at gigs and push each other off the piano bench as part of our good-natured head-cuttin' at gigs."

Playing with Raitt allowed Maxwell to meet and back Sippie Wallace and Arthur "Big Boy" Crudup. Between Raitt and Cotton, Maxwell was either in DC with the Nighthawks or playing in the house bands at the Speakeasy in Cambridge, backing touring Chicago legends like Johnny Shines, Robert Lockwood, Jr., Otis Rush, and Big Walter Horton. The decade closed out when Maxwell joined the original road warriors, Cotton and Murphy.

"In 1980, I was hangin' out and working in Paris for two years. I was playing at this little cave, and one night Memphis Slim and I did a joint gig together. In the 1980s, I was doing music mainly around Boston. I played with Buddy and Junior on gigs. It wasn't a big blues time as far as the commercial scene here. I've always been interested in doing jazz and studying ethnomusicology stuff, like world music and abstract sounds. I listen to more than just blues. I'm listening to all this music to try and be myself.

"When I do play, it's not like I try and imitate anyone like Spann or Pinetop, Sunnyland or Memphis Slim. In my solos, I try to get a little more personally involved so those other influences can come through. You might hear music with Middle Eastern or Indian influences reflected. When I play in a style, jazz or blues, I respect the music and respect the form and really feel like that's an essential part of me."

For those who never sat with Otis Spann or Memphis Slim and soaked up their blues, Maxwell can articulate the experience. "The urgency of Otis, Sunnyland Slim, and Memphis Slim—they were the music. There were times when you viewed their music critically, thinking it's an on or off night. That's the tendency of the mind, to discriminate and be critical, picking out intellectually what is good or bad. Essentially, they were themselves, and they were playing.

"Any performer will rely on certain songs at certain times for the maximum effect. But with them, there was no mistaking, whether it was Skip James, Son House, Memphis Slim, Otis Spann, or Muddy, that there was so much history within a song or note. I just try and bring that same kind of intensity to what I do. It comes naturally with me because of who I am and what I try to give to the music and impart to the listener."

In the 1990s, everything he studied surfaced in his playing. Writing his own original material now gives Maxwell freedom to mix in all his musical influences. "I don't know how that sits with blues purists. I don't consider myself a radical, I'm within the style. I know that I'm dealin' with blues, so I play the language and I'm not really gonna stray from it. I figure there's more honesty for me doing what I do than to string together a bunch of phrases I've copied. I absolutely depend on artistic creation every night I play. That's the reason why I do it, why I'm in this."

Maxwell continues to play in a variety of settings, from a jazz trio to a guitar, piano, harp band supporting James Cotton. Whatever the context, Maxwell naturally tries to involve and affect his audience. "My gigging with Cotton has a certain format. But some nights, even though I'm essentially playing the same tunes, there might be a more inspired turn in my playing. It's really in the way one plays them and communicates with the audience. To be able to really fire up an audience and get their juices flowing and then to follow it up with a slow, introspective piece which brings out a lot of healing vibrations is what I'm more concerned with in music than anything else, to communicate the healing power of the music."

I reminded Maxwell what Eugene Banks told Doug MacLeod, "It's not about you. The blues man is playing to heal the people."

"There you go. It's just naturally what I feel, to create a healing atmosphere for the people. Every once and a while, I become completely selfless and reach places where I'm out on a limb and not sure where I am. That's when the music is coming from another source and just pours through me. At that point there's no conscientious effort involved. I can't think, because when I think about where it's coming from, it stops. The audience knows it and we feed back and forth.

"I would see the showman take place with the older guys, but I would also see the introspective, creative exploration happen as well. People like

Skip James were totally into that. He was aware of what he was doing and very self-absorbed. Son House was also totally into that. Those older guys just did it. Hooker was always very into that. The first time I saw him at a coffee house in Boston, he just came in with a beat-up old guitar case, sat on the chair, and played. A lot of guys were conscientious of how to grab and hold an audience, be the showman. Once you do that, then you can start to communicate with them and build that healing space."

Today, Maxwell takes full advantage of every opportunity to share the bench and watch. "I met Mose Vinson in Memphis in the mid-1990s. What I learned from his 80 years of playing is the approach. It's an intangible feeling that you have to extrapolate. Though he doesn't have the vigor he once had, there is still a certain vigor there. Even at that point, there's a lot that I can learn about phrasing, spaces, and sensitivity. Like watching Pinetop: He doesn't play as many notes as he used to, but I can learn something about overall musicality. Every time I hear Pinetop, I listen carefully. I have a lot of respect for him. The way he approaches music overall and the way he takes what he has and makes something of it is the true mark of a master. Just when you don't expect anything, he hits the spot.

"Charles Brown is another master player I've met. When Bonnie brought him on the road, he had his own dressing room with a piano in it. When I met him, we played about an hour for each other. Before he died, I talked with him whenever he was here.

"Whether it's done through blues or jazz, music makes the whole atmosphere around and among people more harmonious. For me, that's the thing. There's also the personal growth at each gig. I'm never fully satisfied with my playing, so I constantly maintain a critical eye, and I learn more about myself and my playing every time out. That's all part of the process I follow."

Paul
Rishell

The time-honored blues relationship between experienced hands and youthful exuberance is at the heart of Paul Rishell and Annie Raines's connection. Rishell plays master craftsman to Raines's apprenticeship.

"I feel particularly blessed having a partner like Paul, because he's one of the biggest influences on my musical life," said Annie. "To me, he's one of those guys, one of the masters. His understanding of the music and life runs so deep. That's brought up things in me musically that may have taken a lot longer to have surfaced."

Finger-picked, prewar country blues was always at the core of Rishell's soul. Then, in 1992, at his wife Leslie's suggestion, he teamed with Raines's fragile, acoustic harmonica and unwittingly began the transfer of intimate lessons to a willing student.

"The first gig I did with Annie was an acoustic gig. I had played with lots of harmonica players and hated them all, because they all just played everything they knew and force-fit it into everything I was doing. I was surprised that she stayed out of the way so much. When we were done, I thought, 'Well, this was cool—she didn't step on me at all.' It was because she paid attention. I really appreciated that quality," said Rishell.

Within this partnership, Paul's lifetime of studied immersion in the prewar country blues idiom has brought forth a youthful counterpart willing to absorb his lessons and carry them forward. "Paul has taken me into an aspect of the music I'd never really studied. Until Paul, my concept of country blues started and ended with Jimmy Reed. Using Paul's library, I started doing my own homework. From him I learned about Son House, Charley Patton, Blind Lemon Jefferson, Scrapper Blackwell, Leroy Carr, and all these amazing people. What I began to get out of this was why the music

***Paul Rishell says, "If you begin studying blues with Robert
Johnson, you are really starting in the middle. You need to go
. . . to Son House, Charlie Patton and Tommy Johnson."***

has endured all these years. The fact that they were able to make something
so beautiful is really a testimony to the genius of so many of these country
blues players.

"But it's also been learning by playing with him. His knowledge runs
very deep and is very extensive, because he's been studying this form of
blues for his entire life. He has a real talent and an awareness of the nuances
in the music. He's got an ear for the best parts of the music. Those little

nuances in the songs that Paul was aware of are the reasons the music has carried on this long. Those are the parts of him that tended to be overlooked by many people," said Raines. "It's not just the fact that it's 12 bars per verse; there are an awful lot of things on different levels within the music. It's the elegance of the music and the lyrical qualities of it that made it not only enduring but exciting. Too many young players gloss over the good parts and aren't playing the country blues right. Basically they are only playing the easy parts. If they paid attention to the nuances, then they would be playing the music right."

This attention to the details of the music has been central to Rishell's circuitous musical journey. Though he began as a drummer in the early '60s and listened to classic jazz drummers like Max Roach and Slam Stewart, it was a friend's Son House Library of Congress 1941 recordings and *Blues, Rags, and Hollers,* by Koerner, Ray, and Glover on Electra, that turned on the blue light.

"When I heard Son House," remembered Rishell, "I realized, 'Now I get it.' What I heard when I heard Son House play was the drums. Country blues is very percussive. In fact, all black music is centered around the rhythm and percussion. I heard the percussion in his music. So being a drummer, I was very turned on to what House was able to do on a guitar. I think I had an electric guitar as early as 1961, but I really started fooling around with guitar in 1966, when I was about 16. It wasn't until I heard Son House that I realized you could play a guitar like the drums. Back then, I was learning how to play the guitar in a way no one else even knew about. The guys I was in bands with were playing Beatles songs; I'd show them Son House records, and they couldn't stand the sound."

From there, Rishell, like so many white players from the '60s, took the journey backwards. "My line of vision was always going backwards, sort of retroactively. I was learning the music in a solitary fashion, sitting in my bedroom, getting it off the records. I remember my parents coming to me with these concerned looks on their faces because I'd be locked in my room for hours playing and listening," laughed Rishell. His trips from Connecticut to New York City ended up in the funky record shops where blues hounds could find recorded treasures. Rishell's first country blues purchase was the Yazoo *Masters of the Delta Blues, The Friends of Robert Johnson* record, with songs by Kid Bailey, Willie Brown, and Tommy Johnson and seven cuts by Son House before his 1941 sessions. "I didn't know this, but Son House's 1931 sessions were on the *Masters of the Delta Blues* record: 'My Black Mama, Parts 1 & 2' and 'Dry Spell Blues.' I was even more impressed with those recordings because he was a younger guy and it sounded much more urgent."

Through these early country blues recordings, Rishell began to understand the lasting power of the blues. "That music was made at a time when people made things from a different point of view. It was a time when sentimentality was a very prized thing in entertainment. You begin to see how people like Leroy Carr, Tampa Red, and Robert Johnson all made music that was meant to last. The aspect of making something that was made to last was part of the music, part of the work ethic of the time. Lemon Jefferson's been selling records since 1927, and he hasn't stopped yet. The power of Son House singing 'Death Letter Blues' after 60 years is still as intense and passionate as it was when first recorded. That tells me this is music meant to last. Today, you get people making disposable music for today only.

"Blues music is very different. I know the original core of the music will always stand. Blues works simultaneously on so many different levels. Remember, blues is an approach to life and life problems, so you can make anything blues. Blues is music of people waking up to themselves, the quality of introspection. If you're a thinking person, this music will speak to you. Most people who don't know that about blues don't really understand blues. You have to know that it's a profound thing and really study it. Without that people will have trouble really understanding it. I'm afraid that what's happened to blues today."

It was Rishell's meeting Son House in 1972 that solidified the personal delivery of country blues Rishell assimilated from records. Dick Waterman, who was managing House at the time, called Rishell and said to bring his guitar over to Waterman's office. "When I went in, there with his old black guy sitting on the couch. When Dick introduced us, I just had to sit down.

"When people ask me what Son House was like, I tell them it was like meeting Jesse James or one of those Old West gunslingers. I have a lot of respect for these men. I treated him with the respect you would give anyone who lived to that age, especially living the kind of life people like Son did. He told me many stories about growing up down South, about God and the Bible.

"He always talked in a very colorful, beautiful way. He said things to me like, 'You don't have to pound on the guitar, you can play it softly. You're still a young man and you don't have to go down the blues path. It's really a hard road and people will forsake you. People talk behind your back.' He cautioned me every day. The last thing he would say to me would be, 'Think it over, son. It's not too late for you.' There was a lot of that kind of advice.

"My opinions on him and my recollections of him as some disconnected voice I'd heard on the record player when I was 13 years old changed so radically after listening to him in person, playing with him, and talking with him. Those second impressions made me feel like I was doing the right thing by playing this music. If I had any doubts earlier, they had all been eradicated after the last time I said goodbye to him.

"What I learned watching Son House singing, and you don't know this unless you're sitting there actually playing with him or watching him, but what struck me about him and later on Howlin' Wolf or Johnny Shines was they were singing with a tenderness, giving the song a wistful, lilting quality that, if you don't notice, will go right by you.

"The music of Son House is a Zen thing, because if you don't give in to it, then it's not working. The blues is something that you can take out of your pocket, and it'll make you feel better. It'll work. It has all those qualities. It's a science that they invented. Even though there is an aura of self-defense in country blues, the singer is emoting from a position of power. The power is there to protect you, on many different levels. It's like looking into a fire. You can look into a fire forever because it's always changing, and yet it remains constant. That's the blues; it's constant, and like a fire it's constantly changing."

In all his dealings with these musicians, like House, Shines, and Wolf, Rishell always gave them the requisite respect he felt they deserved. "I tried to get a sense of them as people living in the world every day and how their music was a response and reaction to the world. The music I could get off records anytime; the stories about living in Louisiana in 1928 or Mississippi in the 1930s were things I wanted to know about.

"Very early on I absorbed the ideas of what the music was after. Hearing it come from their voices just validated that the thoughts and theories I had were on the right track. It gave me the whole basis to continue. At the point that I met Son, I wasn't particularly in need of any kind of a validation. I was still young at the time and I probably didn't appreciate it. I wish now that I had an opportunity to sit and talk with him, because I would ask him such more penetrating questions than I did.

"I have to say that Son House was the greatest natural musician I ever played with. The way he played, combined with his singing, was very dynamic. House wanted church to be his thing, but he couldn't get into it. I remember his last wife wouldn't let him play blues in the house. She'd hide his slide somewhere in the house to keep him from playing. He once told me, 'Blues must have been a sin, because it looked like so much fun.' He'd be in the basement playing, she'd come downstairs, and he'd change right mid-song into some gospel thing. She felt the blues was not a good thing because if you played blues you didn't belong to the church. And if you didn't belong to the church, you were an outlaw."

Other bluesmen were regulars at the Cambridge club scene. Like so many other young blues guitarists in the '70s, Rishell and his band opened for blues legends when they played Cambridge clubs. This provided Rishell the chance to sit with Howlin' Wolf and learn from Wolf and his guitarist, Hubert Sumlin. "Hanging around with guys like Wolf was another step of learning for me. I started talking to Wolf about Charley Patton. I knew he'd gotten guitar lessons from Charley Patton, and I knew that the howling falsetto thing was from Tommy Johnson. I asked Wolf about Charley Patton in order to get his take on him. Wolf'd say in his gruff voice, 'He was pretty good; I liked his singing.' Wolf told me that once he made Patton give him a guitar lesson all day. He said, 'I learned me more there with him in one day then I would in a whole lifetime.'

"Patton's playing is always high, so I asked Wolf about that. Wolf said he tuned it to where it felt good with his voice. From a clue like that, I really began to realize that singing was the most important playing the blues player could do. To tune the guitar to your voice, instead of trying to sing to the guitar. Then I began to see and understand that these guys would take things and change it around so it would became easy for them to play. They made the instrument work for them. Blues is a singing music. You make the guitar sound like the human voice, not the other way around. The singing part has been hard for me. I never think about the guitar part. If my singing is right, everything else will be right. I've worked very hard to make it nothing more than just honest singing. I try not to embellish it, use an accent, or pronounce words funny. I just try to sound like what I am.

"These were the little tricks I was learning from Hubert Sumlin or Son House. I began to realize that without knowing anything about music or music theory, what they did was that they made it fit what they needed. A lot of the insights I got about the music I got from hanging around these guys.

"To me music is my religion. I say to people I know, 'There's a God because there's music.' The dedication that I've given it for the last 30 years is unswerving. I've never done anything but try to bring the joy that the music gives to me to other people," said Rishell. "I want my records to be records that people are going to listen to in the same way that I listen to those early records."

Immersed for years in country blues, Rishell can easily slip into the master teacher role about other players or songs from the period. Most of his observations can open doors into the prewar country blues musicians and the important role records of the day played in shaping individuals and styles.

"The record labels were making decisions, and at the same time the great musicians who we all know we're taking advantage of those decisions. If you listen to Son House play in those 1941 sessions, 'The County Farm Blues' is actually 'See That My Grave Is Kept Clean.' He told me that he wrote that song at the 1931 sessions in Wisconsin that he recorded 'My Black

Mama' and 'Dry Spell Blues.' The man at the studio asked him if he could write a song with the same melody as 'One Kind Favor.' That was a big hit and the record label wanted people to cover it. House told me he went home and wrote that song overnight. He told me when he came back to the studio the next day, the guy didn't want to hear it, so he didn't record that song until ten years later. That's just another example of how record labels try to duplicate whatever popular melodies were being bought by people.

"If you study blues and begin with Robert Johnson, you are really starting in the middle. You need to go backwards from that. And the farther back you go, the harder it will get. People like Robert Johnson listened to records and took the easiest stuff they could. Kokomo Arnold takes something from Tampa Red and he plays it twice as fast. Then the last verse of his songs he sings, 'I believe I'll dust my broom.' Then Robert Johnson hears that line and he'd write an entire song called 'I Believe I'll Dust My Broom.' Elmore James comes along, records that song, has a huge hit with that, then even names his band the Broomdusters and lays claim to a signature riff. You see? Here's an obscure line from an Arnold song and 30 years later someone like Elmore James makes a career from it. The music is all interconnected.

"I usually write country blues tunes when I'm researching as many as five or six musicians in a row. It's more apt to happen then because as I'm studying and practicing, something different comes out within my playing. I may be copying these guys, but whatever is connecting us all is where my creativity comes out. When I get a judicious blend of guitar styles, I can usually come up with a song. Remember, this is exactly what they did. Robert Johnson took what Skip James recorded on piano as "22-20" and transformed the song into a guitar piece, "32-20 Blues," and made it his own. What you do with blues is take what you can from others and make it your own.

"What you do with blues is you take what you can, change the form, and make it your own. If you're really a great musician, the form will change to suit you. That's the beauty of the blues. You learn the form, you become the form, you change the form, and the form becomes you. This was the greatness of people like Leroy Carr or Tampa Red. I think Leroy Carr was one of the great all-time record makers of any era. He wrote and recorded some of the most beautiful records, like 'Mean Mistreater Blues' and 'How Long Blues,' modern blues that carried along some quality that this guy had in his voice. Carr realized right away that with the new microphone technology, he didn't have to yell on records. He realized the more you shout, the worse it sounds. He realized that he could use the technology to get intimate. I think that's one reason why he was such a phenomenal seller of records. In fact, 'How Long Blues' was such a popular song, it wore out the master and had to be recorded three times."

From the guitar seat, Rishell can speak about Raines and today's blues guitarists. "Annie's a phenomenally musical person with really exquisite taste. She never overplays. There's nothing about her playing that's ever self-aggrandizing. Too much music today, especially blues, is based on this idea of 'Watch what I can do.' To me, that's boring. Remember, blues is a feeling. No one loves guitar solos more than me. But man, I've heard 'em all. I think all the great guitar solos have been taken. So I'm not interested in how many guitar solos a guy can take or how many chords he can play. I play riffs, but it has to be part of the fabric of the music. The more I play, the less solos I take. All I have to do is sit there and play the music. That makes me happy."

What has a lifetime of study boiled down to? "You have to find your own voice and do something with it. I've been playing country blues for a long time. I'm out there to serve the music, to bring the music to people. And in the process I find myself too. Neither Annie nor I have to change who we are very much in order to complement each other in this partnership. We're very committed to serving the music and serving each other."

Duke
Robillard

In a musical genre ruled by the Kings—B.B., Albert, and Freddie—and populated by a wide spectrum of guitarists' styles, approaches, and techniques, one fact is unanimously agreed upon: a Duke named Robillard is in a class by himself.

Acoustic master John Hammond, who toured extensively with Robillard in the 1990s, said, "I just hear what he's doing and it moves me so much. He's just taken it so far. He's the real thing and somebody that I really truly admire. "

Fabulous Thunderbird founder Jimmie Vaughan has known Duke for over 20 years and recalls their first meeting: "I heard that Duke was really into T-Bone Walker. When I finally saw Duke, it was as if I had gone back in time and seen T-Bone as a young man. Ever since then, we've been friends and played a lot of gigs together."

After hearing Robillard, Big Joe Turner told T-Bone's widow, "You see? T-Bone's not dead!"

When Duke Robillard clicks on the guitar amp, he illuminates over 50 years of guitar approaches he has devoted his life to studying and furthering. From his start in 1967 as the 19-year-old founder of Roomful of Blues and his 12 years guiding its success, to his solo career in the '80s, to his replacing Jimmie Vaughan in the Fabulous Thunderbirds in the '90s and back full circle today with Duke Robillard's Pleasure Kings, few musicians have attained Robillard's world-class respect.

In his Roomful days, Robillard was fortunate to share the stage with the music legends he admired, like B.B. King, Freddie King, Muddy Waters, and Big Joe Turner. After Roomful, he joined first Robert Gordon, then Muddy alums in the Legendary Blues Band. Throughout the '80s, Robillard's own

***Says Jimmie Vaughan, "When I finally saw Duke Robillard,
it was like I was seeing T-Bone Walker as a young man."***

recordings alternated between a jazzy swing style and a roots-rock approach. Today, on his recordings, Duke has achieved a striking balance with his guitar. But it continues to be the live arena where Duke thrives.

Though a song list is taped to the floor, it is rarely adhered to. Within the first few songs, Duke feels the direction his performance will follow. At a sit-down club, he will delve into the pre-rock-and-roll swing of the '40s bands, like Buddy Johnson, T-Bone, and Louis Jordan and transport the audience on a jazzy, introspective exploration. At a blues saloon, Duke will channel the white-hot guitaring of Albert Collins, Guitar Slim, or B.B. King and pound a six-string euphoria into the Dukeheads seated at his feet.

"I start shows off with the same three or four songs, because I need a certain common ground to get warmed up. Once I'm warmed up, I like to follow whatever way I feel is right for the room or audience. I don't like to follow a strict direction. On my best nights I feel like I just take hold of it. Sometimes I pull out a lot of tunes nobody knows. That's when I'm at my freest, when I can just do anything that comes to my mind. It may not be at all arranged, but it just works," said Duke.

These are the nights Robillard probes into that unique zone every creative person pursues. "It's a special place that must be balanced with what you as a performer knows works, but with enough leeway so that when the inspirations come, you can follow them. Going to that place is not something that comes up every week for me. But I feel that maybe a small version of that happens every night.

"Then there are the nights where I can completely take a left turn from whatever we usually do. These are the kinds of things that make performing live so interesting. If I couldn't take those left turns, it would be too hard. It wouldn't be as much fun as it has to be to do it as many days as I have to each year. I need to keep it fresh for myself," said Duke.

It is these spontaneous "left turns" that render every Robillard show exceptional. There are live performers who play the same show year after year. Duke is always calling off material from the hip. Sax player Gordon Beadle notes, "His fans tend to be aware of all his records, so he likes to do stuff that the people will know or recognize from an older album."

In one show he may emphasize a 15-minute intro to T-Bone's "Glamour Girl" and then reach back and pluck "Gyp Jam" from his 1987 *Swing* album. Then his strapping string plucks will literally raise Guitar Slim from the dead on "Something to Remember You By." Ever the historian, Robillard may even go so far as to fire off "Floyd's Blues" and then explain to the clamorous bar crowd that it is considered the first song ever recorded on an electric Hawaiian guitar in 1935.

When musicians and fans talk about blues and jazz guitar techniques, they invariably divide into the intellectual and emotional approaches, like a Charlie Christian solo versus one by T-Bone Walker. Beadle explains: "The difference between Christian and T-Bone is their playing over changes. Charlie Christian is more likely to outline the chords by playing these jazzy linear lines that have a shape. You could almost draw a line in the shape of the notes. Where T-Bone is more likely to play a long lazy line or note that cuts through it all and fits over a big portion. Both styles are totally correct.

Some people say that outlining the chords is the more intellectual approach. But many people like the blues style because they say it's more emotional."

Robillard is a virtuoso in both styles. He works around the specifics of every chord and even adds or implies some that might not be there. From jamming with a vast body of blues and jazz players and from his unlimited listening experiences, Duke plays with both authenticity and knowledge of the vocabulary. "Duke shares with Matt Murphy the harmonic sense, the real ability to dig into the chord," continued Beadle. "But he can also play with the rawness of Guitar Slim and be real direct."

Jimmie Vaughan concurs with Beadle. "Duke knows jazz theory beyond the blues. We may be coming from the same place inside, but he knows a lot more technically. I'm more primitive. He can play along with a jazz group because he sat down and studied it."

However, Vaughan points out that it is the spontaneity within Robillard that breeds amazing guitaring. "One time I saw him playing a Strat and he picked the guitar up, put the bridge next to his lips, and blew onto the strings and made them vibrate with this really strange sound I've never seen since or before. It sounded like a harp or something. He's so spontaneous. I don't know if he knows these things are coming," exclaimed Vaughan.

Born in the unlikeliest of blues meccas, Woonsocket, Rhode Island, in 1948, Robillard knew by age six that playing the guitar and performing was the direction he was meant to pursue. "I decided when I was six that I was going to be a guitar player. My parents gave me a plastic ukulele. When I learned how to play it, I just knew this was what I was gonna do. I wanted to get an electric guitar and play. My parents said no. This was in 1954 or '55. That was a really scary period, because guys like Little Richard and Elvis were playing and they scared the hell out of a lot of people. My parents thought this was perverse stuff and were not gonna let their kid do this. I wasn't allowed to have a guitar, but both my brothers had one. When they would be out working or out on a date, I snuck theirs and taught myself to play. By the time I was 13, my uncle had given me an acoustic guitar."

To get his own electric, Robillard took the neck off his acoustic and convinced his father he had a school assignment to build an electric guitar for a science project. "He bought the story, and we built one together. I was in a band a week later," laughed Duke.

Robillard discovered blues from the flip sides of his older brothers' records. Chuck Berry's "Deep Feeling" and "Wee Wee Hours" were the first bite of Duke's blues. "I was 13; I didn't know what it was, but it just moved me. I didn't know what blues meant, but this music just grabbed me inside."

Critics assume that Robillard's encyclopedic knowledge was born of sitting alone in a room practicing for years. Duke explained it differently:

"Because I loved it, it was like a drug to me. For years, I listened to music really hard for a lot of hours a day. By doing that, I absorbed a knowledge that I can't put in words. But what comes out, it is the product of that listening. Muddy Waters, Guitar Slim, T-Bone, B.B., Freddie, Albert Collins, Lowell Fulson, Luther Tucker, Pee Wee Crayton, and Albert King. Even jazz guys like Charlie Christian, Tiny Grimes, and Willie Butler. I emulate those people because I'm just forever thrilled by that sound. When I do a tune that calls for those styles, I can't make up anything better, so I basically try to channel them and improvise within the framework they invented."

Growing up in Rhode Island had its blues advantages: Boston, New York, and the Newport Folk Festival. "I went to Newport when I was about 16 and saw Muddy Waters doing a workshop. It was the kind of thing where you could go up and just put your elbow on Otis Spann's piano. James Cotton was playing harp and Sammy Lawhorn and Pee Wee Madison on guitar, and Muddy. It was so riveting to see Son House, Howlin' Wolf, John Hammond, and Robert Pete Williams up close.

"Boston was a phenomenal scene in the 1960s. I remember taking the train to Boston on the weekends to see Junior Wells, with Lefty Dizz on guitar, in 1967 and then getting back on the train, sleeping on the ride to New York, and catching Muddy or John Lee Hooker that night at the Cafe a-Go-Go, then going back to work on Monday," said Robillard.

Roomful of Blues was born when Duke graduated high school. From its inception in 1967, Robillard's guitar, 15-year-old Al Copley's piano, and Fran Christina's drums dominated the early sound. "Roomful wasn't rock kids playing blues; we had the traditional thing from the start. We played material that really sounded like B.B. King's band minus the horns. Then we added Rich Latille and Greg Piccolo on saxes. We played for about six months with the horns and we thought that was great. I started collecting R&B records and finding Amos Milburn, Roy Milton, Ruth Brown, Wyonnie Harris, and all the R&B music that no white kids I knew ever heard. Then I found *Rock and Roll Stage Show*, by the Buddy Johnson Orchestra, and that record just did it. He was an R&B dance band from the late 1940s. After I heard Johnson, I said, 'This is the sound I've got to do.'"

Given the psychedelic and disco times, their reception in the Northeast was met with a certain amount of skepticism. "People just looked at us and wondered what the hell we were playing." Yet their regular Sunday night gig in the Westerly, Rhode Island, club The Knickerbocker started a jitterbugging trend. The club became the hip, trendy place to be. "Because it was near the beaches of Rhode Island, like Watch Hill and Newport, affluent people from all over the world would end up in those towns, hear about this, and come down. It became this real cult thing. I'll still meet people from all over the world that will yell, 'Play one for the Knickerbocker!'"

During those early years in the 1970s, Robillard was usually found sitting in with his idols. It was the first times he played with Big Joe Turner and Muddy Waters that immediately jump out. "Everything I've learned about music I learned from the older-school guys. For the styles they played, you're talking about two of the most absolute masters—Muddy for his place in Chicago blues, and Big Joe was one of the greatest blues shouters who ever lived. A big part of the blues shouters left in the last 20 years, like Jay McShann, Jimmy Witherspoon, and Jimmy Nelson, are all big fans of Big Joe and still do his material.

"I first played with Big Joe in the 1970s. I was with Roomful of Blues. We knew we were going to love backing him, but he was amazed that we knew what we were doing with his music. That was the night he told me he was going to tape us and bring it back to T-Bone's wife and tell her T-Bone's not dead. That was an important validation for me.

"Muddy was the same experience. The night I played with him for the first time, he said to me, "I don't know who you are, Duke, but if I had you and Hollywood Fats in my band, I could rule the world." After that, he got me onstage with him constantly. That was the validation that I belonged in that group.

"That was in the early 1970s and I was in my early twenties. It was the week that Bob Margolin joined. Dick Waterman had set it up for me to sit in with him, and Dick had cautioned Muddy that Roomful and I were his band and to not get too excited. Muddy was looking for a guitar player, and he said things that night like he was giving me an open invitation. 'Course my band and management all said no. That week, Bob auditioned and joined his band."

It took 12 years and the help of Doc Pomus to produce the first Roomful album in 1979. Immediately following, Robillard left. "At that point there were certain things I was frustrated with. Things really weren't developing in the direction I wanted to go. After doing this for a dozen years, I felt like it was time to make a change and concentrate on the small-band format and my guitar playing."

Though his musical work touched all the musical bases in the 1980s, it was in the 1990s that Robillard's musical stock skyrocketed. In 1990, he replaced Vaughan as the Thunderbird guitarist for two-and-a-half years, only to return to his solo pursuits. "I loved the Thunderbirds; I just missed being Duke." In addition to numerous solo discs, Robillard has been the guitarist du jour on CDs by Kim Wilson, Ruth Brown, John Hammond, Mark Hummel, Tony Z, Jimmy Witherspoon, Pinetop Perkins, Zuzu Bollin, Snooky Pryor,

Jerry Portnoy, Johnny Adams, Al Copley, and others. This barnstorming distinguishes him as one of the most sought-after guitarists in the blues.

As Robillard the player has grown within the music, he has become interested in its subtler aspects: sound and production. "Sound for me is a major thing. The sound of my instrument is something I'm really involved with. The honest truth is that if you are a good guitar player, you should only need one instrument to tell your story on. If I ever got stuck playing on one guitar, I could do that. But I am in love with the instrument and I'm in love with the nuances of tone you can coax out of different types of instruments. On my latest album I feel I've achieved a new level of tonality and coloring and even dynamics, where less notes are more complementary to the song. Though you'd never know it, I used 10 to 12 guitars. There are minuscule differences to the ear, but to me it's the feeling of playing that fits in the music.

"The only distortion effect I use is a tube screamer," continued Robillard. "That basically makes it so I don't have to put my amps on 10 to make the sound distorted. I can play the volume within the proper context of the band, like the Guitar Slim sound. If I were to get that out of an amp without a tube screamer, I would have to play so loud that it would be unbearable. Guitar Slim did and it was cool, but I prefer to keep it in balance within the confines of the band."

Production is the latest area in which Duke is becoming proficient. He has served as producer on recent discs by Hammond, Eddy Clearwater, Jimmy Witherspoon, Beadle, and Jay McShann, as well as his own albums. "As a songwriter, it's important to me to find the proper way to express whatever it is I'm trying to write. I've grown up playing a bunch of styles rooted in the blues, so I try to use whatever parts of the idiom I can. I explore whatever avenue that works for what the song needs.

"I enjoy the challenge of making rock, jazz, or blues music say what it says as well as it can say it. To make the artist sound like themselves is the most important thing a producer can achieve, and to make whatever you are trying to achieve with the music come through, whether it be a really lavish recording where the production end is very complex or the complete opposite, where the music is totally natural. It depends on what the artist is trying to achieve and what the mode of expression is to be. When I'm working with someone else, I always feel like I'm making my own album. If I'm producing, I feel like it's as much my album as it is theirs.

"It's a lot harder when I do both jobs. One thing about me is that I have a real good trust of my intuition. When I'm in a studio, I immediately know if I'm getting a song or track to work. But whenever I do it, I'm absolutely positive of what I'm going for. I really enjoy making the kind of records that expand on the musical knowledge I have. Sometimes I just have to use a certain part of me to get to a point, then go sit in a chair and listen as the producer. Even if it is very skeletal, I know what I need."

As the thrills of playing with Muddy and so many others are weighed against the years of blues dues paid to reach this level, Robillard can find a simple balance. "As I've gone forward and gone through changes, I've kept in touch with where I come from. I can still play things the way I remember playing them from that time. I've kept in touch with that."

Jimmie Vaughan says it best: "He's just an amazing guitarist. He's got it on all different angles. He's got an incredible tone, his technique is amazing, and when he solos he can go on for a week if he wants to and never do the same thing over and over. Though everybody copies somebody, Duke has the ability to get into each person's style and really wiggle around in there as if he was them. But more than that, he plays his own thing. That's how it's come together for him. I'm just tryin' to play my version of this music. It's important for me to have my own style and to play what's inside me. In that way, Duke is busy playin' his own art."

The legacy of Duke's "art" is heard in the countless Roomful-styled bands that have found success in New England and the guitarists who have found Robillard to be both inspiration and model. Many today feel that it was guitarists like Robillard who were responsible for the resurgence of the blues in the mid-1980s.

Within that massive context, Duke appreciates a more precious legacy. "The people I listen to are the people that I always listened to: T-Bone Walker, Freddie King, Charlie Christian, Billie Holiday, and Count Basie. The classics of blues and jazz are still what I draw all my inspiration from.

"Freddie Green always played an acoustic guitar in Count Basie's band and was the connection between the bass and the high hat. It's a really beautiful sound if it's mixed far back. It was like a harmony to the bass, but it also had the high end that connected the high hat. It was the glue for the rhythm section, with four beats strumming to every bar. It was a sound that was abandoned in the 1950s because they didn't want the restriction of the basic chords being laid down like that. I just love that sound and that feel. I could do that all night. It could be all that I do, and I'd be happy. It swings. I love it, and I'm tryin' to keep it alive."

Saffire—
The Uppity
Blues Women

I grew up in a houseful of women; I've deferred at my share of kitchen table discussions. So whenever I talk with the three women of Saffire—The Uppity Blues Women, I know my place. Sit quietly and listen.

"It's been hard to get recognition as musicians, and it still is. People think we're pigs on roller skates, just the novelty act of a major blues label. Nobody took the time to understand the professional musicianship we strive to bring to every show and recording," said Ann Rabson, the piano-machine grandmother who pushes the group.

Gaye Adegbalola, the recently tattooed guitarist, harmonica player, and prime songwriter of the acoustic trio, continued, "Certain press calls us blues lite. I think we've done more in bringing people to the blues than many of the artists out there because we reach such a diverse audience. We've definitely brought in more women. And we touch an older audience too. I think we've really had to fight hard to get beyond the all-women, over-40, culturally diverse, and bawdy labels. Then they'll say, 'Hey, the music's not bad either.'"

"I know they had to overcome the novelty-act label, three middle-age dames leavin' their jobs and traipsing off in a van. A lot of those battles were fought even before I joined," said multitalented "youngster" Andra Faye McIntosh, who joined the group in 1992. "By the time we recorded *Old, New, Borrowed & Blue*, there was a concerted effort to make sure the musicality was up front."

The hardest label to shed was the "too bawdy" sticker that accompanied their shows. "The 'bawdy' label was hard. There aren't any more songs on

***Gaye Adegbalola has worked hard to become
one of the premier songwriters in blues today.***

our albums with sexual double entendres than any other artist's album," said Adegbalola.

"The whole 'woman as a raunchy, sexual come-on' thing hurt," added Rabson. "The old Bessie Smith, Ma Rainey thing, classic blues—we enjoy playing with that. Guys play up that side of the songs too; they just don't get the hassle we do. We still hear, 'We won't hire you because you're too raunchy,' assuming that we can't control that aspect of the crowd."

Raunchy, lewd, and filled with sexual innuendo and double entendre is how these three women initially kick audiences. The first Saffire songs that trapped me were "OBG Why Me Blues," "Ragtime Rag," and "Shake the Dew Off the Lily," from their 1992 Alligator album, *Broadcasting*. Between laughing, I was embarrassed that someone might overhear the explicit lyrics from my earphones.

Watch the explosive reaction of first-timers at any show when Adegbalola sings "Bitch with a Bad Attitude" or "There's Lightning in These Thunder Thighs," two songs Alligator Records' Bruce Iglauer originally deemed too raw. "He felt they weren't bluesy enough, but we felt they were songs that would be another anthem for women to look at themselves through some different eyes," said Adegbalola.

"I think our new hit will be one I just wrote, called 'Silver Beaver,'" continued Adegbalola. "I thought it was time that a new animal was added to the off-color blues menagerie. There are monkeys, roosters, bumblebees, crawling king snakes, and fattening frogs for snakes, so let's bring the beaver in. I ripped off lines from all these different blues songs and hooked up the beaver to them. People just sit with a look of 'Oh my God' on their faces. The last line is, 'Yeah, just leave it to beaver.'"

These are street-smart working girls who realize that once they've got your ears, the other aspects of their musicianship will be hard to avoid. Their seamless recreation of classic blues from the 1920s offers modern rethinks of time-worn standards like "Ain't Nobody's Business" and "Sweet Black Angel," both delivered from the woman's perspective. Each woman is also a powerful vocalist and stage performer. While Rabson and Adegbalola play two instruments, McIntosh expertly handles guitar, bass, mandolin, and fiddle. As the youth in the group, McIntosh assimilates with her stage sisters.

"Ann is the consummate musician and so natural, like she was born with it. She's not a school-taught musician, but she can play any chord you'd want to hear. Gaye is a great teacher and dynamic entertainer to watch. Her songwriting skills are also incredible. Though she will never admit to being a good musician, she's a fine musician."

"I'm not nearly the musician they are," said Adegbalola. "I play well enough to keep from dividing the money by more than three. I have no desire to play lead or learn designer chords. I know that might be a real drawback for the band, but that also puts Ann's piano center stage as the engine to the band. Andra has a powerful soprano voice. Not many people who sing soprano have the power she has."

Rabson countered, "Gaye's got two strengths. First, she's works really well with the audience. From her 18 years teaching high school, she knows how to get people's attention, make them believe what she says, and put the

In addition to singing, Andra Faye McIntosh plays mandolin,
violin, and bass for the group.

story across so that people can't miss the message. Andra's a great singer who I love accompanying. She's an excellent musician who listens hard. If you play a musical joke, she'll play it right back at you and top it. She's a very responsive player."

If the mutual praise sounds too good, check how the democracy works. Onstage, they resemble the Harlem Globetrotters, passin' solos and songs back and forth. Without a nightly set list, the normal procedure is for each woman to perform two songs of her choice and then pass the spotlight.

***Ann Rabson, Saffire's pianist and guitarist, keeps
the music of Big Bill Broonzy, Jimmy Yancy,
and other pre-war blues musicians alive.***

"Because we're women," laughed Adegbalola, "we don't have a testosterone problem. We're one of the few bands that you'll ever meet that is leaderless. Our only rule of thumb is we try and not do the same key or tempo back to back. Then each of us just reads the house."

Andra explained their easy onstage give-and-take. "It's set up as a democracy so everybody gets an equal share of the singing. We alternate interviews and parcel out those chores so nobody feels overwhelmed. Sometimes it might be easier if we'd designate a leader for the day. Ann always says it's easier if there is a leader in the band. But this way, none of us feel like side players; we all feel important to the band. We each choose whatever songs we're going to sing. We draw straws, without straws, to see who'll go first and last. We're all very flexible, accommodating, and nurturing, wanting everybody to be happy."

Their live recording project in 1998 was an exercise in the qualities McIntosh spoke of, for it required each member to distill three nights of tape from their October 1997 Wolf Trap performance for a new live recording. Each day, the women had to listen to the tapes from the previous night and decide which songs needed to be recast. The final 24 songs, some recorded twice, had to be carefully evaluated in terms of both energy and professionalism. On Adegbalola's fourth day she groaned, "It takes hours listening to every note from the different tapes. At first I listened to just the feel, looking for the overall performance, because we really rocked the house. But now the others are writing back with comments about eliminating the takes in which the instruments may have been less than perfect."

McIntosh agreed with the tedium on the process. "Overall, we want the best energy and the best performance musically. Sometimes I think there's no way I can sing that song any better, but there may be a real bad screw-up on the bass."

What does each enjoy most about their shows? "I enjoy accompanying the other people singing," said Rabson. "I enjoy singing too, and I'd never want to give it up, but I really feel good making other people sound good—sort of a Zen thing. The piano's a wonderful instrument to do that with. The piano's got a tremendous range, from hot to warm to icy cold.

"I also love watching the audience. Every now and then when we're doin' a really deep blues, I can look up and see somebody cryin'. I remember once looking over the old upright piano in Blues E.T.C. in Chicago and seeing a guy with tears running down his face. That's a real connection for me," continued Rabson.

"Any part of the show that works," said Gaye. "That varies from night to night. I think it's that moment when I disconnect from what I'm doing and I'm just connected with the audience and with my partners. It's no longer rational, it's just happening and truly spiritual."

Each women has devoted time and energy to the pursuit of musical excellence. Rabson was born in 1945. "Guitar was the first instrument I played. I picked up piano in the early '80s. I was in a band with three guitars, bass, and drums. As the players got better and better, they needed me less and less. I've always wanted to play the piano, so got an old Fender Rhodes and just started bangin' away on it, learnin' by myself. Same with guitar. My first professional job was when I was still in high school, in 1962 or 1963.

"On and off throughout my life, I've made my living playing blues guitar, always blues guitar. Big Bill Broonzy was my first big influence. I heard him sing 'I'm Gonna Move on the Outskirts of Town' on the radio when I was four, and suddenly it seemed that all the other music I'd heard was in black and white and this was in living color. I was also listening to Brownie McGhee, Lightnin' Hopkins, and Memphis Minnie. On the piano, I listened to Mary Lou Williams and the boogie-woogie guys, like Pine Top Smith, Albert Ammons, Meade Lux Lewis, and Pete Johnson. I was fortunate enough in early life to be exposed to Jimmy Yancy and Leroy Carr, and both have become lifelong influences."

In the early 1980s, Ann searched out local hotels to woodshed her piano style. "I'd go to the bar where they didn't even have music and say, 'If you had music in here, you'd have a lot more customers.' I'd play in those places for years, until the government caught up with the people who weren't paying their taxes or the place sold. Then I'd go find another club. Occasionally, I'd go to Charlotte or DC to do a small gig, but mostly it was a little lounge in some hotel. I had a child, and I sure wasn't gonna traipse all over. It was hard enough getting back from a gig at 2:00 in the morning and being mom."

Adegbalola was born in 1944. "I taught science for 18 years, and that was performing with a captive audience every day. Prior to that, I was a bacteriologist and a biochem researcher. There was no music playing at all throughout those years. My father and I ran a small, black experimental theater group for about 25 years. There was always lots of singing and dancing and rhythm and poetry with that.

"Blues caught me as a kid. But when I lived in Boston for four years, I went to school at BU, I bought my current Martin guitar from my old college roommate. She had it under the bed and never played it. I got into folk music. When I lived in New York for four years, I was heavy into jazz, then gospel. Then Nina Simone brought me back to blues again. Early on it was Sonny Terry and Brownie McGhee. My first blues performance was in 1978. I was 34 then. I had only been playing guitar about three years. I had guitar lessons earlier, but it was when I saw Ann doing a solo act in 1975 that I got her to start giving me lessons. We started playing together maybe in 1978 at a Unitarian Church Fellowship. That's when we started playing together. We'd been doing guitar duets for a bit.

"We didn't see each other for a long time. I started playing solo after the 1978 thing. In 1984, I was called to play a Holiday Inn lounge that was too big for a solo act. I called up Ann to join me. She had been playing some piano. She didn't have a piano, so we started sneaking into the local college to practice in their practice rooms. We started playing in this Holiday Inn. Ann was teaching a computer course and Earlene Lewis was in her class. When Ann found out Earlene had a piano, Ann went over to give her a make-up test so we could use her piano. When she finished her make-up test, she joined in on bass and that formed the band. Ann and I had been playing as a duo for a long time before that. We've been together for nearly 20 years. Saffire first played out in June of 1984."

McIntosh was born in 1960. "I started in choir and learned to play violin in sixth grade. Then I dropped out of orchestra and started hanging out with my friends, jamming on Grateful Dead tunes on my fiddle. I went off on that loose direction for a while. People kept telling me that I sang OK, so I decided I really wanted to play. A Bonnie Raitt album turned me on to the blues when I was 16. I also was turned on to B.B. King. Listening to the Stones and the Dead I realized that a lot of the stuff they were doing were old blues tunes. I was one of those people reading the backs of the albums, going backwards. But Bonnie Raitt made me realize that a woman could sing in that style and sound really great too.

"I've been a registered nurse since 1980. I was able to work full and part time. I dropped my day job when Ann and Gaye called and asked me to give it a try. That was in August of 1992. They called a week after I was in Chicago, where I had done some stuff on broadcasting. That was the first time I had worked with them. We met at Blues Camp in 1987. Earlene didn't come that week, but Ann and Gaye did. Earlene came the next year, so I had met them all and sat in with them. It was all very friendly. The recording session went really well. After the recording session, I'd put it out to the spirit and said, 'Wouldn't it be great if they called and I could go on tour with them?' They did. The *Chicago Tribune* called us 'Three refugees from a Tupperware party.' One show labeled us three grandmothers. I haven't even had a baby yet—don't rush us. I'm the youthful, middle-aged one.

"My main influence on mandolin is Yank Rachell. I had heard him play in Indianapolis when I lived there. I already played the mandolin a little, and I noticed everybody had a band with a guitar. I wasn't really into learnin' how to play electric, hot lead guitar at the time. I liked the sound of the mandolin. And then when I saw Yank, I saw you could play blues on anything. When I went to Blues Camp, Rich Delgrosso was there teachin' blues mandolin. He was also quite a mentor in putting the material together. There aren't a whole lot of mandolin players keeping that tradition alive. Rich, Steve James, and Johnny Nicholas are the few out there still playin' it. I try and turn people on to who else is playing that style. It's nice if I can still let people know the instrument is still a tangible instrument in the blues."

In 1989, when they began on the road as Saffire, there was a Top 40 singer also named Sa-fire. To avoid litigation, Rabson and Adegbalola added the Uppity Blues Women tag. "We are officially Saffire—The Uppity Blues Women. But some people think that it's Saffire and The Uppity Blues Women," said Adegbalola. "They think that because I'm the black one, I'm Saffire and Ann and Andra are the Uppity Blues Women."

West Coast

hicago wasn't the only city African Americans carried their music to during the great migration from the South in the early 20th century. Many African Americans from Texas, Oklahoma, and other Southern states moved West, specifically to Los Angeles. Once in the city, the blues styles they carried married with the uptown jazz styles of that hip city.

Blues giants like T-Bone Walker, Pee Wee Crayton, Charles Brown, Lowell Fulson, Johnny "Guitar" Watson, Roy Milton, Amos Milburn, Big Joe Turner, and Big Mama Thornton moved to the city early in their lives and effectively mixed their blues with the stylish jump and swing of the city's jazz to create the R&B that ruled the region throughout the 1940s and 1950s.

When young blues enthusiasts searched out the blues in the mid-1960s, they discovered that these musicians and others, like Lloyd Glenn, George "Harmonica" Smith, Shakey Jake, Eddie "Cleanhead" Vinson, Brownie McGhee, Lightnin' Hopkins, and Roy Brown, were still creating vibrant, fresh music.

If you talk to Chicago bluesmen, they will always tell stories of Little Walter hangin' out in jazz clubs on off nights to assimilate jazz sensibilities into his harmonica phrasing and timing. The young turks from California grew up listening to the smooth jazz styles yet matured into the blues-watching first-generation blues singers playing the music carried within on the journey West. The music these younger players created sifted the West Coast jazz tendencies of Pee Wee Crayton and T-Bone Walker with the blues of Little Walter and Smith. The sound they discovered is as fresh and bouncy today as it was then.

Like any artistic step forward, it took a handful of visionaries to experiment with musical combinations on the bandstand laboratory. From the mid-1970s, the Hollywood Fats band, Rod Piazza and the Mighty Flyers, and the James Harman band were at the front of the stylistic search and development. These young players, who've spent years learning how to play the music, today have developed into the unique voices younger musicians are studying. Whether Rod Piazza or James Harman draws notes on the harmonica or Honey Piazza and Fred Kaplan sprinkle profound piano essence or a young guitar player hears the personality in Junior Watson's string explorations or Al Blake talks with words or music as ethnomusicologist, there is the deep-seated knowledge of a master who has come of age.

Throughout all these profiles, another voice is heard, that of Michael Mann, aka Hollywood Fats. He was the white blues guitar child prodigy from the 1970s. Through him, readers will understand what the real masters perceived and what these younger musicians understood. Fats' life, from musical acceptance to his personal tragedies later in life, is another painful example of how a culture obsessed with appearance, not substance, disregards the talent of its fringe members.

Today, nearly 20 years later, there is a wider circle of acceptance and understanding about where these visionaries were taking the music. Today there is even a name for it: West Coast jump blues. Today, bands across the country shop in thrift stores for bowling shirts, cool suits, and vintage hats to be called West Coasters. Today, there is a swing revival with a band of cool cats on every corner imitating that once-ignored sound. How much did these early bands contribute to this current phenomenon?

But the West Coast isn't all jump and swing. Guitar players on the coast were bred on the constantly touring Albert Collins. The blues revival of the late 1960s in San Francisco, where musicians like Michael Bloomfield, Charlie Musselwhite, Paul Butterfield, Luther Tucker, Buddy Guy, and Albert King played regularly, planted seeds in youngsters like Joe Louis Walker, Coco Montoya, Robert Cray, and Debbie Davies. Today, these guitar players rekindle the spirit of those men with every note they play or word they sing.

There is also an acoustic tradition alive in the West. Doug MacLeod's road to country blues traditions came in Virginia through his association with Ernest Banks, whose simple advice to MacLeod about the nature of the blues and the bluesman is crucial to everything MacLeod believes. He advised MacLeod, "Never play a note you don't believe in." Simple advice we should all heed.

Finally, today there is a new generation of acoustic blues musician, with Keb' Mo' and Kelly Joe Phelps at the vanguard. Instead of waiting for country blues to come to him, Mo' journeyed to Mississippi and lived with 84-year-old Delta guitarist Eugene Powell to comprehend the soul of the blues. Today, he continues to embody the tradition by writing modern blues songs that allow personal experiences to express the universal. Phelps' reliance on the spiritual aspects of the acoustic music he plays recalls in each listener the music of blues entrepreneurs like Blind Lemon Jefferson, Blind Willie Johnson, Mississippi Fred McDowell, and Robert Pete Williams. At the same time, his lap dobro slide bar and smooth baritone can be the perfect way to restore the balance of the soul.

Al Blake

Everybody's speaking the language, but how many people really have the gift? You can't go to Berklee School of Music and learn to play blues," said Al Blake. "It's real simple, but there's no shortcuts to it. Our culture says you can learn something in an hour at home. You don't learn any language in two hours. It takes a lifetime to learn the language of the blues and be able to speak it. You learn it the way everybody has learned it since the turn of the century. The long journey we are all on is symbolized through the blues path. Doc Cheatham, when he died at 92 years old, said that he was always searching, that he was never satisfied.

"This music is different, it's like learning a new language. I probably speak 30 words of Spanish well. But can I write a book or deliver an eloquent speech? A lot of people look at blues from that perspective, if I can play a 1-4-5 progression, I'm playing blues. Those people speak only 30 words, yet they say they're speaking the blues.

"It's an acquired taste. And once you're educated, you'll see that your impressions of the blues were wrong. Blues is like hot sauce or black coffee to a teenager. As you get older and grow, your tastes change, and pretty soon you're putting hot sauce on everything. Blues is bittersweet, something you develop a taste for. Back in the old days, when the masters were playing the music, they had a totally captive audience. Those people didn't have a choice of 20 different radio stations or MTV and VH-1. They had only one, maybe two kinds of music to choose from. Nowadays people are bombarded by so many things in a pop culture. And without education or exposure to real blues, it's almost impossible to get people to even understand it.

"I'm into the study of the roots of the music and the social conditions that produced the music. That's helped me to conceptually understand the

*Al Blake's introduction to hardcore blues came when he
watched Junior Wells's first West Coast performance.*

music better, because I've always had a fascination with going back to the
earliest recordings. One of the things young players lack today is this conceptually understanding the music from A to Z.

"If you study art, they'll tell you that no decade is more important than
any other decade or no period is more important than another period. It's
all relative in the blues. You can't say the Chicago blues is more important
than another period. You can't say that between 1925 and 1935 is less

important than the postwar period. It's all connected. I think it's important to know about it. Some people, however, don't take that approach. But if you were a guitar or a harmonica player like me and you don't know those things, you're going to fall way short."

Al Blake has always been there as a teacher. At a time in the 1960s when young kids in the Los Angeles area were waking up to African American music, Blake was just that much further down the road. To many of those kids—Rod Piazza, Fred Kaplan, Richard Innes—Blake was like an older brother sharing his adult tastes with younger siblings.

Blake grew up in Oklahoma City in the mid-1950s. While his parents worked, the Mississippi woman who took care of the family loved the blues; consequently, the radio played black music all day. When Blake attended military school in the early 1960s, fate put him together with a kid from Kansas City who loved the blues and carried the music with him. "He had Jimmy Reed albums, Muddy Waters's *Live in Newport*, and all those early albums. We used to listen to all those records, and late at night we could get WDIA on the radio. One of the guys in the dorm was a kid by the name of Townes Van Zandt. Though he was singing folk music, he inspired me in wanting to sing and play like that. That was my first vision of being a performer that way."

After graduation, when his family relocated to Los Angeles, the Ash Grove became Blake's hangout. There he took in every bluesman who played the club, in those times before the bandwagon. When younger kids trekked to the clubs, Blake became their primary resource. He advised them on which records to buy and what shows to attend. When Blake witnessed a Junior Wells' Ash Grove show, he began to consider the harmonica.

"At that time I really didn't know whether I was going to devote time to the guitar or harp. But I found myself going more towards the harmonica. I think it was because I'd seen Junior Wells when he first came to the West Coast. It was one of the first times he'd left Chicago and played for only white audiences. He had Little Walter's band with him, Fred Below on drums, Louis and Dave Myers. He was just on fire. He was doing all of his hits, Little Walter stuff, the Sonny Boy stuff, all the classics, even some James Brown. He was spending probably 85 percent of the night playing the harmonica. To be able to make a show of the harmonica in that day and in that setting was just amazing. After I'd seen him a couple of times with that group, I thought to myself, 'That's what I want to do.' I had to have that visual contact, that personal contact of watching. I spent a lot of time watching Big Walter Horton. That was my introduction into really hardcore blues."

He also traveled twice to Chicago and apprenticed in smoky 1960s South Side blues clubs like Theresa's, Pepper's, and the Checkerboard Lounge.

"I went to Chicago twice, once in the late '60s and once in the early '70s. I was a very inexperienced musician when first went to Chicago. My first trip to Chicago was fairly uneventful. I got to spend some time with Louis Myers, but at that time I wasn't really cognitive enough to understand what was going on."

When he returned to Los Angeles, Blake toured as the harmonica player behind a young blues star, Luther Allison. "The mom of a friend was trying to manage Luther's career. I ended up playing harmonica with him when he was out here. Even then, he was a hard-working guy, real personable, always upbeat, and audiences always liked him. In a sense, he was what everybody was looking for. He really had an ability to connect with people.

"The other part for me was being around Hollywood Fats. He was such an incredible musician that he made all of us—Fred Kaplan, Larry Taylor, Richard Innes, and me—the musicians we are today. By experiencing the music through him and playing it from a very straight-ahead, purist view, he made us realize that anything was possible. A lot of people have gone onto tangents because they haven't had a mentor around them to influence them and show them the right way it go. Hollywood Fats for us was the guy. He just had it all. There's no replacement for the effect of an unbelievable teacher on his pupils."

Blake first met Fats, aka Michael Mann, backstage at a Freddie King show. "When I went to the dressing room, Fats was sitting in there. My initial impression of him was that he looked like some overweight Tiny Tim. Freddie says, 'This is Hollywood Fats. He's one of the greatest blues guitar players you'll ever hear anyplace, anywhere.' Freddie had the habit of calling everybody the greatest something, so I'm thinking, 'There he goes again with that "greatest" bullshit.' I'm looking at this guy, thinking it's impossible this guy can play guitar.

"When Freddie went downstairs to play, I was left in the dressing room with Fats and a new, very inexpensive acoustic Gibson guitar. I handed it to him and said, 'Let me hear you play something.' Because it was an acoustic guitar, he started playing exactly like Lightnin' Hopkins. I didn't think there was anybody on the face of the earth that could play like Lightnin' Hopkins. This was the early '70s. Here was this overweight, 17-year-old Tiny Tim-looking guy playing exactly like Lightnin' Hopkins. Because Lightnin' had a certain attack with his timing, it's very difficult for people to get. Fats was playing it exactly.

"Then he proceeded to go downstairs and sit in with Freddie King, doing the electric Chicago thing from a totally different place. And by the end of the night, I knew I'd found this child who held the ultimate secret to life. I knew the talent he had. Freddie King knew, Magic Sam knew, Buddy Guy knew. I made getting to know Hollywood Fats the number-one priority in my life.

"Blues is a very complex music for many people to understand. A guy like Fats had a complete, total, deep grasp of music. It's something that must be genetically coded. It's not something you can teach yourself. You just have to be one of those people. There wasn't anything Hollywood Fats couldn't do on the guitar. He was ten when he began playing the guitar and 12 when his dad would drive him down into the inner city of Los Angeles to begin working in clubs.

"At 15, he had already been under the tutelage of Magic Sam and Freddie King. Muddy accepted Fats into his band in 1973 as Muddy's second white band member. I saw the way they all embraced him because they saw in him something they only saw in the greatest blues musicians. When those guys all came up, they had the experience of meeting and being around some of the greatest players. Most white people didn't have that experience. These players saw in Hollywood Fats something they didn't see in any other musician. They were awestruck by it. They were struck by his ability to absorb everything. People like Paul Butterfield and Mike Bloomfield have been touted as having that same kind of magic. But they were in peewee leagues, while Fats was a full professional. He was a Michael Jordan to their high school abilities. If you really listen and compare Michael Bloomfield to Hollywood Fats and put the two of them together, there is no comparison.

"Fats knew that he could do something that hardly anybody else could do, to attack the music from the source. He had an understanding of the music from the most idiosyncratic nuances of pre- and post-war blues. There wasn't anything he couldn't understand or couldn't execute. That's a huge statement to make: There wasn't anything in the music that he didn't understand. He could just listen to it and do it. Something like that is genetically encoded. In that great spirit and like all brilliant people, Fats took the traditional music to the next level. Then he brought the general population to that level.

The Hollywood Fats band formed in 1975. It brought together Fats's guitar, Kaplan's piano, Innes' drums, Blake's harmonica, and Taylor's bass to play a fresh vision of the blues. Along with the Rod Piazza band of the same time, the Hollywood Fats band was the prototype of today's West Coast sound.

"The Fats band tried to bring the traditional music they had been listening to up to the next level. Through Fats, we were able to do that. Basically we all had ideas and we all had certain tastes that were very much the same, but we weren't capable of executing a lot of those things as fully and totally efficiently as they needed to be done. He knew intuitively how to put our ideas into a musical form. We came to Fats with our ideas and said this is what we want to do, and almost instantaneously Fats would create the whole format for what we wanted to do. And then we all learned and grew from that experience. He wasn't a real leader of men, but he was the consummate bandleader. As a musician there was never an idea that he was at a loss for."

The unique sound the band created was a coupling of those ideas with Chicago blues and a West Coast attitude. "Everybody was focused on Chicago and Memphis, and no one was even thinking Los Angeles as the blues center. So we started really getting into people like T-Bone, Charles Brown, Floyd Dixon, early Ray Charles, Joe Liggins, and Roy Milton. Fats was the medium between that music and us. We were able to begin playing all this incredible West Coast music that no one had ever really looked at as important or viable.

"In retrospect, a lot of the West Coast music had a very profound influence on Chicago musicians who were coming up from Mississippi. If you listen to early Howlin' Wolf, they're trying to combine Johnny Moore and Charles Brown into the Mississippi sounds. We saw that at a time when no one else did. And because we had a guy like Fats in the band, all we had to do was say, 'Listen to this record' and he could play it with its own contemporary touches."

But the public never looked hard enough to see these qualities. Steady gigs were only in the Los Angeles area. At a time when disco clubs ruled the mainstream and punk clubs were bubbling in opposition to the stylish glitter, a retro group like the Fats band was never given a second look. "We were playing both black and white clubs then, and the acceptance in both places was equally poor. Some blacks would hear Hollywood Fats and be absolutely blown away by him. He could make a blues fan out of anybody. But the reception was poor and we struggled over time. We were into the traditional music and into doing it authentically. We must have looked like we were from the Dark Ages at that time. It never got easy. That's why we broke up—we struggled so long and got so good, but we couldn't get jobs and couldn't get paid. We probably had a lot of musical sense and not a lot of business sense, so things just started not working out."

Though the band came apart in 1980 as Fats left to seek out other options, in 1986 Blake and the others retooled for another shot. "Based on the success of Steve Ray Vaughan, the Fabulous Thunderbirds, and Robert Cray, we decided to put the band back together again and give it another shot. We felt that it was the time. It just wasn't in the cards because that night Fats overdosed."

As Blake remembers, when Fats left the world of blues for the world of rock, he became enamored with the availability of the drugs that ease the pain. "He was so brilliant, he just couldn't deal with it. So he chose heroin as his escape. At a time when glamour rock was the thing, he was a large, rotund guy with nothing glamorous about him. So the world was blind to what he had."

The reunion show was a triple bill: the Fats band, Debbie Davies playing with Maggie Mayall and the Cadillacs, and Paul Butterfield's band. "We spent a month rehearsing for it, and everyone was very excited to play again. But unfortunately, Fats had been into heroin and overdosed that night.

"It really shook me. I worked with him from 1973 until his death in 1986. After that night, I stopped playing music until probably 1991 or 1992. I went into deep depression through those years. I saw how completely oblivious the world was to someone so brilliant as Fats.

"Fats was the possibility. He was able to show people. He was able to take the vision and turn it into a reality. All of us were light-years behind him in those days. Like Michael Jordan in the Chicago Bulls, when he was there he brought you up to a level that you just couldn't reach alone."

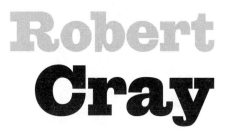

Robert
Cray

The first record I ever bought was Curtis Lee's "Pretty Little Angel Eyes." My father wore out the Coasters' "Yakety Yak" on the hi-fi. Growing up listening to radio DJs Cousin Brucie and Murray the K, I heard my share of Ray Charles, Sam Cooke, and James Brown. When the Beatles arrived, I was more intrigued with the music of the early Rolling Stones, the Animals, and the Yardbirds.

The first group I saw live was Smokey Robinson and the Miracles. The Temptations with David Ruffin was my second concert. Add to that the folk music of Bob Dylan, Phil Ochs, and Pete Seeger, mix in my college days of Otis, Sam, Dave, Wilson, and Aretha, stir in the Airplane, the Dead, the Doors, Hendrix, and Cream, and in retrospect you can see that the musical stew I was cooking was rich in R&B, soul, and blues.

The 1970s turned up the funk, which later turned into disco. Didn't we all think disco would last forever? By the 1980s, most of us had searched through the maze of jazz and rock for an elusive music we once loved.

Fast-forward to 1986. While my family shops, I'm removing wallpaper inch by inch with a steamer and a razor blade. I'm playing a cassette that I borrowed from a friend, by a guitar player I've never heard of named Robert Cray. In a flash Cray hits me dead between the ears and demonstrates that the music I've always loved is still out there. By the time he's lamenting "It's because of me, it's because of me," I'm realizing what a lot of baby boomers on a musical quest were realizing: that in a musical wasteland, the soul, R&B, and blues of this Robert Cray revived the style of music we all once loved.

With Muddy Waters gone and Buddy Guy still playing to tiny crowds outside Chicago, mainstream blues in the 1980s consisted mainly of the

Robert Cray's gospel-like vocals, believable stories, and
stinging guitar rejuvenated blues in the 1980s.

standard set from B.B. King or the butt-kickin', guitar-heavy blues rock from
Texas's new kids on the block, Stevie Ray Vaughan and the Fabulous
Thunderbirds. What made Cray's sound so appealing was the combination
of two elements that had long been overlooked: a gospel-like vocal urgency
and a stinging, Albert Collins guitar approach. Its sales of over two million
rejuvenated the blues and proved to the music world that not all young
black artists were rapping on city street corners.

Cray demonstrated to the music world that blues is fundamentally about telling stories through song. Cray chose to abandon the overworked 12-bar, A-A-A-rhyme song format in favor of crisp, lyrical vignettes about contemporary relationships. His meticulous description of the one-room studio apartment, down to the hotplate, in "I Guess I Showed Her" reeks of the loneliness we all feel when forced to move out of a relationship. Then, in "Still Around," he talks from his bed about his need for the unfeeling woman who has rejected his love and moved out. Again, Cray's bleak images of "Did my best to love you, now do your best to leave" serve the relationship walking papers.

Cray always creates believable characters within his verse and then psychoanalyzes them in his songs. "Smoking Gun" examines the gnawing a man feels when he thinks his woman is seeing another man. Typical blues fare, right? Yet in Cray's voice, listeners hear the emotional pain associated with a bare-your-soul singer like Otis Redding. Flying in the face of 1980s machismo, there is also an honest male admission of fear of the truth. Cray was penning emotional understanding long before men were from Mars. Another song, "Right Next Door," eavesdrops through thin walls on a pending breakup with the man who caused the trouble. The originality here is that the character silently pleads for the woman to stay with her husband and not leave for the fleeting affair. He knows if she leaves, she will be a topic of another song. These are the angles on standard themes and forms that Cray has explored.

"I write more about relationships because it feel like a natural thing to write about, something you learn about over time, and I've found that it's easy to write about those feelings," said Cray. "I think it's the story that is most important. I don't tinker with every word for the right word. That's the lesson I learned from listening to somebody like Howlin' Wolf—lines don't have to rhyme. If I run into a situation like that, I'll just let it go. It doesn't have to rhyme. That's my poetic license."

Today, the meticulous Cray has songs bouncing from notebook to tape recorder until he gets the story elements and realistic images. "Even while we're recording, I'm still working on the lyrics. That's the part that gets really personal. I want to make sure that it's not only understandable to me, but others can understand it also. That's the tricky part."

This kind of maturity didn't happen overnight; beginning in 1980, Cray had already released three albums before lightning struck. Each album subtracted cover tunes in favor of more Cray originals. It was his 1985 Alligator album, *Showdown*, with Albert Collins and Johnny Copeland that readied blues audiences for the Cray explosion. "For years we were inspired by other bands that were playing similar music. We were buying records all the time and diggin' back, trying to find old stuff. I was going back, learning more about blues and doing the same thing with R&B as well. I love the gospel-influenced R&B singers, like Otis Redding and O.V. Wright. I was just really happy that at the time *Strong Persuader* came about was just the right time," said Cray. "As I see it now in retrospect, different musics come and go; that was the right time to do the kind of music we were doing."

Cray was simply the right person playing contemporary blues at the right time. As the blues guitar player population continued to age and younger blacks turned to rap as their outlet, Cray was appropriately anointed as the savior of the blues. From the first show I saw him perform, I will always remember his overwhelming stage presence. Within the first song, I immediately understood Cray's placement in the blues. This revival was not dusty, but thoroughly contemporary and rejuvenating.

His teenage years exposed Cray to the real music he needed to hear. How many people do you know who can claim that Albert Collins played at their high school prom? Maybe only Robert Cray. "This was in Tacoma, Washington, in 1971. We had a choice between Albert and some popular rock band who, at the time, recorded "Evil Woman." Albert had been doin' a lot of club and festival work in the Northwest. I don't know how that happened, but the class voted for Albert Collins. That speaks highly of our class. I knew about him and had the chance to talk to him after the gig. He told me, 'Keep with it, young man.'

"In 1969, he was the first blues guitar player I ever saw. I'd seen all these other rock bands performing. But when Albert Collins came out, he was louder than anybody else. He marched into the audience with his long chord, wore the guitar on the wrong shoulder. I was just turnin' 16, and I thought it was too cool. I'd been playing guitar for four years and thought Albert Collins was the coolest thing on the planet. His hair was really cool too.

"The first time we got up with Albert was after we'd started the band. I believe it was in 1975 or 1976. Our band had been playing at this club and the club owner asked us if we wouldn't mind backing Albert coming through. We did our set, then Albert came on. We'd been doing some Albert Collins songs, like "Don't Lose Your Cool." We did this song "Soul Food" and we talked Albert into doin' it. When I told him he'd played at my high school graduation, he remembered, at least that's what he always told me."

Like so many other young guitarists learning the blues, Cray found Collins to be the perfect mentor. "From watching Albert I was able to realize what the frontman needs from the band. Albert treated us like we were his children. He always made sure we were calling home to our parents. We worked up and down the West Coast with Albert. We'd gone down and played the San Francisco Blues Festival with Albert in 1977.

"We'd get a kick out of watching Albert collect money from club owners and settling up his bar tab. You'd have to sign for drinks at the places we were playing at. Then at the end of the night, you'd settle up. I remember one time, settling up, Richard and I had our names on our tabs, but there were some with no name. At the same time Albert was arguing those weren't his, he was sending the barmaid down to get us another drink.

"Being onstage with him taught me how to do a show. We did a lot of shows with Albert. He'd walk out of the club with this long guitar chord and he'd be outside the club. We'd be playing the song for over 20 minutes, and he'd be on the street jammin' with some kid who'd have his harmonica out. Those were the days we were wearin' platforms, and our feet would hurt so bad that we'd be yellin' at Albert at the end of the night. He'd be out there pretending he was hitchhiking and nobody knew because they couldn't hear the music; all they saw was some nut out there with a guitar and long chord, hitchhiking.

"He had a really great demeanor. I don't think I ever saw him get mad. He was a great example of treating people like you want to be treated. That was the way Albert lived."

But Cray took something from every other player he sat with. "Everybody plays from the soul. You know these people from their music before you even meet them. Everybody I've had the opportunity to play with has been a beautiful person. I think having the opportunity to meet Muddy, John Lee, Albert, and to be accepted by them makes me really feel good about what I'm doing, because they know that I'm not doing the music exactly as they did, that mine has a different kind of groove on it. And yet that they put their arm around me and spent time with me really makes me feel good. They understood where the music in Robert Cray was coming from. B.B. King still introduces me as the future of the blues."

The music on Cray's late 1990s efforts is a subtle return to the successful Cray formula: punctuating Memphis horns, piercing lead guitar, in-the-pocket rhythms, and Cray's "on bended knee" pleading from the gospel/soul tradition. For each tune, Cray, the master of the modern three-minute short story, has compiled fresh characters involved in the daily dilemmas he observes in the world.

Like soul singers in days long past who stood on the dark end of the street, Cray articulates his tale of pain within the confines of each short story. You almost expect Cray to be led away crying, with a cape over his shoulder, only to break free, dash back to the mic, and plead one more time.

Commercial success comes with a price. With every release, Cray battles a narrow-minded press that knows blues is mostly a standard 12-bar, three-line format, and Cray doesn't fit that. Young players are not called the next Robert Cray, because what he writes, sings, and plays is far too complex to be copied. He offers a much wider interpretation of what modern blues encompasses. "When I was a lot younger and I played with local cats, it was a war—who can last the longest?— and nothing good ever came from it. The band realized that a long time ago, to put the emphasis on the band.

"I've found out that it's best to not have any parameters or borders. What comes out of what we play is related to being around the kind of music we've played all these years and the kind of music I enjoy listening to when I'm by myself. I love R&B, I love blues, I love soul, and I love jazz, so my music is always a mixture of what I like to hear. I'm not thinkin' about where to fit it. When we do live sets, we jump over both sides of the fence and walk down the middle of the road."

Debbie Davies

Guitarist Debbie Davies sports one impressive résumé in the blues. Since the mid-1980s, she has spent two years as the guitarist with Maggie Mayall's all-girl band, recorded on John Mayall's *Sense of Place* release in 1990, and played rhythm guitar for three years behind the Master of the Telecaster, Albert Collins, before forging her own solo career full time in 1992.

As the opening band for John Mayall's gigs, Davies developed her deep friendship with guitar soul mate Coco Montoya, Mayall's former lead guitarist. "Coco and I are very close. John has also been so supportive of both of us over the years," said Davies.

It was through her early friendship with Montoya that she was introduced to Albert Collins. "After I left Maggie's band, I started booking my own band again, developing my own stuff, and performing under my own name. I was already about six months into my own band when I got the offer to join Albert Collins's band. I did that for three years."

Collins's untimely death from cancer in 1994 staggered his musical prodigy. "I was devastated when he died. We could tell he was ill, but we didn't know it would spread so quickly," Davies remembered. "Eventually I'm sure the experience put something into my music. That's what the blues is, all of your life experiences and emotions. Both Coco and I felt like we were in a slump for a while.

"He was our older mentor/support person, but also the person who kept me constantly inspired. We always had this thing of showing a riff or a new song to Albert. A lot of people left us in a fairly short period of time. Albert, Albert King, Stevie Ray Vaughan were people that, on some level, we took for granted because they inspired us so much and gave out so much energy. We

As a woman looking to play guitar, Debbie Davies
searched hard for a mentor. "The only woman who did
anything close to what I wanted to do was Bonnie Raitt."

loved them and saw them every moment we could; but it was only when they were gone we realized how much they really were giving us. After a while you realize what you are trying to do and what you are carrying and what your role is. It's a lot harder than you ever think it's gonna be, and you have to pull it out of yourself like these guys did when their mentors left them.

"Albert came up black in the South before Civil Rights. He came up with no money and no family to buy him an instrument or give him lessons. It was that unbelievable drive, that love of what you're doing. He worked tons of other day jobs. By the time he was able to make a living playing music, he had a sense of being grateful about that. That sense of gratitude translated into the warmth and the connections with the people that made these artists so special. I learned stamina, the patience to overlook, and grace as a human being from Albert."

The lessons Collins bequeathed Davies still light her musical direction. "Albert taught me the feeling and roots of the music that can only be picked up touring with master players. Hanging out with Albert and his friends and watching the power and feelings that Albert put into it onstage really taught me the feeling, vibe, and essence of the real blues," said Davies.

"I'd never been in a band like that before. It was a rush! There was always so much energy. I also observed how Albert carried on even when the road became really grueling and difficult, yet no matter what, he found the energy for the gig. He pulled it out from inside himself every night. We might have been stranded for half a day in the heat and Albert was the guy who drove us there. Then he gets up and plays his ass off. That was the biggest thing that affected me from working with him, his ability to reach down inside himself and pull out from somewhere this incredible energy and soul. Even knowing how devastatingly tired he was or what problems had happened in the last few days. That was an invaluable thing to witness, and know that was a goal that I would try and achieve myself."

Though nearly every Davies CD includes a Collins tune, the title track on *I've Got That Feeling* has a special duet between Davies and Montoya on Collins's "I Got That Feeling." "It's a tune that we have both played with Albert. It sure felt like he was with us in the studio. It was one of those magic nights in the studio."

Davies admits there are songs and nights when Collins's presence is strongly felt. "There are certain songs and licks that I do as tributes onstage to Albert. On special nights when I really connect with the crowd and it's really flowin' outta me, I definitely feel him onstage with me. When people say, 'I felt like Albert was here tonight,' that is really special."

As a young girl growing up in Northern California in the late 1960s, Davies found few guitar-playing females to emulate. Her journey into the blues was, as for many of her generation, backward through the British blues invasion. The cutting-edge fierceness of Eric Clapton's solos grabbed her soul for life. "I had an acoustic guitar then, and I was learning some chords, but I really knew I wanted an electric. I didn't know for quite a while why that was. I finally realized that a lot of the music I was drawn to had the blues at its center."

Luckily, Northern California was a hotbed for touring blues musicians, and Davies soaked up every guitar god or blues diva who appeared. "Collins, Junior Wells, Buddy Guy, Etta James, Koko Taylor, Sonny Terry, and Brownie McGhee all regularly played one of the clubs there. The local white blues artists, like Michael Bloomfield, Charlie Musselwhite, and Paul Butterfield, who lived there, also played out a lot. I was really getting a good smattering of all the styles. Then, in 1978, I started playing rhythm guitar in a local band."

But women guitar players were a rare breed. So Davies had difficulty finding female role models in the male-dominated, guitar-slinger world. "It was much more difficult for me to get started fronting a band 20 years ago. There were just no women doing it, so there was no support for it, no understanding, no camaraderie. It was a fight where I felt very isolated. But whatever was inside of me to do this was just stronger. The only woman I ever saw who did anything close to what I wanted to do was Bonnie Raitt. She had a huge impact on me in an inspirational way. Outside of her, I went and saw the men play and learned the licks from them."

In addition to sharpening her six-string craft, Davies distinct songwriting sensibilities also distanced her from the pack. She has contributed originals on each of her releases. Her strapping guitar attack and woman's perspective about human relationships provide a refreshing voice.

"Writing is the thing I really have to do to put myself over as an artist. I have a major regret at this point in my life that I don't have enough time to spend writing. I've only penned three tunes for my new album. When I'm on the road, and I average 200 nights a year, I always come up with ideas or lines or phrases, but I need to workshop an idea to complete it from start to finish. I need to sit by myself with just a tape recorder and a guitar and each day go back to the various ideas I've worked with until it is complete. It's very much a craft to me, and I just haven't had enough time in the last few years to write as much as I would like to. It doesn't come easy and it can be really frustrating, but it can also be really rewarding."

Each new release offers a slight departure from what the blues world has come to expect from Davies. "Each one is a definite growth step for me as an artist. Some of the material stretches me in different directions. I try to make new albums, not all women's blues; otherwise that becomes my MO. I don't want to be pigeonholed as the feminist blues player."

Besides her guitar and writing skills, there is another area where Davies is at the forefront: musician sobriety. She is part of a core group of blues musicians who have chosen sobriety and recovery over drug addiction and alcoholism. In addition to all the normal rigors of a touring musician's world, these musicians faced up to the harsh facts of their addiction and struggle every day to stay clean.

"I literally had been drinking and partying really hard for 21 years. I was a rebellious kid, the kind of female in my generation who would take up electric guitar. Drugs would come and go, but alcohol was the one thing that was there all the time. I loved the feeling I got from alcohol."

For many in the music business, the user's path to addiction resounds identical: acceptance. "When I started playing, there just weren't any other women doin' it. Guys made fun of me, saying, 'What are you tryin' to do?' I thought if I could sit down and keep up with the guys drinking, and believe me I could, I was one of the them. That was part of the rite of passage for me. Everybody was doing it, I know that's not the reason to do it, but we didn't know different back then."

Working in Maggie Mayall's all-girl band in the '80s exposed Davies to both sides of addiction. She played shows with Michael Bloomfield and watched his wrestling with demons, and in 1985 she played on the bill the night guitarist Hollywood Fats overdosed. She also heard the dialogue about the program, because Maggie and John Mayall were in recovery in the program. "I'd heard the dialogue, but I had to say to myself that I couldn't do it anymore. It became a choice of what was more important, my career or getting high."

Finally, in 1990, Davies was able to tap into her inner spiritual strength and go at life clean, without any artificial stimulants. "The whole point is not to numb yourself when you get out there, but to feel the fears, face them, deal with them, and grow. That can produce so much energy. It's all part of your spiritual path. Once you embark on your spiritual path and try and get in touch with that part of yourself, you can then reach out to people so much more in performances."

Davies discovered a clever psychological bait-and-switch to fool what she refers to as her addictive personality. "The feeling onstage was so different that I decided performing was gonna be my new drug. By creating this as a new drug in my mind, I was psychologically tricking myself into enjoying that high more than any other high from drugs or alcohol. That helped me tap into the rush of feelings playing music, instead of the substitute rush of alcohol or drugs. I was focusing on the realer thing."

There is little sermonizing by Davies with friends on the music roads. Davies instead extends a determined support to any musician battling substance abuse, and she displays proof positive of how that decision can turn one's life around. "I don't want to be judgmental. Everybody is an individual with choices to make. If your music is important, make sure that the quality of the music is always the focus. If you see any substances getting in the way of that, that's when you want to question your art and your health.

"It may not be impeding your performance at all now, but that might be a different story in five years. Then it might be really hard to stop. I think I would try and pass on that awareness to face yourself and your shortcomings. Being sober is not the end of the world—it's like the beginning of a new world."

James
Harman

This scene repeats itself in countless blues bars every Friday night across the country: A lead guitarist fronting a four-man guitar ensemble struts forward and rips into the intro of Elmore James's "Dust My Broom." Every arm in the bar thrusts to the ceiling, and every male patron yells, "Yeah!" and high-fives the guys next to him. Another weekend blues-bar orgy commences. Every song is an exercise in lead guitar swagger, bravado, pomposity, and machismo. Some of the musical newcomers are so relentless in their auditory assault that the tones of "Sweet Home Chicago" and "The Sky Is Crying" vanish into identical riffs.

You stand a better chance of turning up alien remains in Roswell than discerning musical dynamics. These forty-something rock musicians cum instantly born-again bluesmen transplant the rock-stage guitar mentality into everything they play.

James Harman learned that to be a creative, artistic force, it is how you paint the song that is important. He emphasizes to any musician he instructs the importance of touch, coloring, and shading. To this barroom bard, each performance is about songs. "A song is like a woman's dress: It's gotta be long enough to cover the subject but short enough to keep you interested. It's about stories being told by a recognizable voice. All the musicians have to be professional so they can play the music that goes behind the story. If you don't have that, you don't truly have a blues artist. It ain't about a guitar player. The guitar to me is like any other instrument or drop of paint that goes somewhere in the picture.

"The blues is so big today because rock went to hell. The new blues audience is about 70 percent rock audience posing as a blues audience; they ran out of music and jumped in on ours. I'm sorry, but on most of these so-called

James Harman recalls, "The time I spent in a car with
Big Walter Horton or George "Harmonica" Smith means
more to me than every record I've ever owned."

blues albums the thinking is that lead guitar is everything. You can't play harp with that rock-edge guitar going. You have to have that harp guitar approach in there, that Jimmy Rogers, Louis Myers, Robert Lockwood, Jr., guitar that goes with a harp, or you might as well play with the Rolling Stones.

"I have no interest in loud lead guitars. Every musician has to be an adequate enough musician to play the changes in the music the way I want it to be played. I tell any musician I'm hiring if he doesn't have that touch, coloring, and shading, he'll either get it or he won't. A band is a band with a bandleader, with his ideas and usually his music and songs. It ain't about a guitar player, and everything else is secondary."

As an active musician since 1962, Harman feels he can express his vision of the contemporary state of the blues. "I've always said, 'You're a blues singer for life.' What disturbs me today is that a group will cut their hair and buy a bowling shirt and now they're bluesmen. I'm glad they came to it, but suits from thrift stores don't make you a blues guy. It's gotta be in your heart. There's a whole lot of guys out there without their hearts in it. You can't lie about the feeling in the song when you've learned it from the real guys. You can't fake that. The beauty of real music is that it isn't a fad or moment thing."

In the contemporary world of blues songs, few writers capture life's quirky side sharper than Harman. Listeners will simply nod in agreement when they see the world through James Harman's eyes. Whether it's motel life on the road or love's pitfalls over a bottle, Harman is a champion at spotting the bizarre in our world and translating it to disc. Early on, B.B. King told Harman, "You've got to do your songs." To that end, his notebook of ideas is never far from reach. "My blues is about storytelling, and I try very hard to have a sense of humor in all I do."

As modern as his lyrics are, there is the impression that the crowd has been transported to a smoky, back-road juke joint. Every night onstage, Harman revives the raw Alabama blues of the 1950s. His equipment—old tube amps and a simple 1940s drum kit—play a large part in the Harman educational mission.

This Alabama boy grew up hanging out in the rural roadhouses, learning. "The blues was all around me when I was a kid in Alabama. I'd turn on the radio and hear Junior Parker, Muddy, Howlin' Wolf, or Jimmy Reed. I loved the magic and the sexiness of it," Harman recalled. "As an eight-, nine-, ten-year-old kid, I heard the rooster in the barnyard and I said, 'Yeah, that's me.'"

Harman grew up with a dad who was a harmonica player, but his mother enforced a piano-first training. "My father played country breakdown harp, and I grew up listening to Noah Lewis and Jaybird Coleman. That's where I come from. His harps were in the piano bench. When I finished my piano lesson, I got to take the harps out and play them. I also wanted to be a racecar driver or motorcycle driver. I studied art too. But every weekend I made money playing music. Art's a tough gig, but there's always a need for music." From there, he first started playing for real in 1962 and first recorded in 1964, at the age of 18.

"I got to Chicago in May of 1965 and Sonny Boy Williamson died in May of 1965 in Arkansas, so I never got to see my mentor. Instead, I hung out a lot with Big Walter Horton. He wasn't the guy after Sonny Boy; he was the same as Sonny Boy. He and Sonny Boy came from the same place; that's why they'll sound the same. Sonny Boy was the poet, Walter Horton was the guy with the greatest tone in the world. He was a genius. If I could tell you what makes his tone stand out, I'd be a genius. I sat in a car, a foot away from him, watchin' his face while he played. I learned more from that than all the records I ever listened to.

"His deal with me was I'd buy him a sack of groceries and a half pint. We'd go and sit in the car and I could watch him play. He didn't teach me anything, but he'd play and let me play. If I tried to do something and didn't quite hit it, he'd kick me in the leg. He bruised me up. He was my mentor."

The blues tradition has always pinpointed the master-apprentice relationship. Older performers will never outgrow the blues, while younger children must possesses the patience to hang in. "The old guys knew they were passing the blues along to guys like me. It was even discussed in the 1960s and 1970s. We were havin' a ball playin' with these guy and hatin' it when they were dyin' off, but we knew sooner or later it'd be us carryin' it on.

"In the 1960s, guys like Matt Murphy and James Cotton were watchin' us and said, 'You guys'll be the ones to keep playing this, because the young brothers don't care.' They thought the white audience would listen to guys like Butterfield, Bloomfield, and Musselwhite. I heard that a thousand times from the old guys: 'We gonna leave this in your hands 'cause nobody else cares.' We all accepted that as the legacy, and they assumed that we inherited the blues. You wake up one day and you're an older bluesman. But, like a bad movie, somebody else runs into the lawyer's office with a copy of the will leaving many of us out."

He played the college frat circuit and opened for soul and blues acts throughout the South before moving to Southern California in 1970. There he formed the Icehouse Blues Band, which backed the likes of Big Joe Turner, Johnny "Guitar" Watson, and others. In 1977, he formed the first James Harman Band, which in the early years included Kid Ramos, Willie J. Campbell, Gene Taylor, Fred Kaplan, Hollywood Fats, and Stephen Hodges. Some have called him the training ground for musicians before they joined some of the most successful bands. Drummer Bill Bateman and Taylor left for the Blasters; later, Ramos and Campbell left for the Fabulous Thunderbirds.

Throughout the 1970s and 1980s Harman was a close musical friend of the late Michael Mann, aka Hollywood Fats. "I came to California in 1970. It was 1970 or 1971 when I went to the Troubadour to do a Hoot Night. After we finished, the guy who ran the Hoot said, 'Next week we'll have Shakey Jake and his All-stars.' I knew Jake was Magic Sam's uncle from Chicago, so I went down to see him. There was this fat kid with long hair playing a Fender Jazzmaster. He was only 16, and he'd been playing for a few years. He was playing a Freddie-King-goes-surfing kind of sound. Fats was hanging around all the shows at The Light House, Ash Grove, Troubadour, and the Golden Bear. Then he started sitting in more often. He got a gig with J.B. Hutto and the Hawks. He went off and lived in the ghettos in Chicago. Then he was with John Lee Hooker, Albert King, Muddy Waters, and Jimmy Witherspoon. Then, in 1975, he started playing weekends with Fred Kaplan and Al Blake at a place called the No Exit Cafe. They got Richard Innes and Larry Taylor to sit in. Within a year, the Hollywood Fats Band was together."

Was he the guitar wizard of the time? "No he wasn't a wizard, just an awfully good guitar player. To me there are all these people, who never heard him and don't know him, have put him on this genius pedestal. Fats would laugh his head off at that. He was a very good, innovative guitar player. He understood all the traditions and learned them all from the right place. Fats could play with the best of them, and the other guys understood and accepted him. One night we were in the studio and Fats was playing this country blues line and I started singing without thinking and Kid Ramos started playing open G fills behind. It was the verse to 'Goat Man Holler.' Fats stopped playing and asked if I was consciously pulling that off of a 1930s 78. He told me I'd found real Delta blues, something Tommy Johnson would have come up with if he'd had more time, a song that was not a copy, but in the real filing cabinet of the world."

The Harman band in the early 1980s featured the one-two guitar punch of Ramos, who joined Harman in 1980, and Fats, who came aboard in 1981. Ramos remembered those days: "When Fats called and wanted to get into this band, James called me and said, 'You're the guitar player in this band. If you don't think it's a good idea, we won't do it.' I give James a lot of credit, because he asked me first. I thought, 'What a great opportunity to learn from this guy. I'm not going to have ego problems with another guitar player like Fats.' He was great to work with. At that time we were playing four sets a night in the bars, so we improvised every night with the music we played. James would get up there and call off a West Memphis kind of thing in a certain key and we would just start playing. Fats played for about three years. He never made me feel like he was the legend and I was nothing. He really was a good guy to be around. He never made you feel like you were beneath him or you didn't deserve to be up there with him."

"Our whole thing," continued Harman, "was to do a two-guitar blues band with R&B and blues roots that would find a way to get over to the rock audiences. We were the only blues band to open for X and the Go-Gos. That's early 1980s. We held our own in that new-age, punk audience. They were throwin' shit at everybody else. Kid came in 1980, Fats in 1981. We killed 'em, murdered 'em. We had a bleak recording life, but live the band was killer.

"We really knew how to write songs. I'd write a lot of the song and go to Kid, who has a great knowledge of voicings. Then Fats would show up and we'd show him what we wanted to happen and ask what he heard. He had this incredible taste in music and could suggest what things he should be doing. We'd orchestrate this two-guitar army.

"People would scream for Fats to shred and rip away, and that pissed him off. When guys'd yell out, 'Play lead,' he'd lean over and tell me, 'No solos on me tonight.' And he'd stand there with a smile on his face and play rhythm guitar all night. He was a musician. He loved the whole picture and he wanted to hear it all being played."

In the studio, Harman makes all the rules. This allows him the freedom to sculpt textures in the exact way he hears them. "The CD has to be James Harman from start to finish. That's why I'm a nightmare to these guys. When I tell record labels what I need to produce a CD, they laugh at me. Give me the money and leave me alone. That's the only way to handle me. That's what the Scott Brothers did at Black Top. When I'm finished, I don't want to thank anybody; I don't want to blame anybody. You have to have your own visions of where you're going, or else you'll be manipulated by someone else. I already did that for the first 20 years. Bob Rivera allowed me to become what I've become now." In 1984, Rivera wanted to finance a Harman live CD; James agreed, but only if he could record a studio album too. Those landmark *Extra Napkins* and *Strictly Live* recordings from the mid '80s are now being released in CD format by Cannonball records. *Extra Napkins* showcased James's dedication to tradition by recording each tune with the musicians who would best deliver the sound he wanted. Everybody's tryin' to recreate the ambient sound of the 1950s today; Harman was doin' it in 1984.

Since his Rivera work, Harman the artist tries to paint an album every two years, but always with different color schemes and textures. "I never know what my next release will feature. One of the reviews for *Cards on the Table* came from a reviewer who'd probably heard one of my records, and he wrote, 'This record represents a big change in direction for Harman.' Hey, every record's a change in direction. Every record is different from the last, and yet they are the same because texture's my name. I might play bongos with the rest of us on bagpipes in the Sistine Chapel."

Harman the teacher does not neglect his responsibility to teach today's young musicians and audiences the history of the music. "I was lucky growin' up down there. Somebody showed me the ropes, so I'll show somebody else. It's a beautiful thing to pass on." Spectators who've watched Harman work with his young guitarist, Robbie "Sugar Boy" Eason, can see the special pride James feels in passing the legacy along. "I remember Robbie's first tour. He was 17 and we were playing the King Biscuit Festival in Helena in 1993. He was playing for thousands of people like he'd been doin' it all his life. Then James Cotton needed a band and I volunteered my band. First tour, 17 years old, and he's playin' with Cotton and Pinetop like he'd done this his whole life. He's got the soul of a 50-year-old black musician."

But the most vivid memory Harman has of that weekend happened after hours in Sonny Boy's Hall. Sam Carr and Frank Frost were playing and he remembers seeing Robbie watching the guitar player and listening to how it worked. "I saw the hairs stand up on my arm because I thought I'm doin' exactly what they did to me. Older guys taking me out to joints to hear the real thing. This is good. This is how it's supposed to be, a master-apprentice deal.

"You can't get it all off the records; you've really got to absorb it from the master players. The time I spent sitting in a car with Big Walter or George "Harmonica" Smith means more to me than every record I've ever owned. There was always an unwritten apprenticeship deal that you had to go through. I think if we lose that, we've lost something important."

Fred Kaplan

"**B**lues is not so much music you study, it's painting an emotional portrait," said Fred Kaplan. "When you can paint that portrait and it hits
someone, then you've done your job. Blues wasn't designed for people
to sit around and discuss the finer points eclectically. It ain't about that. It's
about people jumpin' up and dancin'.

"For me, the traditional and contemporary are always running together.
The music I love is all traditional in nature and timeless music. Bach is as
timeless today as he was 300 years ago because he had something to say
musically. Intelligent conversation is still intelligent 500 years later. People
will immediately hear the timeless character of the blues."

Encompassed within his philosophy of keeping traditions alive, Kaplan
has another agenda: to keep the piano alive on the bandstand. When the guitar moved to center stage, it pushed the piano and sax into the background.
From his deep knowledge of the idiom, his friendship with pianist Lloyd
Glenn, and his ensemble work with the Hollywood Fats band, Kaplan
attacks music and mission with intelligence and heart.

"The piano has been shoved to the back of the stage with the screaming
electric guitar. I've been fighting that all my life. Like a sax, the piano has a
purity that you can't change. The piano doesn't have tone and volume
knobs; it's a pure, acoustic instrument like the human voice. It's a percussion instrument, like drums, but with tone as well. It's a five-dimensional
instrument. It has percussion, tone, sustain (like a horn or human voice),
multinote capability, and the pianist can play a whole band by himself. A
guitar can do some of that. But I can play the bass, drum, vocal, and horn
parts all together. That's why piano players were the blues in the 1920s.
Bring one piano player into a house and he could do it all. As soon as you

*As part of the Hollywood Fats band, Fred Kaplan backed
people like Percy Mayfield, Big Joe Turner, Roy Brown,
Lloyd Glenn, and Lowell Fulson.*

add a band to the piano, you have to pare it down and adjust the piano to
fit. As the guitar came more to the front, the piano took a backseat."

Kaplan's deep reverence for the piano came from his association with
West Coast piano legend Lloyd Glenn. Glenn was a piano player from the
1930s. He played with B.B. King in the early 1950s. He cowrote and played
on many of Lowell Fulson's songs. "He was the influence for guys like Ray
Charles and Charles Brown. His biggest recording came out in 1955, called
'Chick-a-Boo.' I modeled a lot of my playing after Lloyd Glenn. I soaked up
Lloyd's West Coast style and Otis Spann's Chicago blues styles. I once took
Lloyd to a show with Charles Brown, B.B. King, and Ray Charles. None of
them called him Lloyd; they all called him Mr. Glenn.

"I met Lloyd at the benefit following T-Bone Walker's funeral. It was at
the Musicians' Union. Lloyd got up with a trio, and 30 seconds into the song
the whole room went dead quiet. My mouth hit the floor. These were all
musicians, people like Johnny "Guitar" Watson and Joe Liggins. It was like
God stepped on the stage; people just shut up and listened. He was a musicians' musician. People realized he had something to say musically.

"We became more than friends; he took me on as his son. I would go to
his house a lot. I spent holidays there. Whatever I could do, I did for them.

He allowed me to become part of his life. He didn't sit down and say, 'Here, play these notes.' He would let me sit at the piano bench while he would play. I absorbed by osmosis what he did into my playing."

As with so many others, Glenn not only offered Kaplan musical lessons, he also provided subtle life lessons. "The biggest thing he taught me was how to listen to music. One thing he said early on that didn't hit me until later was, 'If you can't hear it, you can't play it.' When I finally understood that, he said, 'If you can't play it slow, you can't play it fast.' At the time these were beyond me. But as our relationship and my playing matured, I realized what this man was giving me."

In retrospect, Glenn offered Kaplan the solid foundation to build his style upon. "Lloyd taught me two very important things: Always know where the 'one' is—time—the 'one' beat. Michael Jordan understands where the 'one' is. He knows how many beats go by before he comes back on the ground. Musicians do the same thing. You can throw the tempo in the air and juggle it, but you need to know where the one is so you can put it back down again. In blues, in jazz, time is everything. You have to start there. If you don't have time, you don't have anything.

"The second thing Lloyd told me was what separates the good musicians from the greatest. It's not what they play—it's what they leave out. Pick and choose your notes properly. Don't say it all in one sentence. Use a whole paragraph or page if you like. I didn't comprehend that until years later when I started listening to people like Count Basie. He didn't play much piano—he didn't need to. Muddy Waters is another good example. What he had to say was to the point. All those guys weren't incredible guitar technicians. They knew what they could do and they did it with authority.

"Before I met Lloyd, Otis Spann was my biggest influence. He was on records, so I knew about him and studied him. Through both of those guys, I went backwards in time to Big Maceo, Walter Rolands, Blind John Davis, real obscure piano players who influenced blues piano in the 1920s and 1930s. Then I studied the boogie-woogie school, like Meade Lux Lewis, Albert Ammons, and Jimmy Yancy. I started realizing that piano players were really more isolated then regional guitar players. I learned quickly to identify what part of the country a piano player is from by the way he plays."

Kaplan's road before meeting Glenn had its share of serendipitous twists and turns. Born in 1954 in Southern California, Kaplan had his musical tastes decided early. His father, a furniture salesman, won a piano as a sales perk, so by age five, Kaplan started lessons. Teachers labeled him an incorrigible student who only wanted to play his own music. When another salesman offered the young Kaplan discarded 45s from jukeboxes for five cents each, Kaplan bought 20 for a dollar. "This was pre-Beatles. I was listening to the records of guys I never heard of, like Bo Diddley, Amos Milburn, Chuck Berry, and Little Richard. That was when I got my first taste of blues, through early R&B and rock and roll. That stuff was so different from the surf music and Beach Boys I heard on the radio. Most of the time I listened to the records, then I'd try and play what I'd heard.

"By the time I was in high school, my tastes of what I wanted to learn were very defined. I lived in a Hispanic area, so cruisin' was real big in the late 1960s. These guys knew I played piano, so I'd get asked to their parties. I was in a Hispanic band at these low-rider parties. We'd play strictly R&B stuff. I cut my teeth at these little house parties. It was after high school I met Al Blake, and he sorted the wheat and chaff."

Kaplan's first in-person mentor was the slightly older Blake. "Al'd been in the blues a long time. He would put me on to guys I didn't know. He was more responsible for helping me understand the origins of where the music itself came from. He explained the differences between Texas, Chicago, West Coast, and Piedmont, so he started hipping me to a lot of that stuff stylistically. I knew to pay attention to his knowledge."

Through his friendship with Blake, Kaplan was introduced to the third member of his blues trinity, Hollywood Fats. One night, Blake took Kaplan along to hear Muddy Waters. "He introduced me to Hollywood Fats, this big fat kid with a ponytail. He said, 'He plays guitar.' I'm thinking, 'Yeah, whatever.' This kid got up onstage and just blew my mind. It was one of those things where the picture didn't match the sound. It was like watchin' a Chinese movie where the mouths move in perfect Chinese, but the words are off. I'm thinkin' what's wrong with this picture. Later I realized this kid had a gift. I was still so young that what he was playing was beyond me at the time.

"This was in 1973, and Fats was 19, maybe 20. He'd just come off the road with J.B. Hutto. He had gigs playing with blues guys since he was 15. First guy to give him a job was Shakey Jake. It was through Shakey that Fats got turned on to other guys. Shakey was Magic Sam's uncle. When Sam came to the coast, he'd introduced Fats to him. Magic Sam was a big influence on Fats's playing. Freddie King also influenced Fats a lot in the early '70s. Freddie was also very magnanimous with his playing. He'd sit Fats down for hours and let him pick his brain.

"More than that was the fact that Fats was a gifted individual. He had the type of mind to facilitate anything he could hear. You could put on any old blues album—it didn't matter whether it was Blind Blake or T-Bone Walker—Fats would listen to it a few times and then pick up the guitar, duplicate the tone, and play exactly what he'd heard. He had the broadest musical spectrum of anybody. He could hear and execute whatever he wanted to in the blues idiom.

"The older black guys who saw Fats immediately saw that in him. Freddie King, Johnny Shines, Jimmy Witherspoon, Muddy, they all saw that right away. It only took them a couple of minutes to figure out this guy had a gift. He was beyond anything. Fats was the kind of guitar player who would come up with a part so powerful that it forced you to pay attention to him. It wasn't done with volume. He had such command and authority over the instrument that he made you sit up and listen. Older guys who came to see us saw that right away. I figured that even if I couldn't hear everything he was doing, if they could hear it, I better start listening too. Over the years, I became more of a believer in what the guy had to say musically."

What began as a duo added Fats to the band when he was home. "We were known as the Head Hunters and modeled ourselves after the early Head Hunters, Little Walter and Jimmy Rogers." Then, in 1975, Kaplan formed the Hollywood Fats band.

Strange musical happenings began occurring in Southern California. The mixture of acumen from Kaplan, Blake, and Fats—along with the visionary approach that evolved from Piazza's work before his surgery and expanded in the newly formed Rod Piazza band with Honey, Bill Stuve, and Junior Watson—pioneered a new blues sound, what we today call West Coast blues.

"We all dug blues and listened to blues, but we also listened to straight-ahead jazz people like Art Blakey, Sonny Stitt, Red Garland, Lester Young, Bird, Coltrane, Miles, anybody on the Blue Note label. That's who we heard, blues musicians who played from a jazz perspective. When I talked to Lloyd and T-Bone and Louis Myers, they all had this common thread— they all dug jazz. I found out the guys I liked were jazz players who played blues. That was the approach to our playing. When we play together, we listen to each other the way jazz players listen and play more like a jazz ensemble. The approach to the music is not turn it on, turn it up. It's more turn it on and listen."

That band started backing up people like Joe Turner, Albert Collins, Pee Wee Crayton, Percy Mayfield, Lloyd Glenn, and Lowell Fulson. In 1976, they recorded the Hollywood Fats record, re-released today on Black Top. "Because everybody in blues knew Fats, we quickly developed this reputation. I was booking bands to come out, people like Turner, Fulson, Collins, Otis Rush, Louis Myers, Freddie Robinson, Joe Willie Wilkins, Margie Evans, Eddie "Cleanhead" Vinson, and Johnny Shines. As soon as you said it was the Hollywood Fats band, they were eager to come out and play Los Angeles.

"We had the opportunity to be blues entrepreneurs, so we felt it was our obligation to support the people who influenced us and were responsible for the music. It was a share-keeper thing."

"When we play, then and now, it's like having a conversation with people in the same room. If you're gonna be in a roomful of people having intelligent conversations, you need two things: a vocabulary and the knowledge about what they are speaking about. Without both, you can't play blues like we play it. I was fortunate that by being around the original sources, the people who created the vocabulary, I have the vocabulary. I also had the availability to exercise my vocabulary over the years. I had the good fortune to be with other conversationalists who could sit at the same table with me and say, 'Let's have a conversation right now in the music.' I had all the ingredients at the right time in my life.

"A lot of the younger people coming up today haven't taken the time to learn how to listen. They need to make themselves sensitive enough to not be the lead guy all the time, to be part of the conversation instead of the entire conversation."

Like other blues bands in the late 1970s and early 1980s, survival was tough. Disco and punk were attracting mass audiences, and blues bands suffered through extremely lean times. "We were playing traditional, hardcore, straight-ahead, unadulterated, pure blues, and we couldn't find work to make a living. Fats began playing with James Harman. Then Fats joined the Blasters when they were on the verge of becoming a major rock and roll deal. He got burned out on that really bad. He didn't like the music and the volume. Then he started playing around with different drugs. After he left the Blasters, we decided to give it another shot. Punk was just starting, so they put the Hollywood Fats band on with bands like X upstairs in Chinese restaurants. They didn't know where to put us because we didn't sound like anybody else."

At a moment when the band regrouped for another try, tragedy struck. Kaplan, like Blake, recalls Fats's final gig. "The last time I ever saw Fats, December 9, 1986, we played at the Music Machine in West L.A. as a reunion gig to kick-start the band. It was the kind of performance where we all thought we were gonna do something again. After the gig, I packed my gear and split. I got a phone call Sunday morning saying Fats was gone. I was concerned about Fats's health because of his drug abuse at the time. He never did any hard drugs until he went off to the rock thing near the end. He was around people with money and hard drugs in the last three or four years of his life.

"Blues is a learned cultural music. You need to find the root source and spend time studying it. The music is there; you have to put the time into the study. In order to learn the language, you have to learn the vocabulary.

In order to learn the vocabulary, you have to learn the ABCs. And in order to learn how to put it together, you have to learn the phonics. They all tie together. I'm not taking anything away from the guys who think Stevie Ray Vaughan is the blues. But if he were alive today, he'd be the first to say, 'What I know came from these sources back in time.' It's very important to understand the traditions of the music. If you want to study blues, you have to go find it. It's not promoted in the culture where you can just flip it on. You have to love it. You have to look through the bins and begin to educate yourself."

Keb' Mo'

In the 1960s, Taj Mahal introduced new audiences to the blues. It was Robert Cray who did the same in the 1980s. It is likely that years from now, Keb' Mo' will be the name most identified with attracting younger audiences to the blues in the 1990s and early 2000s.

His Okeh releases seem to enjoy unrestricted airplay in almost any radio format; they and he have been honored with both Grammy and Handy Awards. His velvety voice appears on commercials (like the AT&T effort with dad and kid stuck in their car during a snowstorm while Keb' sings, "Oh, the weather outside is frightful"), his songs show up in movies like *Tin Cup*, and he may even turn up singing or acting on a show like *The Rosie O'Donnell Show, Tonight Show,* or *Touched by an Angel.* He hopes this massive pop culture exposure, coupled with his accessibility and welcoming personality, can lure unfamiliar audiences into acoustic music that grew from Mississippi seeds.

Though he's been a musician in Los Angeles since 1970, Kevin Moore was baptized by the soul of acoustic Mississippi blues only in 1989. From that starting point, he has traveled the back roads of apprenticeship to discover the source.

"I always touched on the blues when I played. But when I heard real acoustic Delta blues, that put a whole different slant on things. Blues is the sound of culture. There's a real pull in the acoustic Delta. These guys were closer to the source. I felt their blues was coming from a place that was more of an honest place. For me, the acoustic is closer to the feel and source. I hear that closeness when I listen to Fred McDowell or Big Bill Broonzy," says Keb'.

There have been two musical epiphanies for Keb'. His brush with Big Bill's records in 1989 illuminated facets of this music he'd never understood. "I was at a friend's house listening to jazz records like Sonny Rollins, Miles, and Herbie Hancock, this really eclectic mix of bebop. All of a sudden he pulled out Big Bill Broonzy. I had been playing at the blues, but when I heard that blues, I knew that was the real blues, the blues from the cot-

When Grammy winner Keb' Mo' was in high school, he cut
classes to see Taj Mahal perform at an assembly. Today, they
perform side by side at festivals around the world.

ton field, the root, one guy plucking and singing. I could hear his soul so
clear. I could hear the soul of a man who was not seduced by Hollywood.
His music was something that was a part of him. After you work all day, you
come home and pick that guitar up and sing about what your day and life
was like. When I heard Big Bill, my mouth hit the floor, and I thought,
'There it is!'

"Music always hypnotized me. I was playing music at an early age. My early musical experience was playing steel drum in a steel band when I was 10. I played in that band all the way through high school. At the same time, I was playing the French horn in the orchestra, and I was playing guitar in a cover band at the school. We played covers of Motown, Stax, Wilson Pickett, Sam and Dave, and the Rascals. The one rock song we did was 'Sunshine of Your Love.'

A little-known singer, Taj Mahal, came to a high school in Compton in the mid-1960s. In the audience sat one Kevin Moore. "I'll always remember my drafting teacher in my senior year of high school, because he had the foresight and wisdom to let me go see Taj twice. He singled me out because he knew that I liked music. No one in the school, including me, had ever heard of him, but I was totally getting it.

"But I never thought of music as a calling. I always saw myself with a tie on working in an office somewhere from 8 to 5. I'd get a track house in one of the outlying areas of Compton. That's what I saw people doing. And music would be something I could do after a day at work. But it was just always there. I supported myself through most of my life with music. It seemed that the call was always music."

Today, in retrospect, Keb' says he knew to accept the call and follow his path. "When you catch on to your path in life, everything lays out perfect. It flows like a river. I discovered my path in my mid-30s. I just thought, 'God wouldn't have given me this gift of music if I couldn't take care of myself.' Once I surrendered to it, the flow totally changed. There's a flow to it, and when you try to control it or overthink it, it won't work, like swimmin' against the river. Once you discover your calling, your calling will take care of you, your calling will not let you down. From that day on I was never without work in music.

"The earlier you find that groove, the better it is. It doesn't matter when you find it. But if you can find it real early on, like Stevie or Jonny Lang, that gives you the confidence in who you are and the confidence that you have a unique place in the world, the confidence that you are a valid part of society. Finding that groove early gives you more time to develop its uniqueness and separate you from the rest of the pack."

The second awakening on this journey was his trip to the Delta in 1993 to live with Eugene Powell, aka Sonny Boy Nelson, for ten days in order to absorb more about the spirit from which the music originates. Powell (who died in November 1998, at 89) and Keb' sat knee to knee and lived the Mississippi life.

"Prior to my record deal, Steve Lavere told me he wanted me to go study with this guy Eugene Powell. He sent me to Mississippi for 10 days to study with Eugene. As we talked, I realized his life, not music, is the real education. It wasn't what he was telling me as much as what I witnessed about who this man is. You learn so much by sitting there and watching him play. I could feel his soul coming through in the music. I could see how the music and man became one. He plays, starts to talk, and I could understand where the licks came from. There was so much to absorb in those ten days."

With his musical calling now focused, Kevin understood that he could ensure his success only if he took full responsibility. "It showed the label [Sony] that if I was gonna get out there and work, they'd get behind me. You gotta be focused with a goal and plan of how to get there," says Keb'.

This sounds like a plan concocted by a newcomer to the music industry. Born in 1951, Keb' has been playing the guitar for 33 years. "Nobody knows who Kevin Moore is. I was virtually unknown. I made my living in L.A. playing a combination of clubs, sessions, theaters, and film work. I used to play with Papa John Creach in 1972–73. I played with him for three years on the road."

In 1993, armed with the passion and direction, Keb' charted his blues course. That plan included nonstop touring both as a solo acoustic performer and as an opener for diverse acts ranging from Santana, Joe Cocker, and Celine Dion to Bonnie Raitt and B.B. King. In January and February of 1995, he performed in a play adapted from three Zora Neale Hurston short stories at the Hartford Stage Company, playing the guitar and singing original blues tunes written for these pieces. He also wrote the original music for Keith Glover's play *Thunder Knocking on the Door*, which played at the Yale Rep Theater in 1997.

"The touring has enriched my life, but it's a struggle to keep up with things at home. The goal today is to really get into life. I've done enough touring. I toured my brains out. Now, it's time to kick back on the touring a bit and get more into life, give myself more time and be selective about the gigs I take. I have to do more of my own shows."

The other key element was to record his own original acoustic-flavored music rather than re-record ad nauseam more covers of country blues. After leaving Creach in 1976, Keb' began honing his songwriting skills. In the early 1980s Keb' spent five years in what he terms "Songwriting College," working in a workshop setting with other writers, for Casablanca Records. "I learned skills like structure, lyrical quality, and content. At that point, I'm free to do whatever I want within that structure. There are certain formalities and basics about composition you follow. Then I add my creativity. That's what I wanted to be first, a songwriter. I didn't really want to be a singer. I would much rather stay home and write for the people."

In that sense, Keb' embodies the bluesman of yesterday enclosed in the skin of today. Powell and Broonzy put their personal experiences into paradoxically happy-sad songs that reached out universally. Keb' writes from that perspective, only it's from the context of today. "A lot of blues artists try to live in the past, playing the classics. That's just as valid as what I do. I just do the same thing they did.

"Everybody's got a heart and feelings. That's where you have to go. If you put heart and sincerity, put your all in there, that overrides the whole deal—as long as you're speaking your truth for the moment. That's what the blues gave me. Those guys were speaking the truth all the time.

"Blues is the truth. Before it was called the blues, we used to call the blues 'the reals.' The blues talks about stuff that's gonna happen to everybody. When you have a problem, you think that nobody's havin' it but you. When you listen to the blues, then you find out that other people are havin' the same kind of problems that you have. It's a feeling of 'I'm not alone.' It's a healing process. When you hear the blues, you don't feel alone."

In that respect, Keb's songs will become vignettes of the modern world, to be looked at in the future in the same way ethnomusicologists study the country blues of the 1930s for an understanding of life then. As a debut blues disc, his first CD was a runaway chart buster. It includes songs like the beautifully written "City Boy," the minor-key lament of every city dweller that explores every person's search for a home where freedom is prized, and "Victims of Comfort," which takes our overindulgent society to task.

Keb's third disc, *Slow Down*, offers nearly perfect snapshots of the world and relationships at the millennium's end. It opens with the gentle swing of "Muddy Waters," a song that explains why he and others have fallen captive to the blues spell. The images Keb' summons on "Henry," a personal tribute to Taj Mahal, recall a rural South when African Americans sharecropped and cuts precisely to the heart of the history of the blues. Both of these songs touch on the core of intense feeling in Delta blues and are pure reminders of why we all love and feel the blues.

"When my second album came around I was scared, because I'd seen enough fail. When I recorded the second one, there were a lot of things going on with my life that were hard to deal with. I realized that no one was going to pay more attention to my record than I was. Too many people were making decisions, and it was starting to get away from me. The take on 'Love You So' isn't the right take I wanted. What saved me were the songs. (Many are his most requested live show staples.) On *Slow Down*, I was there and responsible for everything. I coproduced it with John Lewis Parker, so I got what I wanted. The second one could have been of that quality.

"I'm a one-track-mind kinda guy. I have to focus on what's at hand. That's why when I perform, I only perform; when I'm writing, I'm writing. I discovered that about myself in the late 1980s. I have to get one thing right. That's why I could pull these last three records off, because when I'm recording, that's all I concentrate on. When you write a song for an album, the song tells you what it's gonna be. I don't go into the studio until I'm finished writing. I'm empty after each record. I blurted out everything I had for *Slow Down*. If I was asked to do another record right now, I ain't got no more.

"The acceptance of my original songs lets me know that I've touched listeners with my heart. I never get tired of playing my songs because all those songs have a personal story. Every song has a little experience for me that I relive each time I play one. It feels good when people holler out requests at shows, because then I know what songs the people are really getting into.

"The critics, however, are very interesting animals. There are ones who really listen to your stuff, ones who are jaded, ones who think you suck if you're not at the forefront, ones who think you suck if you are at the forefront, ones who love to chop you down if you re at the top. But one thing about a critic—and really anybody who listens to music—is that everybody's got a heart and feelings. That's where you have to go. If you put heart and sincerity, your all, in each song, even the most jaded critics will feel it. The music keeps growing with life. You have to keep the music in tune with who you are because the music is you and you are the music. I'm a servant to the people and a servant to the music; that's how I would describe my music. As long as you're speaking your truth for the moment, that overrides the whole deal."

Doug
MacLeod

Doug MacLeod will freely share the story: "I wanted to be a bluesman and write blues, but I didn't know about cotton, crossroads, or hellhounds. One-eyed Ernest Banks said, 'Ever been hungry? Ever been broke? Ever miss a woman, boy?' I said, 'Yes sir.' He said, 'Be honest and write about what you know. That's the blues.'"

Since that talk in the mid-1960s, MacLeod has dedicated himself to the perspective of originals. Hiding behind no covers, MacLeod, like the bluesmen of old, bares his writer's soul, in hopes that his songs will soothe and heal. The final cut on MacLeod's 1997 *Unmarked Road* CD offers thanks to MacLeod's blues teacher Banks. Playing without pick, MacLeod uses his heavy thumb to pluck crashing chords. Shrill treble and silvery slide tones all swirl behind MacLeod's lonesome nighttime blues walk.

MacLeod was born in 1946 in New York City. It was when the family moved to St. Louis that the music took hold of MacLeod. "What I heard growin' up in New York was doo-wop. When I got to St. Louis, the guys took me down to Gaslight Square. B.B. King was the first guy I heard." After that, MacLeod took to playing bass in local bands before enlisting in the Navy. Stationed in Virginia, MacLeod first played acoustic blues in the coffee house circuit there. He's very honest about what the motivating force was, women. "When I started, there was no art involved or chills up the spine—it was the women. If the folk guys were doin' great with the girls, that's where I was. If the blues band was doin' great, that's where I was," laughed MacLeod.

All that changed when he met Banks. "Ernest Banks gave me some of the best advice I ever had, not only about the blues, but about how to live my life," remembered MacLeod. "He told me, 'Don't ever play a note you don't

Blues songwriter Doug MacLeod offers one piece of sage
advice: "Don't ever play a note you don't believe in."

believe. That's how you live your life too. Don't ever say anything you don't
believe.' That's some heavy livin'.

"When I first met Eugene, I was a 19-year-old, hot-headed, wise guy. I
went to him not to learn, but to show him what I already knew, because I
was a well-seasoned 19-year-old bluesman. I had my blues uniform and
made sure I looked like a bluesman: Had my beat-up blues hat, my beat-up
jeans, my beat-up shirt, my beat-up shoes, my beat-up blues guitar case I'd

run over concrete walls to get the look. I got there and played a fast and loud Elmore James riff. Banks took my guitar and proceeded to blow rings around everything I played, took me right to school. He looked at me with that one eye and said, 'See what I mean, boy?' I said, 'Yes sir.' Nineteen-year-old, well-seasoned bluesman, and I was humbled.

"When you play alone, you gotta sound like you're more than one guy. That goes back to the old guys, like Ernest and how he played. When he played, he made sure the foot sounded like a bass and a drum, you get the slap on the guitar. You know how Son House played? That's what Ernest sounded like. He sounded like there were three guys playing. It just came natural to him. When this 19-year-old saw that, I was astounded.

"He told me the idea of a bluesman is not about the bluesman, it's about the giving. By reaching other people and making them feel something, you help them get through the world easier.

"Some of my favorite bluesmen are what I would call singer-songwriters, like Big Bill Broonzy, Leadbelly, and J.B. Lenoir. They played guitar in their own way, sang in their own way, and wrote songs in their own way."

Bare-boned blues is how MacLeod delivers his musical vision. The journey recorded is the circuitous path every writer and artist walks in the artistic recreation of self. Musically, MacLeod's arrangements mix the colors and textures of his acoustic finger-picking with explosive percussive rhythms, haunting vocal calls-and-response, soothing brushes, a dominating acoustic bass, and rollicking piano to uniquely paint each song. Those who know MacLeod understand he sings each story with a wide smile. MacLeod's vocals, which effortlessly coast from falsetto to gruff, old man, possess a low-pitched strength perfectly suited to the personal narratives he recounts.

"Ernest taught me about music. He was probably the best guitar player I ever saw. He could play all the styles, from Delta to Piedmont. He would never teach somebody; he would just take the guitar and tune it down. I'd ask him, 'What tuning are you in?' He'd say, 'Vestapol.' I'd go, 'What's that?' I didn't know what that was. I was just tryin' to watch his hands. He figured if you got it, you were supposed to get it, and if you didn't, the hell with you. About seven months later, he'd warmed up to me and we became close friends. Finally, he said, 'You startin' to get a handle on this.' I have no idea why he took to me.

"The apprenticeship really was talkin' together. We'd split a bottle of wine up against my car and talk about what the feeling of blues is. He was more concerned that I get the feeling. I can see it now. He was saying that if you've got the talent, you can play the notes. But what you have to get is the meaning and the feeling behind the music. I think that was what he was teachin' me."

Today, Doug MacLeod is the only one keeping Ernest banks alive. "Ernest froze to death in a snowstorm in 1968. I'd only been with him a couple of years, but I felt a major loss then. In some ways I still feel it today. But I have fond memories and I'm really glad he took a shine to me.

"Norfolk, Virginia, was a rough crowd to play acoustic blues for, so I went away from my solo career. I heard a Kenny Burrell record and said, 'That's what I want to play like.' I met jazz guys and saw the gentler lives they lived and said, 'This is where I'm going. I can live like this.' So I tried my hand at blues-type organ jazz. I moved to Boston and enrolled at Berklee. I was good enough to survive in Boston. Then I came out to California and I ran into some real jazz players. I met Joe Pass. He plays outside, but he can sing it. If your key is F, Joe could sing it in B-flat against that F. Guys who have the education can play the notes on it but can't sing it. He could sing it. I knew if that was a jazz guy, I didn't have a prayer. I don't hear that. It didn't make sense to me. Joe asked me what I heard. I said, 'Blues' and he said there was nothing wrong with that. He said, 'You gotta play what you hear.' That's when I started getting my band together and getting back into the blues."

After moving to Southern California, MacLeod met his other mentor and musical influence, George "Harmonica" Smith. "George taught me more about how to handle a crowd. I never saw anybody do it better. When I see Rod Piazza, I see so much George in his show. I was just a guitar player with George. But every time I played with him, I'd tell my wife, 'I learned a lot today.' The main thing was he honestly cared for people. For George, it was all about entertaining the people with a show, so his core was always, 'I really care for these people.'

"I started with him in 1978 and played on and off with him until he died, in 1984. We used to do this thing at a little 50-seat club on Redondo Pier. For the price of a drink, you could see George, Pee Wee Crayton, Lowell Fulson, Big Joe Turner, Big Mama Thornton, and Shakey Jake. I played behind all these guys, met 'em all. Pee Wee had a great saying. He used to always say, 'Take your time. You're not gonna die right away. Take your time and live with every note,' which is sorta like what Ernest Banks said."

Like so many others on a search for the artistic voice, MacLeod was wearing the wrong clothes, an acoustic bluesman wrapped in the clothes of an electric band. His welcome back to the acoustic traditions happened as many conversions do, late at night and in the desert. "Around 1991, I was in Sedona, Arizona. An agent had come to see the band and didn't like the show. I was crushed. I went up and did this cross on a hill in Sedona. I fell down on my knees. I'm not this religious man, but I said, 'God, I don't know what you want me to do. Whatever your will is, let me know so it can become my will. Help me please.'

"My wife was there and said, 'You just said something from the heart.' After that day, I felt the urge to go back to playin' acoustic solo and writing songs that meant something. I got tired of getting people drunk. In 1992 I dissolved the band, and in 1994 I recorded my first acoustic record, on Audioquest. That's when I started coming back full circle. Now, with my acoustic style of playing, there is some jazz surfacing in the funk and rhythms I'm playing.

"The real secret is that I don't think, I just let it flow. It becomes a very unique, unorthodox way of playing, but it has become my own original style, a voice that sometimes takes people a lifetime to discover. I discovered it quite by accident, by taking that circuitous road. Now I've come back to this style. I know that I'm not traditional, so I get nervous being around traditional-sounding players. To be so well accepted at the King Biscuit Festival has been one of the highlights of my life. Now I feel wonderful and confident about my singing and playing."

Also sharing space at the center of MacLeod's originality is the discovery of his unique song composition. "I consider myself a modern blues songwriter. You have a certain responsibility when you have the pen. Whatever you write—song, book, or article—you have to be responsible. That's something else I learned from Ernest. I've been writing for over 30 years. The growth I've seen is that I'm getting deeper and more introspective. One guy wrote a review saying I'm too introspective about things. What the hell do you want me to write about? I'm writing about what I know. You want me to make up stuff and write it out? Ernest's advice years ago has been a strength and pillar. Even though I may be around people that I sense don't understand blues, it never takes away the fact that I was fortunate to learn from a man who was a master at it. He taught me important things. That's what those guys wrote about.

"The writing process is a gift. I have to honor it when it comes. Sometimes it comes when I don't want it to come, like at 3 A.M. But I honor it when it comes. I know guys who can get up at 10 A.M. and write for three hours. It's never been that way for me. I might go a couple of months with nothing, then all of a sudden, in one week, they'll be six to seven songs. I know that it's just a temporary stop.

"I've given up trying to fit songs into 12-bar forms. They come as they come. I feel that I don't have any right to mess with them as they come through. When I first write, I try and get it out as fast as it's coming. Then I look it over to make sure I'm not saying the same thing twice. I try to consolidate and, like writing poetry, say as much as I can with few words, letting the images do the work. I've written 325 that I know of and another 160 instrumentals we did in my band that have never been recorded. Some of the highlights have been writin' 'Your Bread Ain't Done' for Albert King and 'The Working Man's Blues' in 1984 for Albert Collins. The other highlights have been havin' songs on the TV show *In the Heat of the Night*.

His intensely personal style and personal songs set MacLeod apart from other traditional approaches. However, in the magazine cover world of popular culture, acoustic players like MacLeod are either totally ignored or pushed into loud bars, where the bar banter overpowers the music.

"A bar worries about how much alcohol it can sell. I'm concerned that acoustic blues singers may have to go the folk route until they can hook back up with the blues audience. Somehow there must be a way that the electric blues guys can carve a niche for the acoustic players so that audiences can hear this music too. I would love to see a good electric band carry an acoustic opener. That would be a great show."

But MacLeod is willing to accept any musical challenge in order to continue playing. "Acoustic players going into a bar have to accept that challenge. That's what the original guys did. If you can handle a bar or the club scene, it only makes you stronger. When I do play a loud bar, I'm always surprised that at the end, people are coming up tellin' me they really liked what I played. That's the bluesman touching that one person; that's what it's all about."

The old country road he has walked, good and bad, has shaped him into the total bluesman package: songwriter, vocalist, and guitar player. "I had to come through that stuff to get to where I am today. Somehow, we need to let people know that you can get the education without the scars. We need to save the musicians when they're young. So very few shine when they're old, we need to make 'em shine when they're young. If you can keep the light burning, they can take the music to the places today's musician cannot see or hear."

Coco Montoya

oco Montoya has been given precious traditions to carry on. Montoya, aka Albert Collins's adopted son, accepts the responsibility of keeping Collins alive in every note he plays. Though Montoya played drums and some rhythm guitar with the Iceman from 1972 through 1976, Montoya's shoulders are broad enough to perpetuate Collins' spirit and intensity.

"Albert was very much a father. I try and say it often: I had two fathers, and I was really blessed," whispered Montoya. "The gifts I've received from him were soul, compassion, faith in myself, faith in the music, and how to continue on. I've watched him be strong through a lot of things, and I've watched him be weak too."

His first venture into the blues came before Collins. He went to see an Iron Butterfly show and Albert King was the opener. "When I first got wind of the blues, it was through the British. I thought Clapton was playing Clapton. Crossroads? I thought a friend of Eric's wrote that. When I first heard 'Born Under a Bad Sign' and Cream was playing it, I thought it was theirs. I had no idea, until I saw Albert King, and that was purely by chance. I never intended to go to see King. I went to see Iron Butterfly and Creedence Clearwater. Albert was between the two. He opened, then it was Creedence, then Albert played again, then it was Iron Butterfly.

"He had the kids in the palms of his hands. He came walking up with a pipe in his mouth. He picked up that guitar and did 'Watermelon Man,' and my jaw dropped when I heard his voice. When he was done with his set, I was sweating and totally forgetting about Iron Butterfly. I realized that this is where it all came from."

Whenever Coco Montoya straps on the guitar, you can feel the
spirit of Albert Collins throughout the emotional show.

Montoya's first meeting with Collins came in 1971 when Coco went to
see the Buddy Miles Express at the Whiskey a-Go-Go. Collins was in the
crowd and offered to take Montoya backstage to meet Miles. "After the
show we go back to his house, pop a few beers, play guitars and dominos,
and talk. I leave at 6 A.M. and don't think another thing about him."

Their next meeting wasn't as friendly. Montoya's drums were lent to
Collins and his band for a show. "I got really pissed off when I found my

drums set up different. Me and the club owner got in an argument about it. Albert called me up to apologize. He was so nice about it, I let him use them. I came down to see him play.

"He just floored me. He got in your face. It was incredible. He walked out of the club, and I had goose bumps everywhere. I've never had a drug do me like that. My jaw dropped. When I heard his voice, it was religious. When he was done with his set, I remember being blown away. Then he insisted that I come sit in and play! I came to find out years later, Albert asked everyone to sit in and play. I'd be playing, turn around, and a guy with a guitar in his hand would be pluggin'. I'd look over at Albert and he'd say, 'I told him he could.' He never could say no."

After that gig, Collins called in need of a drummer, and Montoya nervously accepted. "I've never been so scared. I've never been so doubtful but at the same time so exhilarated. I figured I'd have rehearsals. Albert just said, 'I'll be by in three hours.' Went to Oregon with no rehearsals. He talked me through the whole thing. Every time I went on the road with him, every day, he'd ask, 'Did you call your mother?' He used to call her to check that I wasn't lying about calling her. He loved my mother. Seriously. I'd call my mom and Albert would talk to her. It was that close.

"What a beautiful, wonderful, incredible human being to know. Out of the Third Ward of Houston, which is a death sentence. Black and from one of the poorest places in the world, there's really not much hope for you to become the man that he did, and that's amazing—to deal with the racial crap that he grew up in, like every black man did, and to still be the man he was. He loved everybody. He would sit at the end of the bar after a gig and talk to the drunks and have the patience of a big dog playing with a puppy," told Montoya.

"Once we played a festival and Albert came back with tears in his eyes after talking with the promoter. He told me they were trying to cut his money in half. He looked at me and said, 'I'm tired of it being done this way.' I said, 'Pop, I want to play this thing so bad, but don't let them do this to you no more. You gotta make a statement. Let's get out of here. You're better than this.'

"He looked at me, gave me a hug and said, 'Fuck you guys.' The guy went out and announced, 'Albert Collins has chosen not to be a part of this festival because he doesn't want to work with us.' He was making it sound like it was Albert's fault. I ran out there and grabbed the mic real quick and said, "If you'd have paid him what you promised to pay him he'd be playing right now.' That was my proudest moment.

"Albert always used to say, 'If you throw me a brick, I'll hand you a piece of bread,' all the time about turnin' the other cheek. That goes through my head when I'm pissed off at people in this business. When he's telling me that, he's telling me let go, don't get mad anymore, make your peace and live well.

"An Otis Redding ballad called 'Nothing but Love' had the line 'Nothing but love here in my heart and soul.' I realized that was one of the last things Albert ever told me before he died. I remember him standing there, skinny as a rail, and he said, 'I don't hate nobody. I got nothing but love in my heart for everybody.'

"I'll always remember him saying, 'Take you time, son.' That goes through my head almost every day. I'll do something and I'll catch myself rushin,' and I'll stop myself and whisper, 'Take your time.' He did that musically and in life for me. Before you take a solo, take your time. Before you open that door, take your time and wait a minute. Don't be in such a rush.

"From the day I met him to the day I buried him, I heard him saying, 'Thank you for accepting me.' It was what the man ended his shows with every night. A perfect album would be a great picture of Albert looking out at a live audience saying, 'Thank you all for accepting me.' All those things Albert did or said are constantly hitting me in the head all the time.

"When I left him, I went up to Seattle thinking I had my whole career happening up there. I fell flat on my face. I just remember Albert coming into town and me and him sittin' in the old Denny's up there, where we used to sit all the time. I remember I was tryin' to lie to him. I was a kid, broke and livin' in my van. He looked at me and said, 'You just a boy doin' what you had to do. Everybody makes mistakes.' He reached in his pocket and gave me $200 and said, 'Use this to buy gas to go home and regroup and get it together.'"

Collins had an incredible sense of humor, especially when it came to head-cuttin' with any young guitar in the house. "'Pops'll cut you a brand new one. You go up there only if you're ready to get an education.' I remember standing onstage with Stevie Ray in Texas and Albert sank both of us real well. Stevie looked at me and smiled, 'You gotta love getting your ass kicked just like that.' I said, 'It happens every night.' You couldn't get over on that old man, he'd cut your ass. Then he'd come offstage, humble as can be. Those are the lessons you learn from the masters. But you've got to be open and receptive to all that. A lot of guys don't pick up on all the subtleties of those things. You have to see what they go through, see what makes them like that, see what makes them happy, sad, or pissed off before you judge."

From 1976 until 1984, Montoya had lost some of the feel for music and worked bartender jobs to survive. In 1984, his second mentor, John Mayall, was celebrating his birthday in a bar where Montoya was performing. Montoya's from-the-hip version of "All Your Love" caught Mayall's ear, and

Coco was asked to pack his Strat and join the Blues Breakers. "During my stint with the Blues Breakers, I was really a miserable player, yet John hung in there with me. What I learned from Johnny was self-confidence in myself. Through John I've learned how to say it's OK to make mistakes. I could never do that before. I owe John a lot."

Montoya is a self-taught guitar slinger who plays with an emotional intensity few possess. Playing left-handed and upside down, like Albert King, Montoya learned his guitar techniques from his years with Collins. "I never had a lesson in my life. It's more from just hanging out in the hotel rooms. Albert would grab his guitar and I would pick up one and we'd play. I just learned by listening, all by ear. I just play it the way I hear it. I don't know anything about music. I don't know all the licks in the world, but I know the ones I can express happiness or sadness or emotion with.

"I would watch other guitar players to catch what they did. I would wait for that one moment when they would do it, and just stare at them and try and remember where their hand was, where their fingers were. And that night I would go home and find that place on the neck and try to find out where the fingers went. Blistered fingers, are you kidding? But that was the kind of thing I had inside me. I don't think everybody has that drive," revealed Montoya.

"I can only play what I play. When you call me, you're getting Coco Montoya—that's all I got. There's a very limited menu here," laughed Montoya. "I owe that acceptance to John especially. Today, I accept whatever I do good and whatever I do mediocre; I accept me for me. I can't worry about who's quicker on guitar or who sings better. This is me, vocally and musically. When I was with John I was always upset that I wasn't in any of the blues Who's Who books when I'd see all the young guys there and no Montoya. That used to bother me, but no more."

November 1994 is a month of double meaning for Montoya. It is the anniversary of his sobriety and the death of Collins. "It really helps that I don't drink anymore. We have to let the young kids coming up know that they don't have to live the blues lifestyle. Those people lived that life because that was the way life was then. I was up there in it, and I don't regret a minute of it. But that lifestyle doesn't make you a great player. A bottle of Jack Daniels is not gonna make you a great player. Your heart makes you great. The bottle holds you back. You're sloppy, you don't give a damn. You're saying, 'I'll show up when I show up, sing if I want.' You get these attitudes. You just don't care. You can't see that when you're drinking.

"Talk about nuts! I just think about those days with John Mayall. I'd come offstage, go in the dressing room, and swing a bottle against a wall. Walter Trout would take this guitar stand and start beating the wall with it.

Just a lot of uncontrolled anger, especially with the liquor in me. There was no controlling that. That kind of stuff is so negative. I know that now and I am so glad that I'm better. I do still get angry, but I try and channel it into more positive outlets. I'm ready to accept my faults.

"I've apologized to Mayall a million times for what I put him through—drunk on my ass, screamin' at him. Today the good nights far outweigh the bad ones. And I'm getting better and better each day. What's really neat about not drinking is that when I'm playing, I'm actually hearing myself. It's amazing how good it feels now. The music feels so powerful. My mind is a lot better, my attitude too. I can make mistakes and accept that."

It was also a time of personal loss, for Albert Collins died of cancer in that same month and year. "I think everything at this point is for him. I think part of me being sober is attributed to him, because it came when he was dying. There are times I feel Albert's presence onstage. Spooky stuff. There's times I come off the stage and look at my manager, who was also Albert's manager, and I'm shaking. There are times, I swear to God, that he visits. He crawls inside me and it's like he still wants a piece of it. I really feel that."

Coco Montoya is fortunate to have learned his lessons from two classy mentors. One time, he was in a tour bus between Collins and Mayall. As they talked, Montoya realized he was the child sitting between his two "fathers," the youth who is designated to carry forward their life's work. "It just hit me when I was watching them. I am the product of it. I'm the child who's asked to take it to the next generation. I'm the one who's getting so much from this. Without them I wouldn't be here. Without those two main guys in my life, I would not be here. There would be no Coco show; it just wouldn't be happening."

The growth in Montoya as singer and guitarist is crystal clear throughout every live show. When fans flock to a Montoya performance, they come to partake in his naturally flowing hour of joy. They see a show where Montoya goes on spiritual, soulful journeys with music and touches people.

"My live shows are flowing so much more like a journey. When it's comfortable and everything's right, I just go at it with no pretenses in my mind about what or how it's gonna be. I'm really glad to be there playing. I look at myself as a player who just entertains. I don't look at myself as a virtuoso of any kind. I entertain. I have fun being up there. I enjoy people enjoying the music, not saying things like, 'you're so technically happening.'"

One irony in a life full of twists and turns is that in May of 1996 at the Handy Awards, after over 29 years supporting Collins and Mayall and forging a solo career, Montoya was honored as New Blues Artist of the Year. Looking skyward, Montoya's first words were, "Thanks, Pop."

Kelly Joe
Phelps

As technology hurries us forward and the pop culture rapidly searches for the next icon, traditions of our past shuffle off quietly to extinction. Kelly Joe Phelps is one of a dying breed: lap-style slide guitar players. There may be no more than a handful who embrace this antiquated approach to guitar playing. This is not flashy, MTV guitaring young players will embrace; consequently, this style will vanish as those few older masters depart.

"As far as I know, I'm one of the very few playing lap style acoustically. I don't see anyone else doing that," Phelps acknowledges. Sonny Rhodes, David Lindley, Ben Harper, and Jeff Healy all play some electric lap slide, but Phelps plays the style exclusively. "The lap steel that I play is not really that common. Initially, I was experimenting with slide guitar, and I was playing both lap style and bottleneck style. I kept finding little things playing lap style that I liked more. Tonally, there was a certain sweetness that I really liked about using a slide bar. By having it in my lap, I started seeing what I could do technically. The only notes I could play are with the slide bar, which gave me the freedom as far as nuance and shading. I like a larger tone, a bigger body sound. It took making the decision to play that style exclusively. All my guitars are lap guitars. I've got them all set up like dobros. I haven't played standard guitar in years."

Coming from a musical family that resided in Sumner, Washington, Phelps began playing guitar at the age of 12. Early on he gravitated to jazz guitar playing. "My folks started me playing music because they both played. But they were playing real early country and western and their brand of gospel music. As I got a little older I was better able to understand

The spiritual guitar musings of Kelly Joe Phelps attempt to
discover the perfect union of guitar and voice.

the emotional side of that music, in terms of the creative and spontaneous approach. Up to that point I was doing a little bit of finger-picking, but mostly using a pick and strumming without any specific style. I was about 16 or 17 when I ran across this guy who started me playing finger-style guitar. He introduced me to some of the harmonic concepts of jazz that piqued an interest in me. At that point, my limited knowledge was you either approached music creatively or by rote. The rote thing left me dry fast. I just went full speed ahead into exploring the creativity, and it consumed me for quite a long time. It was solitary study from 17 to 21."

Then Phelps started getting out and playing in the Portland, Oregon, jazz scene. For six years he played bass in three-piece bands that played the bebop style he liked. It was the freer forms of the music he heard from bass players Dave Holland and Charlie Hayden and the later recordings of Ornette Coleman and John Coltrane that lead him back to the guitar. "In Portland, there was a pretty strong jazz community. There were a lot of great jazz musicians, and also there was enough support to keep a number of them working. It was a very straight-ahead scene. Bebop was the thing. There wasn't any fusion. There was a lot of work, but there wasn't a lot of money, which meant that most of the groups were small. I picked up the bass at that point. I ended up working around town in jazz as a bass player. It was six or seven years before I picked the guitar back up. Fortunately, the two instruments are close enough. I did all that straight-ahead stuff as a bass player, and that included the freer forms that were going on. And that sort of led me back into the guitar. It got to the point that I was playing bass more as a guitar player, in terms of the melody, so I kinda worked back into guitar.

"Paul Chambers, Ron Carter, and a lot of the upright players were the people I was listening to. From there I listened to Dave Holland, Charlie Hayden, the later Coltrane and Ornette Coleman records, and some of the ECM stuff that was coming out, like Conference of the Birds. Mostly it was other musicians, like Keith Jarrett and Bill Evans.

"The jump back to the blues never felt like it was a jump back. Musically I got farther and farther into playing free music and losing my interest in playing over changes, so to speak. What still was motivating me musically was being completely in touch and in control with spontaneous creation. The farther I went into that, the more things I heard that I wanted to do. Playing with other people started feeling uncomfortable to me, because I wanted to free up the music as much as I could. So I started exploring approaches to the guitar that were free in nature. But at the same time I was heading towards purer melodies and purer rhythms, not simpler.

"Somewhere along the way I got a hold of a Fred McDowell record that opened this door for me. I had probably heard it a few times before, but I'd put it on and it was as if I was listening to any of the free jazz musicians I was listening to at the time. To me he was a singing Ornette Coleman. All of a sudden—the freedom that he had and his approach to something that, if it were to be boiled down, was a relatively simple approach initially, but misleading too. Very complex in its simplicity. In retrospect, I can see that he also opened up the door that allowed me to come full circle with myself musically, because what I do now feels like it's a culmination of all the things clear back to listening to my parents play music," he recalls.

Phelps remembers, "Once I was bit by that bug, I immersed myself in the older Delta players, the common guys, like Fred, Skip James, and Robert Pete Williams. Robert Pete and Fred give the feeling that they just sit down and play music and sing. In another corner it was the country thing, with the way Joe Callicott or Herman Johnson played, real straight forward and very moving."

An emotionally artistic player himself, Phelps is also a technician who searches for the perfect mix or union of himself with his instrument. This honest dedication to a personal growth within a style empowers Phelps to transport audiences to places they never expected to go. His debut Burnside release, *Lead Me On*, is a treasure chest filled with 70 minutes of back-porch-style gems. His eerie images, coupled with his evocative slide, are marvelous renderings of what Robert Johnson might have sounded like today. Phelps' slide is not of the icy Delta style; it is more chordal, and very effective in concert with his baritone voice.

His subsequent recordings on Rykodisc continue Phelps' search for the perfect union of guitar and voice. At times, notes from his lap dobro cascade like a mountain waterfall; at other times, his notes will lighten the night sky like a summer meteor shower. Many times his voice soars in its own direction, while dark and ethereal shadings finger picked on every string of his lap dobro gyrate in a solitary dance to meet its vocal counterpart. There are CDs to turn up the volume and boogie a Friday's worth of joy; there is other music that is more introspective and restorative. Like an antique kit bought to restore the luster in vintage wood that has withstood the ravages of time, Phelps' simplicity puts steel wool and tongue oil to the stains time has put on our spirits.

"Right now I'm at a point where I understand the importance of the music and the creative process. I've got a long road yet to go down, and I've already been down a long road. There's a resolution there that this ain't gonna change; I'm on this road and I'm not getting off. If I was 20, I could say if this isn't working out I could get off this road and do something else. But now there's no choice. I had a kid come up to me the other day and ask, 'What's your advice on making it big?' I laughed, 'Shit, man, put the guitar away! Don't do it because of that!'

"At this point, it feels like a whole different instrument to me, that I've got this very personal connection with the instrument. I can now see that there's a world before me and a lifelong study if I want to find out what's in it."

There is also Kelly Joe Phelps the songwriter. "Writing music is a continual focus as part of the process of getting closer and closer to a more pure expression. My writing process is getting into a space with a handful of stuff at the same time. I tend to work on writing words more than writing music. I'll spend a lot of time just writing and trying to develop that side of what I want to do and not even touch the guitar. It always amazes me when people tell me that my songs soothe or comfort them in the ways that other music touches me. I hope my CD says to the public that it's honest and heartfelt emotion. I mean this stuff with every breath I take. You may or may not like it, but I sure meant it."

The common reaction to Phelps' music notes the sad and doleful nature of his songs, to a fault. "I deal with that subject matter or feeling more than others," answers Kelly. "There is a cathartic nature underlying it all, just as there is under all good music. Even though I sing of despondency and despair, there is an underlying sense of hope. I'm not saying, 'I'm gonna jump off that bridge'; it's more like you're saying, 'Man, this is horrible where I'm at, but there's always tomorrow.' In a spiritual nature, you can sing about the Lord with a very sad tone of voice because you're saying 'I want to meet the Lord in the sweet by-and-by,' but you're also feeling the fact that you are tired and hungry."

As a performer, Phelps is close to the spontaneous visions of a Keith Jarrett. "The way he plays and creates is very inspiring and very moving. He is instrumental in turning that light on for me. He does that; he goes way down inside there and you just hang on every note. He's an amazingly beautiful musician. He may have shown me what a person can strive for with that spontaneous creation. He also is amazing in that I don't necessarily think about playing the blues when I'm playing, and I would imagine it is the same with him, because it's not always jazz that he is playing—it's just music. So all of my influences are coming from my soul through my hands. Playing, many times, is more for me than the audience. Taking a listener to a place is all a side effect to me going there—or trying to get there. Then anybody that chooses to follow along is more than welcome. Performing music is my support system. If I'm traveling, I hear myself thinking, 'If I could just get to that gig and start playing, everything'll be gone and it will all be OK.' It feels very prayerlike, because it's retreating into some kind of meditation that lets the sighs of the world fall away and focuses in on that light."

Phelps' deepest musical philosophies surface when he expounds on the creative processes that occur within any musician who creates from inner visions. His descriptions of the rooms within that he must reach are appropriate to anyone who follows artistic paths. "Every song has the potential of taking me to that place. And on a good, connective night, where I'm really in tune with those impulses, all of the songs I do will fit. The first one or two will take me to the place; the rest will show me all the rooms. It is always the same place, but there are different little corners to look into. When things aren't happening, it feels like the house is way up on the hill and you can't quite get there 'cause the road's slippery. There are times when I'm playing and I have to resort to almost autopilot. That can happen for a variety of reasons, but the most common reason is that someone in the audience isn't particularly enjoying what they are hearing and they might be hollering out, 'Rock and roll!' or 'Play something fast!' or 'Lightnin' Hopkins!' when it's the last thing you want to do that night. The problem is that you might have 100 people in the room, and 99 of them are in church and one of them is hollering for Lightnin' Hopkins and that's the one I hear and respond to. So that can throw me off.

"In that respect, each song is different each time, because that is one of the tools I use to get me to the house. If I play a song the same way twice, I don't get to go to that place. That's strictly personal, because there are songs that are composed and set down in stone that may move me a certain way every time I hear them. It's not the fault of the music in that regard. But for me to go to the place I want to go with music and if I'm playing music, it has to be the energy of the forward motion and momentum of the music and the feeling of walking that I get only from not knowing where the next step is gonna hit."

And will this ever lead Phelps to perfection of inner stirrings and outward expression? "There is no such thing, because each song is in the moment. I would never consider it perfect. As a musician, you know when you're flowing; I know when it's happening, I can feel the magic. That's what I'm always driving for. So it can be magic an infinite number of ways. That's why it can't be perfect. For example, if I played a song that brought the house to tears one night, tomorrow night if I tried to play the same song the exact same way, chances are it wouldn't affect the audience the same way, because all the circumstances are different. There's a magic about music that sometimes brings the audience along with you, which could make any given performance magic. Even if technically it wasn't necessarily happening, the people can respond to that thing spiritually. I've had those experiences too where all of a sudden the whole room just slipped into that space. It lasts for so long and then it's done. You all shared in that and it's over."

In the world of music, there are those who itch for instant fame and those who spend a lifetime in quest of clarity, perfection, and union of sound and idea. Kelly Joe Phelps is the latter.

Rod and Honey
Piazza

Recognition always comes slow in BluesWorld. After starting on the road in 1975, Los Angeles' Rod Piazza and the Mighty Flyers have built themselves into a musical El Niño that continues to storm clubs and festivals with their top notch West Coast brand of swinging jump blues and their breathtaking show. In 1998, he band was nominated in six W.C. Handy award categories. Rod won his first Handy as Harmonica player of the Year and shared the stage with the all star band assembled at the show. Then the next night, in true Mighty Flyer fashion, the band blew the top off the Blues Tent at the Beale Street Music Festival. In 1999, they were again nominated in five major Handy categories, winning as Blues Band of the Year. Ditto 2000. All proof of the ensemble philosophy Piazza learned while apprenticing with blues masters in the 1960s.

To follow the intertwining blend in harmonies and textures, you almost need five sets of ears to discern the individual contributions that snake in and out of any song. From Honey Piazza's two-fisted solo piano boogie-woogie to Rick Holmstrom's fat T-Bone Walker–style guitar phrasing to Bill Stuve's seasoned bass to the double shuffles by drummer Steve Mugalian to Piazza's ultra smooth vocals and harmonica solos atop tables, the show is a highlight reel of precision. Even if you're a veteran of the show, you will still feel compelled to holler "Yeah!" whenever Rod demands it.

"Whether it is 5 or 5,000, we make the audience a part of our show. For us it's a 50/50 share with the audience. We're actually reaching out and grabbing hands, empowering the audience to participate in our show," said Honey. "Rod always says, 'You can't put across a good night in a blues club without a good crowd.'"

The primary force behind the band's success has always been the hep cat, sunglassed vocals and harp work of Piazza. Whether his throat vibrato holds a note longer than it seems possible or he deals out squealin' chromatic

For Rod and Honey Piazza, it's always about the people.
"You can't put across a good night in a club without
a good blues crowd," Rod says.

tones or he draws bent notes from the depths of his experience, Piazza
always plays with an intensity born deep within his soul.

"For me, it's always been to play what I love," said Piazza. "I always felt
that if I was moving the crowd and playing what's in my heart that I was doing
it right. The music was always first and if the people followed it that was great.
I've always tried to play the music I love in a way that they can love it too.

"Playing music is like building a house built of straw. It's a slow process.
When you are just playing traditional blues with spirit and fire, you still
gotta realize that it's not gonna appeal to everybody. I've been doing it since
1965. The Mighty Flyers have been together since 1980. That's a long time
for people to hear about you."

Rod was born in Riverside, California, in 1947. In the 1950s, his first
recorded harmonica influences were Jimmy Reed, Slim Harpo, James
Cotton, and Junior Wells. It was when he was given *The Best of Little Walter*
that Piazza found the harp style suited to him. "Even before I was a bandleader, from playing guitar at seven or eight years old and seeing popular guys
play on TV, I knew that music really was my destiny and it was what I wanted to do. And then getting in the first band I got in, it wasn't much different than it is today as far as trying to please the people and please yourself."

In 1965, he formed a group, the Mystics, and later turned it into the Dirty Blues Band. His primary musical education began when he and a teenage Richard Innes began hangin' in the blues clubs throughout Watts and meeting George "Harmonica" Smith. "George was like a dad to me. We used to hang around or drive around in the car together. That's when he talked about lot of different things that I didn't have a grasp on, being a young white kid.

"Musically, he had larger than life approach to playing blues, one that commanded respect. He showed me to believe in yourself, to be larger than life, and also someone who people can relate to. When I saw guys like Muddy, George, Big Mama, and Wolf, when they were still really doin' it, they were giants. Just walkin' up there before they played a note, they could command this respect. To me, it seemed like if I ever wanted to be some-body, I had to learn how to do that. Before that, I thought I could just stand up there and play. But these guys gave off such a vibe it just had everybody goin' before it even happened," remembered Rod.

Piazza's first time onstage with Smith happened at the Ash Grove in 1968. From his audience seat, Piazza had hollered to Smith that he wanted to play. Midway through the set, Smith handed the 20-year-old Piazza the harp and mic and said, "You said you can blow, so blow!" Piazza first played diatonic, then was handed George's Big Mama, the chromatic. "I played two progressions on the regular harp, but could barely make the changes on the chromatic." Months later, while Piazza was opening for Howlin' Wolf, Smith forced Piazza to repay him and took the stage with Rod. It was from this that Piazza's double harmonica band, Bacon Fat, was born.

In 1969, the two harp approach allowed Piazza to tour the country with Smith and Big Mama Thornton. The Piazza show we see today is a direct descendant from playing gigs with Smith. "I realized that the only way to really succeed is to have the whole cake, not just the frosting. You had to have everything to really make it work. I strive for that with the group. I'm always thinking, 'What's in the show that people really like?' I think that came from being on shows in the late 1960s with George Smith."

The unselfish approach of Piazza's band comes from being around Smith. "I think playing with George helped me the most as a bandleader. I heard how the other guys had screwed up and I learned what not to do from their mistakes. He always let everybody do their thing and wouldn't hold anybody back. A lot of people have come and gone from this band and I think they have gotten better from being in it; they've left a whole better player then they came into it. You might think, if you're the bandleader, that one of the guys might drop the ball. Or if I let this guy have a solo, he might take over the show. By keeping the unit together, we wouldn't lose our momentum toward the overall goal of recognition and success. Those are the natural human instincts of a bandleader. For 30 years, I'd labored under the guilt of playing my solos too long. But in the last few years I've realized that I give everybody else plenty of time to do their solos, I also need to be doin' mine too. You have to be able to lose yourself as a player, but you also have to be conscious up there as a bandleader about what else is going on with the group."

"The first time I sat in with Muddy Waters was in 1968. George had told him about me. He was playin' Shelly's Manhole in L.A. Paul Oscher was playin' harp and Otis Spann was on piano. I asked Paul to let me up there. He said, 'You can't do it.' I said, 'Give me a chance.' He handed me the harp and I started playin' and the band went wild. Muddy came out from the back and got on the bandstand and started the next tune by saying, 'Let me listen to the boy blow.' I got to play with him that night and sat in with him a few more times. I ended up playing in Spann's group. He had a big show in New York at the Electric Circus in 1968. It was Muddy, John Lee Hooker, Buddy Moss, Otis Spann. I was hangin' there for the week and playin' with Spann and S.P. Leary and Johnny Young. That was really great."

Piazza's prime blues mentors in those days were Smith, Pee Wee Crayton, and Shakey Jake. "Pee Wee and I were born on the same day. I called him my godfather. He was always telling people that I was his son. Pee Wee loved me from the minute we got together. He was playing with George Smith when I started playing with him. They were always at each other, but they were still good buddies. Pee Wee'd say, 'George, you can't play no harp, get Rod up here.' There was no rookie test I had to pass. When I joined up with these guys, they really thought I was something. When George realized there were a few things on the harp I couldn't do, he just looked at me kinda cross-eyed. That was how I'd figure out that wasn't right. Shakey told one of the blues magazines, 'I thought Little Walter was dead when I came out to the West Coast, but he ain't. He's living here in Rod Piazza.'"

"Hangin' with those guys was a great life. We'd be at George Smith's house, Shakey Jake's house, Pee Wee Crayton's house. In 1968 and 1969, we'd be backin' up Joe Turner, T-Bone Walker, Eddie "Cleanhead" Vinson, Roy Brown, Big Mama Thornton, and everybody else who came out here. A lot of guys like J. B. Hutto or Sunnyland Slim would stay at George's house. They'd usually play the Ash Grove in L.A., that was a white club. Then after their gig, they'd come down to the black club and sit in after their shows."

In those late 1960s experiences, Piazza was the kid looking over the fence at George Smith and Muddy Waters, while younger players like Kim Wilson and Mark Wenner were looking up at Piazza. "It was just a matter of being a little bit older and bein' there first. Al Blake was older than me and he had the Little Walter records before me and he could play to them. Al was turning me on to that stuff. Charlie Musselwhite and Paul Butterfield were both older than me, and they used to always come around. In fact, I played chromatic on one of Charlie's records in 1969.

"When me and George Smith used to play with the Bacon Fat band in 1969 at the Santa Monica college campus, Kim Wilson was a college student up there. He told me ten years later at Antone's that it was watching me and George Smith playing that 'made me decide to strap on my guns and I wanted to play harmonica.' I remember the first time I met Mark Wenner of the Nighthawks at a show at the Golden Bear. When he walked in during the sound check, he came in and said, 'Man, I learned off those old Bacon Fat records of yours.'" In fact, today there are legions of harmonica players from novice to advanced who look to Piazza's records and performances in the same way Piazza listened and watched Smith and others.

"You have to sit down with those old records with your harps laid out, lock yourself in a room for an hour or two, and play along to learn some of the great music that's already been done. I'd take one song and learn it all the way through. Even years later when I thought I'd gotten Little Walter, whom I loved, years later I could hear notes a half step different than what I'd been playing. At first listen you can't even fathom how much he did on the harp.

"I think the tone in blues is the most important thing you need. It doesn't come right away. It's a development thing. Whether your tongue is on or off the harp, how you hold your hands, all effects your tone. You can watch people play a guitar or piano, but you can't watch a harmonica player play. All you can see is his hands and his face, so it's harder to pick things up.

"I remember in the old days playing with George Smith that he would come up behind me and reach around with his arms and grab my hands and squeeze 'em. He wouldn't say anything to teach me, he'd do things. He'd look at me and if I still wasn't doing it, he'd take the harp during the song and start blowin' it and look at me as if to say, 'Are you getting this, son?' Then, he'd hand it back to me to see if I was catchin' it and shake his head. That was part of going to school."

As more younger players began to link Chess Chicago with the West Coast sound, Piazza recalled the role of the guitar child protégé of the early 1970s, Michael Mann, aka Hollywood Fats. "I gave him his first job in 1970 with the Bacon Fat band. He originally was calling himself Robert Junior Jr. He used to come around to our gigs or go over to Shakey Jake's house in Hollywood. Magic Sam would come out there and hang out for a couple of weeks and Fats would go up there those weeks and hang out too. He got Magic Sam to show some stuff on the guitar. That's when Shakey started calling him Hollywood Fats, because he lived in Hollywood and Fats was overweight so Shakey said, 'You ain't Robert Jr. you're Hollywood Fats.' Fats took that name from then on.

"One of the guys in the Bacon Fat band was murdered and Fats had been wantin' a gig so I hired him. I remember the first rehearsal he came to we were playing a Little Walter song. He was supposed to learn the lead guitar lines. He started off half-assed and really didn't know it. Then he went home and came to the rehearsal the next day and knew it cold, note for note. His solo work was always way beyond anyone else's. He had the timing and the depth to his playing that went with the notes, and the guy was just great rhythmically. I ain't heard no white guys have it like he had it.

"Thirty years ago, in 1970, Fats was way out in front of everybody. Those were tough times in 1971. We were playin' whatever gigs we could get. When Fats had a chance to play with Albert King and asked to go, my answer was, 'Go ahead man, maybe you got a shot at it.' When he came back, and after he and Al couldn't get anything going, me and him and Finis Tasby and Larry Taylor and a drummer played down in Watts at the Chantelly Lace Club with Shakey Jake. The we moved over to Smokey Wilson's Pioneer Club and added Honey, Smokey, and a couple of guys."

Honey Piazza joined Rod's band in 1973. She remembers first asking "Harmonica Rod" for an audition in 1973 and how different Rod was then. "When I met him I said that I played piano like Otis Spann. He said that was the only thing the band was missing. I was in the band because I respected him as a musician. But he was really mean and cold.

"He gave me a tape with three Little Walter songs to learn. He and Richard Innis came to my house a month later. So then we started playing one of the locals and I had to start learning the songs. He was real demanding. He'd say, 'You got tomorrow night to do right or you're out!' He was like a whole different person. But that was the nature of the business as he saw it back then. Rod became a real human being when he got so sick in 1975 and went in for the surgery. He almost died. At that point he saw that you can't stress out with temper and anger. He saw what was important. Facing death makes you evaluate your whole life and look at what you do. I didn't like him at all before the surgery. After that he became a different person."

The ulcerative colitis surgery could not have come at a more inopportune time, the exact moment Muddy Waters was looking for Piazza to fill his harmonica seat. When Piazza left the hospital, that opportunity had passed and half his band had jumped ship to form the Hollywood Fats band. That was when Piazza added guitarist Junior Watson and bassist Bill Stuve to the lineup and launched the Chicago Flying Saucer band, the first incarnation of the Mighty Flyers.

From that moment, it was like a race into space between USA and the USSR. The Hollywood Fats band and Rod's band were nearly simultaneously discovering what today is labeled West Coast jump blues.

The West Coast swingin' sound that is so popular today didn't hatch over night. Piazza and others were experimenting in tiny petri dishes throughout Los Angeles in the 1970s. Cool jazz and big band R&B were prominently displayed, and it was up to the young blues players to discover how to fit these styles together. Older transplanted Chicago bluesmen like Smith fashioned the chromatic harp to mimic the horn lines and young disciples like Piazza followed. Guitar players like Hollywood Fats and Junior Watson uncovered the swing guitar of people like Johnny Moore and T-Bone Walker. Throw in the swing attitude of Louis Jordan and you had all the right ingredients. But when these young bands began playing their unique brand of West Coast jump blues over 20 years ago, no one really got it.

"It was the sound Little Walter had been trying to do in the '50s," said Piazza. "That was where I was coming from. I always wanted a band that played arrangements and had some validity. We knew our sound was different than everybody else we heard, but to us it just felt right."

That's when the Mighty Flyers played at tiny saloons up and down the Pacific Coast Highway. They played gigs six night in a row where Rod could book them. Rod said, "I came up playing for an audience in the 1960s that was at sit-down folk clubs where people watched the band play. We played that music differently than you would play at the bar in Watts where people wanted to get up on the dance floor. And same thing today. You need to read your audience. What has made this band successful has been that we learned to adjust to what the audience hears. We mainly set the tempos, the groove, the type of beat the drums play to pace the show for each different audience."

During the 1980s, thanks to beach clubs and a few die-hard blues joints in California, the Piazza band continues to refine the sound and show. Many of the blues clubs had shriveled and died, and the ghetto taverns in South Central L.A. didn't get where the approach was headed. In those early years, the Fabulous Thunderbirds's Texas shuffle on Telecasters was the sound most associated with blues. It was when the kids at the Southern California beaches began craving the Mighty Flyers' brand of danceable roots rock that the band started gaining widespread regional popularity. "We were using hollow body guitars and a string bass. Nobody was doing it then. That gave us a quieter, jazzier form," said Stuve.

"Almost from the beginning, the crowds of kids out here accepted us. Back East and throughout the Midwest, they really didn't know what to do with us. When we started touring in 1980," recalled Piazza, "I can remember playing in Niagara Falls, and everybody would be standing at the back of the club wonderin' 'What's this?' They wanted that Chicago shuffle Jimmy Reed kind of thing and nothing else."

Today, Piazza has become one of the few modern harp players who has crafted his own original voice into a recognizable harmonica expression that separates him from his oft-praised influences. This identifiable harp voice has new and young players listening in the same way Rod listened to George Smith and Little Walter. Piazza watches these younger harmonica players with a nod of respect. "These guys can play technically note for note better then I ever could. Early on I said to myself not to let my head get in the way of my heart. Not to take the music apart in a way where I lose the feel. I may not be able to always hit the music technically right, but I always worked to get the feeling I wanted.

"It's scary the first time you begin to dabble and put your own brush strokes on the music. Pete Welding wrote on one of my records, 'Rod is not an interpreter of the blues, he is the blues man.' You can play for a number of years and become pretty good on your instrument and singer and you can pick someone else's tune out and do a really good job, play it pretty spot on. I hear a lot of these guys and they're playing a song by somebody and they're playing it pretty close to the original as they can, but that's all they do with it. They don't never put none of themselves into it. I think you got to have something of yourself to tag on to change it up a little bit to make it you or you're just an interpreter of this. Once you've mastered enough of the instrument where you're confident creating on it, then you can do your own thing.

"I was lucky coming up when I did, seeing all those guys. When I wasn't playing, I'd sit on the bandstands and watch what they did. I'd see pitfalls that I didn't want to step into and I'd try to juggle all that and keep it in my mind and make my decisions accordingly to what I had learned. A lot of these young players are real talented at their instruments, but unfortunately, they never got to see any of these guys who were bigger than life and commanded attention. I think that's one thing that I was so lucky to do. Those experiences always add something to whatever I do. I don't know if I'm a big enough icon to younger players where they'll take something from me like I did from the guys I grew up with. I don't know if they'll envision me and the music the way I envisioned those guys."

From her perspective on the boogie-woogie piano seat, Honey can bear witness to Rod's change and growth. "He has gotten so good musically as he shed the other weights. Any harp player will tell you that he's a genius. He plays with such deep soul and with a sensitivity to what's going on. It comes from this place that is so deep. You just don't hear it when you listen to other people play. They might be playing the great notes, they might be playing the great licks, but where is that something that twists you down deep inside.

That thing that puts the bumps on your skin. Or chills up your spine. I always listen for that because that's what I need to hear. He still can do that for me during a show. Give him a slow blues and he can do that anytime he wants.

"The most amazing thing I've seen him do is when he comes up on the gig with just the head to these instrumentals. He'll play the head, and we'll all recognize it, and then he'll go off progression after progression and get more out there with different licks. A normal person hears the normal way the licks go. Rod puts them backwards, reverses them like Little Walter did. He takes Walter apart and twists the licks around and does it the opposite way. I can see harp players in the audience with their mouths hanging open," said Honey.

Working with this solid musical foundation, coupled with the George Smith showmanship, Piazza experienced has merely increased the Flyers' popularity here and abroad. There is no band working harder than Piazza to keep the crowd in the show. His constant yells of, "Let me hear you say yeah!" never allow the audience's attention to wander too far. Honey is quick to explain the Flyer formula for success. "We have a real obligation to our fans, so we put out a lot of energy up there. That's the only way we can play. I've seen Rod so sick, but he is still up on the bar doing his thing. We just have it in us to do the best possible show we can do. We won't let ourselves do any less. We feel we owe it to the people in the audience who have driven a long way to see us or who have spent their money to see us."

Rod agreed, "Believe it or not, if you listen to my shows, you'll hear the home runs, but if you listen hard enough, you're gonna hear some different stuff throughout the night. You're gonna hear different tunes that you haven't heard before. I would love to play nothing but old blues, but I don't want to disappoint the fans who've never seen us."

Because of this heartfelt obligation, the band is always surrounded by a crowd of old friends who turn out to rekindle this special relationship. Honey describes the family feeling generated. "We have built a loyal following over the years that is just like a family. We've seen people meet at our gigs then gotten married, had kids, and now their kids are coming to our shows."

Most fans of the band know Rod's history, but Honey Piazza's road to blues piano followed a more circuitous route. Born in 1951 in Northern California, Honey studied classical piano from seven into her teens, but it was a Texas great-grandmother who exposed her to boogie-woogie. Like so many afflicted with the love of the blues, Honey remembers her conversion.

"I was 19 when I first heard Otis Spann. That's what made me fall in love with the blues. I got every record I could of his and worked for a couple of years mastering what I could from him. His records were my main teacher. He died in 1971 when I was 20. Shortly after that some friends and I went to Chicago. We were just young kids staying on the South side with some relatives of the Spanns. We just put a mattress down in a small apartment they used as storage. We met Louis Myers and he took us around to a lot of the clubs and introduced us to a lot of people. I played with the Four Aces in Chicago. I tried to capture his passion. I did capture a small percentage of his licks, but his passion, his attack, his heart are within the spirit of his music.

"It was kinda the end of the reign of the blues. A lot of the blues players were getting older and a lot of the clubs were closing down. But we were in awe of those people, we were saying, 'Why couldn't we be old like them. Why couldn't we be blues musicians.' We stayed about a month and had to get back. I had my kids to care for. I wanted to move there and stay there forever because that was where you had to go to play the blues. But when I saw what it was like out there on the South Side of Chicago, when I realized that it wasn't the paradise I'd made up in my mind, I knew it would be too hard to move there and raise my kids out there. I said I can do it in California where my roots are."

One constant show highlight is the poundin' piano boogies Honey hammers out twice a show. "Much later, I developed my boogie piano as a side bar. It's ironic that now I'm more identified with that but it's really not what I started out to be. It's a mystery where that inspiration comes from inside the player. I know with "Buzzin'" is about eight minutes and just goes forever and really sends people from these high places and these quiet places. It works them over. It works me over too. Creating as you go takes people on a different trip. It allows people to go to this special world together. As a musician, you hope to go there every night, but some nights it isn't as good as others. Sometimes we can only go to the edge of the place, but we can't go through the door. We always try to, but you cannot get in the door every night. We can be right on the threshold, but we won't feel satisfied because we always want to get beyond the door. There's nothing you can do about it. Practice 24 hours a day, seven days a week—it doesn't matter. It picks and chooses when you are gonna get there.

"I've entered a new time in my life where things are just coming to me when I'm playing. It's not from studying with records or practicing, new things are just coming out. Any musician will tell you that certain licks get predominate in your brain and you go to them. If you play them too much, it can become uninspired. That's why it's so exhilarating when these new things are coming out. I don't even know where they came from or how to tap it. It just came out of me. Whatever's happening, don't all of a sudden end so I can't do it anymore.

"We're all real good at listening to each other. I'll listen really hard to what Rick's playing and what Rod's playing and when my solo comes, play off of that, so to bring a new idea into it. Because we play off each other, whenever anyone finds something new to play, it makes it into a fun battle up there. I might play a piece of someone else's solo to start off mine and go off that."

Though to everyone, Honey appears super confident during performances, she is always plagued by self-doubts. "Music is a challenge I put on myself. I have very high standards for myself. I'm always trying to be better than the night before, always try to outdo myself. Succeeding is wonderful, but sometimes I wear out under the challenge.

"I have to admit that every night, I am worried that I won't hook up to the "Blue Zone." When I do—and I know within the first few seconds of the first song—my playing just flows and there are so many surprises. It's as if the notes are coming from another source. If I just stay out of the way, and don't try too hard or think too much, I can solo all night long without ever repeating myself. But when it doesn't come to me, it's pure torture and I can't imagine ever playing good again.

"At this stage of my life, it's easier to get there. Some nights it will be magical. When you all have that night between five people, it's a rush that is indescribable! Those audiences are just so lucky. When they come up and say, 'It was great tonight,' I say, 'You got a special night, don't forget that.'

"The object of blues is how you play in this most simple art form. Not how much, but how beautiful, how touching, how you can combine what you know. It could be just one note, but it's how you hold that note. In that way, there's an infinite number of soloing and improvisational parts that could go on forever."

Honey's strength does not go unnoticed by the legions of women fans who attend every gig. She doesn't occupy the typical woman singer role; she plays a very active part in the success of the Mighty Flyer band. "Women who see me up there tell me it is an inspiration for something they want to do; they see that now they can go out there and do it. They love seeing a woman up on the stage, and one that kicks ass too! I'm glad to be representing so many people up there and I always try make them proud."

Rod agrees, "I really love to watch the crowd's response to Honey's boogie. For so many years, she was vastly overlooked. There were guys who didn't want to play in a group with her. Now, she's getting her rewards."

Current guitarist Holmstrom has followed the band since the mid-1980s and can view the strengths of Rod and Honey from an inside perspective few of us will ever experience. "Because Rod gets on the road to towns once or twice a year, he feels like he wants to give them the best show possible. A lot of people think the show is the same, but the only thing that is the same is Honey's boogie-woogie number and "Southern Lady." The rest differs every night. You never know what he's gonna pull out. Each night, he turns a song over to Bill and me to sing. There aren't many bandleaders who'll do that. Rod feels, 'If you got something to add to the show, I'm not gonna hold you back.'

"Rod hears everything that's going on all time. I'll play one little note, then later on that night he'll come to me and ask, 'Were you a little sharp on that part in the song we opened with?' I remember the first time ever played within the band, and we played "Mean Old World" by Little Walter. I was filling in for Alex Shultz at the time. I was playing a Muddy Waters chording I thought that was right. Later, Rod said, 'I don't think it's that three-note Muddy Waters chord. I think it's more major sounding.' His explanations are not theoretical, but he was right, he knew what his ear heard. So many times he'll tell me something and I think he's wrong, when I go back and listen to the record, I hear that he's right on the money.

"He's like that with every instrument in the band, especially drums. I think he's probably the best teacher for blues drummer there is. When Jimi Bott came to the band, he was a raw, unfinished product. Look at what he's become. Steve Mugalian has grown so much in his years with Rod. Rod is able to teach Steve and Jimi all the little subtleties and dynamics and every little feel a drummer can have and use. I think that's one of Rod strengths. He went beyond and decided he had to learn what others in the band were supposed to do. That suggests a lifetime of listening to the older players on Rod's part," said Holmstrom.

On Honey, Holmstrom said, "I've learned professionalism from Honey. Honey is very disciplined when she plays a tune. Because Honey has classical training, she can figure things out on the piano that Rod doesn't understand the music theory behind. She can tell him that the guitar is supposed to be playing this dominant or minor chord."

Flyerheads, fans who travel to every festival and show the band plays in a region, look forward to every aspect of their live show. We love to see Honey's boogie, Rick and Bill singin', Rod on tables and bar tops, and anticipate the "Southern Lady" explosion. Many of these aspects are present on every Mighty Flyer CD, from the early ones on Hightone to the 1990s discs on Black Top to *Live At B.B. King's*, a high energy xerox of a Flyers' live set to their current Tone-Cool recordings.

"It's just the fans and the friends that I have made through the music have made my life full of meaning," said Honey. "That's what has given meaning to my life. In the beginning it was more, 'I'm gonna be a musician, people are gonna watch me on stage.' I never expected to get their love back. I ended up discovering people."

Rod also continues to play his blues with an intimate, emotional emphasis. That personal commitment to the music he and the band love surfaces the more you listen and understand. "People interpret you as a serious artist when you've done something for a long time. The artist himself is just trying to pursue the same thing he was after all along. When you are playing traditional blues with spirit and fire, it's gonna be a slow climb. I've been in this music since 1965.

"To me, the music is a love and art form and it's a whole world unto itself. When I see myself nominated in a category for Entertainer of the Year with B.B. King and Buddy Guy, it makes me think that maybe all of this hasn't been just for my own ears. This has always been an effort to spread the music that we love out to the people."

Joe Louis Walker

I
s there a more prolific musician than Joe Louis Walker? By recording ten CDs in little more than ten years, Walker epitomizes the artist's drive within to deliver.

"You could say that I'm more driven than most other guys. I did 10–11 records on my own, but I've also produced some and have been on over 15 other things: two albums with B.B. King, a couple of things with Otis Grand and House of Blues. I lose count," laughed Walker.

The compelling need to deliver surfaces in many different places. "Once I hear someone play and it inspires me, I go home and try to come up with something. It doesn't matter if it's B.B. or Carl Weathersby. I always tell the guys playing with me, 'If this ain't where your heart is, go do something that's your heart, but do it 110 percent'"

As the new century opens, Walker is finally coming into his own as a writer, producer, and singer. He continually writes most of the songs on his recordings. As a producer, Walker is not only in constant demand because he brings out the best of the artist, but Walker also feels that producing brings out new aspects of his own musical spirit. "I like to work with other people. Like a friend of mine once told me, one of music's best qualities is to inspire you."

Walker's inspirations know no limits. He continually discovers a comfortable balance between acoustic and electric musical voices. At times Walker has performed solo with only guitar and harmonica rack; his other gigs center around his ever-changing backup group, the Boss Talkers ("There's strength in numbers. I think it brings out the best in me."). How does Walker balance this double-guitar identity?

***When B.B. King was honored by President Bill Clinton
at the Kennedy Center in 1996, Bonnie Raitt asked
Joe Louis Walker to plan the evening's show.***

"Playing acoustic, I can hear my voice and I can do subtle things with my voice and the guitar. On electric, you can bring the band up or down, but that can become old hat after the first one or two times. Acoustically, you can hear everything much better, which can inspire me to sing better. I don't get self-conscious being out there alone; I just have to practice and practice, over and over. Most guitar players go in their room and turn on their amp and play for 4–5 hours. That's easy. But on the acoustic I have to sing the songs all the way through every day until it becomes like second nature."

Walker's acoustic drive springs from the older acoustic blues musicians around the San Francisco scene with whom Walker worked during the 1960s and 1970s, primarily Mississippi Fred McDowell and Lightnin' Hopkins. "I'd see them all the time. I was only 16 when I played with Fred. Everybody else would go outside to smoke a joint, and I was sitting backstage trying to figure out that damn guitar. I only played once with Lightnin' onstage, but I used to follow him around too.

"My band opened up for Fred, so I'd play the first set. Once, after our set, Fred said, 'Son, you played all your good guitar licks on the first song. What you gonna play now?' I said I was gonna play the same thing, just backwards. He told me I had to learn how to slow down and pace myself. That didn't mean doing a show with half the energy. That means you have to really pace yourself. He told me that on several occasions, and it's so true. I know guys today who play their hot licks on the first song and spend the rest of the night regurgitating it." Important lessons for a 16-year-old kid learning the music. The blues is easy to learn but so hard to master.

Growing up, Walker listened and watched. When Walker left home at 16 and moved in with Michael Bloomfield, the music world presented itself to him. "There were a lot of Chicago guys out here. Jimmy Reed died out here. Lowell Fulson, Jimmy McCracklin, Charlie Musselwhite, Bloomfield, Barry Goldberg, and Nick Gravenites were all out here. If you went to Oakland, they had Little Joe Blue and some of the older guys who had been out here. It was a good scene for the blues.

"You could follow Muddy around then. I met the Wolf and Magic Sam. I played Freddie King's guitar. I've been knowing John Lee Hooker since I was 17. I played with Earl Hooker for a couple of weeks. So I got to know a lot of those guys. Most of them were very giving of their time to young players. They were real understanding. I think they saw in me when they were that age, so they always had time for me.

"I never did ask for any lessons. I thought if I could just watch 'em and pick something up, that would be cool. I've never had another guitar player give any formal lessons. The majority were very giving with what they knew."

Walker remembers those first steps when invited onstage with any of his idols. "Sometimes I'd make a fool of myself and sometimes I wouldn't. The best time I ever had onstage was playing with Earl Hooker. After the song was over, he would give me little pointers, especially about slide guitar. To me, playing with Earl was a real learning ground. So is playing the first time with John Lee, because he's so unique. You gotta keep your ears open. I've played with guys who jump time and play 13-bar blues, so you just have to really listen."

Walker also recalls the days of onstage headcuttin' and ass whoopin', which don't happen anymore: "I remember once, when I was older, playing with Mel Brown. He's the one guy who did teach me something. He's probably one of the greatest guitar players in any style. I remember playing at Antone's and all these hotshot Austin guys had played before him. Mel just came up and slaughtered all of us, including me, just murdered everybody. That doesn't happen much today because everybody's nicey nice. Nobody tells anybody, 'You need to work on that.' Nobody cuts you down, makes you go home and learn. Most kids nowadays want to get up and play guitar. But there's a lot more to it. It's not just notes; it's what's behind the notes.

"When I go into surgery, I don't want a doctor who just came out of med school. I want a guy who's been out there doing surgery more than 15 years. A kid on guitar may be doing the right thing, but later on in his life he'll be mo' better."

Walker was born on Christmas day 1949 in San Francisco. His father was from Cleveland, Mississippi, and his mother was from Little Rock, Arkansas. They brought the music West with them. His father loved the pianomen, like Meade Lux Lewis and Albert Ammons; his mother favored B.B. King. "It was B.B. King all the time." His four older siblings were buying all the Sun Records, Elvis and Jerry Lee Lewis. So Walker's childhood cemented his adult direction.

"I knew when I was seven that music was what I was gonna do. I took home every instrument from the school: violin, accordion, bass, harmonica, drums, you name it. Some of them I was too lazy to learn, like the violin. I had four cousins and three were guitar players, so the guitar came easy. I started playing with my cousins when I was about 14. I left home at 16 and started answering ads in the paper. They were always blues-based groups looking for a guitar player. At 16, I was opening for many of the blues acts who came to play in San Francisco. Before I left home, my mother did send me to a music teacher for about a year. That worked out really good.

"He taught me keys, chord structures, majors, minors, augmented and diminished. In our kind of music I think it's more important to capture the feeling than the technicality. But knowing the technical aspects does help when you get in the studio with people like Branford Marsalis or Charlie Hayden. When they say, 'Let's go to a flattened fifth,' you need to know what that is. The rest of my musical education was sitting home playing along with the records."

In those years, the teenage Walker befriended Chicago transplant Michael Bloomfield and roomed with him in Mill Valley, California. That exposed Walker to the guitarist many call *the* greatest blues guitarist of the 1960s and 1970s. "The nights he was the best were when he was playing with Paul Butterfield. Most of the time I saw him, it was one of those things where you didn't know what was gonna happen next, because he didn't know what was gonna happen next. He was flying without a net. That's the way Buddy Guy used to be. He still plays parts with flashes of that. Michael and Buddy were the two who impressed me, because from note 1 it was extremely exciting. Michael used to get loose every song, every solo. It was like somebody's got you pinned to the wall. I was young when I heard that and I thought, 'I've been listening to blues records since I was two, and he just brought a different image to me.' For just sheer excitement, Michael burned. I don't think Michael was ever captured on record like he played live onstage. The closest thing that I think ever came to it was 'Mellow Down Easy' and 'Got a Mind to Give Up Living.'

"I thought Michael and Taj were bookends of American music. On weekends at the house we'd have country western Saturday, stride piano Friday, bottleneck Thursday. Everybody who came to town came to the house to pay homage to Michael. He was the only guy I know who could come out of a studio doing *Highway 61* with Bob Dylan, then go and do *Fathers and Sons* with Muddy, go play with the Woody Herman Orchestra, come back and play with Sunnyland Slim and Eddie "Cleanhead" Vinson, then play with Moby Grape and not miss a beat. That doesn't even touch on the stuff with Al Kooper, Stephen Stills, Dr. John, John Hammond, and the Electric Flag."

These were also the fast times of overindulgence, and Walker embraced that lifestyle. "I was living the blues lifestyle when everything was excessive. I got tired of the lifestyle, and I had to find another way to live. A lot of my friends were in deep, serious trouble with the lifestyle and so was I. I needed to change or I'd become a statistic. I was fortunate that the right thing came along at the right time for me to find a way out, and it still was music." In 1975, Walker returned to the purity of music and joined a gospel quartet, the Spiritual Corinthians.

At the same time Walker was cleaning his musical soul, he cleaned his system of substances. "I had to go through the program. I've been drug free since 1982. When I cleaned up, I noticed the difference in the music was in the clarity. My head was clearer. I could set goals and time frames. I could plan better. I had more energy. That was the number-one asset in leaving that stuff behind."

Then, surrounded by blues stages at the 1985 New Orleans Jazzfest, the blues again spoke to Walker. "I had a great time in gospel for 10 years, until gospel got a little bit restricting for me. I left it and went back to the blues.

I was writing a lot of songs. We did one and it sounded great, people liked it. But some of the older guys in the group were saying, 'Joe's got too much blues and rock in it.' That's when I figured I gotta be on my way."

Walker was asked to tour Europe with the Mississippi Delta Blues Band and jumped at the chance. Guitar player Cool Papa of the band couldn't go to Europe, so he asked Walker to fill in. In those two months, Walker rebuilt his blues foundation. "The fortunate thing about being with the Mississippi Delta Blues Band was that I was bandleader for half the show. Before I toured, I was playing with a quartet in little places around the Bay Area. After touring Europe, I felt like I could handle it. I could set goals for myself about what I wanted to do for myself. I used the money I made in Europe and made demos to send out to labels. I was trying to get a contract from about six record companies. And I wanted to get a nice band together too. I never put a time limit on things. I knew when positive things started happening, that would spur me on."

Before Walker left for Europe, an interesting twist that could derail most young guitarists reinforced his personal convictions. "Before I left San Francisco, I was playing with Steve Ehrmann and a sax player named Nancy Wright. I didn't know she knew anybody in the business. She sent a live tape to Alligator's Bruce Iglauer. He was coming out to this area, and so he said he was interested in seeing me. That was very encouraging in itself. When he came out to see me, I wasn't playing with my group, I was playing with Cool Papa. He couldn't make any decision from that gig, so he asked me to make him a tape when I came back from Europe. When I came back, I sent him a tape and thought, 'I'm gonna be with Alligator!' But he passed. To this day, I thank him for passing. I signed with Hightone, and they let me do what I wanted to do. If I'd signed with Alligator, my music would have ended up different. Sometimes something you think is bad can really be something good."

The good started happening the moment Walker returned from Europe. He formed the first incarnation of the Bosstalkers, met producers Bruce Bromberg and Dennis Walker of Hightone, and in 1986 released his first album, *Cold Is the Night*, on Hightone. As other albums followed, so did the honors. Handy voters honored Walker as top Contemporary Blues Artist in 1988, 1989, and 1990.

The musical sound that Walker was hearing was a combination of things. The song is the story, and Walker tells the story using his voice and guitar. "I've been raised on putting whatever the song takes. I like to play with subtleties. In the past, blues was two verses, a guitar solo, and out. Too much hard-rockin' stuff is like having sex all the time. For me, that don't work. My thing is more song oriented. If a song calls for a hot guitar solo, I can step into that."

When Walker hit the scene in the mid-1980s, there were the inevitable comparisons between him and another Bay area guitarist, Robert Cray. "When I was playing in 1985, there was no competition with Robert Cray, other than the critics saying there was. I always say that I've got a foot in the old blues and the new blues. The difference between me and Robert and a lot of guys is that I was around all the old guys. Ninety percent of them came out this way, and I got to see them and hang with them. I learned my blues first hand. A lot of the younger guys learn their blues off records. Ain't nothing wrong with that, but it's hard to get a sense of the feeling and the history of the music. Just bein' able to talk to them showed me so much.

"Some guys don't have the personality to be around those cats. They take stuff like Robert Lockwood, Jr. hollerin' at you personally. It ain't no big thing. Next thing, he's asking you to come upstairs and play for him. That's how they communicate. They was tough and you had to be tough too. Now everybody's real nice to each other. That ain't the way I learned how to play. I learned from my failures. I didn't have guys pattin' me on the shoulder."

Stories of blues legends roll from Walker's personal who's who of the blues. "Jimmy Rogers was one of those special guys. Everyone who was ever around Jimmy left with a real positive feeling about his music and the history about it. He's like his playing. You don't know how good it is unless you were to take his guitar playing out of all the Muddy Waters songs. Then you just have gutbucket blues. With him in there, you had a little jazz taste to it. It was amazing what his personality added. He was just like a godfather to all us younger guys. Take away everything else, just consider the history of him and Kim Wilson, and you'll understand what I mean.

In another of the odd twists in the blues, Walker's greatest friendship is with the man whose records he was weaned on growing up, B.B. King. "B.B.'s the encyclopedia. I'm not talking about only music. I'm talking about how to handle yourself. B.B.'s always telling me, 'There are things you've got to do so you don't feel like you're laggin'. If you're gonna do this, you gotta get your rest, take a nap, eat right.' B.B. is always real informative about stuff like that. He tells me stuff I don't wanna hear.

"I opened for him in the mid-1980s, probably 1986. I lived with Bloomfield, and if you didn't like B.B. King, you couldn't live there. I was there when Bloomfield got him to play the Winterland Fillmore the first time."

Walker smiles and tells the story of a guitar given him by King in 1987. King told Walker to choose any guitar from a wall of over 40. When Walker got the guitar home, King told him, "Joe, one of these days when I'm gone, you gonna hear that guitar playing."

The responsibility towards old and new, to preserve and at the same time create, drives Walker today. "That's why I did *Great Guitars* in 1997. I've done shows with 90 percent of those people. They know me and they knew that I wasn't doing it to use them to further my career. I consider them the architects and pioneers of blues guitars. My idea was to showcase how they influenced music from blues to rock to jazz and rockabilly."

Walker comes to the music in the 1990s also wearing the producer's hat. As someone who understands how the music should come from the musician, Walker is the producer of choice of many. "There are hands-on producers and ones who aren't. I'm hands-on, looking to get the best performance from the musician. The musician has to trust me so I can get the best out of them. It's not so much work as it is making somebody feel comfortable. If they do something I don't think is their best, I have to be able to tell them. A lot of producers don't do that.

"It's like a coach, I can't destroy somebody to bring out the best. I've been around producers whose whole attitude changes when there was something happening they didn't get. You're not supposed to get everything. There are some things guys are tryin' to do to make his own style, his own name. A lot of things like that happen by accident. It takes time to find your sound.

"I enjoy it when something that doesn't normally happen happens in the studio. Producing a lot of different people takes me out of my security blanket, and I have to come up with something that fits both me and the person I'm producing. I really have to listen hard as a producer. The most fun I ever had was working with Scotty Moore. A lot of people don't realize Scotty produced all the old Elvis stuff the old way, everybody standing in the same room, the mic's up, and they'd start singing. He said to me, 'Don't go in the booth Joe. We're gonna do it right here.'"

Throughout his resurrected blues life, Walker searches to discover the unique songs, arrangements, or personnel fitted to his concepts or visions. "Every album has a different twist and tries to avoid being pigeonholed. I feel like this, if there is a musical avenue that I think I can do something good in or that I'm versed in, then I'll do it. The only way I can do it is if my heart's in it." Whether you go back to his Hightone recordings, like the riveting *Live at Slim's, Vols. 1 & 2* or the critically acclaimed *The Gift* or you search out Walker's Verve releases from the mid-1990s, like *Blues of the Month Club*, *Great Guitars*, or *The Preacher and the President*, or check out his stripped-down approach with James Cotton on *Deep in the Blues* or his own unadorned acoustic gem *Silvertone Blues*, there is no escaping the fact that Joe Louis Walker remains one of the few chosen to carry the past into the new century.

Junior
Watson

When the West Coast blues guitar tree is constructed, Hollywood Fats and Junior Watson's names will be the limb off of which younger guitarists like Kid Ramos, Alex Schultz, Rick Holmstrom, and Rusty Zinn branch. West Coast Guitarist Junior Watson's introduction to the blues happened as a teen, in 1962. "The surf music was going wild, and I was getting into the instrumental bands like the Ventures. I went to a garage sale and bought a 45, 'Bed Bug Blues' by Lightnin' Slim. That was my introduction to the blues. It was hypnotizing when I first heard it. It gave me a feeling like you've sunk into a realm that was mysterious, and you want to tell everybody but no one wants to listen. That's all we were talking about early on.

"I had just got a guitar with two strings on it and I'd figured out how to play songs like "Walk Right In." My grandparents, who I grew up with, figured I really had some talent and thought they'd better buy me the rest of the strings. I'm self-taught; I never took lessons. These Mexican kids had a band called the Gaylords. They were doing a lot of R&B stuff, so I got to see a lot of it right there.

"The most available stuff were things like Jimmy Reed. All the Mexican kids loved Jimmy Reed. Then Muddy Waters. When I first heard Little Walter in 1966, I realized I was already playing a lot of that guitar style, like sliding on the ninth chords and adding jazz to the rock and roll, bluesy things. It was really strange how I developed that without hearing too much of that. When I heard that style on the Walter songs, everything flew into place. I said, 'This is tailor-made for me.' Once I made that statement, I started listening to Luther Tucker and Robert Lockwood, Jr."

Like the others who came of musical age in the 1960s, Watson was seen

***After he left the Mighty Flyers in 1987, Junior Watson spent
ten years as the lead guitarist for Canned Heat.***

as just another weirdo in high school, part of a small subculture. "I'm
Portuguese, so I got along with the Mexican kids more than the other kids.
We were the outcasts. You could go see the blues, but it was always the
Mexicans and the blacks in the audience. I was 45 miles from Fresno. I was
too young, and it was way on the other side of town, but I saw a lot in the
VFW halls. All these bands came through there. Jim Dovell and the
Gauchos. I remember seeing them playing R&B with driving horns. And if

I had only known what the blues scene was like there in the mid-'60s, the records they were putting out 45 miles from where I was."

Watson was another teenager fortunate to catch first-generation blues players in the mid-'60s. "In 1965, the packages of folk guys were coming through Berkeley, and I could see guys like Mance Lipscomb, Furry Lewis, Bukka White, and Fred McDowell. I saw a couple of those shows. It wasn't my thing, but I sure was fascinated by it. That's when John Lee Hooker was playing by himself and he would kill all of them. He was great. Listening to those guys talk was one of the most fascinating things. The shows were crowded with students. I don't think half those people knew what they were seeing, but at least they were there. Then there was the hippie scene, where you could see Magic Sam opening for the Grateful Dead.

"I remember seeing Buddy Guy in 1967 with Junior Wells. He had this old, beat-up bassman amp in the Fillmore, where you were used to looking up and seeing a wall of amps like a train car. There he was with that little amp, sounding better than anybody. He was an unbelievable showman back then. At that time, 'Purple Haze' or 'Sunshine of Your Love' was out, and he would say, 'Jimi Hendrix can't do it like this,' and he'd play it with a handkerchief over the guitar."

Watson discovered the John Mayall, Paul Butterfield music, then he got on the Delta track. One of his earliest bands included Gary Smith on harmonica and Steve Gnomes. "We were only into the old stuff. That would have been 1968–69 in San Jose. I got all the records, and from that point on I was totally into that. Stuff like Cream, Hendrix, or the Beatles really didn't interest me."

Watson stayed with Smith until 1974. In that time they were the house band in San Francisco for people like Good Rockin' Robinson, Lowell Fulson, Sonny Rhodes, and Luther Tucker. He was a big foundation of the scene, playing with Musselwhite a lot and John Lee Hooker in the early 1970s. "On any given night in San Francisco, you'd have Johnny Winter, Mike Bloomfield, and Elvin Bishop playing, and we'd be backing them up."

As those days became the foundation of the friendship between Watson and Tucker, they also served as Watson's advanced course in the blues guitar style he was already proficient in. "Luther Tucker is the biggest influence on me. I would say there was a good five years of very hot to an intensive learning from Tucker. You learn by watching him play and seeing the whole attitude he brought with him. There was this double-picking style, this flurry he always did. It was a style where you move your hand in a mandolin style of picking. He was the king of that. Tucker took Lockwood's things and put his own touch to them. It's kinda a nervous style, but he played it very relaxed.

"When people asked Tucker where he got this stuff from, he'd answer, 'Tiny Grimes.' That was the first time I'd ever heard the name Tiny Grimes. I would be at the record store the next day looking him up. I made that connection between blues and swing way back then. I couldn't play it all that good, but watchin' Luther Tucker and hearin' him talk about Tiny Grimes' approaches showed me the connection. There weren't any bands really swinging that heavy. It was more of a hard, Chicago-type sound. The Little Walter approach was about as jazzy as you could get. Then you had to go a step further to T-Bone and Charlie Christian to really get that stuff. The study of Christian delves more into the notes and harmonics instead of merely playing a long, lazy note over everything."

The early 1970s had Watson following the blues up and down the California coast. That blues quest exposed Watson to more of the legends but also put him in touch with the generation of young players who were learning with an eye toward developing individualistic approaches. "Rick's was in Venice Beach and everybody came to it. The first time I went there, in 1971, T-Bone Walker was there. There wasn't much money to play there, but they treated you like a king. That's when I saw Hollywood Fats for the first time, playing on a jam night with Rod Piazza. I know that I saw Fats with Albert King in 1970. I think he was 16. I didn't know who he was. I just saw a big fat kid up there with long hair looking like Tiny Tim. He sounded great."

But there was also a dark side to these days, as young white players tried to emulate the rough-and-tumble lifestyle of their blues mentors. "In 1973, I was stabbed by Rick Estrin. He cut me in the jugular vein over this girl. We were backing up Luther Tucker that night. I was in intensive care, and they had to block the vein off. They flew in a specialist. I lost about three and a half pints of blood, and they thought I was going to die. About two and a half weeks later, I was playing with Gary Smith at a place. Tucker walked in and saw me onstage, and it was like he'd seen a ghost. Later he told me he'd seen so many guys in Chicago die from the same kind of knife wound. I didn't even press charges against Rick; I filed for him to have to go to some psychiatric care. It's incredible how much Rick has cleaned up since then. He's totally done a 180."

After this incident, Watson left Smith's band (1974) and teamed with bassist Bill Stuve in an R&B band. "That was when I basically learned how to play songs with changes in them instead of playing only three cords. That was where Bill and I really got together. The offshoot of that was we were working with one of the Globetrotters, going to Las Vegas and Reno, and making good money. At the time, it was a very good learning situation."

At this point, in the mid-'70s, something unique was about to happen.

Having spent at least ten years learning from the fathers of the music, the younger West Coast kids were ready to fly in their own bands with their own unique mix of approaches. The right amounts of Chicago blues and West Coast jazz would lay the groundwork for today's immensely popular West Coast jump blues.

The two competing bands were the Hollywood Fats band and Rod Piazza and the Mighty Flyers. When Piazza came out of the hospital from his surgery, Watson and Stuve were Piazza's choices to replace the departed guitar and bass. "It was called the Chicago Flying Saucer band when I first joined. Steve Gnomes called to tell me that Rod Piazza was coming up to play a few gigs in Berkeley and San Francisco. Gnomes told me that Piazza'd heard me on a Bay Area compilation with Musselwhite, Sonny Rhodes, and Smith from 1976 called *Blue Bay*. Rod heard one instrumental I did called 'Blues for Mr. P.' for Oscar Peterson. At that time I was into Albert Collins, so it had that feel. The other instrumental was more Little Walter. Rod heard that and said, 'That's all the guitar I need to hear.' So he called me up and asked me to play with them up in San Francisco. Because I was in between bands, I accepted immediately. He was a cult figure back then."

The competition heated up as each band laid claim to which was the first to play West Coast jump blues and which band copied. "I think Rod was doing that sound before the Fats band. When I got in the band in 1977 with Rod, there were tapes of Larry, Richard, and Fats with Rod and it sounds great. I remember Fats had a slick sound, a lot slicker than the actual sound of most of the West Coast sound."

For Watson, the early days with the Flyers centered on Piazza's harmonica playing. "I think I've heard every harmonica lick there is, through all the years with all the guys I've played with. I've never really been able to get away from it. I remember right when I got in the Flyers, there were a lot of Little Walter songs. I don't think I've ever played that many Little Walter songs in one night. A lot of the early shows were with George Smith, who wanted a completely different thing.

"When I look back at those days, I realize that George never liked the way I played. He wanted to hear the guitar soloing while the harmonica was going and while the vocals were going. He wanted to hear the guitar soloing every second, and I wanted to be sympathetic to what he was singing and only play in the holes. He kept making faces and telling Rod, 'I don't like this guy, man,' while I was trying to do everything I could to please him. The more you listen to a lot of his late 1960s stuff, the more you hear Marshall Hooks constantly playing. That's what I realized he wanted from me. George was an amazing musician, and I never regret playing with that guy. He was another mentor, like Luther Tucker.

"I never felt overshadowed by playing with all these harmonica players. Almost all of them liked the guitar because they played the Chicago style where the guitar and harmonica are so intertwined. Rod used to tell me George would say that if you could hear the guitar, it was too loud. I never believed that, because George always wanted to hear the guitar," laughed Watson.

Watson had spent ten years with the Flyers when a better offer came across his table, Canned Heat. "Larry Taylor recommended me to the band in 1987. It seemed like the band was fairly sharp when I got in. But it seems to have gotten progressively worse, more rocked out. It was a lot of fun at the very beginning. But as time has gone on, it seems to have leaned more to the uglier side of commercial appeal. I realized that the direction for the Canned Heat was to simply recreate all the hits, to be a nostalgia band totally livin' off the past. You only get people to respond to the hits. Even on the worst night, you always know you can rev an audience up when you launch into a hit. I quit in October of 1997, after Henry Vestine died. When we found Henry dead in his hotel room on October 20, 1997, I thought it was an omen that I should get out of there. Of the three guitars—Robert Lucas, Henry, and myself—Henry was the guy who really got over to the audiences. Henry owned that sound of the band. He had the squawky, identifiable Canned Heat sound. Since he's been gone, it started having no direction. There was nothing to look forward. Now there's only Larry Taylor and Fito de la Parra left. It's just played out.

"Today, I prefer the blues crowd, because they seem to be more educated and know what they came for and respond more to the music."

At the core of anything Watson's associated with is his inventive guitar ideas, which sprout like wildflowers in an Alpine meadow. Just when you think you know where he's going, Watson speeds off road for a bar or two and then returns. From the shivery, distorted, squawking tones he gets from the vintage equipment he uses, to the mandolin-style up-and-down string picking, to his ultrahip, ultraclean solos, Watson plays with all the excitement of a kid turned loose at a nude beach. Rather than lock into imitation, Watson brings a playful sense of humor to the music. In the middle of a song, he may quote "Here Comes the Bride" and then leap right back into some 1950s blues tune.

To achieve that signature sound, Watson turned himself into the king of retro arch tops and tweed amps. "I basically discovered it. I had a 1961 Birdland guitar with VAF pickups when I played with Rod Piazza. I'd be saying, it sounds pretty good, but it still sounds too modern. We were playing a ski resort with George Smith, up in Oregon, and I went to this music store. There on the wall was an Espanada guitar made by Harmony. That's basically a big, fat, 16-inch-body black guitar with aluminum bindings on it. It looks really peculiar. I pulled it off the wall, and it had the tone I was going for acoustically. It was $50, and I didn't have the money because I was just starting to work with Rod. He paid for it, and that's been my guitar all these years. I've got all kinds of guitars for different situations, but that's the guitar for me to really have the Tiny Grimes–type tone when I'm recording. It's a really powerful bassy tone that's distorted."

Watson's 11 years with the Flyers lightened up the serious and deep blues guitar everybody else was playing. He brought a sense of humor to the role of the guitar and popularized cheap, vintage guitars. Watson's pupils include the likes of Alex Schultz and Rick Holmstrom. The best description of Watson's approach may come from Holmstrom: "Just the choice of cheap Silvertone, Harmony, and Kay guitars he used was a new thing. He played with an off-the-wall approach that made people laugh. He has a definite sense of humor in everything he plays. You can't go away from watching Junior and not smile. He took the notion that everything had to be serious, soulful, and deep all the time and lightened it. I think a lot of guitar players latched onto that.

"He was finding the old tweed amps, trying to get that the fat, spongy sound. Junior was playing quiet underneath. Once he asked me to try playing without bending any notes for as long as I could. He told me to slur everything or go chromatically. He wanted me to do that because those guys in the old days couldn't bend strings as easily as we do today because the strings were so thick. That's why players back then played the way they did. The limitation was placed on them by the equipment. Junior is actually one of the best note benders there is, but that was an exercise, a way to develop a style, something that was different from what everyone else was playing. Junior forced himself to do things that were different. He got me thinking about that," said Holmstrom. "Junior Watson's advice to me was to play two- and three-note little chords, not huge chords. The voicings on the guitar have to be sharp, close, and direct."

Holmstrom summed up Watson's place on the guitar tree: "Bill Clarke used to tell me that Fats was the king, the baddest, toughest out here, until about the early 1980s. Then Watson caught up to him and, in Bill's eyes, passed him as far as ideas and original sound to become an influence on everyone who came after."

DISCOGRAPHY

Allison, Bernard, *Hang On*, Inak, 1993

Allison, Bernard, *No Mercy*, Inak, 1996

Allison, Bernard, *Keeping the Blues Alive*, Cannonball, 1997

Allison, Bernard, *Times Are Changing*, Ruf Records, 1998

Allison, Bernard, *Across the Water*, Tone-Cool, 2000

Allison, Luther, *Love Me Mama*, Delmark, 1969

Allison, Luther, *Bad News Is Coming*, Motown, 1973

Allison, Luther, *Luther's Blues*, Motown, 1974

Allison, Luther, *Night Life*, Motown, 1975

Allison, Luther, *Love Me Papa*, Evidence, 1977

Allison, Luther, *Live in Paris*, Ruf Records, 1979

Allison, Luther, *Power at Wire Blues*, Charley, 1979

Allison, Luther, *Serious*, Blind Pig, 1987

Allison, Luther, *Hand Me Down My Moonshine*, Ruf Records, 1994

Allison, Luther, *Soul-Fixin Man*, Alligator, 1994

Allison, Luther, *Blue Streak*, Alligator, 1995

Allison, Luther, *Reckless*, Alligator, 1997

Allison, Luther, *The Motown Years*, Motown, 1996

Allison, Luther, *Where Have You Been? Live in Montreux*, Ruf Records, 1976-1994

Allison, Luther, *Love the People, Live at the Barrymoore*, Self-issued, 1997

Allison, Luther, *Live in Chicago*, Alligator, 1999

Ball, Marcia, *Soulful Dress*, Rounder, 1983

Ball, Marcia, *Hot Tamale Baby*, Rounder, 1985

Ball, Marcia, *Gatorhythms*, Rounder, 1989

Ball, Marcia, *Dreams Come True*, Antone's, 1990

Ball, Marcia, *Blue House*, Rounder, 1994

Ball, Marcia, *Let Me Play with Your Poodle*, Rounder, 1997

Ball, Marcia, *Presumed Innocent*, Alligator, 2001

Blake, Al, *Mr. Blake's Blues*, Blue Collar Music, 1997

Block, Rory, *The Early Tapes, 1975-1976*, Alkazar, 1976

Block, Rory, *High-Heeled Blues*, Rounder, 1981

Block, Rory, *Best Blues and Originals*, Rounder, 1981-87

Block, Rory, *Blue Horizon*, Rounder, 1983

Block, Rory, *Rhinestones and Steel Strings*, Rounder, 1983

Block, Rory, *I've Got a Rock in My Sock*, Rounder, 1986

Block, Rory, *House of Hearts*, Rounder, 1987

Block, Rory, *Mama's Blues*, Rounder, 1991

Block, Rory, *Ain't I a Woman*, Rounder, 1992

Block, Rory, *Angel of Mercy*, Rounder, 1994

Block, Rory, *When a Woman Gets the Blues*, Rounder, 1995

Block, Rory, *Turning Point*, Munich, 1996

Block, Rory, *Tornado*, Rounder, 1996

Block, Rory, *Gone Woman Blues*, Rounder, 1997

Block, Rory, *Best Blues and Originals, Volume II*, Munich, 1997

Block, Rory, *Confessions of a Blues Singer*, Rounder, 1998

Block, Rory, *I'm Every Woman*, Rounder, 2001

Brooks, Lonnie, *The Crawl*, Charlie, 1955-1959

Brooks, Lonnie, *Live at Peppers, 1968*, Black Top, 1968

Brooks, Lonnie, *Sweet Home Chicago*, Evidence, 1975

Brooks, Lonnie, *Let's Talk It Over*, Delmark, 1977

Brooks, Lonnie, *Bayou Lightning*, Alligator, 1979

Brooks, Lonnie, *Turn On the Night*, Alligator, 1981

Brooks, Lonnie, *Hot Shot*, Alligator, 1983

Brooks, Lonnie, *Wound Up Tight*, Alligator, 1986

Brooks, Lonnie, *Live from Chicago*, Alligator, 1987

Brooks, Lonnie, *Satisfaction Guaranteed*, Alligator, 1991

Brooks, Lonnie, *Roadhouse Blues*, Alligator, 1996

Brooks, Lonnie, *Deluxe Edition*, Alligator, 1997

Brooks, Lonnie, *Lone Star Shootout*, Alligator, 1999

Brooks, Ronnie Baker, *Golddigger*, Watchdog Records, 1998

Brooks, Ronnie Baker, *Take Me Witcha*, Watchdog Records, 2002

Brown, Kenny, *Going Back to Mississippi*, Plum Tone, 1996

Brown, Kenny, Can also be found on most R.L. Burnside CD's on Fat Possum

Copeland, Johnny, *Copeland Special*, Rounder, 1981

Copeland, Johnny, *Texas Twister*, Rounder, 1983

Copeland, Johnny, *Showdown*, Alligator, 1985

Copeland, Johnny, *Brining It All Back Home*, Rounder, 1986

Copeland, Johnny, *Houston Routes*, Ace, 1988

Copeland, Johnny, *Ain't Nothin' but a Party*, Rounder, 1988

Copeland, Johnny, *Collection Volume I*, Collectibles, 1988

Copeland, Johnny, *Boom Boom*, Rounder, 1990

Copeland, Johnny, *Collection Volume II*, Collectibles, 1990

Copeland, Johnny, *Flying High*, Verve, 1992

Copeland, Johnny, *Further up the Road*, Aim, 1993

Copeland, Johnny, *Catch Up with the Blues*, Polygram, 1994

Copeland, Johnny, *Jungle Swing*, Verve, 1996

Copeland, Johnny, *Live in Australia*, Black Top, 1997

Copeland, Johnny, *Honky Tonkin'*, Bullseye Blues, 1999

Copeland, Shemekia, *Turn the Heat Up*, Alligator, 1998

Copeland, Shemekia, *Wicked*, Alligator, 2000

Cray, Robert, *Who's Been Talking?*, Atlantic, 1980

Cray, Robert, *Bad Influence*, High Tone, 1983

Cray, Robert, False Accusations, High Tone, 1985

Cray, Robert, *Showdown*, Alligator, 1985

Cray, Robert, *Strong Persuader*, Mercury, 1986

Cray, Robert, *Don't Be Afraid of the Dark*, Mercury, 1988

Cray, Robert, *Midnight Stroll*, Mercury, 1990

Cray, Robert, *Too Many Crooks*, Tomato, 1990

Cray, Robert, *I Was Warned*, Mercury, 1992

Cray, Robert, *Shame and a Sin*, Mercury, 1993

Cray, Robert, *Some Rainy Morning*, Mercury, 1995

Cray, Robert, *Sweet Potato Pie*, Polygram, 1997

Cray, Robert, *Take Your Shoes Off*, Rykodisc, 1999

Cray, Robert, *Heavy Picks*, Mercury, 1999

Cray, Robert, *Shoulda Been Home*, Rykodisc, 2001

Davies, Debbie, *Picture This*, Blind Pig, 1993

Davies, Debbie, *Loose Tonight*, Blind Pig, 1994

Davies, Debbie, *I Got That Feeling*, Blind Pig, 1996

Davies, Debbie, *Round Every Corner*, Shanachie, 1998

Davies, Debbie, *Tales From the Austin Motel*, Shanachie, 1999

Davies, Debbie, *Love the Game*, Shanachie, 2001

Funderburgh, Myers, *Talk to You by Hand*, Black Top, 1981

Funderburgh, Myers, *She Knocks Me Out*, Black Top, 1985

Funderburgh, Myers, *My Love Is Here To Stay*, Black Top, 1986

Funderburgh, Myers, *Sins*, Black Top, 1987

Funderburgh, Myers, *Rack Em Up*, Black Top, 1989

Funderburgh, Myers, *Tell Me What I Want To Hear*, Black Top, 1991

Funderburgh, Myers, *Through the Years, a Retrospective*, Black Top, 1992

Funderburgh, Myers, *Live at the Grand Emporium*, Black Top, 1995

Funderburgh, Myers, *That's What They Want*, Black Top, 1997

Funderburgh, Myers, *Change in My Pocket*, Bullseye Blues, 1999

Hammond, John, *Big City Blues*, Vanguard, 1964

Hammond, John, *Country Blues*, Vanguard, 1964

Hammond, John, *So Many Roads*, Vanguard, 1965

Hammond, John, *Live*, Rounder, 1983

Hammond, John, *The Best of John Hammond*, Vanguard, 1989

Hammond, John, *Got Love If You Want It*, Charisma, 1992

Hammond, John, *Live*, Rounder, 1992

Hammond, John, *Mileage*, Rounder, 1980

Hammond, John, *Frogs for Snakes*, Rounder, 1982

Hammond, John, *Trouble No More*, Virgin Point Blank, 1994

Hammond, John, *Found True Love*, Virgin Point Blank, 1996

Hammond, John, *Long As I Have You*, Virgin Point Blank, 1998

Hammond, John, *Wicked Grin*, Virgin Point Blank, 2001

Harman, James, *Those Dangerous Gentlemen*, Rhino, 1987

Harman, James, *Extra Napkins*, Cannonball, 1997

Harman, James, *Extra Napkins, Vol. 2*, Cannonball, 2000

Harman, James, *Live in '85 Volume I*, Rivera and Cannonball, 1990

Harman, James, *Do Not Disturb*, Black Top, 1991

Harman, James, *Two Sides to Every Story*, Black Top, 1993

Harman, James, *Cards on the Table*, Black Top, 1994

Harman, James, *Black and White*, Black Top, 1995

Harman, James, *Taking Chances*, Cannonball, 1998

Hollywood Fats, *Rock This House*, Black Top, 1993

Johnson, Big Jack, *The Oil Man*, Earwig, 1987

Johnson, Big Jack, *Daddy, When Is Mama Coming Home?*, Earwig, 1991

Johnson, Big Jack, *Live in Chicago*, Earwig, 1997

Johnson, Big Jack, *We Got to Stop This Killing*, M.C. Records, 1996

Johnson, Big Jack, *All the Way Back*, M.C. Records, 1998

Johnson, Big Jack, *Roots Stew*, M.C. Records, 2000

Johnson, Big Jack, *Memphis Barbecue Sessions*, M.C. Records, 2002

Johnson, Big Jack, and the Jelly Roll Kings, *Rockin' the Juke Joint Down*, Earwig, 1979

Johnson, Big Jack, and the Jelly Roll Kings, *Off Yonder Wall*, Fat Possum, 1997

Johnson, Big Jack, and the Jelly Roll Kings, *Jelly Roll Blues*, Paula, 1973

Kaplan, Fred, *Signifying*, Blue Collar Music, 1997

Kubek, Smokin' Joe, and Bnois King, *Steppin' Out Texas Style*, Bullseye Blues, 1991

Kubek, Smokin' Joe, and Bnois King, *Chain-Smokin' Texas Style*, Bullseye Blues, 1992

Kubek, Smokin' Joe, and Bnois King, *Texas Cadillac*, Bullseye Blues, 1993

Kubek, Smokin' Joe, and Bnois King, *Keep Comin' Back*, Bullseye Blues, 1995

Kubek, Smokin' Joe, and Bnois King, *Got My Mind Back*, Bullseye Blues, 1996

Kubek, Smokin' Joe, and Bnois King, *Take Your Best Shot*, Bullseye Blues, 1998

Kubek, Smokin' Joe, and Bnois King, *Cryin' For the Moon*, Bullseye Blues, 1995

Kubek, Smokin' Joe, and Bnois King, *Bite Me*, Bullseye Blues, 2000

Lane, Jimmy D., *It's Time*, Acoustic Sounds, 2002

Lane, Jimmy D., *Legacy*, Acoustic Sounds, 1998

Lane, Jimmy D., *Long Gone*, Acoustic Sounds, 1997

MacLeod, Doug, *Come to Find*, Audio Quest, 1994

MacLeod, Doug, *You Can't Take My Blues*, Audio Quest, 1996

MacLeod, Doug, *Unmarked Road*, Audio Quest, 1997

MacLeod, Doug, *Fifty-Forth and Vermont*, Self-produced, 1989

MacLeod, Doug, *Woman in the Street*, Self-produced, 1987

MacLeod, Doug, *Live As It Gets*, Macombo Records, 1999

MacLeod, Doug, *Whose Truth, Whose Lies*, Audio Quest, 2000

Mahal, Taj, *Natch'l Blues*, Columbia, 1968

Mahal, Taj, *Giant Step*, Columbia, 1969

Mahal, Taj, *Taj Mahal*, Columbia, 1968

Mahal, Taj, *The Real Thing*, Columbia, 1972

Mahal, Taj, *Sounder*, Columbia, 1973

Mahal, Taj, *Oh So Good in Blues*, Columbia, 1973

Mahal, Taj, *Mo' Roots*, Columbia, 1974

Mahal, Taj, *Anthology, Volume I, 1966-76*, Columbia, 1976

Mahal, Taj, *Like Never Before*, Private Music, 1991

Mahal, Taj, *Taj's Blues*, Columbia Legacy, 1992

Mahal, Taj, *Dancing the Blues*, Private Music, 1993

Mahal, Taj, *Phantom Blues*, Private, 1996

Mahal, Taj, *An Evening of Acoustic Music*, Ruf Records, 1996

Mahal, Taj, *Señor Blues*, Private Music, 1997

Mahal, Taj, *Sacred Island*, Private Music, 1998

Mahal, Taj, *In Progress and in Motion, 1965-1998*, Columbia, 1998

Mahal, Taj, *Kulanjan*, Rykodisc, 1999

Mahal, Taj, *Blue Light Boogie*, Private Music, 2000

Mahal, Taj, *Shoutin' in Key*, Hannibal, 2000

Margolin, Bob, *The Old School*, Powerhouse, 1988

Margolin, Bob, *Chicago Blues*, Powerhouse, 1990

Margolin, Bob, *Down in the Alley*, Alligator, 1993

Margolin, Bob, *My Blues and My Guitar*, Alligator, 1995

Margolin, Bob, *Up and In*, Alligator, 1997

Margolin, Bob, *Hold Me to It*, Blind Pig, 1999

Maxwell, David, *Maximum Blues Piano*, Tone Cool, 1997

McClinton, Delbert, *Delbert and Glenn, Clean*, 1972

McClinton, Delbert, *Victim of Life's Circumstances*, ABC, 1975

McClinton, Delbert, *Genuine Cowhide*, ABC, 1976

McClinton, Delbert, *Love Wrestler*, ABC, 1977

McClinton, Delbert, *Second Wind*, Mercury, 1978

McClinton, Delbert, *Keeper of the Flame*, Mercury, 1979

McClinton, Delbert, *The Jealous Kind*, Capital, 1980

McClinton, Delbert, *Playing from the Heart*, Capital, 1981

McClinton, Delbert, *The Best of Delbert McClinton*, Curb, 1989

McClinton, Delbert, *Honky Tonkin'*, Alligator, 1989

McClinton, Delbert, *Live from Austin*, Alligator, 1989

McClinton, Delbert, *I'm with You*, Curb, 1990

McClinton, Delbert, *Never Been Rocked Enough*, Curb, 1992

McClinton, Delbert, *Delbert McClinton*, Curb, 1993

McClinton, Delbert, *Classics Volume II, Playing from the Heart*, Curb, 1994

McClinton, Delbert, *Classics Volume I, The Jealous Kind*, Curb, 1994

McClinton, Delbert, *Great Songs Come Together*, Curb, 1995

McClinton, Delbert, *One of the Fortunate Few*, Rising Tide, 1997

McClinton, Delbert, *Nothing Personal*, New West, 2001

Mo', Keb', *Keb' Mo'*, Epic, 1994

Mo', Keb', *Just Like You*, Epic, 1996

Mo', Keb', *Slow Down*, Epic, 1998

Mo', Keb', *The Door*, Epic, 2000

Mo', Keb', *The Grin*, Epic, 2001

Montoya, Coco, *Got a Mind to Travel*, Blind Pig, 1995

Montoya, Coco, *Ya Think I'd Know Better*, Blind Pig, 1996

Montoya, Coco, *Just Let Go*, Blind Pig, 1997

Montoya, Coco, *Suspicion*, Alligator, 2000

Musselwhite, Charlie, *Stand Back, Here Comes Charlie Musselwhite's South Side Band*, Vanguard, 1967

Musselwhite, Charlie, *Stone Blues*, Vanguard, 1968

Musselwhite, Charlie, *Charlie Musselwhite*, Vanguard, 1968

Musselwhite, Charlie, *Louisiana Fog*, Cherry Red, 1968

Musselwhite, Charlie, *Tennessee Woman*, Vanguard, 1969

Musselwhite, Charlie, *Memphis Charlie*, Arhoolie, 1969

Musselwhite, Charlie, *Taking My Time*, Arhoolie, 1974

Musselwhite, Charlie, *Going Back Down South*, Arhoolie, 1975

Musselwhite, Charlie, *Leaves the Blues to Us*, Capitol, 1975

Musselwhite, Charlie, *Times Gettin Tougher Than Tough*, Crystal Clear, 1978

Musselwhite, Charlie, *Harmonica According to Charlie*, Kicking Mule, 1979

Musselwhite, Charlie, *Tell Me Where Have All the Good Times Gone*, Blue Rocket, 1984

Musselwhite, Charlie, *Memphis, Tennessee*, Mobil Fidelity, 1984

Musselwhite, Charlie, *Mellow Dee*, Cross Cut, 1986

Musselwhite, Charlie, *Ace of Hearts*, Alligator, 1990

Musselwhite, Charlie, *Signature*, Alligator, 1991

Musselwhite, Charlie, *In My Time*, Alligator, 1993

Musselwhite, Charlie, *Rough News*, Virgin Point Blank, 1997

Musselwhite, Charlie, *Blues Never Die*, Vanguard, 1998

Musselwhite, Charlie, *Continental Drifter*, Virgin Point Blank, 1999

Musselwhite, Charlie, *One Night in America*, Telarc, 2002

Neal, Raful, *I've Been Mistreated*, King Snake, 1991

Neal, Raful, *Old Friends*, Club Louisiana, 1998

Neal, Kenny, *Big News from Baton Rouge*, Alligator, 1987

Neal, Kenny, *Devil Child*, Alligator, 1989

Neal, Kenny, *Walking on Fire*, Alligator, 1991

Neal, Kenny, *Bayou Blood*, Alligator, 1992

Neal, Kenny, *Hoodoo Moon*, Alligator, 1994

Neal, Kenny, *Deluxe Edition*, Alligator, 1997

Neal, Kenny, Blues Fallin' Down Like Rain, Telarc, 1998

Neal, Kenny, *What You Got*, Telarc, 2000

Neal, Kenny, *One Step Closer*, Telarc, 2001

Neal, Kenny, *Homesick for the Road*, Telarc, 1998

Peterson, Lucky, *Lucky Strikes*, Alligator, 1989

Peterson, Lucky, *Triple Play*, Alligator, 1990

Peterson, Lucky, *I'm Ready*, Verve, 1992

Peterson, Lucky, *Beyond Cool*, Verve, 1994

Peterson, Lucky, *Lifetime*, Verve, 1996

Peterson, Lucky, *Move*, Polygram, 1998

Peterson, Lucky, *Lucky Peterson*, Blue Thumb, 1999

Peterson, Lucky, *Double Dealin'*, Blue Thumb, 2001

Phelps, Kelly Joe, *Lead Me On*, Burnside, 1995

Phelps, Kelly Joe, *Roll Away the Stone*, Rykodisc, 1997

Phelps, Kelly Joe, *Shine-Eyed Mister Zen*, Rykodisc, 1999

Phelps, Kelly Joe, *Sky Like a Broken Clock*, Rykodisc, 2001

Piazza, Rod, *Stone Dirty*, ABC Bluesway, 1968

Piazza, Rod, *Rod Piazza*, Bluesman, LMI, 1973

Piazza, Rod, *Chicago Flying Saucer Band*, Gangster Records, 1979

Piazza, Rod, *Radioactive Material*, Right Hemisphere, 1981

Piazza, Rod, *File under Rock*, Right Hemisphere, 1984

Piazza, Rod, *From Start to Finish*, Right Hemisphere, 1985

Piazza, Rod, *So Glad to Have the Blues*, Murray Brothers, 1988

Piazza, Rod, *Heartburn*, Black Top, 1986

Piazza, Rod, *Blues in the Dark*, Black Top, 1991

Piazza, Rod, *Alphabet Blues*, Black Top, 1992

Piazza, Rod, *The Essential Collection*, High Tone, 1992

Piazza, Rod, *Live at B.B. King's Blues Club*, Big Mo, 1994

Piazza, Rod, *California Blues*, Black Top, 1997

Piazza, Rod, *Tough and Tender*, Tone Cool, 1997

Piazza, Rod, *Live in '75*, Tone Cool, 1998

Piazza, Rod, *Here and Now*, Tone Cool, 1999

Piazza, Rod, *Beyond the Blues*, Tone Cool, 2001

Rishell, Paul, *Blues on a Holiday*, Tone Cool, 1990

Rishell, Paul, *Swear to Tell the Truth*, Tone Cool, 1993

Rishell, Paul, *I Want You to Know*, Tone Cool, 1996

Rishell, Paul, *Moving to the Country*, Tone Cool, 1999

Robertson, Sherman, *I'm the Man*, Atlantic, 1993

Robertson, Sherman, *Here and Now*, Atlantic, 1995

Robertson, Sherman, *Going Back Home*, Audioquest, 1998

Robertson, Sherman, *Sherman Robertson*, Alligator, 2002

Robillard, Duke, *Too Hot to Handle*, Rounder, 1985

Robillard, Duke, *Rockin Blues*, Rounder, 1988

Robillard, Duke, *You Got Me*, Rounder, 1988

Robillard, Duke, *Swing*, Rounder, 1988

Robillard, Duke, *Duke Robillard and the Pleasure Kings*, Rounder, 1989

Robillard, Duke, *Turn It Around*, Rounder, 1990

Robillard, Duke, *After-Hours Swing Session*, Rounder, 1990

Robillard, Duke, *Temptation*, Virgin Point Blank, 1994

Robillard, Duke, *Duke's Blues*, Virgin Point Blank, 1996

Robillard, Duke, *Dangerous Place*, Virgin Point Blank, 1997

Robillard, Duke, *Plays Jazz, The Rounder Years*, Bullseye Blues, 1997

Robillard, Duke, *Plays Blues, The Rounder Years*, Bullseye Blues, 1997

Robillard, Duke, *Stretchin' Out Live*, Stony Plain, 1998

Robillard, Duke, *Conversations in Swing Guitar*, Stony Plain, 1999

Robillard, Duke, *Jimmy Witherspoon with the Duke Robillard Band*, Stony Plain, 2000

Robillard, Duke, *New Blues for the Modern Man*, Shanachie, 1999

Robillard, Duke, *Explorer*, Shanachie, 2000

Robillard, Duke, *Livin' with the Blues*, Stony Plain, 2001

Rogers, Jimmy, *Chicago Bound*, MCA Chess, 1976

Rogers, Jimmy, *Feelin' Good*, Blind Pig, 1995

Rogers, Jimmy, *Ludella*, Antone's, 1990

Rogers, Jimmy, *Live with Ronnie Earl*, Bullseye Blues, 1994

Rogers, Jimmy, *Blue Bird*, Acoustic Sounds, 1994

Rogers, Jimmy, *The Complete Chess Recordings*, MCA, 1997

Rush, Bobby, *One Monkey Don't Stop No Show*, Waldoxy, 1995

Rush, Bobby, *She's a Good Un*, Ronn, 1995

Rush, Bobby, *Lovin' a Big Fat Woman*, Waldoxy, 1997

Rush, Bobby, *Southern Soul*, Cannonball, 1998

Rush, Bobby, *The Best of Bobby Rush*, LaJam Records, 1999

Rush, Bobby, *Hoochie Man*, Waldoxy, 2000

Saffire, The Uppity Blues Women, *Saffire, The Uppity Blues Women*, Alligator, 1990

Saffire—The Uppity Blues Women, *Hot Flash*, Alligator, 1991

Saffire—The Uppity Blues Women, *Broadcasting*, Alligator, 1992

Saffire—The Uppity Blues Women, *Old, New, Borrowed, and Blue*, Alligator, 1994

Saffire—The Uppity Blues Women, *Cleaning House*, Alligator, 1996

Saffire—The Uppity Blues Women, *Live and Uppity*, Alligator, 1998

Saffire—The Uppity Blues Women, *Ain't Gonna Hush*, Alligator, 2001

Shannon, Tommy, *Double Trouble, Been a Long Time*, Tone-Cool, 2001

Vaughan, Jimmie, *Strange Pleasure*, Epic, 1995

Vaughan, Jimmie, *Out There*, Epic, 1998

Vaughan, Jimmie, *Do You Get the Blues*, Artemis Records, 2001

Vaughan, Stevie Ray, and Double Trouble, *Texas Flood*, Epic, 1983

Vaughan, Stevie Ray, and Double Trouble, *Couldn't Stand the Weather*, Epic, 1984

Vaughan, Stevie Ray, and Double Trouble, *Soul to Soul*, Epic, 1985

Vaughan, Stevie Ray, and Double Trouble, *Live Alive*, Epic, 1986

Vaughan, Stevie Ray, and Double Trouble, *In Step*, Epic, 1989

Vaughan, Stevie Ray, and Double Trouble, *The Sky Is Crying*, Epic, 1991

Vaughan, Stevie Ray, and Double Trouble, *Live at Carnegie Hall*, Epic, 1997

Vaughan, Stevie Ray, and Double Trouble, *Greatest Hits Vol. 1*, Epic, 1995

Vaughan, Stevie Ray, and Double Trouble, *Greatest Hits Vol. 2*, Epic, 1998

Vaughan, Stevie Ray, and Double Trouble, *Blues at Sunrise*, Epic, 1999

Vaughan, Stevie Ray, and Double Trouble, *In Session with Albert King*, Stax, 1999

Vaughan, Stevie Ray, and Double Trouble, *SRV* (boxed set), Epic, 2000

Vaughan, Stevie Ray, and Double Trouble, *Live at Montreux 1982–1983*, Epic, 2001

Vaughan Brothers, *Family Style*, Epic, 1990

Walker, Joe Louis, *Cold As the Night*, High Tone, 1986

Walker, Joe Louis, *The Gift*, High Tone, 1988

Walker, Joe Louis, *Blue Soul*, High Tone, 1989

Walker, Joe Louis, *Live at Slim's Volume I*, High Tone, 1991

Walker, Joe Louis, *Live at Slim's Volume II*, High Tone, 1992

Walker, Joe Louis, *Blues Survivor*, Verve, 1993

Walker, Joe Louis, *J.L.W.*, Polygram, 1994

Walker, Joe Louis, *Blues of the Month Club*, Verve, 1995

Walker, Joe Louis, *Hello Everybody*, Verve, 1995

Walker, Joe Louis, *Great Guitars*, Polygram, 1997

Walker, Joe Louis, *Preacher and the President*, Polygram, 1998

Walker, Joe Louis, *Silvertone Blues*, Blue Thumb, 1999

Watson, Junior, *Long Overdue*, Black Top, 1994

Watson, Junior, and Lynnwood Slim, *Back to Back*, Crosscut Records, 1998

Watson, Junior, and Lynnwood Slim, *Lost in America*, Atomic Theory, 1997

Watson, Junior, *Blues Harp Meltdown*, Mountain Top, 2001

Weathersby, Carl, *Don't Lay Your Blues on Me*, Evidence, 1996

Weathersby, Carl, *Looking at My Window*, Evidence, 1997

Weathersby, Carl, *Come to Papa*, Evidence, 2000

Weathersby, Carl, *Restless Feeling*, Evidence, 1998

Williams, Lil' Ed, *Roughhousing*, Alligator, 1986

Williams, Lil' Ed, *Chicken, Gravy and Biscuits*, Alligator, 1989

Williams, Lil' Ed, *What You See Is What You Get*, Alligator, 1992

Williams, Lil' Ed, and Dave Weld, *Keep On Walkin*, Earwig, 1996

Williams, Lil' Ed, and Willie Kent, *Who's Been Talking?*, Earwig, 1998

Williams, Lil Ed, *Get Wild*, Alligator, 1999

Wilson, Kim, *Tiger Man*, Antone's, 1993

Wilson, Kim, *That's Life*, Antone's, 1994

Wilson, Kim, *My Blues*, Blue Collar, 1997

Wilson, Kim, *Smokin' Juke*, MC Records, 2001

Wilson, Kim, and the Fabulous Thunderbirds, *Fabulous Thunderbirds*, Crysalis, 1979

Wilson, Kim, and the Fabulous Thunderbirds, *Butt Rockin*, Crysalis, 1981

Wilson, Kim, and the Fabulous Thunderbirds, *Tough Enuff*, Epic, 1986

Wilson, Kim, and the Fabulous Thunderbirds, *Powerful Stuff*, Epic, 1989

Wilson, Kim, and the Fabulous Thunderbirds, *The Essential*, Crysalis, 1991

Wilson, Kim, and the Fabulous Thunderbirds, *Walk That Walk*, Epic, 1991

Wilson, Kim, and the Fabulous Thunderbirds, *Hot Stuff, The Greatest Hits*, Epic, 1992

Wilson, Kim, and the Fabulous Thunderbirds, *Roll of the Dice*, Private Music, 1995

Wilson, Kim, and the Fabulous Thunderbirds, *High Water*, High Street, 1997

For more information on the blues programs, contact the Blues Foundation, 49 Union Ave., Memphis, TN 38103.

For information on the contemporary blues scene, subscribe to *Blues Revue*, Rt. 1, Box 75, Salem, WV 24626; *Living Blues*, c/o The Center for the Study of Southern Culture, University, MS 38677; and *Blues Access*, 1455 Chestnut Pl., Boulder, CO 80304.

PHOTO CREDITS

ABOUT THE AUTHOR

Art Tipaldi received his B.S. from Central Connecticut State University in 1973 and his M.A. from Springfield College in 1984. He has been teaching American literature, writing, and speech communication at Minnechaug Regional High School in Wilbraham, Massachusetts, since 1973. In 1992, he began teaching a blues curriculum as a way for his students to understand African-American literature and explore the music and culture of African Americans.

In 1997, he pioneered a Blues and Literature course, which focuses on the Southern culture that produced the blues, blues musicians, and African-American literature. Today, he teaches four sections of Blues and Literature. Musicians like Keb' Mo', Corey Harris, Honeyboy Edwards, Shemekia Copeland, Kelly Joe Phelps, and Eddie Shaw have come to Art's classes and added crucial insights to his student's Blues in the Schools educational experience. In 1999, B.B. King and his band came to Minnechaug and held a one-hour blues workshop for 100 students.

Tipaldi presented this curriculum at the National Council of Teachers of English in November 1994, at the House of Blues Teacher Institute at the University of Mississippi in July 1995 and 1996, and three times at the Blues Foundation's Blues Symposium in 1993, 1994, and 1998. In 1999, he presented "Cross Road Blues," a five-day workshop that showed 25 Connecticut teachers the various methods of incorporating blues into their curriculum. He has written numerous articles about teaching blues in the classroom. In 2000, he authored the *Blues Time Line, Blues Men and Women Guide* and extensive profiles for the House of Blues Curriculum Guides.

He is a six-year member of the Blues Foundation's Board of Directors, serving as chairman of the Education Constituency, and a member of the Boston Blues Society. He is currently a senior writer for *Blues Revue*, where he writes profiles, reviews, and the column "T'ain't No Body's Business." He also contributes to the Boston Blues Society's newsletter and the *Hartford Advocate*. He is the Blues Foundation's 1996 Keeping the Blues Alive award winner for excellence in Journalism.

When not at a blues show, Art and his wife, Bonnie, live in western Massachusetts.

INDEX

Longhair, Professor, 109, 113
Lucas, Robert, 311

M
MacLeod, Doug, 226–227, 267–272
Maghett, Magic Sam, 257, 289
Magic Sam. *See* Maghett, Magic Sam
Mahal, Taj. *See* Taj Mahal
Mann, Michael "Hollywood Fats." *See also*
Hollywood Fats Band
  Al Blake and, 231–234
  Albert King and, 290
  Fred Kaplan and, 257–259
  Freddie King and, 231, 232, 257
  James Harman and, 250–252, 259
  Junior Watson and, 309, 310
  Michael Bloomfield and, 232
  Rod Piazza and, 289–291
  West Coast blues and, 226
Marcia Ball and the Misery Brothers, 112
Margolin, Bob, 164, 186–193, 213
Maxwell, Dave, 164, 194–199
Mayall, John, 241, 245, 276–278
Mayall, Maggie, 234, 241, 245
McClinton, Delbert, 107, 130–135
McDowell, Mississippi Fred
  Joe Louis Walker and, 300
  Keb' Mo' and, 261
  Kelly Joe Phelps and, 281–282
  Kenny Brown and, 46–47
McIntosh, Andra Faye, 216–223
Memphis Slim. *See* Chatman, Peter
  "Memphis Slim"
Merriweather, Big Maceo, 256
Mighty Flyers. *See* Rod Piazza and the
  Mighty Flyers
Milburn, Amos, 257
Miles, Buddy, 274
Misery Brothers, 112
Mississippi Delta Blues Band, 303
Mississippi Fred McDowell. *See* McDowell,
  Mississippi Fred
Mississippi John Hurt. *See* Hurt, John
  "Mississippi"
Mitchell, George, 46
Montoya, Coco, 226, 241, 273–278
Moore, Johnny, 233
Moore, Kevin. *See* Keb' Mo'
Moore, Scotty, 305
Morganfield, Big Bill, 193
Muddy Waters. *See* Waters, Muddy
Mugalian, Steve, 285, 296
Mulvehill, Mikki, 17
Murphy, Matt "Guitar," 197, 211, 250
music, blues

Chicago blues, 9–10, 233
Delta blues, 261, 265
East Coast blues, 163–164
Texas blues, 107–108
West Coast blues, 225–227, 233, 258
West Coast jump blues, 226, 291, 310
Musselwhite, Charlie, 10, 62–70, 226, 289
Myers, Louis, 183–184, 231, 294
Myers, Sam, 115–122
Mystics, 287

N
Neal Brothers Blues Band, 74–76
Neal family, 72–73
Neal, Kenny, 71–78
Neal, Raful, 71–75, 77–78
Nelson, Sonny Boy, 263–264
Nelson, Tracy, 110, 113
Newhouse, Jackie, 147
Nighthawks, 289
Nulisch, Darrell, 115, 116–117

O
Oscher, Paul, 288

P
Papa John Creach. *See* Creach, Papa John
Parker, Charlie, 4
Pass, Joe, 270
Patton, Charlie, 54, 55, 167, 175
Paul Butterfield Blues Band, 234. *See also*
  Butterfield, Paul
Paul, Les, 139
Penniman, Richard Wayne. *See* Little
  Richard
Perkins, Pinetop, 193, 194, 199
Peterson, James, 79–82
Peterson, Lucky, 10, 79–84
Phelps, Kelly Joe, 227, 279–284
Phillips, Dewey, 65
Piazza, Honey, 226, 258, 290, 292–296
Piazza, Rod
  Al Blake and, 288–289
  Albert King and, 290
  Doug MacLeod and, 270
  George "Harmonica" Smith and,
    287–289, 291–293
  Hollywood Fats Band and, 290–291
  Junior Watson and, 310–312
  Little Walter and, 288, 289, 292, 293
  Muddy Waters and, 290
  Otis Spann and, 288
  West Coast blues and, 226
Piccolo, Greg, 212
Pickett, Wilson, 262

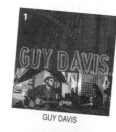

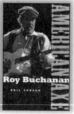